The Doctrine of the Holy Spirit

The Doctrine of the Holy Spirit

An Examination of the Person, Gifts, and Works of the Holy Spirit in Biblical Teaching and Historical Christian Teaching and Practice Through the Centuries

YACOB GODEBO

Foreword by Veli-Matti Kärkkäinen

WIPF & STOCK · Eugene, Oregon

THE DOCTRINE OF THE HOLY SPIRIT
An Examination of the Person, Gifts and Works of the Holy Spirit in Biblical Teaching and Historical Christian Teaching and Practice through the Centuries

Copyright © 2025 Yacob Godebo. All rights reserved. Except for brief quotations in critical publications or reviews, no part of this book may be reproduced in any manner without prior written permission from the publisher. Write: Permissions, Wipf and Stock Publishers, 199 W. 8th Ave., Suite 3, Eugene, OR 97401.

Wipf & Stock
An Imprint of Wipf and Stock Publishers
199 W. 8th Ave., Suite 3
Eugene, OR 97401

www.wipfandstock.com

PAPERBACK ISBN: 979-8-3852-4332-7
HARDCOVER ISBN: 979-8-3852-4333-4
EBOOK ISBN: 979-8-3852-4334-1

06/30/25

Unless otherwise noted, all biblical quotations and references in this publication are from The NIV Study Bible, With Study Notes and References, Concordance and Maps, Copyrighted © 1985, by The Zondervan Corporation, Edition 2000 by Hodder and Stoughton, London.

This book is dedicated to the glory of the Triune God. In order to express my profound and profusely deep praise and gratitude to God without whom nothing is possible, I want to adapt King Solomon's praise to God: "Praise be to the Lord, the God of Israel, who with his own hand has fulfilled what he promised with his own mouth . . ." (1 Kgs 8:15). For God spoke with his own mouth, promised to provide the necessary resources from his treasury, and initiated the writing of this book. He alone has been the initiator, provider, and builder of everything all the way through the journey of this study. He has fulfilled his promise by providing resources and by enlightening, guiding, and helping me to accomplish the work. His is the praise, glory, and majesty now and forever!

Contents

Foreword by Veli-Matti Kärkkäinen | ix
Acknowledgments | xi
Abbreviations | xv
Introduction | xvii

PART I. THE PERSON, GIFTS, AND WORKS OF THE HOLY SPIRIT IN BIBLICAL TEACHING | 1

Chapter 1 The Old and New Testament Teaching | 3

Chapter 2 Reception of the Holy Spirit and His Gifts at and after Pentecost | 23

Chapter 3 Manifest Connection of the Holy Spirit with Charismatic Gifts | 43

Chapter 4 The Holy Spirit in Funding, Organization, and Shaping of the Life and Ministry of the Church | 58

PART II. THE PERSON, GIFTS, AND WORKS OF THE HOLY SPIRIT IN HISTORICAL CHRISTIAN TEACHING AND PRACTICE FROM AD 100 TO 1900 | 79

Chapter 5 The Apostolic Transmission and Post-Apostolic Church's Teaching and Practice | 81

Chapter 6 The Patristic Period Church's Teaching and Practice | 112

Chapter 7 The Emergence of Tension and Division over the Experience of the Presence, Gifts, and Works of the Holy Spirit | 140

Chapter 8	The Medieval Western Church's Teaching and Practice	162
Chapter 9	The Reformation and Post-Reformation Protestant Churches' Teaching and Practice	184
Chapter 10	The Overall Image of the Christian Teaching and Practice of the Person, Gifts, and Works of the Holy Spirit from AD 100 to 1900	214

PART III. THE PERSON, GIFTS, AND WORKS OF THE HOLY SPIRIT IN CONTEMPORARY CHRISTIAN TEACHING AND PRACTICE | 235

Chapter 11	The Rise, Emphases, and Expansion of the Pentecostal and Charismatic Movements	237
Chapter 12	Expansion and Influence of the Charismatic Movement on the Established Churches' Traditional Teaching and Practice of the Person, Gifts, and Workings of the Holy Spirit	254
Chapter 13	Summary, Personal Reflections, and Conclusions	276

Bibliography | 301

General Index | 313

Scripture Index | 319

Foreword

I CANNOT THINK OF any theological topic beyond pneumatology, the doctrine of the Holy Spirit, to which the statement by the late statesman of African studies Andrew F. Walls that "anyone who wishes to undertake serious study of Christianity these days needs to know something about Africa" applies so well![1] Not only because that continent currently houses more Christians than any other but also because the interest in spirituality, sensitivity to the spirit world, and openness to spiritual manifestations is prevalent across the ecumenical spectrum. The Spirit is alive and well in African Christianity!

All that said, most of the studies and treatises on pneumatology throughout the centuries—and even in the beginning of the third millennium—have been penned by theologians with little or no knowledge of the rich spiritual reservoir of African Christianity. Even worse: how many textbooks or introductions to the biblical, historical, and contemporary pneumatologies at large you have seen written by an African scholar? Almost without exception, even African students are still studying the theology and spirituality of the Holy Spirit from the texts produced outside their own milieu.

Here comes a long-awaited comprehensive treatise on the Spirit written by an African scholar: Dr. Yacob Godebo's *The Doctrine of the Holy Spirit* which provides a succinct, well-researched, and pedagogically useful . . . *Examination of the Person, Gifts and Works of the Holy Spirit in Biblical Teaching and Historical Christian Teaching and Practice through the Centuries*. Far from being merely a report about the Holy Spirit's work and presence in his own continent—a worthwhile project in itself, for that matter—this Ethiopian Lutheran theologian and seminary professor cartographs the whole history of the Spirit of God in biblical, historical,

---

1. Walls, "Eusebius Tries Again," 106.

and contemporary perspectives. In other words: he is providing an African Christian leader's reading of the texts concerning the Spirit in the Bible and throughout church history about the person, work, and empowerment of the Spirit.

This is a book meant not only for Africans—as highly useful and needed it might be there—but to students, ministers, and interested lay persons across world Christianity. Certainly I, a European theologian teaching in the US, badly need this kind of tutoring!

Not only that! There is more good news available in this important book. Written by a representative of Africa's and, in fact, the world's, largest Lutheran Church, the Ethiopian Mekane Yesus Church, Dr. Godebo also pays close attention to an important topic of pneumatology almost routinely ignored in standard primers, namely, the dynamic charismatic work of the Spirit of God. Not only is that theme essential to contemporary world Christianity as well as all African Christianity; it is also a felt need in Dr. Godebo's own rapidly growing church tradition which beginning from the early 1990s has incorporated within its structures a vibrant charismatic way of Lutheranism. And let me add this bonus: that the question of spiritual gifts and charismatic endowments is placed in the widest possible framework of historical and contemporary developments of pneumatology makes a unique contribution to both scholarly and pedagogical literature.

This is a pneumatological feast, a carefully researched and richly-documented primer on all-things-Holy Spirit. *Tolle, lege!*

VELI-MATTI KÄRKKÄINEN, DR. THEOL. HABIL.
Professor of Systematic Theology, Fuller Theological Seminary
Docent of Ecumenics, University of Helsinki, Faculty of Theology

Acknowledgments

FIRST AND FOREMOST, I want to acknowledge the role of my beloved mother, Lombo A. Ordolo, in my religious, social, and academic life. She offered me to God as a votive offering in my childhood at Lalo Mekane Yesus, the church of my birth place. She then brought me up with an unfailing love and unceasing prayer in the presence of God. In answer to her prayer, I believe, God has called, trained and appointed me to his service. I will forever owe an immense debt of gratitude to her.

My profoundly felt thanks and gratitude also go to All Saints Parish Church, Hoole, Chester, UK, which, together with the University of Chester, supported my postgraduate research degree study in the UK and enabled the honour of my receiving a doctorate degree of Philosophy (PhD) from the University of Chester. Without first achieving such an academic qualification, thinking about undertaking a postdoctoral research study, such as this one, would have been impossible for me. All Saints Parish Church has made this possible for me. I will forever owe a great debt of thanks and gratitude to this Church. Similar heartfelt thanks and gratitude go to the Mekane Yesus (MYS) Seminary Senate for the repeated granting of research leave. I want to express my special thanks to all of them both individually and as a team.

There are several others to whom this research study is indebted. Special heartfelt thanks and gratitude are due to the Reverend Dr. Bruk Ayele, MYS President, from 2016–2024, who encouraged the doctoral degree holders to engage in further research work and to make contributions to the academic life of the institution. He not only encouraged them to engage in further research work but has also striven to provide them with the means such as granting research leave and finding short- and long-term scholarship grants from partner churches and institutions. I was fortunate to become the first beneficiary of this, which eventually resulted in the completion of this book. Indeed, without his commitment and support, the successful completion of this book would have been impossible. I owe a debt of special gratitude to him.

I would also like to express my deepest thanks to Rev. Debbie Braaksma, the head of the Presbyterian Church of United States World Mission Africa Desk. Her office sponsored my research leave and enabled me to stay at the Louisville Presbyterian Theological Seminary (LPTS) and to make use of its resourceful library for this study. I want to say a special thank you to her personally and her office collectively. Similar deepest thanks go to the LPTS. The LPTS, with its park-like compound, is a wonderfully silent and safe place to conduct an independent research study. In addition to such an intriguing compound, I received a great deal of help from the LPTS leadership, faculties, librarians, and Furlough House Board members through what they did for me both individually and collectively during my stay at LPTS. I am deeply grateful to all of them. While I will owe a deepest thanks to them all, I want to say a special thank you to two individuals: Prof. Cliff Kirkpatrick and Prof. Susan Garret. They were so generous with their time, constantly visiting me and generously providing whatever needs I had at hand. I want to say special thank you to both of them. My special thanks are also due to those friends and families who assisted and supported me during my health crisis at LPTS. I would also like to express a similar heartfelt thanks and gratitude to the Concordia Theological Seminary St. Louis Leadership and staff for supporting my research work during my stay in their Seminary at a time when the COVID-19 pandemic was sweeping the world.

I am also indebted to Professor Veli-Matti Kärkkäinen, who has kindly committed to reading and reviewing this book's drafts and has made many helpful and constructive comments. As an insightful evangelical scholar and extremely elite writer in systematic theology, he distinctly perceives the particular characteristics of the pneumatological issues and comments accordingly. He has offered me quite helpful evangelically insightful and academically sound comments on this work. Having his priceless comments and advice is both honour and privilege. I cannot thank him enough but I owe a debt of special gratitude to him! My special and deepest gratitude goes to Dr. Elaine and Mr. Rick Hemmings for the many ways in which they have given support for this study. Dr. Elaine, in particular, has read the draft text of this book and made expert linguistic and grammatical diagnosis. Her academic comments and thorough amendments on the draft text were profoundly helpful and useful. Without her commitment and expert help, the text of this book would not have taken its current flavor or made the taste it does now. I will forever owe a great debt of special thanks and gratitude to her!

I also owe a debt of gratitude to the Norwegian Mission Society (NMS), whose generous sponsorship made the publication of this book possible. I want to say a special thank you to my colleagues, the College of Theological Studies faculty at MYS. All of them have been supportive and encouraging throughout the course of writing this book. My special heartfelt thanks are also due to the students I taught in the Masters of Arts (MA) in Theology class. MA students, especially those on the "Issues in Pneumatology" course in the years from 2014–2020, have been so inspirational and an encouragement to me in writing this book. Their questions, comments, and arguments during our class discussions and the challenges they have encountered have been the reason and inspiration for the writing of this book. I want to say a special thank you to all of them both individually and collectively as a class.

Last but not least, I would like to thank most especially my wife Demewoz Ayele and our children Israel, Loza, Tekledlot, and Aksan. Their prayer and manifold and steady encouragements have provided immeasurable spiritual and emotional support for the successful completion of the book. I remain immensely grateful to them all.

Abbreviations

I. GENERAL ABBREVIATIONS

ABC	Addis Ababa Bible College
AD	Anno Domini (i.e., to refer to years after Jesus Christ was born)
BC	(i.e., to refer years before Jesus Christ was born)
ca.	circa (i.e., to refer approximate dates or to say approximately)
cf.	confer (i.e., to say "compare")
CoTS	College of Theological Studies
Ed. (s)	edition, editor, editors,
EECMY	Ethiopian Evangelical Church Mekane Yesus
EGST	Ethiopian Graduate School of Theology
ETC	Evangelical Theological College
etc.	*et cetera* (to say "and other similar things")
i.e.	that is
MA	Master of Arts
MABTS	Master of Arts in Biblical and Theological Studies
MYS	Mekane Yesus Seminary
PCM	Pentecostal and Charismatic Movement(s)
PTC	Pentecostal Theological College
Trans.	translator, translation, translated
Vol.	Volume/s

II. BIBLICAL ABBREVIATIONS

Gen	Genesis	Matt	The Gospel of Matthew
Exod	Exodus	Mark	The Gospel of Mark
Lev	Leviticus	Luke	The Gospel of Luke
Num	Numbers	John	The Gospel of John
Deut	Deuteronomy	Acts	Acts of the Apostles
Josh	Joshua	Rom	Romans
Judg	Judges	1 Cor	1 Corinthians
1 Sam	1 Samuel	2 Cor	2 Corinthians
2 Sam	2 Samuel	Gal	Galatians
1 Kgs	1 Kings	Eph	Ephesians
2 Kgs	2 Kings	1 Thess	1 Thessalonians
1 Chr	1 Chronicles	Phil	Philippians
2 Chr	2 Chronicles	1 Tim	1 Timothy
Neh	Nehemiah	2 Tim	2 Timothy
Job	Job	Tit	Titus
Ps	Psalms	Heb	Hebrews
Isa	Isaiah	1 John	1 Epistle of John
Jer	Jeremiah	1 Pet	1 Epistle of Peter
Ezek	Ezekiel	2 Pet	2 Epistle of Peter
Hos	Hosea	Jas	James
Mic	Micah	Rev	Revelation
Zech	Zechariah		
Mal	Malachi		

Introduction

My theological education career began with the diploma in theology programme at the Mekane Yesus Seminary (MYS) of the Ethiopian Evangelical Church Mekane Yesus (EECMY). In this programme I studied thirty courses, but no independent course focused on the Holy Spirit, his gifts, and workings. After four years of service, I joined the bachelor of theology programme at the MYS. In this programme I studied thirty-five courses, but, again, there was no independent course focused on the Holy Spirit, his gifts, and workings. The only course that considered the doctrine of the Holy Spirit was the course entitled "Christian Doctrine." In this course, the subject of the Holy Spirit was merely touched upon, but not taught in depth. However, since 2011 the subject of the Holy Spirit, his gifts and works have become a matter of strong attention within the EECMY as a whole and at the MYS in particular.

It was in the fall of 2011 that the MYS leadership invited me to teach in the masters of arts in theology programme, after I had completed my doctoral study in the summer of that year. I accepted the invitation and joined the MYS in January 2012. To some extent, the subject of the Holy Spirit and his gifts was related to the field of research for my doctoral dissertation. By virtue of this, I was assigned to teach a course entitled "Issues in Pneumatology" in the MA programme. I was also asked to teach the same course in the Ethiopian Graduate School of Theology (EGST) in the Masters of Arts in Biblical and Theological Studies (MABTS) Programme. Thus, the purpose of this study and the writing of this book draws its roots from my teaching of a course entitled "Issues in Pneumatology." Accordingly, the subject of this study is the Christian doctrine of the Holy Spirit (Pneumatology)[1] with special emphasis on the historical

---

1. It is understandable that traditionally theological and academic conceptions of the Holy Spirit, his gifts, and workings are generally referred to as the doctrine of the Holy Spirit or Pneumatology.

Christian perception, teaching, and practice of the presence, gifts, and workings of the Holy Spirit. The impetus for the study of this subject arose from three major factors:

The first impetus arose from my readings of the literature in this field. When I began to teach this course, I checked for literature written in this field and available at the MYS library. I found only a limited number of books, which were helpful for the course but raised some serious questions for me. For example, some of the authors argue that the doctrine of the Holy Spirit "belongs to the uncompleted doctrines of the church."[2] Some argue that in the history of the church the Holy Spirit was treated as the "stepchild of the Trinity"; the "Cinderella of the Trinity"; and the "dark side of the moon" in theological practices. Some argue that the Holy Spirit was "subordinated to the other two persons of the Trinity," "made the shy/silent member of the Trinity," and "eclipsed."[3] These arguments raised such questions in my mind: What do these arguments refer to? Do they mean that the Holy Spirit was not given his proper place and role in the belief, teaching, and practice of the church? Or do they mean that the church lacked interest in the presence, gifts, and workings of the Holy Spirit and excluded from its theological teaching and practice? If so, what factors might have led the church to do so? I felt that the writers of these arguments do not adequately explain the reasons why this neglect of the Holy Spirit occurred in the church. This raised such a question in my mind: where can one find answers about the place and role of the Holy Spirit in Christian belief, teaching, and practice in the history of the church? The search for answers to these and similar questions was the first impetus prompting this research study.

The second impetus arose from class discussions. The master's-level students I teach at MYS are mostly EECMY ministers in the units and institutions of the church. All of them have earned their bachelor of theology degrees either from the MYS or the regional seminaries. Some of them are presidents, executive secretaries, department heads, and programme leaders in their respective church units. Some are instructors in the regional seminaries and Bible schools. Some are long-serving ministers in districts, presbyteries, parishes, and congregations. We sometimes have a few students from other evangelical churches such as Kale Heywot, Mulu Wongel (Full Gospel), and Meserete Kristos. The

---

2. Sasse, *Letters to Lutheran Pastors*, 3:219.
3. For the explanation of these terms and related arguments, see ch. 10.

students I taught at EGST came from these churches and many other denominations and nondenominational fellowships. All of the students I teach in the MA class are almost in a comparable level of education and work positions and are mature in age and the Christian ministry. When I open the floor for discussion following each lecture, they raise critical questions about the theology, doctrine, baptism, and experience of the gifts of the Holy Spirit. The reason why their questions focus on these areas is, at least locally, understandable. Since 1991 the evangelical churches of Ethiopia have been experiencing challenges resulting from the influence of the Pentecostal and Charismatic Movements (PCMs). The students' questions reflect those challenges and their effects on the lives of their respective churches. When discussions on these issues become heated, some students insist on the traditional evangelical position that adheres to and advocates the objective reception and doctrinal belief of the Holy Spirit. Some students, however, favor the subjective experience of the Holy Spirit.[4] Most often class discussions end with divided views and unanswered questions. The divisions are not always based on bias toward denominational positions but are also mixed with interests in the subjective experience of the Holy Spirit.

These discussions led me to ponder such questions as: Why does the subject of the Holy Spirit, his gifts, and workings lead to tension and division? What does the Bible teach about the Holy Spirit, his gifts, and workings in the church? What did the presence, gifts, and workings of the Holy Spirit look like in Christian belief, teaching, and practice in the history of the church? Have divisions over the presence, gifts, and workings of the Holy Spirit been present in the history of the church? If division over these features was the case in the history of the church, then what of these features might have caused the divisions? Might these divisions be common issues among other churches in other parts of the world at present? If so, might there be suggested possibilities or documented solutions in response to the cases of the other churches so that we may draw on them to overcome such divisions when and where they occur locally? And so on. As I was caught up in such anxious thoughts with these and similar other questions raised in class, I had to go back to the available books at MYS library and read them again, to see if any similar story is recorded in church history and if any proposed solution or measure taken can be found. However, none of the available books contained a

4. For the definitions of the terms "objective reception," "doctrinal belief," and "subjective experience" of the Holy Spirit, see chs. 2, 3, and 6.

single page addressing these issues. Further, I had to visit other local libraries such as that of EGST, Evangelical Theological College (ETC), Addis Ababa Bible College (ABC), and Pentecostal Theological College (PTC) and read available books in the field to see if any similar story has been recorded. But, again, none of the available books contained satisfactory answers to my questions. Rather, I found the views of the writers of the books divided into two categories.

The first category of books was written from a perspective of the historical doctrinal belief of the Holy Spirit. Their authors do not mention the gifts and workings of the Holy Spirit in church as an issue. In those rare cases where they do mention them, the authors criticize such experiences for being in contradiction to orthodox Christian belief, teaching, and practice of the Holy Spirit. The second category of books was written from a Pentecostal-charismatic perspective. Some of the writers of this category criticize the other party's view for being merely obstinately dogmatic. Hence, I could not retrieve from the available books possible answers to the students' questions. Yet my students, though not knowing that I was more confused than they were, expected me to come up with answers to their questions in the next class. I was caught between their expectations and my lack of possible answers from the available books. Sometimes I was driven to stop teaching a course "Issues in Pneumatology." Accordingly, after teaching only two different classes, I stopped teaching the course at EGST. However, due to the lack of qualified faculty in the field, I couldn't stop teaching it at MYS. Yet the subject left me with many challenging questions.

Along the way, the subject led me to realize three things. *First*, the division of the writers of the books into two categories reminds me that there have been *two distinct Christian views* on the doctrine of the Holy Spirit. *Second*, I realize that a lack of knowledge of the biblical teaching about the Holy Spirit, his gifts, and workings in the church and historical Christian perception, teaching, and practice of these features is a dominant factor underlying our questions and confusions. *Third*, the gap between my students' expectations and my own lack of answers to their questions often drew my attention to realize that I had never been taught about the doctrine of the Holy Spirit during the whole course of my theological studies from diploma to PhD. Neither have I had personal experience of the fresh reception and experience of the Holy Spirit and his gifts. Thus, I found myself far behind in producing appropriate expectant answers to the complicated pneumatological and charismatic questions my students raised. Hence, the subject led me to continuously ask such questions as: How should my students be provided with possible answers to their questions? Whom can I consult on this confusion? And so on. Thus, the search for answers to these and similar questions is the second impetus prompting this study.

The third impetus prompting this study is the EECMY's recognition of the challenges and threats posed by PCM. The EECMY is grounded on the Lutheran theological tradition, which emerged from the sixteenth-century Reformation theological tradition. The reformers' theological tradition does not emphasize the presence, gifts, and workings of the Holy Spirit as a mandatory part of faith practice.[5] For this reason, the EECMY's congregations have not been taught about these issues and their experience through Pentecostal-charismatic form of worship. Nevertheless, since 1991 EECMY congregations have been impacted by the PCM and immersed in their religious experiences. This impact has resulted in an acute challenge to the EECMY's theological identity and poses a threat to its prospective future. There is documented evidence that constitutes an example that there is a concern about the prospective future of EECMY's theological identity resulting from the impact of the PCM. Consequently, the church's thinking seems to have been occupied with the question: what should be done in response to the challenges? The aim of adapting a course "Issues in Pneumatology," in the MYS curriculum, was to find possible solutions to respond to as well as to overcome such challenges.[6] Thus, the search for answers to such pressing issues is the third impetus that has prompted this study.

The purpose of this study, therefore, is to examine the Christian doctrine of the Holy Spirit with a particular aim to provide theological, biblical, and historical practical answers to the questions and confusions that prompted this study and led to the writing of this book. To accomplish this purpose, the study is laid out in three major parts. Part I examines biblical teaching about the theology, manifestation, gifts, and works of the Holy Spirit as an independent divine person. Part II will engage in a broader exploration of the historical Christian understanding, teaching,

---

5. For a detailed explanation of the sixteenth-century Reformation theological tradition, see ch. 9.

6. The subject of the EECMY's concern about the impact of the Charismatic movement is a vast one with its own independent contextual nature and characteristics that cannot be covered within the limits of this book. Therefore, it will be pursued in the subsequent book of the study.

and practice of the person, gifts, and works of the Holy Spirit from AD 100 to 1900. Part III examines the nature of contemporary Christendom's teaching and practice of the person, gifts, and works of the Holy Spirit from 1901 up to the present time. Amidst all this, there are a few things worth noting while reading this book:

First, this study does not engage in any particular denominational perspective. While the book is written by a Lutheran theologian for the Lutheran theological milieu, for the EECMY theological institutions in particular, it does not focus on the Lutheran theological and ecclesiastical tradition of the subject of the study. Rather, this study intends to be a neutral academic work that focuses on the biblical teaching and historical Christian perception, teaching, and practice of the person, gifts, and works of the Holy Spirit in the church. Lutheran theological perspective of the subject shall be considered in the subsequent book of this study.

Second, the subject of the doctrine of the Holy Spirit is very vast by nature. Every anticipated aspect of his nature, manifestation, gifts, and works cannot be covered within the limitations of this study. In particular, the study does not engage in discussion of the presence and works of the Holy Spirit in the wider world, in the creation and social spheres of human life. The scope of the study is limited to the biblical teaching and historical Christian perception, teaching, and practice of the Holy Spirit, his gifts, and works in the church. Even in this scope, every anticipated aspect of the subject cannot be discussed in detail, because the study does not attempt to provide an in-depth examination of the subject nor to seek definitive answers to the questions or solutions to the problems identified and addressed in it. The study, therefore, does not attempt to claim to be exhaustive. However, the most conspicuous features of the root causes of the subject of the study are given careful consideration. Some reliable sources and helpful directions are also highlighted for possible theological, biblical, and historical practical answers to the questions and solutions to the confusions that prompted this study.

May God grant that the endeavors of this study will be of benefit to his church as a whole and to individual believers who read this book.

PART I

The Person, Gifts, and Works of the Holy Spirit in Biblical Teaching

As indicated in the introduction, some authors argue that the doctrine of the Holy Spirit "belongs to the uncompleted doctrines of the church." This may raise such questions as: Why is the doctrine of the Holy Spirit viewed as an incomplete doctrine of the church? If it is to be viewed as an incomplete doctrine, then where does such evaluation come from? Does it come from a genuine examination of the biblical teaching about the theology and doctrine of the Holy Spirit? Or does it come from a genuine examination of the historical Christian understanding, teaching, and practice of the Holy Spirit? And son on. In order to answer these questions with the most probable answers, examining what the Bible teaches about the theology, doctrine, and workings of the Holy Spirit is indispensable. Thus, part I of the book examines what the Bible teaches about the person, manifestations, gifts, and workings of the Holy Spirit in the church. The Bible may not provide us with case-by-case answers to the questions or solutions to the confusions identified and addressed in this study. However, it provides initial theological grounds and practical guidance about the person, manifestation, gifts, and workings of the Holy Spirit. The examination, therefore, focuses on four major features, among many others. First, it examines what the Old and New Testaments teach about the person, manifestation, gifts, and works of the Holy Spirit from inception of the creation up to the end of earthly ministry of Jesus. Second, it examines the ways of reception and practice of the Holy

Spirit at and after Pentecost in the early church. Third, it examines the manifest connection of the Holy Spirit with the charismatic gifts of ministry. Fourth, it examines the presence and role of the Holy Spirit in the foundation and organization of the church, as well as in shaping of the methods of its ministry.[1] This will be examined in chapters 1 to 4.

---

1. It's noteworthy that the biblical examination of these chapters does not consider an exegetical, interpretative, and argumentative approach to the texts used as references in the discussions.

CHAPTER 1

The Old and New Testament Teaching

As mentioned above, the Bible may not provide case-by-case answers to the questions or solutions to the confusions identified and addressed in this study. However, it offers initial and appropriate theological grounds and guidance about the person, gifts, and works of the Holy Spirit in biblical times. This chapter will examine the Old and New Testament teachings about the person, presence, gifts, and works of the Holy Spirit beginning in the inception of creation up to the incarnation, life, and ministry of Jesus. Before turning to this examination, however, the chapter will briefly examine the etymological origin and development of the term "Spirit" by examining its root words—the Hebrew word *ruah* and the Greek word *pneuma*.

THE LINGUISTIC AND THEOLOGICAL MEANING OF THE TERM "SPIRIT"

Linguistic studies of the etymological roots of the term "Spirit" describe that the term draws its roots from the Hebrew word *ruah* and the Greek word *pneuma*.[1] In the Old Testament, the basic meaning of the Hebrew word *ruah* is understood as "wind, moving air, and breath."[2] In the sense of "wind," the term stands mainly for the "wind" that swept over the face of waters (Gen 1:2) and in the sense of "breath" it is "identified with the

---

1. F. W. Horn, "Holy Spirit" in *Anchor Bible Dictionary*, 3:261.
2. Horn, "Holy Spirit" in *Anchor Bible Dictionary*, 3:262.

breath of life or soul itself,"[3] which is given to all creatures (Gen 1:30), and breath of life which God breathed specifically into the man—Adam (Gen 2:7). Accordingly, the term "Spirit"/*ruah*, is understood as a "vital force divinely breathed into the man that formed a distinct part of his being" and took the meaning healed by the term "soul—God-breathed substance,"[4] which also is the "principle of life (like *nefesh*) directly derived from the wind at the bidding of God" and that "distinguishes a living from a dead."[5] Accordingly, the term *ruah* is understood to have employed three words for the "*breath-soul, nefesh (ruah),* and *neshamah*" of which the first two indicate the "personal soul and the invading Spirit."[6] This life-giving breath of God is understood as "*ruach Elohim,*" which indicates that God created all creatures not only through his word "Let there be," but also by his breath, "*ruach Elohim,*" which in turn indicates the "transcendence of the *Ruach Elohim* and his active participation in the creation process."[7] This creator *ruah Elohim* stands for the "Spirit of God" which is God's life-giving breath and continues to sustain life and without which human beings, in particular, cannot live. In this sense, *ruah* can be understood and described as "human vitality, the quality that marks off a living person from a dead person."[8] Thus, the gift of the "Spirit of God" came to be understood as "analogous to creation" in which the term *ruah* came to be understood as a term "for life itself."[9]

In the Old Testament *ruah* is also understood as the "spirit of Yahweh" which is "God's power in action" which seems to mean that "Yahweh's spirit is God himself present and at work." Accordingly, the "Spirit of Yahweh" is understood to "shape creation, animate animals and mankind, direct nature and history."[10] It is also understood as a means of "divine judgment in which God commands the wind, which accompanies or represents God's self-manifestation, and thus symbolically heralds God's coming."[11] For example, the concept of the winds from the four directions

3. Robinson and House, *Analytical Lexicon*, 286–87.
4. E. Kamlah, J. D. G. Dunn, C. Brown, "Spirit, Holy Spirit" in *New International Dictionary*, 3:692.
5. Robinson and House, *Analytical Lexicon*, 286–87.
6. Robinson and House, *Analytical Lexicon*, 287.
7. Yong, "Ruach," 190–92.
8. Green, *I Believe*, 20–21.
9. Horn, "Holy Spirit" in *Anchor Bible Dictionary*, 3:262.
10. Packer, "Holy Spirit," in *New Dictionary of Theology*, 316.
11. Horn, "Holy Spirit" in *Anchor Bible Dictionary*, 3:262.

of the world appears to imply the life-giving breath, which specifies the "Spirit of God" that animates and revives the dead (Ezek 37:1–14). Thus, following these essential meanings, the term *ruah* is used to express the concept of "dynamic power beyond human control" and to refer to "qualities of human being, God, . . . and supernatural spirits."[12]

Linguistics suggest that the Old Testament Hebrew *ruah* is characterized in the New Testament by its Greek equivalent *pneuma*. The basic meaning of the Greek noun *pneuma* derives from the verb *pnewo* which denotes "air in movement, experienced as wind, breeze, or breath."[13] Following this basic meaning, the term *pneuma* is used with four different meanings: "wind, breath, life, and metaphorical extension of these."[14] This indicates that both Hebrew *ruah* and Greek *pneuma*, originally describe the same reality of wind, moving air, blowing, breathing, breathing out, breeze, etc.[15] Linguistics further suggest that the term *pneuma* stands also for "air in motion . . . aspect of humans immaterial being [which gives life to the material body] . . . an incorporeal supernatural being . . . [and] divine person, the third member of the godhead."[16] The term also stands for a supernatural independent being that "differentiates God from everything that is not God, . . . the divine power that produces all divine existence, . . . the divine element in which all divine life is carried on, . . . the bearer of every application of the divine will."[17] These suggestions seem to remind us that the New Testament expression of the Greek term *pneuma* is precisely related to the "Spirit of God," "God-Spirit," and "God the Holy Spirit."

In the New Testament *pneuma hagion*, the "Holy Spirit," is presented as the divine person distinct from the Father and the Son in the Christian baptismal formula (Matt 28:19), which is traditionally believed as biblical assurance for the Christian doctrine of the Trinity. The unity, independent personality, and mission of Christ and the Holy Spirit are clearly expressed by Jesus himself when he identified the Holy Spirit as "he" and the "other Paraclete" who continues the presence and works of Jesus after his departure. It is evident in the Gospel of John that Jesus asserted that the Holy Spirit is the divine person distinct from the Father and the Son,

12. Horn, "Holy Spirit" in *Anchor Bible Dictionary*, 3:261–62.
13. Horn, "Holy Spirit" in *Anchor Bible Dictionary*, 3:263.
14. Horn, "Holy Spirit" in *Anchor Bible Dictionary*, 3:261.
15. J. Kremer, "Pneuma" in *Exegetical Dictionary*, 3:117.
16. Decker, *Reading Koine Greek*, 652.
17. Arndt and Gingrich, *Greek-English Lexicon*, 682.

with his own distinct functions, given to the church as another *Paraclete* by taking over Jesus' roles as counselor, comforter, helper, adviser, advocate, guide, etc (John 14:16). Hence, comprehensive impartation of the Holy Spirit occurred on the day of Pentecost in which the outpouring of the Holy Spirit was accompanied by empowering of the disciples to preach the gospel in foreign languages (Acts 2:1–4). The Holy Spirit poured out on the disciples at Pentecost is identified with the Old Testament *ruah*—the Spirit of God (Joel 2:28, Acts 2:15–21). Accordingly, the Christian is viewed to be the "product of the divine *pneuma*" which is "mediated to him by the Messiah" which characterizes the new covenant of the new age of the Spirit.[18]

1.2. THE OLD TESTAMENT TEACHING

The Old Testament emphasizes different roles of the Spirit of God. However, this study will examine only the most conspicuous and common features of the Old Testament belief and practice about the Spirit of God, his gifts, and works. In the Old Testament, there are a few references to the designation of the "Holy Spirit" such as those mentioned in Ps 51:11 and Isa 63:10–11. In Ps 51:11 the psalmist appeals for a continuous experience of the life-giving, renewing, and empowering presence of God the Creator, which he thinks is possible by the presence of the Holy Spirit. In Isa 63:10 the Holy Spirit is understood as a personal being that can be offended by human behavior and aggressively avenges it. Besides these two references, the Old Testament does not employ the designation "Holy Spirit" as such. There are, however, corresponding designations such as the "Spirit of God" (Gen 1:2; Exod 31:3; 2 Chr 15:1; Job 33:4; Joel 2:28); the "Spirit of the LORD" (Judg 3:10; 11:29; 13:25; 14:6; 1 Sam 10:6; Isa 11:2); the "Spirit of the Sovereign LORD" (Isa 61:1); the "Spirit of skill, wisdom, and knowledge" (Exod 31:3; Deut 34:9; Isa 11:2); the "Spirit of power and might" (Judg 14:6, 19; 15:14–16), and the "Spirit of prophecy" (1 Sam 10:6, 20:14, 24:20). From these designations, it can be noted that what is referred to as the "Spirit of God" in the Old Testament is what is believed and described as the "Holy Spirit" in the New Testament. Hence, the Old Testament teaches about five major features of the Holy Spirit: (1) his presence and role in creation; (2) his giving supernatural gifts for divine-related activities; (3) his giving prophetic ministry gifts; (4) his

---

18. Robinson and House, *Analytical Lexicon*, 287.

acting as a divine agent of renewal and transformation, and (5) about the future coming of the Holy Spirit in a different status.

1.2.1 The Holy Spirit in the creation process

In the Old Testament, the first manifestation and activity of the Spirit of God appear in the creation story: "The earth was formless and empty, darkness was over the surface of the deep, and the Spirit of God was hovering over the waters" (Gen 1:2). This account indicates that the Spirit of God was active in the process of creation. The Old Testament community seems to have believed that God continued to manifest himself, act in creation, and sustain life through his Spirit. What Job and the psalmist declare can constitute examples of this. Job, for instance, declared that if God withdrew his "Spirit and breath, all mankind would perish together" (Job 34:14–15). For Job, every person's life is dependent on the life-giving Spirit of God. Therefore, to take away God's Spirit from a human being, for Job, means equally removing life and leaving lifeless flesh behind, which then returns to its origin—dust—and perishes.[19] Similarly, the psalmist declares that when God sends his Spirit, creatures are created and the face of the earth is renewed (Ps 104:29–30). Both Job and the psalmist speak of the Spirit of God as a direct presence and direct action of God the creator in giving life, sustaining and renewing it, but by the work of his life-giving and sustaining Spirit. They asserted that "no creation can stand without the Holy Spirit."[20] These instances remind us that in the Old Testament, the presence and action of the Spirit of God were equivalent to the presence and action of God the Creator. Accordingly, the Spirit of God was perceived as the creative, life-giving, and life-sustaining divine agent. This indicates that in the Old Testament, the being and doing of the Spirit of God was understood as entirely one with God the Creator.

1.2.2. The Holy Spirit endowed people with different kinds of supernatural gifts

The Old Testament indicates that the Spirit of God descended on certain individuals who were chosen by God to carry out special tasks for or

---

19. Hartley, *Book of Job*, 454.
20. Wesselschmidt, *Ancient Christian Commentary*, 239.

on behalf of him. In such incidents, the Spirit of God came upon the chosen individuals and possessed, gifted, empowered, and guided them to act on behalf of the divine. Some examples can be cited: Bezalel was chosen by God and was filled with the Spirit of God which resulted in his having particular skill, ability, and knowledge in all kinds of crafts to make artistic designs for the construction of the sanctuary (Exod 31:1–4; 35:30–35). The Spirit of the LORD came upon Othniel and made him Israel's judge (Judg 3:10); upon Gideon and empowered him (Judg 6:34); upon Jephthah, empowering him and advancing his war against his enemies (Judg 11:29). The Spirit of the LORD also came upon Samson, awakened and empowered him (Judg 13:25) whereby he tore the lion apart with bare hands (14:6), slew thirty people at Ashkelon (14:19), caught three hundred foxes and tied them tail to tail in pairs (15:4–5); the ropes in his arms became like charred flax and the bindings of his hands simply dropped off (15:14); he slaughtered one thousand people with the jawbone of an ass (15:15), and he killed more than three thousand people at once (16:28–30). The Spirit of God came upon David and empowered him beginning from the very point of his anointment (1 Sam 16:13). These references remind us of two things. First, in each of these events, the Spirit of God was manifested as God's manifestation and presence among his people. His manifestations and actions were perceived and presented as the ways of God's manifestation and execution of his particular purpose in a particular time and place. Second, such gifts and empowerments were not permanent, but temporary and limited to particular occasions and actions as destined by God and delivered and guided by the Spirit of God. Persons had to be specially chosen by God for a special task to be endowed with these kinds of extraordinary gifts and empowerments.

1.2.3. The Holy Spirit endowed people with prophetic gifts

The Old Testament presents four functions of the Spirit of God concerning the prophetic gifts and ministries: (1) generalized prophetic ministries; (2) people-targeted and response-required prophetic ministries; (3) no people targeted or response required but spontaneously inspired prophetic utterances; and (4) prophetic messages that seem to hang between people-targeted prophetic and spontaneous ecstatic utterances.

Generalized prophetic life and ministries: In the Old Testament there was a concept of general prophetic life and ministries. For example, Abraham was considered to be a prophet of God and God's spokesman (Gen 20:7). Isaac, Jacob, and Joseph were generally recognized as God's prophets (Ps 105:14-15). Moses was recognized as a prophet-leader (Num 12:6-8; Deut 18:15-19; Hos 12:13). Although there is no textual indication at what specific time the Spirit of God came upon Moses, before or after deliverance from Egypt, God said to him, "Bring me seventy ... elders ... I will take of the Spirit that is on you, and put ... on them" (Num 11:16-17). This indicates that Moses had been given the Spirit of prophetic ministry and leadership. During the time of Judges, Deborah was a prophetess who was filled with the Spirit of the LORD and turned the hearts of her people to God (Judg 4:4-20). Elijah can be categorized among the general prophets (1 Kgs 17). Although the specific time and manner of his call and appointment as a prophet are not mentioned in Scripture, Elijah's prophetic status was confirmed by God through the prophet Malachi (Mal 4:5). These references indicate that the Spirit of God came upon those individuals and gave them the prophetic status of life, leadership, and ministry power.

Invasive, people-targeted and response-required prophetic ministry: Invasive and people-targeted prophecies were directed from God to people at particular times and places, for particular purposes, and required a response from the receiving people. These kinds of prophetic ministries began mostly after the time of Israel's division into the Northern and Southern Kingdoms (1 Kgs 11-13). In this aspect, Isaiah was sent by God to speak his message to his people (Isa 6:8). Jeremiah's call and commissioning (Jer 2) were analogous to that of Isaiah. The majority of the prophets, both preexilic and postexilic, however, did not claim to be possessed, gifted, and guided by the Spirit of God. Yet, some references indicate that the true prophets were indeed possessed, gifted, inspired, and guided by the Spirit of God to deliver God's message to their people. For example, Nehemiah declared, "By your Spirit you admonished them through your prophets" (Neh 9:30). Speaking of his call, Isaiah attested "The Sovereign Lord and his Spirit sent me" (Isa 48:16) and "The Spirit of the Sovereign Lord is on me" (Isa 61:1). Hosea declared a prophet to be a "man of the Spirit" (Hos 9:7). Micah declared, "As for me, I am filled with the Spirit, power ... and might of the Lord to declare ... to Israel his sin" (Mic 3:8). Zechariah generalized that the people of his time hardened their hearts and did not listen to the words that the LORD had sent by his

Spirit through the prophets (Zech 7:12). These references indicate that in the process of the reception and utterances of prophetic messages, the Spirit of God always takes the lead and begins to possess, gift and inspire the prophet concerned. This reminds us that the true prophets of the Old Testament were chosen and called by God, and then possessed, gifted, empowered, inspired, and guided by the Spirit of God.

Spontaneously inspired prophetic utterances: Some Old Testament accounts inform us that the Spirit of God sometimes gave spontaneous and ecstatically inspired prophetic utterances. For example, when the Spirit of God rested on the seventy elders chosen to assist Moses, they prophesied (Num 11:25). The Spirit of God rested on Eldad and Medad and they prophesied (Num 11:26). Although Balaam was not from among the Israelites and was heading to them with a wicked purpose, the Spirit of God came upon him, inspired him, and he prophesied (Num 24:1–2). The Spirit of God also came upon Saul in power and he was changed into a different person; he met a procession of prophets and prophesied with them (1 Sam 10:6–11). When the Spirit of God departed from him, Saul moved with a plan to kill David and sent messengers to bring David to him. When his messengers found David with Samuel, the Spirit of God came upon them, inspired them, and they prophesied (1 Sam 19:20). When his messengers delayed in bringing David to him, Saul followed them and found them with Samuel and David. Amidst his surprise at what was going on, the Spirit of God came even upon Saul, inspired him and he also prophesied (1 Sam 19:23–24). In 1 Sam 10 we are told that Saul prophesied following his anointment at the beginning of his reign. In the latter case, however, he seemed to prophesy in "shame as God stripped him of his dignity, along with stripping him of the kingdom."[21]

These Old Testament references indicate that the Spirit of God came upon certain individuals on certain occasions and gave them spontaneous, inspired prophetic utterances, which were different from the prophetic utterances that targeted specific people with a specific purpose. This reminds us that in the Old Testament, the Spirit of God sometimes inspired incidental, charismatic, and ecstatic utterances that did not bear messages targeted to audiences or require responsive action from audiences. While the content and substance of such kinds of spontaneous utterances were unclear, the individuals concerned were possessed by the Spirit of God and inspired to speak what the Spirit put in their mouths. As

---

21. Steinmann, *1 Samuel*, 377–78.

the practitioners did not repeat their utterances, it seems that these kinds of prophetic utterances broke out momentarily for a purpose understood by the Spirit of God alone. These experiences indicate that in the Old Testament spontaneous prophecy and exuberant experience were bound together in response to the possession, gifting, and inspiring of the Spirit of God. These experiences seem to correspond to or are analogous with the experience of speaking in different tongues in New Testament times as spontaneous praise to God as a response to the reception of the gift of the Holy Spirit (Acts 2:4).

Messages that seem to hang between invasive and spontaneous prophetic utterances: Some empowerment and utterance experiences are attributed to the possession and inspiration of the Spirit of God. For instance, the Spirit of God came upon Amasai, one of the chiefs of David, and he spoke an encouraging, ecstatic prophetic message to David as someone possessed and inspired by the Spirit (1 Chr 12:18). The Spirit of God came upon Azariah, son of Oded, and he boldly spoke to Asa as someone also possessed and inspired by the Spirit of God (2 Chr 15:1–2). The Spirit of God came upon Jahaziel, son of Zechariah, and possessed and inspired him to speak to King Jehoshaphat and the people of Judea and Jerusalem (2 Chr 20:14–17). The Spirit of God came upon Zechariah, the son of Jehoiada the priest, and inspired him to admonish the people for their disobedience to God's commands (2 Chr 24:20). The messages of these speakers seem to hang between people-targeted prophetic messages and spontaneous prophetic utterances. In Amasai's case, it seems to be a spontaneous utterance but in Jahaziel's and Zechariah's cases, their utterances lean more towards being invasive, with people targeted to hear the message and act accordingly.

Similarly, the anointment of divinely chosen individuals was understood to be and referred to as resulting from possession and empowerment by the Spirit of God. Certain leaders of Israel were chosen, anointed, empowered, and guided by the Spirit of God to lead their nation (Deut 34:9; Judg 6:34; 1 Sam 11:6, 16:23; Ps 89:19–24). Isaiah understood and declared that the Spirit of the LORD anoints and empowers the servant of God to bring justice to the nations and to proclaim God's jubilee of grace and peace to the world (Isa 42:1–4, 61:1). The role played by God in choosing and anointing kings and empowering them for servanthood and just leadership as a sign of God's presence was attributed to the Spirit of God. Furthermore, the extraordinary knowledge and activities of certain individuals were also attributed to the Spirit of God. For example, God declared Joshua a man in whom the Spirit of God resided/dwelt (Num 27:18); speaking of Joseph's extraordinary ability, Pharaoh said, "one in whom is the Spirit of God?" (Gen 41:38); and speaking of Daniel's extraordinary ability, Nebuchadnezzar said, "One in whom is the Spirit of Holy God" (Dan 4:8). These instances indicate primarily that certain individuals committed themselves to God and were enabled by God to perform extraordinarily. In virtue of this, those individuals were perceived as possessed, gifted, empowered, and enabled by the Spirit of God. Secondly, these instances indicate that prophetic utterances, servant leadership, and performing extraordinary things of the Old Testament period were understood, by the beneficiaries, to follow the possession, gifting, empowering, and initiation of the Spirit of God, and the messages or acts were perceived as gifts of the Spirit of God. None of these experiences was perceived to be a result of human enthusiastic prompting. Thus, it seems reasonable to conclude that the manifestation, movements, gifts, and activities of the Spirit of God in the Old Testament were available only when and where God wanted to intervene or to introduce or enact his purpose among his people.

1.2.4. The Holy Spirit in renewal and transformation activities

In the Old Testament, the Spirit of God played a role in the divine renewing activities of people's lives and was understood as an agent or executor of renewal. Prophets such as Isaiah, Jeremiah, Ezekiel, and Joel predicted that God would renew and transform his people's ethical, spiritual, and social status by pouring out his Spirit upon them and putting his Spirit within them so that they might walk in his way in a new relationship with him (Isa 11:1–2; Jer 31:31–34; Ezek 36:27; 37; Joel 2:28). Isaiah's prediction of the transformation of the hopeless wilderness into a fruitful field (32:15–20) shows a metaphoric expression of divinely intended renewal for Israel. Jeremiah predicted that God was due to bring a new time and a new covenant that would involve people's knowledge of God. The word of God would no longer be external to God's people, written on tablets of stone, but written inwardly on their hearts by the Spirit. Jeremiah hoped that this would happen when God established a new covenant and a new relationship with his people (Jer 31:31–34). Ezekiel heard God speaking to him saying that he was going to bring a renewal specifically attributed to the Spirit of God. Ezekiel foresaw an appointed time when God would sprinkle clean water upon his people, remove a heart of stone from his people, put his Spirit within his people, and give a new heart to his people (Ezek 11:18–20, 36:25–32). Ezekiel had another vision of this hope when God gave him a vision of the valley of dry bones as a divine assurance that the long-awaited days for the renewal of the nations would take place when the Spirit of God would come and infuse new life into the dry bones, bringing them out of their graves and giving them a new and transformed life (Ezek 37:1–14).

These prophetic predictions point to the fact that in the Old Testament, the Spirit of God was at work in the world bringing renewal and transformation. The prophets declared that there was an appointed time when God would put his Spirit in his people's hearts in a new way and that the Spirit's dwelling within them would make a new covenant and a new relationship between God and his people. This would distinguish between the nature and quality of the people's obedience to God's law and the resultant blessings. Hence, humankind would be united to God in a new relationship by and through the Spirit of God as God himself declared, "neither by might nor by power," but by his Spirit (Zech 4:6). Thus, these accounts indicate that the divine challenging, changing and transforming the moral, ethical, spiritual and social status of the wicked people and restoring a new relationship between God and his people with a new heart and new obedience to the Law of God was attributed to the Spirit of God.

1.2.5. The Old Testament anticipates the future coming of the Holy Spirit

The Old Testament was the period heading toward the anticipated age of the Spirit. For Isaiah that particular age of the Spirit would be realized with the arrival of the expected one—the anointed one of the Spirit of God (Isa 11:1–5; 42:1–5; 61:1–4). He also predicted that God would pour out his Spirit in a new way on Jacob's offspring (Isa 44:3). Parallel words of anticipation are noted in Isa 59:21, Ezek 39:29, and Hag 2:5. The latter anticipations differ in content from the previous ones, but they simultaneously point to the appointed time when the Spirit of God would be permanently available to God's people. Joel prophesied that the appointed time would come when the people of God, all men and women, irrespective of their race, age, and social standing, would be filled with the Spirit of God and they would prophesy, dream dreams, and see visions (2:28–29). Joel's prophecy appears to be an anticipation of the gift of the Holy Spirit radically different from that of the Old Testament and includes all people on earth. Such inclusive sharing of the Spirit of God was inseparably connected to the new age of the Spirit and the new community of the Spirit through the particularly endowed figure of the Spirit (Isa 11:1–4; 42:1–4). Joel's prophecy, in particular, became a fundamental word for the New Testament period's development of the theology and doctrine of the Holy Spirit. From the Christian point of view, Joel's prophecy was fulfilled on the day of Pentecost when the Holy Spirit poured out on the 120 who were waiting in Jerusalem. The New Testament accounts such as John 1:33 and Acts 2:33 appear to be the fulfillment of the Old Testament anticipations, being identical with Joel 2:28–29. These kinds of anticipation of the Spirit-filled people of God are major themes that run from the Old Testament tradition through to the New Testament tradition.

Given the above discussions, two things seem worthy of nothing in light of the Old Testament accounts of the Holy Spirit:

First, although the Old Testament does not directly call the Holy Spirit "God," it attributes to the Holy Spirit the same divine nature, manifestation, power, gifts, and activities beginning in the inception of creation. The Spirit of God was implementing the divine purpose for creation from day one and exercising the continuous function of giving and sustaining life. All divinely initiated actions and events were enacted, illumined, empowered, and guided by the Spirit of God. Accordingly, the being, manifestation, and deeds of the Spirit of God were understood to be and identified as those of God the creator. This indicates that in the Old Testament, all the activities exclusively belonging to God were attributed to the Spirit of God. Besides the miraculous activities in the Israelites' deliverance from Egypt, the Old Testament community knew God's presence, gifts, power, and activities only through the manifestation, possession, gifts, empowerment, inspiration, and works of the Spirit of God. This seems to affirm that God himself was present and enacting his purpose through his Spirit. This marks who the Holy Spirit is and what he does. Thus, since the Spirit of God was manifest in absolute divine nature and acting only with absolute divine purpose as God's presence, it can be conceived that there is no difference between the being of God and the Spirit of God. God the creator and the Spirit of God might not be technically one and identical but they are utterly inseparable by nature, manifestation, authority, and activities. Their distinction seems to be simply a distinction of personality without any separation of essence. Thus, these Old Testament teachings about the Spirit of God have provided the church with a clear grounding for the pre-Christian view of the essence, presence, manifestations, gifts, and activities of the Holy Spirit. It was on this grounding that Christianity illustrated the image of the doctrine of the Trinity in which the Holy Spirit is acknowledged to be a distinct and equal member of the Triune personality of God's being.

Second, in the Old Testament, the Spirit of God was identified with divinely provided gifts of wisdom, knowledge, skill, power, awakening, inspiration, prophecy, spontaneous ecstatic utterances, vision, dreams, renewal, and transformation. The Spirit of God came upon certain individuals possessing (controlling), gifting, empowering, inspiring, and guiding them to carry out what God wanted to be done at a particular time, place, and in a particular manner. All the divinely provided and delivered messages, utterances, and actions were understood to follow the coming of the Spirit of God; to result from the possessing (controlling), gifting, empowering inspiration and initiation of the Spirit of God, and to be experienced as the gifts of the Spirit of God. These experiences seem to be the essential character of the coming of the Holy Spirit upon individuals and resulting Spirit-initiated subjective experiential appropriation of the coming of the Holy Spirit. Thus, these Old Testament claims run parallel to the New Testament's claims of the Spirit-initiated subjective experiences of the reception, gifts, power, and activities of the Holy Spirit.

Despite the above-discussed theological and biblical facts, three things seem to be worth noting: first, the Holy Spirit was manifest and acted only as a visiting divine agent from time to time as occasions or events required but not as a permanently indwelling gift of God. Second, the Holy Spirit was conveyed from one person to another, from Moses to the seventy elders (Num 11:25); from Moses to Joshua (Num 27:18–21; Deut 34:9); and from Elijah to Elisha (2 Kgs 2:15). Third, despite the presentation by Isa 63:10 of the Holy Spirit as a personal being that can be offended by human behavior and aggressively avenges it, the Old Testament's understanding of the independent personality of the Holy Spirit seems to be unclear. These features may remain debatable for academic studies.

1.3. THE NEW TESTAMENT TEACHING

The Old Testament era was an era moving toward the divinely appointed age of the Holy Spirit. As we shall see, Joel's prophecy, in particular, described the era in which the coming and reception of the Holy Spirit would be radically different from that of the Old Testament period. The New Testament Scriptures claim that this particular prophecy was fulfilled in the New Testament era: primarily in the person of Jesus, and secondarily in the church at and after Pentecost. The examination of this section, therefore, focuses on three major issues: the presence and role of the Holy Spirit in the life and ministry of Jesus; the ways that Jesus' teachings established the doctrine of the Holy Spirit; and Jesus' promise about the future coming of the Holy Spirit and its fulfillment.

1.3.1. The Holy Spirit in the life and ministry of Jesus

In the conception of Jesus: According to the Gospel of Luke, the presence and role of the Holy Spirit in Jesus' life and ministry began from the time of his conception. Luke informs us that the angel told Mary that the process of Jesus' conception would be a distinctively and radically new mystery in history in which both the divine nature and human nature would be brought into union by the power and action of the Holy Spirit. The angel said, "The Holy Spirit will come upon you, and the power of the Most High will overshadow you" (Luke 1:35). The angel assured Mary that by choosing her to host this incomprehensible mystery in her womb and making her the mother of the Holy One, the Most High, God, has done a peculiar and a very great and high favor for her. Her son was to be named the Son of the Most High, Jesus—a savior, which later came to be known as the name above all names in the universe (Phil 2:9–11); nothing is left outside his authority and everything is put in subjection to him who is crowned with glory and honour (Heb 2:8). While the formation of every child in his/her mother's womb in natural procreation and the entrance of the breath of life (*ruah, nefesh*) into the fetus in the womb is a divine mystery in human nature, the mystery of Jesus' conception is more incomprehensible. The nature of his conception, says Max Turner, "removes Jesus' origins from the sphere of human possibilities" and "locates him in the divine realm."[22] In the context of the angelic annunciation,

---

22. Turner, *Power from on High*, 158.

Michael Horton notes, the "Holy Spirit gave Jesus to the world in the Incarnation."[23] The Holy Spirit, therefore, according to Robert Letham, is the Spirit of "Incarnation, the one in whom and through whom the Word of God breaks into history."[24] This event makes Jesus' conception miraculous and makes Jesus a unique divine person in history which is where the theology and language of *Emmanuel—God with us* draws its roots.

In Jesus' anointment and ministry: During the Old Testament period, there was a tradition of anointing prophets, priests, and kings as was the case with Aaron (Exod 28:41), Saul (1 Sam 10:1), Elisha, and Jehu (1 Kgs 19:15–16). The Old Testament predicted that the Spirit of the LORD would rest on the future coming Messiah and that the Messiah would also be anointed with the Holy Spirit far more bountifully than anyone in the Old Testament (Isa 11:1–2, 42:1–2, 61:1–4). John the Baptist saw the fulfillment of this prediction when he witnessed the Holy Spirit descend and rest upon Jesus at his baptism (Matt 3:16; John 1:33). At the beginning of his ministry, Jesus himself declared in the synagogue in Nazareth that the Spirit of the Lord was upon him, anointing him to preach good news to the poor and to rescue people from bondage and deformity (Luke 4:18–20). In virtue of his unique anointing, Jesus was able to deliver the message of God in a far-reaching new way which "no human being had ever been able to declare before."[25] He was uniquely anointed to fulfill the entire hope expected from the Old Testament's priestly, prophetic, and royal lines. For this reason, he is greater than all before him and performed all things with his "decisive authoritative Spirit-imbued command . . . dramatic power, effecting both judgment and salvation."[26] Furthermore, he is

- the one whom the "winds and the waves obey" (Matt 8:27);
- the one who has "authority on earth to forgive sins" (Matt 9:6);
- "greater than the prophet" (Matt 11:9);
- the "Lord of the Sabbath" (Matt 12:8);
- the one in whom God is present in his power to free people from their wretched state of life (Luke 4:18–19);

---

23. Horton, *Rediscovering the Holy Spirit*, 85.
24. Letham, *Holy Trinity in Scripture*, 56.
25. Brunner, *Christian Doctrine of Creation*, 275.
26. Turner, *Power from on High*, 183.

- ← the one who spoke and acted in absolute divine authority saying, "Truly, truly, I say unto you" (John 5:19–24);
- ← the one who did only what God the Father does (John 5:19–22);
- ← the one who came to "save the lost" (Matt 18:11);
- ← the light of the world to those who want to come to God (John 8:12; 14:6);
- ← the one who incarnates, proclaims, and delivers God's grace by which alone the world can be saved (John 1:12, 16–17; 3:16; 10:9);
- ← the one who is "the way, the truth, and the life" for those who want to come to God (John 14:6).

Indeed, it is conceivable that Jesus can do these things by his authority as a divine person. Yet, his declaration in Luke 4:18–20 demonstrates that he was uniquely anointed by the Holy Spirit in such a way as to enable him to do what he has done. His unique anointing by the Holy Spirit clearly demonstrates the very being and the very action of God in his being and doing. This is his "moral difference from humankind."[27] In virtue of this anointing, the entire content and quality of Jesus' mission and ministry was vastly different from that of his predecessors. His earthly life and ministry were surrounded by the presence, power, and empowerment of the Holy Spirit, and his ministry was the joint working of himself and the Holy Spirit. In general, as Letham notes, Jesus was "governed and directed by the Holy Spirit" in all that he became, lived, and did.[28] This reminds us that the work of redemption as a whole involves the Holy Spirit, who remains together with Jesus in bringing about salvation for the lost world,[29] and that Jesus and the Holy Spirit are "inseparable companions in the history of salvation, working together in a joint mission to bring sinners into communion" with God.[30] Thus, the story of Jesus' conception, anointment, and earthly ministry informs us that the identity of Jesus was determined through his conception by the Holy Spirit; through his anointing by the Holy Spirit; through his empowerment by the Holy Spirit; through his equipment throughout his temptations and sufferings, and his joint ministry with the Holy Spirit.

---

27. Badcock, *Light of Truth*, 160–61.
28. Letham, *Holy Trinity in Scripture*, 57.
29. Beckwith, *Holy Trinity*, 227.
30. Nafzger et al., *Confessing the Gospel*, 555.

1.3.2. Jesus' teachings of the theology and doctrine of the Holy Spirit

Along with his emphasis on the presence and role of the Holy Spirit in his ministry, Jesus' discourses also laid a strong foundation for the doctrine of the Holy Spirit's deity, independent personality, and divine role in the church and the world. According to the Gospel of John, four of Jesus' sayings can be identified as examples:

(1) Jesus said that "The Spirit gives life" (John 6:63), which seems to be a corresponding idea to the role of the Spirit of God in the inception of the creation (Gen 1:2).

(2) Jesus said, "I will go, he will come" (John 14:25–26). In this statement, Jesus declared the Holy Spirit to be an independent person in the Godhead by referring to the Holy Spirit as "he." Jesus was the only figure in history that attributed a personhood designation to the Holy Spirit. In this strange personification of the Holy Spirit, Jesus assured his audiences that the Holy Spirit would replace him as a person and take over all the roles he had begun to perform as a person. Post-Pentecost accounts of the New Testament show that the Holy Spirit himself proved his independent personality and operation through both his presence and the role he played in the early church. The accounts present the Holy Spirit as an independent divine person in his own right with consciousness, will, absolute authority, and a personal sense. As it can be noted from the book of Acts, in particular, the Holy Spirit played a divine role as an independent person in every detailed aspect of the inward life and outward acts of the early church. His acts extended to acting as a primary guide in leadership and episcopate appointment (Acts 6:1–6, 20:28); willing or forbidding people to do something (Acts 8:29, 16:6–7); and giving intelligence and guidance for the apostolic missionary movement (Acts 18:9–10, 20:22–24, 23:11) including approval and disapproval of it (Acts 8:26–29, 10:19–20). He also acted in church discipline along with the apostles (Acts 15:28–29). He spoke to the apostles in the way only a person can do (Acts 8:29; 10:19, 11:12, 16:6–7) and commanded the church to separate individuals for the ministry he wanted them to carry out (Acts 13:1–4). He was described as having a mind, knowledge, and intelligence (1 Cor 2:11–12); he teaches the ways of God (1 Cor 2:13); gives to Christians the mind of Christ (1 Cor 2:16); he intercedes (Rom 8:27); gives supernatural gifts for life and ministry (1 Cor 12:4–11); and he can be grieved as a personal being (Eph 4:30). These references ascribe

to the Holy Spirit attributes that are characteristics of a personal being who can think, feel, will, speak, and act with independent authoritative activities but as an invisible personality and transcendent being.[31] This evidence indicates that the Holy Spirit owns a real personality and does things only a real person can do. This evidence provides us with clearly annotated basic guidelines for understanding the origin, essence, personality, authority, and independent operations of the Holy Spirit.

(3) Jesus said generations will be baptized in the name of the Father, of the Son, and of the Holy Spirit (Matt 28:19). As a further affirmation of the identity, dignity, and authority of the Holy Spirit, Jesus declared that gentiles in all generations will be baptized in the name of the Holy Spirit. The Old Testament's one and singular name "God" takes the names of three distinct divine persons together, Father, Son, and Holy Spirit. Accordingly, Jesus instituted holy baptism to be performed in the name of the Triune God.

(4) Jesus said that "he who speaks against the Holy Spirit will not be forgiven, either in this age or in the age to come" (Matt 12:32). Here Jesus asserted two things: the absolute significance of the Holy Spirit's presence and power in his ministry and the identical dignity of the Holy Spirit with God the Father, which God himself ordered not to be misused (Exod 20:7). With these words Jesus also affirms that anyone who speaks against the Holy Spirit stands forever outside the boundaries of God's mercy. This affirmation seems to mean, as Beckwith notes, that "the work of creation and redemption involves the Spirit as much as the Father and the Son" and that there would have been "no access to the salvation purchased by the Son except by the Holy Spirit."[32] Jesus' strong words here seem to further affirm that salvation is the work of the Triune God.

These identifying characteristics provide convincing theological, biblical, and doctrinal grounds to formulate the doctrine of the Holy Spirit as a person of the Trinity distinct from the Father and the Son. Given this biblical evidence, the issue of the Holy Spirit's divinity, independent personality, and independent authoritative operation of the divine purpose seems to be *incontestable*. The church fathers based their rationale on this biblical evidence when formulating the doctrine that acknowledges the Holy Spirit to be an independent person of the Trinity, equal and one with God the Father and the Son (see chapter 6).

---

31. Nafzger et al., *Confessing the Gospel*, 553.
32. Beckwith, *Holy Trinity*, 237, 229.

1.3.3. Jesus promised the future coming of the Holy Spirit

Jesus' mission was to be shared with his followers who would stand on his authority to represent him and to act on his behalf. At the beginning of his ministry, Jesus called a group of twelve people to be with him, trained, and sent out to extend his mission (Matt 10:1-4; Mark 3:13-19). These followers exercised this mission when Jesus sent them out to preach the good news of the kingdom of God just as he had begun to do (Luke 9:1-6, 10). Jesus then commissioned them, before his ascension, to continue his mission, beginning from Jerusalem to the ends of the world and to make the kind of disciples he had made for the kingdom of God (Matt 28:18-20). Hence, the question that might be asked here is: if Jesus served with the presence and power of the Holy Spirit, how much more would his messengers need the same Holy Spirit in his physical absence? Being conscious of this need, Jesus promised to equip his disciples with gifts and power from on high which would be realized in the coming of the Holy Spirit. Jesus taught his disciples for three consecutive years by using various ways and methods of teaching. Yet he was aware that they were not adequately empowered in the way he would have liked them to be. Thus, he told them to wait in Jerusalem for the baptizing, transforming, and empowering gift from on high, which would take place along with the coming and reception of the Holy Spirit (Luke 24:49; Acts 1:4-8).

The account of John's Gospel, in particular, clearly reports how Jesus promised the future coming of the Holy Spirit and what his activities and relationships would look like. When speaking about the Holy Spirit's relationship with the Father, Jesus said that Holy Spirit proceeds from the Father (John 15:26) and that the Father would send him in response to Jesus' prayer (14:26). When speaking about the Holy Spirit's relationship with himself, Jesus said that the Holy Spirit is the other counselor, comforter, and guide who replaces Jesus and acts on his behalf (14:16, 26); he will be given at the prayer of Jesus and given in Jesus' name (14:16, 26); he will come only after the departure of Jesus (16:7); he will bear witness to Jesus and will glorify Jesus (15:26; 16:14); he will receive and deliver only what is of Jesus and does nothing on his own (16:13-15); he will recall to the minds of Jesus' followers what Jesus had taught them during the course of his physical presence with them (14:26). In speaking about the Holy Spirit's relationship to his followers, Jesus said that he is what God promised to give to Jesus' followers (Luke 24:49; Acts 1:4); he will be "sent to them" (16:7); he will be "with them forever" (14:16); he will be "in them and dwells with them" (14:17); he will "teach them" (14:26); he will "guide them into all truth" (16:13) and he will alert them about what is to come (16:13). Finally, in speaking about the Holy Spirit's relation to the world, Jesus said, "The world neither sees him nor knows him" and therefore cannot receive him (14:17) and he will confront the world with regard to sin, righteousness, and judgment (16:7–11).

In the light of these gospel accounts, it may be concluded that Jesus is the unique God-man, through whom the Old Testament's Spirit of God gave full revelation. His conception was the work of the Holy Spirit; his anointing as Christ, Messiah, was by the Holy Spirit; his baptism was a combination of water and Spirit; he was anointed, empowered, and guided by the Holy Spirit during his earthly life and ministry, and the Holy Spirit continues to bear witness to him and glorify him to the end of the ages (John 15:26; 16:14). Jesus, as Turner asserts, was not only "filled with the Spirit, but owes his very existence to the Spirit."[33] He and only he, in Michael Green's words, is the "funnel through whom the Holy Spirit becomes available" to the world.[34] The long-ago predicted and long-awaited time and age of the Spirit, which inaugurated the dawn of the new age of the new covenant, was brought about by the person Jesus. The fuller knowledge and realization of the person, power, gifts and activities of the Holy Spirit were made known and made possible to the world only after and through Jesus. He, and only he, opened the way for the ever-dwelling reception and realization of the gifts, power, and works of the Holy Spirit. Thus, the fulfillment of the promised and expected reception of the Holy Spirit came at the feast of Pentecost following Jesus' ascension. To this, we will turn our discussion.

---

33. Turner, *Power from on High*, 158.
34. Green, *I Believe*, 50.

CHAPTER 2

Reception of the Holy Spirit and His Gifts at and after Pentecost

WE HAVE SEEN HOW Jesus promised the future coming of the Holy Spirit and how his followers would be baptized in the Holy Spirit and clothed with power from on high when the Holy Spirit was poured out upon them. This chapter examines how that promise was fulfilled at Pentecost. The examination focuses on features such as: (1) the nature of the coming and reception of the Holy Spirit at Pentecost; (2) what the term "baptism in the Holy Spirit" means and what the New Testament teaches about its origin, theology, and practice; (3) how reception of the Holy Spirit continued to occur in the post-Pentecostal life and ministry of the church; (4) the relationship between baptism in the Holy Spirit, water baptism, and laying-on of hands, as well as differences between these phenomena; and (5) how repeated reception of the Holy Spirit was experienced by the apostles.

2.1. THE COMING AND RECEPTION OF THE HOLY SPIRIT ON THE DAY OF PENTECOST

The day of Pentecost, according to the Old Testament, was an annual Jewish festival which fell on the fiftieth day after the Passover. In the Old Testament Pentecost was called "Feast of Weeks" because of the seven intervening weeks between Passover and Pentecost and the "Feast of Harvest" or the "Day of the Firstfruits." At the beginning of the first seven weeks that led to the Pentecost, the first sheaf of the barley crop was offered to the Lord. On the day of Pentecost, the fruits of the wheat harvest were offered to the Lord (Exod 23:16; Lev 23:9–14; Deut 16:9–12). It was on that "Feast of Harvest" that the Holy Spirit was poured out on the followers of Jesus in Jerusalem. From that day on the Holy Spirit gifted, empowered, and guided the receivers into the new harvest of the kingdom of God in the new covenant through the presence, gifts, workings, and guidance of the Holy Spirit. The book of Acts attests that all those who were in the upper room were "filled with the Holy Spirit and began to speak in other tongues as the Spirit enabled them" (Acts 2:4). This coming and reception of the Holy Spirit was accompanied by what sounded like a mighty wind from heaven filling the house and something that seemed like tongues of fire resting upon those who received the gift of the Holy Spirit. Referring to the apostolic witness of the event at Pentecost and their guidance to the early church regarding how to celebrate the day of Pentecost in the future, the writers of the *Constitutions of the Holy Apostles* wrote this: "After ten days from the ascension . . . do [you] keep a great festival: for on that day, at the third hour, the Lord Jesus sent on us [the apostles] the gift of the Holy Ghost, and we were filled with his energy, and we spoke with new tongues, as that Spirit did suggest to us; and we preached both to Jews and Gentiles."[1] The phenomenon of the day of Pentecost reminds us of three features:

1. There was an objective gift of the Holy Spirit from God as fulfillment of his long-awaited promise (Joel 2:28)—objective impartation of the Holy Spirit to indwell believers.

2. There was subjective experience of the presence, gifts, power, and workings of the Holy Spirit. When God imparted the Holy Spirit to his people, he had also given them charismatic gifts. As a proof of this, the Holy Spirit enabled the receivers to speak in different tongues unknown to them, and which made them appear drunk to their observers. It was the divine, objective impartation of the Holy Spirit that was initiating the charismatic form of spiritual experiences in the lives of the receivers of the Holy Spirit. Having given them charismatic gifts, the Holy Spirit then inspired and moved believers towards practical implementation through subjective experience. Hence, subjective experiential movement was initiated by the Holy Spirit and practiced by people as a response to the gifts endowed and power imparted along with the impartation of the Holy Spirit.

---

1. *Constitutions of the Holy Apostles* 5.20.

The receivers experienced simply Holy Spirit-initiated subjective experience. This clearly reminds us about the objective gift and subjective experiential contents of the manifestation of the Holy Spirit.

3. The gift of the Holy Spirit contained the gift of special power, as the fulfillment of Jesus' promise (Luke 24:49), and special and unprecedented supernatural gifts. Unprecedented power was imparted along with the impartation of the Holy Spirit, which traditionally came to be known as "Pentecostal power." The receivers of the gift of the Holy Spirit were empowered and inspired to go forth among the nations to persuade people to believe in Jesus Christ crucified and to receive the gift of the Holy Spirit. From among those gifted and empowered, Peter took the lead, stood up, and explained to the crowd, who were observing them in puzzlement, that the phenomenon was the fulfillment of the long-awaited prophecy of Joel (Acts 2:14–18).

This indicates that the reception of the Holy Spirit at Pentecost resulted in tangible empowerment and new charismatic experiences in the lives of the receivers of the Holy Spirit. Peter assured his puzzled audience that this was the fulfillment of the divinely appointed, predicted, and awaited coming of the Spirit of God differently from that of the Old Testament times. He assured them of two main things: that that pattern of reception of the Holy Spirit means the simultaneous reception of the forgiveness of sins, salvation, and power, i.e., as one event of the same moment; and that the Holy Spirit confronts the recipients with supernatural power, gifts, inspiration, and audible and visible physical movements. The power of the Holy Spirit had an impact on Peter's audiences and quickened their response to the message resulting in three thousand believing in Jesus and being baptized in his name (Acts 2:37–41). Such an effective evangelization was inseparably connected to the outpouring of the Holy Spirit upon them and their resultant empowerment. On that historical day, the church was born and through that notable event, the entire content of the mission and ministry of Jesus was handed over to the disciples, together with the gift of the Holy Spirit and power from on High. James D. G. Dunn considers the event at Pentecost as the beginning of the new age and new covenant in the reception and experience of the Holy Spirit and that Jesus is the one who brings in the new age and new covenant and initiates into them by baptism in the Holy Spirit.[2] Kilian McDonnell considers it that "like Christ, the Christian is anointed

---

2. Dunn, *Baptism in the Holy Spirit*, 41, 43–44.

by the Spirit," which is a sign that indicates that a "believer has entered with Christ into the Messianic age."[3] History, therefore, is "divided not only by the incarnation and messianic mission of Jesus but also because of the pouring out of the Holy Spirit upon God's people in an unusual inundation"[4] at Pentecost.

Dunn's and McDonnell's observations seem to be accurate because Pentecost has sharply differentiated between the old age and the new age ways of the Holy Spirit's coming, reception, and resulting practice. Reception of the Holy Spirit at Pentecost would clearly initiate the receivers' entry into the new age of the Spirit and the new covenant of a new heart and new obedience to God. The reception of the Holy Spirit at and after Pentecost clearly marks the believing community's entering into the new age and new covenant and sharing in the benefits and blessings in a greatly different way to that of the old age experience.[5] In this dramatic event, Pentecost established such new things as: (1) a new era, the age of the Holy Spirit, which constitutes the new covenant people of God; (2) Christian entry into Abba relationship with God the Father through the gifts and acts of the Holy Spirit; (3) the sacramental rite of water plus Spirit baptism; and (4) the birth and realization of the church in the world. These features are the characteristics of the new age and new covenant which came into being after Pentecost, and thereafter the Holy Spirit became available to fill all the people of God.

2.2. THE TERM "BAPTISM IN THE HOLY SPIRIT"

As mentioned in the introduction, the concept and practice of baptism in the Holy Spirit have been viewed as one of the complicated and perplexing issues within the doctrine of the Holy Spirit. Understanding, interpretation, and application of this phenomenon have become even more controversial in contemporary Christian spiritual experience. This raises the question: why has the concept and practice of baptism in the Holy Spirit become one of the points of tension within the doctrine of the Holy Spirit? The search for an answer to this question is one of the impetuses prompting this broader study and this section of the chapter specifically. A search for an answer to this question, again, requires addressing

---

3. McDonnell, *Holy Spirit and Power*, 73.
4. Horton, *Rediscovering the Holy Spirit*, 138.
5. Dunn, *Baptism in the Holy Spirit*, 44, 48–49.

questions such as: (1) What does the term "baptism in the Holy Spirit" mean? (2) What does Scripture teach about its theology, doctrine, and practice? (3) Does baptism in the Holy Spirit differ from the reception of the Holy Spirit in the sacramental rite of water baptism? (4) How should it be understood and defined from theological, biblical, and practical perspectives? And so forth. Scripture does not provide us with clear-cut answers to these questions but it does provide certain key themes, indications, and concepts of baptism in the Holy Spirit as promised by God and as occurred at and after Pentecost. These rare themes and indications have acted as a cue and biblical guide for some Christians in the formulation of the doctrine of baptism in the Holy Spirit in contemporary Christianity. Identifying and analyzing these themes and indications is important to answer the questions raised concerning baptism in the Holy Spirit within the doctrine of the Holy Spirit.

As we shall consider in chapter 4, the concept of baptism in the Holy Spirit was as taught by Jesus and is recorded in John 3:1–11. This text seems to suggest that baptism in water + the Spirit is one event that takes place at one moment, and that reception of the Spirit is inseparably connected to the water baptism. The water is the outward visible element in which people are visibly baptized. The Spirit is the inward invisible element in which they are invisibly baptized by the redeeming, transforming, and saving divine. Hence, both elements together yield the same result: rebirth in the Holy Spirit. For Jesus, this baptism bears mysterious power to transform the sinful nature of a natural man into a spiritual man. It is for this reason that Jesus emphasized this baptism as the primary requirement to belong to the kingdom of God. This baptism, for Jesus, is essential and conditional for salvation. In this discourse, Jesus has constituted a theology and doctrine, as well as a practice of initial sacramental baptism as a means to give the gift of salvation and the Holy Spirit. The sacramental principle of water baptism draws its roots from this divinely disclosed pattern of saving baptism. Nevertheless, a different concept of "baptism in the Holy Spirit" is used by John the Baptist. The Baptist uses the term to differentiate his ministry of repentance through mere water baptism from Jesus' ministry in which Jesus baptizes with fire and Holy Spirit (Matt 3:11). Indeed, the Baptist declares that the term "baptism in the Holy Spirit" has not been coined by him, but learned by him from a heavenly voice that spoke to him saying, "The man on whom you see the Spirit come down and remain is he who will baptize with the Holy Spirit" (John 1:33). This shows that the term "baptism in the Holy

Spirit" was primarily coined by the heavens and introduced to the world at the moment of Jesus' baptism. John the Baptist's witness discloses that the origin, designation, concept, and practice of "baptism in the Holy Spirit" are from God. Theologically, therefore, baptism in the Holy Spirit and its practice is objective. Jesus too recognized the term when he referred to John the Baptist's discourse in the words, "you will be baptized with the Holy Spirit" (Acts 1:5, 8). Scripture does not, however, give any clue about whether Jesus gave a further explanation about what the term "baptism in the Holy Spirit" means or what the precise nature of its experience would look like.

Luke for his part uses different terms or phrases to describe the nature of the reception of, or baptism with, the Holy Spirit in the early church: "you will be baptized in the Holy Spirit" (Acts 1:5; 11:16); the "Holy Spirit comes on you" (1:8; 19:6); "filled with the Holy Spirit" (2:4; 9:17); the Spirit "poured out" (2:33; 10:45); to "receive the Holy Spirit" (2:38; 8:15, 17; 10:47; 19:2), and the "Holy Spirit came on them" (11:15), etc. These different expressions may raise a question: are these terms and phrases expressions of different events or different expressions of the same event—i.e., reception of the Holy Spirit? From their context, these different expressions appear to be nothing other than descriptions of one event, the reception of the Holy Spirit. The experiences of the coming and reception of the Holy Spirit may differ only according to the time, place, and conditions in which the event occurred. Otherwise, these different expressions seem to refer to the one and single reception experience of the Holy Spirit, which was predicted as "baptism in the Holy Spirit." Larry Christenson suggests that Luke might have used such different expressions "synonymously" which altogether have been "narrowed down to a single term baptism with the Holy Spirit."[6] This appears to be the case because Luke seems to be simply using a variety of verbs to express the same event without noticing the meaning each expression may give. These different expressions seem to be metaphors that underlie a common biblical expression for giving the Holy Spirit, namely, to "pour out" the Spirit (Joel 2:28–29). The central common meaning of these different expressions seems to be "you will be filled with the Holy Spirit," which is generally referred to as "baptism in the Holy Spirit." What might be noted from these different expressions of the same event is that Luke may not have written the accounts of these events at one time. Rather, he

---

6. Christenson, *Charismatic Renewal*, 51–52.

collected them on different occasions, and so appears to be using different linguistic expressions following different occasions of data collection thereby creating a lack of uniform linguistic treatment for different occurrences of the same phenomenon and using interchangeable expressions to describe "manifest demonstration and working of the Holy Spirit in terms of manifest experience."[7] Thus, these different expressions, for Luke, define and present the whole concept and practice of what is meant by the term "baptism in the Holy Spirit." This seems to be the reason why he does not repeat the term again and again except for where it is mentioned twice in the book of Acts, i.e., Jesus' words in Acts 1:5–8 and Peter's reference to this in Acts 11:16.

A question that might be asked here is: how do scholarships understand and interpret the term "baptism in the Holy Spirit"? It would seem that contemporary scholars have not yet reached a consensus on the understanding and interpretation of the term "baptism in the Holy Spirit." For example, for Frank D. Macchia, the term is a "metaphor used by John the Baptist to characterize and inaugurate the person and work of Jesus" and is a "metaphor that can function imaginatively in ways other than doctrinal conceptualization."[8] For Karl Barth, it is the best possibility of the "self-attestation and self-impartation of Jesus Christ himself" and is a "magical infusion of supernatural powers by whose proper use a man can do what he cannot do in his own strength."[9] For Donald Bridge and David Phypers, it is a "distinctive work of Christ" that "adds to human experience what was unknown before Christ" and is one of many ways in which God works to bring changes in the lives of believers.[10] For Turner, it is the messianic "immersing of people in a flowing river of fiery Spirit" and "pouring out of the eschatological flood of Spirit and fire from on high that transforms . . . the people of God and consumes all evil."[11] For Karl Rahner, it is an "ultimate fullness of the Spirit"[12] and for Anthony C. Thiselton, it is "neither partial nor conditional" but a "complete filling with the Spirit."[13] For Michael Welker, it is an experience that "surpasses all the previously experienced effects of and previously awakened

---

7. Christenson, *Charismatic Renewal*, 51–52.
8. Macchia, "Kingdom and the Power," 111–12.
9. Karl Barth, *Church Dogmatics*, 4/4:32.
10. Bridge and Phypers, *Spiritual Gifts*, 137–39.
11. Turner, *Power from on High*, 181.
12. Rahner, *Spirit in the Church*, 10.
13. Thiselton, *Holy Spirit*, 56.

expectations of the Holy Spirit" that "exerts an influence on an experience of objective powerlessness, of mutual forgiveness, speechlessness, and inability to achieve understanding." In it, Welker adds, the "fullness of the Holy Spirit's action is really present and effective" and that the term "cannot be comprehended in an essential and structure-giving manner."[14] And yet, says Thiselton, by referring to other sources, "it is a doctrine still in the making."[15]

Now, who is right among these scholars about the term "baptism in the Holy Spirit"? To which of these interpretations are we to consent? Well, all of these scholarly interpretations seem to be valid and valuable. On the one hand, since the phenomenon of baptism in the Spirit is only the fulfillment of the Old Testament's prediction of the pouring out of the Spirit of God (Joel 2:28), all the interpretations offered by these scholars apply to it. On the other hand, however, there seems to be much perplexity about translating the term "baptism in the Holy Spirit" into a common and understandable interpretation. In this respect, what Thiselton refers to as a "doctrine still in the making" seems worthy of attention because it points out that there is still ongoing complexity in understanding and interpretation of the term. Since Scripture reports the phenomenon as an experience at Pentecost but does not make it clear from conceptual, doctrinal, or practical perspectives, it is surely difficult to know how to define the term in any clear-cut way. Particularly when viewed in light of the great variety of the presentations in Acts regarding the different ways of reception of the Holy Spirit, it is indeed formidable to give an exact definition or conclusion to the term "baptism in the Holy Spirit." Its mystery, on the one hand, seems to fall outside a human finite conceptual framework. Therefore, an ultimate definition of the term, beyond those offered by these scholars, may not be possible unless one receives the content of God's heart that may lead towards a true definition of the term. Given this complexity and the range of terminology, finding a definitive definition may remain as complex as ever. On the other hand, however, the search for the most likely definition should not lead us to confusion. Without going into the depths of the intricacies of the term, it may be fair to perceive it as nothing different from, or other than, the Holy Spirit's coming in power upon, and penetration of, the lives of the receivers.

---

14. Welker, *God the Spirit*, 234–5. See a similar view offered in detail by Hurt, "Spirit Baptism."

15. Thiselton, *Holy Spirit*, 457.

2.3. RECEPTION OF THE HOLY SPIRIT IN THE POST-PENTECOST EARLY CHURCH

Reception of the Holy Spirit at Samaria (Acts 8:4–17)

Biblically, Samaritans were understood as mixed-race Jews and were viewed by the Judean Jews as hostile because they had both Jewish and gentile blood. Here it is important to raise questions such as: When did their hostility begin? From where did it draw its roots? How and why did it continue until the time of the apostolic ministry? If their enmity was still strongly in existence during the time of the apostles, then how did Philip, being a Jew, dare to enter into the territory of the enemy to preach the gospel? According to Scripture, the hostility between Samaritans and Judean Jews drew its roots from the division of the Israelites into the Northern and Southern Kingdoms during the reign of Rehoboam the son of Solomon (1 Kgs 11–12). Ten of the twelve tribes of Israelites became the Northern Kingdom, with its capital in Samaria and with Jeroboam as its king. Scripture indicates that these tribes continued to rebel against God (1 Kgs 14:1–16; 16:21–34) and God called the Assyrians to punish them. The Assyrians invaded and conquered the Northern Kingdom in the early eighth century BC (2 Kgs 17:7–22; 18:9–16) and carried the people away to their own countries. The Assyrians then brought some foreign races and settled them in Samaria. When the ten tribes were transported to Assyria, a few were left in Samaria. Those left behind in Samaria intermarried with the foreign races who had been brought to the land by the Assyrians (2 Kgs 17:24–41). Thus, they were known as Jewish and gentile mixed race, both in blood and religion (Ezra 9).

The remaining two tribes of Israel continued as the Southern Kingdom with its capital in Jerusalem. Scripture indicates that they too continued to rebel against God (1 Kgs 14:21–24) and God brought the Babylonians to punish them. The Babylonians invaded and conquered the Southern Kingdom in the sixth century BC and carried them away to the Babylonian lands (Jer 25–29). Unlike the Samaritan Jews, perhaps on account of the Lord's promise to bring them back to their own land after seventy years of captivity (Jer 29:10–11), the Judean Jews strongly defended their Jewish identity and remained as Jews in the land of captivity. When they were allowed to return to their country, they continued to return to their land and rebuild their city and temple under the leadership of individuals such as Zerubbabel, Ezra, and Nehemiah. Thus, when the Judean Jews returned and settled in their land, they began to discover the Samaritans' interrelationship with those considered to be alien races. From then on they began to disdainfully look down on the Samaritans and reject them for no longer being pure Jews. When the Judean Jews began to rebuild their city and temple, the Samaritans wanted to join in and offer their help. However, the Judean Jews rejected their offer and the Samaritans were prohibited from taking part in rebuilding the temple.[16] It is from this historical incident that the long-standing hostility between the Judean Jews and Samaritan Jews draws its roots. During the early New Testament times, it was well understood and even proverbial that the Judean Jews had no dealing with the Samaritan Jews. This was well disclosed even by Jesus himself. For instance, when Jesus appointed the twelve apostles and sent them out to proclaim the gospel, he alerted them not to enter any of the Samaritan towns (Matt 10:5). He regarded a Samaritan man, who was healed by him, as a "foreigner" (Luke 17:15–19). When Judean Jews engaged in controversy with Jesus concerning his identity, they viewed him as a "demon-possessed Samaritan" (John 8:48). This hostility was further disclosed by a Samaritan woman when Jesus asked her to give him water in Sychar, a city of Samaria (John 4:4–9; cf. Luke 9:52). Despite this long-lasting hostility, Jesus entered Samaria, conversed with a Samaritan woman, and paved the way to break down the barrier between Judean and Samaritan Jews and later instructed his disciples to take the gospel to the Judeans and Samaritans respectively (Acts 1:8).

According to Acts 8, the evangelist who brought the gospel to Samaria was Philip, one of the first elders of the Jerusalem church (Acts 6:5). In the *Apostolic Constitution* he is referred to as a "fellow-apostle" who by the "gift of the Lord and the energy of the Holy Spirit performed the miracles of healing in Samaria" by which Samaritans were "affected and embraced the faith . . . of the Lord Jesus, and were baptized into his name."[17] The content and power of Philip's preaching seem to be the same as that of the apostles, which was accompanied and confirmed by supernatural manifestations common to the apostolic evangelization enterprise. The response of the Samaritans also seems to have been positive and similar to the response of the three thousand converts at Pentecost. Their baptism in the name of Jesus was fully Christian in the context of the apostolic ministry of the time. Ironically, the Holy Spirit did not come upon them

---

16. Clement, *Pentecost or Pretense?*, 181–83.
17. *Constitutions of the Holy Apostles* 6.9.

when they were baptized in the name of Jesus, but they received the Holy Spirit only when Peter and John arrived in Samaria and laid their hands on them and prayed for them. The event is echoed in the *Apostolic Constitution* through reference to Peter's speech: "When we heard of the grace which was working among Samaritans by Philip, we came down to them and enlarging much upon the word of doctrine, we laid our hands upon all that were baptized, and we conferred upon them the participation of the Spirit."[18] Nevertheless, the Samaritans' case raises some questions. For example, if Philip's preaching was confirmed by supernatural manifestations common to the apostolic ministry; if the Samaritans' response in believing in Jesus was similar to the response of the three thousand converts at Pentecost; and if they were baptized in the name of Jesus, then why was their baptism unable to confer on them the gift of the Holy Spirit? Why did God allow all those miraculous manifestations to accompany Philip's proclamation, but withheld the gift of the Holy Spirit from the Samaritans? Was it a case of waiting for apostolic recognition and authorization? If this was so, then did the reception of the Holy Spirit depend on the apostolic authorization only in the case of the Samaritans, while it did not in all other cases? May this also mean that belief and baptism in the name of Jesus did not always result in the gift of the Holy Spirit, which is contrary to Jesus' own teaching and apostolic ministry (Acts 2:38)? Thus, the reason why the Samaritans' reception of the Holy Spirit awaited apostolic confirmation seems to remain obscure and debatable.

On the other hand, however, there appears to be an issue worthy of attention regarding Philip's authority. The *Apostolic Constitution* contains an indication that there was a problem in Philip's authority. Referring to the discourse of the apostles, the *Constitution* contains this statement: "If some do blame Philip our deacon and Ananias our faithful brother, that the one did baptize the eunuch and the other one Paul, these men do not understand what we [the apostles] say. . . . Philip and Ananias did not constitute themselves."[19] What does it mean here that these two men did not "constitute themselves"? This seems to suggest something required to fully constitute Philip's and Ananias's authority was missing, on account of which those who made that statement considered Philip's authority status to be defective. For a reason not made clear to its readers, the *Constitution* sometimes affirms and sometimes denies Philip's authority status.[20] If this

18. *Constitutions of the Holy Apostles* 6.9.
19. *Constitutions of the Holy Apostles* 8.46.
20. *Constitutions of the Holy Apostles* 7.7.

is so, then it raises other questions such as: If Philip's authority was still in question, then what was the purpose of the apostles' previous laying hands on him to serve in the Jerusalem church? If the apostles' laying on of hands does not play a role in his formal constitution, then what was its value? Even if the apostles' laying on of hands might have been defective for one or another reason as fallible human beings, then what should we make of the release of the supernatural signs, wonders, and miracles that accompanied Philip's gospel proclamation, which came from a universally absolute source to constitute apostolic authority in the evangelization enterprise? When viewed in line with the miracles and healings that accompanied Philip's gospel proclamation in Samaria, whatever was missing from his qualification indeed remains obscure.

Some scholars have struggled over how to understand and interpret this particular incident. Among them is Horton who suggests that the reason the Samaritans were not given the gift of the Holy Spirit at the moment of their baptism was that they were baptized only in the name of Jesus and that their baptism was not done in the "Triune formula that Jesus mandated in the Great Commission."[21] Would this be the case? Viewed in the overall context of the apostolic ministry of the time, Horton's suggestion may be argued to be pointless. The reason is that, on the one hand, there is no indication in Scripture whether the apostles baptized other converts of the time in the Triune formula. While they were aware of the Great Commission of baptizing in the Triune formula, the apostles were professing faith in Jesus and baptizing their converts in his name. On the other hand, as we shall see here, at times converts received the gift of the Holy Spirit even before professing faith in Jesus and being baptized in the name of Jesus or in the Triune formula. Rather, Bridge and Phypers offer a reconciliatory notion when they suggest that this is an "admittedly difficult chapter" of the New Testament and that the whole situation of this event was "highly abnormal."[22] This observation is shared by other scholars. Christenson calls it a "notoriously difficult passage to interpret."[23] Dunn calls it "the Riddle of Samaria." He adds that this is a "mutually exclusive" and "wholly irreconcilable" event with the rest of the New Testament teachings.[24] Dale F. Bruner calls it "the

---

21. Horton, *Rediscovering the Holy Spirit*, 194.
22. Bridge and Phypers, *Spiritual Gifts*, 145–46.
23. Christenson, *Charismatic Renewal*, 43.
24. Dunn, *Baptism in the Holy Spirit*, 55.

Samaritan puzzle."[25] It was, as cited by Dunn, a "unique situation and one of the chief turning points in the missionary enterprise" of the time.[26] These scholarly interpretations and suggestions of the incident indeed seem relevant, because the Samaritans heard the gospel accompanied by signs, wonders, miracles, and healing; they responded to it by believing in Jesus and were baptized in his name. However, they have not been given the gift of the Holy Spirit at the moment of their baptism, which is contradictory mainly to Jesus' teaching (John 3). This arguably makes the Samaritans' case "abnormal," "exclusive," "a riddle," and "puzzling." In agreement with Dunn, it may simply be concluded that the case of the Samaritans was a "distinctive and exclusively unique experience even in the divine role in the evangelization movement" of the time, which still remains "irreconcilable" with the rest of the New Testament's teaching.[27]

Reception of the Holy Spirit at Caesarea (Acts 10:44–48; 11:15–17)

Acts 10:44–48 informs us that Cornelius already possessed standard piety to the extent that God communicated with him personally. Nevertheless, he was advised by an angel to call for Peter and to learn further from him. Following this advice, Cornelius called Peter, who responded by coming to his house and preaching the gospel. While Peter was preaching the gospel, the Holy Spirit came upon all the listeners and they spoke in tongues and praised God. In this incident, it seems that the reception of the Holy Spirit happened even before Peter made any appeal for repentance and believing in Jesus. It seems that the hearers were simply listening to the preaching and they did not yet respond to the gospel message by faith or in believing in Jesus, but they were filled with the Holy Spirit and spoke in tongues and praised God. Jewish believers who had accompanied Peter were astonished when they saw that the gift of the Holy Spirit was also poured out on the gentiles, and when they heard them speaking in unknown tongues and praising God. According to the story of the event, it was after being baptized in the Holy Spirit that the recipients were led to the sacramental water baptism (10:44–46). Peter recognizes this phenomenon as the gentile equivalent of the Jerusalem

---

25. Bruner, *Theology of the Holy Spirit*, 175.
26. Dunn, *Baptism in the Holy Spirit*, 62.
27. Dunn, *Baptism in the Holy Spirit*, 55.

Pentecost and assures his audiences in Jerusalem that the event at Cornelius's house was precisely the same as the experience of the 120 people at Pentecost (11:13–18). When viewed in the light of Peter's preaching at Pentecost repentance of sin, the forgiveness of sin, belief in Jesus, and reception of the gift of the Holy Spirit seem to have been perceived, by the apostles, to be inseparably united initial conditions for salvation. This does not, however, appear to be maintained at Cornelius's house. Rather, the Holy Spirit seems to have taken another method by which he intervenes to save the people in a situation seemingly urgent from the divine side.

Reception of the Holy Spirit at Ephesus (Acts 19:1–6)

Acts 19:1–6 indicates that when Paul arrived in Ephesus he met a group of twelve "disciples" who were also "believers." They were believers who had not received the Holy Spirit. When Paul asked them the question, "Did you receive the Holy Spirit when you became believers?" they replied that they had not even heard there was such a thing as the Holy Spirit who they could receive. "In what then were you baptized?" asked Paul. They replied, "Into John's baptism." Paul enlightened them by explaining the difference between John's baptism and the baptism of the one who was to come after John, namely Jesus. When Paul told them about Jesus, they were then baptized in the name of Jesus, and the moment Paul laid hands on them, the Holy Spirit came upon them, and they began to speak in tongues and prophesy. Dunn argues that they were not fully Christians before they met Paul. He says that "they are disciples, but do not yet belong to *the* disciples; that is, they are not yet Christians." He adds that this is the reason why Paul did not accept them as Christians with complete initiation experience and instructed them "to go through the full initiation procedure."[28] Dunn's observation could, on the one hand, be plausible. On the other hand, however, this event seems to indicate that Paul was aware that people could be Christians and yet not receive the Holy Spirit for one or another reason. This event, as was the case with the Samaritans, seems to indicate that in the early church's experience, believing and baptism in Jesus' name was not always accompanied by, or did not always result in, the reception of the Holy Spirit. Sometimes there was a time interval between believing and baptism in Jesus' name and

---

28. Dunn, *Baptism in the Holy Spirit*, 85–86.

reception of the gift of the Holy Spirit. Thus, in the event at Ephesus, the reception of the Holy Spirit was conditioned by baptism in the name of Jesus and the apostolic laying-on of hands.

2.4. RECEPTION OF THE HOLY SPIRIT AND ITS RELATION TO WATER BAPTISM AND LAYING-ON OF HANDS

We have seen that baptism in water + the Spirit is one event that takes place at one moment and that reception of the Spirit is inseparably connected to the water baptism. When considered from the above discussions, however, the rite of water baptism does not appear to be the only decisive means of reception of the Holy Spirit in the early church's experience. When considered through the window of the book of Acts, baptism with water + Spirit and baptism in the Holy Spirit seem sometimes united and sometimes separate phenomena. There are occasions when reception of the Holy Spirit appears to be mediated by the preaching of the gospel, as it was in Cornelius's house where it occurred spontaneously upon nonbelievers. On other occasions, the laying-on of hands stands as a means of reception of the Spirit, as it was in Samaria and Ephesus. At times those who were baptized in water baptism were led to be baptized in the Holy Spirit, by laying-on of hands, as was the case in Samaria. Conversely, at other times, those who were first baptized in the Holy Spirit were led to be baptized in water baptism, as it was in Cornelius's house. When observed from those experiences, it seems that there was no precise order or set formula or means or precondition for the reception of the Holy Spirit. Thus, based on the book of Acts, it may be fairly concluded that reception of the Holy Spirit can take place before, alongside, or after the conferring of sacramental water baptism, and with or without laying-on of hands. Despite these complexities, the reality is that whether the reception of the Holy Spirit took place before, at, or after water baptism, and with or without laying-on of hands, the Holy Spirit was coming continuously, giving the gift of salvation and ministry, and mobilizing the missionary activities of the church. Hence, it appears that the setting of a rule formula or precise order is not required by the divine for the dispensation of the Holy Spirit.

2.5. REPEATED RECEPTION EXPERIENCES OF THE HOLY SPIRIT IN THE EARLY CHURCH

There are Scripture references that indicate that there were repeated reception experiences of the Holy Spirit in the early church such as those mentioned in Acts 4:8, 31; 13:9, 52. If this was the case, it may lead us to ask such questions as what similarities and differences are there between the ways the apostles received the gift of the Holy Spirit before Pentecost (John 20:22), at Pentecost (Acts 2), and after Pentecost (Acts 4:31)? Did the apostles, who were breathed on by Jesus and received the Holy Spirit before his ascension, and who received the gift of the Holy Spirit at Pentecost, receive the gift of the Holy Spirit at Jerusalem for the third time (Acts 4:31) and at Iconium of Antioch for the fourth time (Acts 13:52)? Were there then at least four different occasions where the apostles experienced reception of the Holy Spirit? Further, was Peter, who received the Holy Spirit at least four times in a group, refilled with the Holy Spirit privately a fifth time (Acts 4:8)? Is the experience of reception of the Holy Spirit something that can be renewed and repeated over and over again? Do these repeated reception experiences indicate one baptism with the Holy Spirit, at Pentecost, and successive continuous refilling with the Holy Spirit at the moment of every important event and purpose? Do these repetitive reception experiences serve as a biblical model for conceiving that there can be one baptism but repeated fillings in the Holy Spirit? If this repetitive reception experience of the Holy Spirit did indeed exist in the early church, can it be theologically justifiable to conceive that baptism with the Holy Spirit at Pentecost was simply a door opening to continuous refilling experiences of the Holy Spirit? If this is so, then does it not challenge the teaching of Jesus that the once-received Holy Spirit will indwell believers forever (John 14:15–17)? Does it not challenge the Christian doctrine that the one Pentecost holds the assurance for Christians of all ages that the Holy Spirit has been given to them, indwells them, and works in, with, and through them? This is one of the features that cause confusion and complexity within the doctrine of the Holy Spirit.

Now, the question is: how should the whole concept of the apostolic repetitive reception experience of the Holy Spirit be understood and interpreted? Should it be understood in agreement with Rudolf Bultmann, who argued that "inconsistency can to a large extent be called appropriate to the nature of the Spirit," and that the Holy Spirit is the "power given now and again for the occasion, enabling him [the believer] to accomplish an extraordinary thing"?[29] Or with Brunner, who argued that the "operation of the Holy Spirit cannot in the last resort be conceptually grasped. It transcends all that can be said, it is in its depth and fullness that cannot be uttered"?[30] Or with Barth, who argues that such experiences are "subject only to his [God's] control" and that "so great is the mystery" of the events?[31] Or with Dunn, who argues that these repeated reception experiences of the Holy Spirit may indicate that the Christian may enter into the new covenant and new age at one moment through one baptism with the Holy Spirit, but he/she may be filled and empowered with the Holy Spirit as many times as necessitated?[32] Indeed these are likely relevant suggestions. Three further possibilities may be suggested in concluding this subject. First, it may be concluded in agreement with Dunn that the Christian may enter into the new covenant through one baptism with the Holy Spirit but may be filled and empowered with the Holy Spirit as many times as necessitated. Second, this story may alert the church that the ways and forms of reception of the Holy Spirit are thoroughly unpredictable. Third, it is true that the Holy Spirit is free to move and act by God's sovereign will and purpose, in whichever way, mode, case, or moment of the given salvation act or missionary activity. Therefore, in any case, no matter to what degree people may receive the Spirit in one baptism or on one occasion, there seems to be the possibility for further filling and empowerment with the Holy Spirit.

2.6. SUMMARY

Given the above biblical accounts and discussions, there are four points to be identified and underlined in concluding the chapter.

First, one of the major questions raised above is: how should the concept and practice of baptism in the Holy Spirit be understood, interpreted, and applied? When the New Testament records of the concept and practice of the term "baptism in the Holy Spirit" are examined, the term is used only three times: firstly, when the heavenly voice introduced its concept to John the Baptist (Matt 3:11; John 1:33); secondly, when Jesus cited John the Baptist's speech (Acts 1:5–8); and, thirdly, when

---

29. Bultmann, *Theology of the New Testament*, 1:160–62.
30. Brunner, *Christian Doctrine of the Church*, 15.
31. Barth, *Church Dogmatics*, 4/4:4.
32. Dunn, *Baptism in the Holy Spirit*, 54.

Peter referred to Jesus' speech (Acts 11:16). When its theological origin is examined, it is evident that the term "baptism in the Holy Spirit" was primarily coined by God and introduced to the world through John the Baptist. Its origin, therefore, is God and theologically it is objective. Despite the term appearing to be beyond comprehension, as above discussed, the whole event related to the concept and practice of baptism in the Holy Spirit is God's communication and touch to save, renew, transform, gift, empower, and guide his people. The claim and experience of baptism in the Holy Spirit, therefore, is not only based on the mere claim of people and driven by mere subjectivity but is an accurately, divinely destined gift and divinely arranged experiences of the church. Despite these theological and biblical facts, there have been acute problems related to the understanding, interpretation, and application of this doctrine. This, on the one hand, is due to the lack of clear, biblically set standard forms of both the concept and practice of baptism in the Holy Spirit. On the other hand, it is due to the difficulty of differentiating between the reception of the Holy Spirit in initial sacramental baptism and subsequent empowerment baptism in the Holy Spirit. This difficulty has often caused tensions and conflicts between objective, conceptual, doctrinal belief and subjective, experiential appropriation of the Holy Spirit. From a genuine hermeneutical perspective, this dilemma seems hard to resolve and may remain open for misunderstandings, misinterpretations, and misapplications, as well as the ignoring or rejecting of its claim and practice, thus causing perennial tensions and divisions within the doctrine of the Holy Spirit.

Second, there was a diversity of ways in which God poured out his Spirit and worked to cause people to participate in the fortunes and destiny of faith and salvation. These diverse ways of the Spirit's reception seem to be indicators of God's fulfillment of his appointed time for the pouring out of his Spirit upon all people (Joel 2:28). As a demonstration of the fulfillment of those promises, the Holy Spirit came upon different groups of people, at different times and places, and for all classes of people without discrimination. These diverse ways of the Spirit dispensation may appear puzzling because they contain both shared and different elements when compared to the experience of one reception at Pentecost. Yet, in each case, people were initiated into the benefits of the new covenant through the gift of the Holy Spirit. Viewed in the light of these diverse ways of reception of the Holy Spirit, it appears that the original Pentecost did not deliver a once-and-for-all reception and experience of the coming and working of the Holy Spirit. Rather, Pentecost seems to be only initiating an ongoing reception of the Holy Spirit.

Third, there was a history of repeated reception of the Holy Spirit in the early church. According to the book of Acts, repeated reception of the Holy Spirit sometimes occurred to enliven worship with power and praise, sometimes to enliven and empower upcoming evangelization activities, and sometimes in times of crisis. Most of the repeated reception incidents were not a fresh and first-hand reception of the Holy Spirit but were a kind of re-awakening, re-empowering, and re-inspiring of the receivers with supernatural resources. This may signal a persistent need for the continuous impartation and fresh awakening of the Holy Spirit on every needful occasion, for enhanced spiritual life and empowered ministry as the major purpose of his indwelling believers. In light of this, reception of the Holy Spirit at Pentecost and/or at water baptism does not seem to be a decisive settlement of reception of the Holy Spirit once and for all. Receiving the Holy Spirit once and for all in sacramental baptism and experiential appropriation of his permanent indwelling in the Christian life seem to be different issues in content, context, mission, and values. It seems that no matter to what degree people may receive the Holy Spirit in water baptism, there is the possibility for further filling, awakening, empowerment, and inspiration, as was the case with the apostles but only when deemed necessary by God. Hence, it seems likely to assume that those who have already been filled with the Holy Spirit may again experience an ongoing fresh awakening, empowerment, and inspiration from the Holy Spirit. If this is to be conceived, then it may lead us to believe in the possibility of multiple encounters with the Holy Spirit as the ongoing gifting and empowering in Christian life, ministry, and mission as the purpose of his indwelling.

Fourth, when considered from the book of Acts, both the apostles and Luke seem to have understood the concept and practice of baptism in the Holy Spirit as a fulfilled, finished, and closed promise at Pentecost. Thereafter, the claims and practice of baptism in the Holy Spirit seem to have been out of their thought, which appears to be the reason why none of them mentioned it in their writings as a continued experience of the church.[33] Viewed in the light of their omission, baptism in the Holy Spirit appears neither conditional for salvation nor normative or mandatory for Christian spiritual experience, apart from sacramental baptism. As a

---

33. See ch. 5 for further explanation.

consequence of their omission, there is no explicit biblical or historical practical evidence about its concept and practice. It does not even seem to be part of the second-century Montanist movement's core spiritual emphases. Its concept and practice, therefore, remained at the center of question, confusion, and debate among those who ask "what does it mean to be baptized in the Holy Spirit?" Since Pentecost, the only person who emphasized, prayed for, claimed, and experienced baptism in the Holy Spirit seems to be the Holiness movement evangelist Charles F. Parham at the end of the nineteenth century (see chapter 11). Hence, when considering the reappearance of the observable experience of baptism in the Holy Spirit in the early twentieth century, accompanied also by audible utterances and visible performances of charismatic gifts, it would seem that the church's long-lasting lack of interest in or rejection of the experience of baptism in the Holy Spirit does not necessarily mean that the substantive content of the Spirit baptism does not exist in faith practice. On the contrary, its existence seems to be convincing. It might fairly be concluded, in agreement with Dunn, that "Pentecost can never be repeated" but the supernatural experience of the day of Pentecost "can and must be repeated" in the experience of Christians of all ages.[34] If this conclusion is to be reached, then it must be noted that while the sealing of the Holy Spirit, given to believers in sacramental baptism, should also be regarded and maintained as the Spirit baptism, the Christian spiritual experience should not avoid the particular experience of baptism in the Holy Spirit.

---

34. Dunn, *Baptism in the Holy Spirit*, 53.

CHAPTER 3

Manifest Connection of the Holy Spirit with Charismatic Gifts

IN THE INTRODUCTION, WE have noted that tension arising from the practice of the Spirit-charismata has been viewed as one of the trends of tensions within the doctrine of the Holy Spirit. This situation raised a question: why has the practice of Spirit-charismata been viewed as a point of tension within the doctrine of the Holy Spirit? A search for answers to this question is one of the impulses prompting this study. This chapter will examine this particular issue. The examination will address four main features: (1) linguistic origin and development of the term *charisma* or its plural form *charismata* or *charismatic* gifts; (2) biblical teaching about the theological origin, meaning, and experience of the charismatic gifts; (3) biblical teaching about the manifest connection between the Holy Spirit and charismatic gifts and power from on high; and (4) whether there is any biblically grounded reason that leads the charismatic experience to a point of tension within the doctrine of the Holy Spirit.

3.1. LINGUISTIC ORIGIN AND DEVELOPMENT OF THE TERM CHARISMA/CHARISMATA

Scholars who have explored the etymology, origin, and development of the English terms charisma or charismata suggest that the New Testament Greek word for these terms is "charis" which means "grace." For example, V. D. Verbrugge explains that the terms "*charis, charisma,* and *charizomai*" are formed from the Greek root "*char*," which indicates something that produces well-being. This in turn effects *chara*, "joy," which is the individual experience or expression of this well-being. Verbrugge explains that *charis* means grace, gracefulness, graciousness, favor, thanks, gratitude, etc; *charisma* means a gift given out of goodwill, spiritual gifts; and *charizomai* means to show favor or kindness, give as a favor, and be gracious to someone. He states that from this basic meaning of the root, the individual meanings of *charis* are derived. *Charis* can, therefore, describe the attitude of both the gods and human beings but the derived noun *charisma* describes only gracious gifts and donations solely from God to humans, while the verb *charizomai* means to give graciously. When applied to human dealings with one another, says Verbrugge, *charisma* means to do something pleasant for someone, to be kind or gracious, to oblige or gratify someone. Verbrugge adds that the Old Testament equivalent to "*charis*" is the noun "*hen*" which clarifies the biblical meaning of *charis* as grace in action that denotes the coming of the stronger to help the weaker in a voluntary decision. Often this term can only be understood as the result of the special intervention of God, who supplies grace to weak mankind. Verbrugge concludes that when *charis* is used in the context of the activity of God, it is largely in the sense of God's undeserved gracious gifts in election.[1]

Other scholars also interpret the term in conformity with Verbrugge. Gordon D. Fee, for instance, suggests that the noun *charisma* has been formed from the root word *charis* to refer to concrete expressions of God's "grace" received.[2] For Thiselton the term *charismata* is entirely related to, and a particular expression of, *charis*, "grace."[3] For Yves Congar the term *charismata* can be understood only in connection with the word *charis*, "grace," because *charismata* are gifts that Christians owe to the grace of God, and which aim at the realization of salvation.[4] From these scholarly presentations, it can be noted that the etymological root of the term *charisma* or *charismata* can be understood with the Greek root word *charis* meaning "grace" which stands for and refers to, God's gracious gifts of the church's life and ministry.

---

1. Verburgge, *NIV Theological Dictionary*, 1331.
2. Fee, *God's Empowering Presence*, 32–35.
3. Thiselton, *First Epistle to the Corinthians*, 930.
4. Congar, *I Believe*, 2:161–62.

3.2. BIBLICAL TEACHING OF THE THEOLOGICAL ORIGIN AND MEANING OF THE CHARISMATIC GIFTS

Scholars who have examined the theological origin and meaning of the term charisma/charismata unanimously suggest that this term derives from Pauline understanding and discourses about the gifts and activities of God's grace through the gospel. Siegfried Schatzmann, for example, considers charismata as the most intrinsic concept by which Paul expresses God's fundamental gift of salvation and subsequent functional gracious gifts. He considers them to be the outpouring of God's grace; individuation of God's grace; the ways of concrete actualization of God's grace; and the expressive diversity of God's grace bestowed upon the charismatic community, "concretions and individuations" of his grace.[5] Christian Duquoc and Casiano Floristan consider charismata as the function of salvation theology to put into order and illuminate the data of faith.[6] H. H. Esser notes that charismata flow from God's grace in Christ to minister the gospel in words and deeds and to accompany and empower the missionary activities of the church.[7] Charismata, for David Middlemiss, are the "imminence of the beyond; of grace impinging on the human experience through the gifts of the Spirit" which also indicates direct and continuous revelation of God where he speaks through human tongues.[8] Charismata, for Jurgen Moltmann, are the gifts of grace springing from the creative grace of God, given by the Holy Spirit for the crystallization and individuation of the one grace given in Christ.[9] For Larry Christenson charismata are divinely appointed means or instruments of the manifestation of God's grace. God's grace is conveyed and received by, with, in, and through charismata. They are the divinely set, absolute means of the realization of God's grace.[10] According to Paul's understanding and expression, says Dunn, charismata do not refer to any particularly defined gifts of grace but, being synonymous to "*diakonia* (ministry)," they refer to every word, act, or gift that mediates God's grace to the believing community. Dunn further generalizes by saying that all ministries given to all members of the body of Christ by the Pentecostal

---

5. Schatzmann, *Pauline Theology*, 2, 8.
6. Duquoc and Floristan, *Charisms in the Church*, 6–7.
7. H. H. Esser, "Grace, Spiritual Gifts" in *New International Dictionary*, 119.
8. Middlemiss, *Interpreting Charismatic Experience*, 13.
9. Moltmann, *Church in the Power*, 295.
10. Christenson, *Welcome Holy Spirit*, 110–11.

Spirit are charismata.[11] From these scholarly analyses, it may be concluded that all charismata are the gracious gifts of God to serve the aims, objectives, and purpose of the message of salvation. They are the way, means, and instruments through which the grace of God can be observably manifested and practically realized for the life, ministry, and mission of the church. Thus, the theological meaning of the term charisma or charismata can be seen to be comprehensively derived from Paul's general perceptions of, and discourses about, the gifts and activities of God's grace through the works of Jesus Christ and the gospel.

The Old Testament provides important background to the New Testament term charismata and how these were experienced. Some references indicate God's miraculous intervention and protective actions to his people during the Old Testament times. For instance, ten miraculous plagues were inflicted on the Egyptians on the account of the deliverance of Israel from Egypt (Exod 7–12); the Red Sea parted (Exod 14) and the bitter water of Marah was sweetened (Exod 15:25). In the course of the forty-year journey in the wilderness, manna was provided from heaven (Exod 16); water was provided from the rock (Exod 17); the earth opened its mouth and swallowed Korah, his accomplice, and their possessions (Num 16:31–5), and the clothes and sandals of the people did not wear out throughout the forty-year journey in the wilderness (Deut 29:5). During Joshua's leadership the river Jordan was parted (Josh 3:16); the sun stood still and the moon stopped (Josh 10:12–14). Samson was provided with water in the wilderness (Judg 15:19). Elijah was fed by ravens; the dead son of the widow was raised to life by Elijah's prayer; the oil in the jar increased (1 Kgs 17); and he repeatedly saw fire fall from heaven (1 Kgs 18:38; 2 Kgs 1:10–12). Elisha healed the water (2 Kgs 2:19–22), raised the dead (2 Kgs 4:32–35), healed leprosy (2 Kgs 5:12–14), made an iron axe head float in the water (2 Kgs 6:6–7) struck the enemy blind (2 Kgs 6:18–19), and by his bone, a dead person was raised (2 Kgs 13:20–21). The sun reversed its movement in the heavens as the sign of assurance of Hezekiah's healing (2 Kgs 20:8–11); three Hebrew young men were preserved in the blazing fire (Dan 3:16–17); and Daniel was delivered from the lions (Dan 6:16–24).

These Old Testament references remind us of two things: (1) Although the recorders of the events did not refer to them as charismata, all of those occurrences were charismatic phenomena that assured God's

---

11. Dunn, "Ministry and the Ministry," 82–85.

audible/visible interventions in the lives of his people. (2) Although the references do not overtly associate the events with the Spirit of God, they resulted from divine manifestations and miraculous interventions. As discussed in chapter 1, it was these and other similar divine traditions of manifestation and intervention that the Old Testament often associated with the coming, possession, gifting, empowering, and initiation of the Spirit of God. Therefore, all these events can be recognized as Old Testament background for the New Testament charismata and their functional manifestations in connection with the manifestation of the Holy Spirit. This pre-Christian experience of charismatic manifestations provides us with a window to see the continuity of the charismatic dimension of God's work between the Old and New Testaments.

In the New Testament, the detailed lists of charismata are presented in Rom 12:6–8 (gifts of prophesying, serving, teaching, encouraging, compassion, leadership, and mercy); 1 Cor 12:8–11 (gifts of wisdom, knowledge, faith, healing, miracle-working, prophecy, discerning spirits, speaking in tongues, and interpretation of tongues); 1 Cor 12:28 (apostles, prophets, teachers, miracle workers, healing, helping, administration, and speaking in tongues); and Eph 4:10–11 (apostles, prophets, evangelists, pastors, and teachers). It is only in Rom 12:6–8 and 1 Cor 12:8–11 that Paul uses the term to describe specific gifts of ministry, commonly referred to as "gifts of the Holy Spirit" or "charismatic gifts" or "spiritual gifts." In Rom 12:6–8, he describes them as the gifts of grace. In 1 Cor 12:8–11, he refers to them as the gifts of the Holy Spirit and in v. 28 as ministry gifts and/or offices already destined for the church by God. In Eph 4:10–11, Paul considers charismata as the gifts of the risen, ascended, and glorified Lord. The latter case seems to be a biblically ascertained fact because Jesus was giving charismatic gifts such as healing, miracle-working, casting out demonic spirits, etc., to the apostles during the course of their training (Matt 10:7–8; Luke 9:1–6). In his discussion of 1 Cor 12:4–11, Athanasius of Alexandria comments that these gifts are distributed by the Holy Spirit, but they are "one activity of the Trinity." In assertion of this conviction, he states, "Whatever gift is given is given in the Trinity, and all the gifts are from the one God."[12] Veli-Matti Kärkkäinen insightfully combines the perceptions of both Paul and Athanasius, by citing from a other source, "The charismas bestowed by the Spirit on the people of God are a point of concrete Trinitarian correspondence in the

---

12. Athanasius of Alexandria, *Letters to Serapion on the Holy Spirit* 1.30.4—1.31.

church. The nature of the Trinity is imprinted on the charismas."[13] In light these suggestions it would indeed make better sense for charismata to be recognized and referred to as the "gifts of grace" or "gifts of God" since this term would embrace the gracious gifts of the Triune God distributed by the Holy Spirit, instead of referring to them as the gifts of the Holy Spirit in a single sense.

In the book of Acts, Luke also mentions some of the charismata listed in 1 Cor 12 such as speaking in unknown tongues, prophecy, healing, exhortation, miracle-working, teaching, administration, and discerning the spirits. However, he does not term them by the collective name "gifts of grace" (charismata) like Paul. Since there are no textually indicated uses in the New Testament other than by Paul, it would appear that Paul is the one who coined the term charismata, "gifts of grace," over and over again. Such scholars as Turner, Fee, and Schaztmann unanimously affirm that the term charisma is exclusively Pauline because he is the first evangelist to designate this distinctive theological term without defining the meaning of the term to his audiences.[14] Schatzmann, in particular, notes that charisma is a complex concept even for Paul himself with a wide range of applications.[15] This observation is surely right because Paul uses the term "grace" or "gifts of grace" or "works of grace" at different times, in different contexts, in different terms and to express different kinds of messages. Indeed, throughout his Epistles, Paul uses the word "grace" more than ninety-five times.[16] It is one of the dominant themes of Pauline theological conviction and teaching of the gracious saving acts of God. For example, he sometimes uses the term in opening and closing salutation; sometimes to express his own miraculous call and appointment for gospel ministry by divine grace; sometimes in contrast to sin which pays its wages of death; sometimes to define God's gracious gift of salvation through Jesus Christ; sometimes to refer to Israel's gracious privileges of divine choice; sometimes about God's promise to provide the church with all its needs; sometimes to refer to moral, ethical, and social dimensions of the Christian life; sometimes to encourage his audiences to praise God;

---

13. Kärkkäinen, *Constructive Christian Theology*, 5:407 in particular and 5:406–12 in general.

14. Turner, *Holy Spirit*, 256–59; Fee, *God's Empowering Presence*, 32; and Schatzmann, *Pauline Theology of Charismata*, 4.

15. Schatzmann, *Pauline Theology of Charismata*, 9.

16. Pauline use of the term "grace," "gifts of grace," and "works of grace" was intentionally checked throughout his Epistles for the purpose of this study. Therefore, this suggestion is based on tangible biblical evidence.

sometimes to witness God's unique favor in delivering him from danger in a particular place; and so on. In all these instances Paul does not use the term in connection to the ministry gifts of the Holy Spirit but simply designates a variety of ways in which God's grace is evidenced in the lives of his people.

3.3. MANIFEST CONNECTION OF THE HOLY SPIRIT WITH CHARISMATIC GIFTS

Numerous biblical examples indicate that manifestations of the Holy Spirit and charismatic gifts were tightly connected. The Scriptures attest that charismata, their manifestations, and dispensation are connected to the manifestation and activities of the Holy Spirit. In the religious practices of Judeo-Christian traditions, as discussed in chapter 1, the Spirit of God was understood to be the Spirit of power, wisdom, knowledge, signs, wonders, miracles, healing, prophecy, tongues, vision, dream, inspiration, awakening, etc. In both Testaments, the Holy Spirit is understood and presented as the divine agent through whom these supernatural gifts are delivered to God's people, and their experiences are initiated. Three things can be presented as examples of this.

First, we have seen in chapter 1 that the Old Testament is clear enough in attesting that the Spirit of God dispensed different kinds of supernatural gifts and empowered individuals for divine-related actions. The Spirit of God came upon individuals by possessing, gifting, empowering, inspiring, and guiding them to carry out what God wanted to be done at a particular time, place, and manner. He endowed them with audibly uttered and visibly performed gifts and initiated their experiences. All the supernatural messages, utterances, and actions followed the coming of the Spirit of God; resulted from the possessing, gifting, empowering, inspiration, and guidance of the Spirit of God; and were experienced as the gifts of the Spirit of God. The Old Testament predicted that in the future the Spirit of God would be poured out upon God's people and would enable them to receive and experience these gifts. This evidences that it was God himself who was connecting the manifestation of the Holy Spirit with the manifestation of the charismatic gifts, empowerment, and inspired utterances of audible charismata or performances of visible charismata in the Old Testament.

Second, at the beginning of his ministry, Jesus declared that the Holy Spirit had anointed him to proclaim the gospel accompanied by supernatural signs, wonders, miracles, and healings (Luke 4:18–20). This was practically fulfilled in his ministry. From beginning to end, a range of charismatic manifestations accompanied his ministry (Matt 11:4–6; Luke 4:31–41). This aspect of Jesus' ministry gave assurance of the fulfillment of the long-predicted and long-awaited age of the Holy Spirit and the characteristic charismatic content of his ministry. It was these characteristic charismatic experiences of Jesus' ministry that the apostles later collectively named "gifts of grace" or "gifts of the Holy Spirit." Jesus trained his disciples to adopt the same concept, content, and characteristics of ministry (Matt 10:7–8; Luke 9:1–6). He then promised that the Holy Spirit would come and would indwell, empower, and guide them to serve in the ways he had served and would have served. This divinely revealed mystery of divine acts discloses a manifest connection between the Holy Spirit and charismata and provides a safe and secure theological and biblical basis and model for the characteristic charismatic content of Christian worship, life, ministry, and mission.

Third, the church's experience of the charismatic phenomenon at and after Pentecost affirms that the manifestations of the Holy Spirit were connected with, and resulted in, audible utterances and visible performances of the Spirit-charismata. For example, at Pentecost, the recipients of the Holy Spirit began to speak in unknown languages as a result of the Holy Spirit's gifting, empowering, inspiring, and initiating of the speeches. The Holy Spirit, the one who anointed, gifted, empowered, and guided Jesus also anointed, gifted, empowered, inspired, and guided the apostles as well as the early church. He who animated the gospel proclamation of Jesus by charismatic manifestations also animated the gospel proclamation of the apostles with the same manifestations and acts (Acts 3:1–10; 8:5–13; 9:39–41; 14:3–11). Thus, beginning from the day of Pentecost the audibly uttered and visibly performed charismata occurred along with or following the coming of the Holy Spirit. Thereby, the apostles' prayers addressed the miraculous intervention of God through these gifts (Acts 4:28–30). As a demonstration of God's response to their prayers, miracles were performed (Acts 2:43; 5:12; 8:4–7), the crippled were healed (Acts 3:1–11; 5:12–16), the dead were raised (Acts 9:32), and authentic prophecies occurred (Acts 11:27–28). In the same manner, Paul's gospel proclamation was accompanied by charismatic manifestations (Acts 14:1–3; 15:12; 28:8–12; Rom 15:19). Based on his own experience, Paul asserted that the Holy Spirit, his gifts and power are inseparably connected (1 Cor 12:8–11; Gal 3:5; 1 Thess 1:5–6). The author of Hebrews attests that God confirmed the gospel proclamation of the time by the gift of the Holy Spirit and connected charismatic manifestations (Heb 2:4). This biblical evidence assures us that from the day of Pentecost, the gospel proclamation of the church was accompanied by charismatic gifts such as signs, wonders, miracles, healings, prophecies, raising the dead, exorcising demonic spirits, speaking in different tongues, and with the confidence of power and authority. They evidence that in the early church when people were given the gift of the Holy Spirit, they were also given the gifts of audibly uttered or visibly performed charismata as demonstrations of the Holy Spirit's presence, gifts, and working among them. The presence of these supernatural phenomena in the life and ministry of the early church reminds us about the dynamic continuity between the ministry of Jesus and the apostles. Thus, it is in this sense that the term *subjective experience of the Holy Spirit* is used hereafter throughout this study.

In light of this biblical evidence, some scholars who have examined the manifest connection between the Holy Spirit and charismata also remind us that they are inseparably connected. Among them is Dunn who perceives the Holy Spirit as a *"fact of experience"* in the lives and worship of Christians.[17] He considers charismata as the "manifestation of supernatural power and act which takes place only when the Holy Spirit manifests." They are the experience of "being permitted by the Holy Spirit to see into realities beyond human mind and sight." He asserts that as the gift is the "manifestation and concretion" of the giver, it is inseparable from the giver.[18] Rodman J. Williams adds to this by stating that the Holy Spirit is "on the scene in dynamic self-manifestation" through the charismata because "charismata alone are *the* manifestation of the Spirit."[19] For Hendrikus Berkhof, charismata are the instruments by which Christians "partake in the wider ecclesiastical and cosmic dimensions of the Spirit's work" and are the "missionary witness" of the Holy Spirit to the world.[20] These scholarly observations are in agreement with the biblical evidence since Scripture affirms that charismata were manifested and experienced as the Holy Spirit's self-manifestation and as the expression of the gifts and power imparted by the Holy Spirit. The expression of the reception of

17. Dunn, *Baptism in the Holy Spirit*, 225.
18. Dunn, *Jesus and the Spirit*, 253–55.
19. Williams, *Renewal Theology*, 2:331.
20. Berkhof, *Doctrine of the Holy Spirit*, 89.

the Holy Spirit, his gifts, and power took place only through the expression of audible and visible charismata. The Holy Spirit, who is invisible by nature, manifested himself audibly and visibly through the manifestation of charismata. The manifestation of charismata seems, therefore, to be the means or instrument of the Holy Spirit's objective manifestation and believers' subjective experience it.

3.4 IS THERE ANY BIBLICALLY GROUNDED REASON THAT LEADS THE CHARISMATIC EXPERIENCE TO A POINT OF TENSION WITHIN THE DOCTRINE OF THE HOLY SPIRIT?

We have already said that the expression of the reception of the Holy Spirit, his gifts, and power took place only through the expression of audibly uttered and visibly performed charismata. The Holy Spirit, who is invisible by nature, manifested himself audibly and visibly through the manifestation of charismata. The biblical accounts discussed in chapter 2 and the current chapter are clear enough in presenting images, themes, and indications of genuine charismatic experiences and related exuberance in praise as a result of genuine communication with God and a genuinely inspiring awakening of the Holy Spirit. As briefly presented in chapter 2, some biblical accounts indicate that in biblical times the coming of the Holy Spirit sometimes equally entailed both objective manifestation of divine reality and subjective experience of the gifts, power, and works of the Holy Spirit. Sometimes when God imparted the Holy Spirit to his people, his gracious charismatic gifts and power were also imparted along with the impartation of the Holy Spirit. There was both objective imparting of the Holy Spirit from the divine side and subjective experiential movement from the people's side, which resulted from the gift endowed and the power imparted along with the Holy Spirit. In biblical times it was the divine objective impartation of the Holy Spirit that was initiating the charismatic form of spiritual experiences in the lives of individual believers. Having given them either verbally uttered or visibly performed charismatic gifts, the Holy Spirit then inspired and moved believers towards practical implementation through subjective experience.

In those Spirit-provided and Spirit-initiated subjective experiences, believers' experiences were accompanied by genuine unprecedented and unpredicted exuberant worship, praise, and spontaneous movements.

In such incidents, the practitioners' subjective experience took place only as a result of the genuine objective gift of the Holy Spirit and the resulting endowment and empowerment beyond the practitioner's consciousness and calculation. The recipients of the gifts and empowerment of the Holy Spirit were just objects of divine purpose and their subjective experiences were genuine charismatic experiences. These patterns of subjective experiences spring up from within practitioners as inner compulsion without any self-validating calculation. In such genuine subjective experiences, exuberant worship, spontaneous praise, and utterances were thus apparently divinely provided and divinely initiated. Thus, in the light of the biblical accounts, initiating reception of the Holy Spirit, endowing people with audibly uttered and visibly performed charismatic gifts, and moving people in power toward subjective experience ever remains the divine possession of and divine provision for the church. Therefore, subjective experiences of biblical times had authentic theological and pneumatological roots and edifying practical affirmation. Reception of the Holy Spirit, in biblical times, therefore, seems to mean equally an experience of evident gifts, power, and acts of the Holy Spirit. Consequently, this seems to be a clearer theological and biblical ground for why the Holy Spirit has traditionally been associated with and represented by practices of charismatic experience, power, praise, emotion, spontaneity, awakening, inspiration as well as audibly uttered and visibly performed charismatic experiences.

When observed from the book of Acts, in particular, it was not human enthusiastic experiences that constituted the subjective experience of the Holy Spirit. Nor was it the subjective spontaneous movements through mere sentiment by those who were given the gifts of the Holy Spirit. Rather, it was God himself who constituted both objective impartation and subjective experiential dimensions of the Holy Spirit's manifestation. It was God who made his own arrangements, gave gifts of grace, empowered, inspired, and moved his people toward subjective experiences by his own initiative. The biblical times' subjective experience, therefore, was only God's initiative and input that burst forth as an assurance of the reception of the gifts and power of the Holy Spirit. This indicates that when God encounters people for something purposeful, he gives them gifts, empowers, equips, and enables them to either utter verbally or perform something visible through different gifts in subjective experience. The subjective experience of the Holy Spirit in biblical times, therefore, was divinely initiated for the fulfillment of the divine purpose and was attained only as engagement and participation of people in God's purpose and action. Therefore, both an objective gift and subjective experience of the Holy Spirit through charismatic gifts were utterly divine favor and divine gifts. This may remind today's reader of the Scriptures that both the objective gift of the Holy Spirit and the resulting subjective experience are the objective theological way for Christians to manifest the presence, gifts, power, and works of the Holy Spirit working in, with, through, and among them. This is a fundamental theological and empirical experience of the Holy Spirit.

Given this biblical evidence, a question that might be asked is: should the reception and practice of charismatic gifts cause tension, confusion, and conflicts within the doctrine of the Holy Spirit? Viewed from a biblical perspective, a possible answer to this question seems to be "No! It should not!" Biblical accounts indicate that there was no rift, tension, or confusion between the doctrine of the objective reception and subjective experience of the Holy Spirit in biblical times. In biblical times, when audible or visible charismatic manifestations occurred, they often did so as an affirmation of manifestation of the Holy Spirit and his specific activities intended to meet a specific target of the missionary needs of the church or to accomplish a specific divine purpose. Through those manifestations, the Holy Spirit convincingly catches the attention of unbelieving people, permeates their hearts and lives, and breaks through specific salvation targets. An experience of the Spirit-charismata in biblical times, therefore, was divinely destined, divinely delivered, and divinely initiated for the fulfillment of the divine purpose. They were genuine occurrences as a result of the genuine objective gift of the Holy Spirit and the endowment of believers. They were beyond the receivers' consciousness and calculation towards a certain targeted end. When considering the accounts of the apostolic evangelization movement, it was not only because of the objective reception of the Holy Spirit that resistance to the gospel message was overcome but also because of the resulting subjective charismatic experiences. When the objective gift of the Holy Spirit was followed by audibly uttered or visibly performed charismatic experiences, people who might otherwise resist the gospel message instantly become open to it (Acts 5:1–12). Reception of the objective gift of the Holy Spirit and the experiencing of resulting audible and visible charismatic gifts, therefore, was the best means of attraction and winning power in the apostolic worship and evangelization enterprise (Acts 2:47; 5:12–14). Scripture accounts are clear enough in demonstrating that in biblical times

Spirit-charismata manifested only as the divine side of reality, were quite different from the human side, and were never a two-party affair. They were objectively given and received, faithfully experienced, and enabled the practitioners to demonstrate the saving power of the gospel through a supernaturally provided means. Therefore, in biblical times, there was no tension, confusion, or ambiguity related to, or resulting from, the realization and demonstration of Spirit-charismata.

3.5. SUMMARY

Given the above-discussed biblical accounts, a few points appear to require particular consideration and underlining to conclude the chapter.

First, given the biblical accounts discussed both in chapters 2 and 3 a question that might be asked concerning the subjective experience of the Holy Spirit is: does Scripture make subjective experience normative and mandatory? A possible answer to this question is "No, it does not." Scripture does not make the subjective experience as normative as the objective reception of the Holy Spirit. As we shall see in chapter 4, Scripture dogmatizes the objective reception of the Holy Spirit, commonly received through sacramental baptism, as mandatory and normative. While objective reception remains the central presupposition of the doctrine of the Holy Spirit for the church's life and mission, according to John 3:1–11, subjective experience, from a Scriptural viewpoint, cannot be made normative. While the theological reality and practical significance of the Spirit-initiated subjective experience cannot be questioned, Scripture does not dogmatize it as a mandatory component of the church's teaching and practice. In the meantime, it must also be noted that the subjective experience of biblical times was not God's response to human enthusiastic expectation and nagging prayers, but God's initiation.

Second, given the biblical accounts discussed in chapters 2 and 3, a question that might be asked is: does filling in the Holy Spirit really open up possibilities for the reception of the charismatic gifts and empowerment? A possible answer to this question seems to be "yes sometimes, but not always." Biblical evidence indicates that filling in the Holy Spirit at times worked as the gateway to the reception of certain charismatic gifts. This sometimes happened immediately as indications of the Holy Spirit's coming and filling in individuals, as was the case at Pentecost, at Cornelius's house, and at Ephesus. In these incidents the comings, filling in, gifting, empowering, and workings of the Holy Spirit were displayed through the manifestations of certain audibly uttered charismata. Accordingly, manifestations of the Holy Spirit appear to be manifestations of the Holy Spirit + charismata. This seems to be the reason why Paul generally coined charismata as the gifts of the Holy Spirit, which in turn developed into the traditionally known term "Spirit-charismata." Nevertheless, filling in the Holy Spirit did not always play a role as a precondition for the reception and demonstration of charismatic gifts. Sometimes filling in the Holy Spirit seems to have acted as affirmation of his permanent dwelling, empowering, equipping, inspiring, and guiding (Acts 4:31; 13:52). As it can be noted from biblical accounts, charismatic gifts could occur along with, or immediately after reception of the Holy Spirit, or in progress as part of the growth process of the Christian life—depending on God's choice and decision. Therefore, those who advocate that the reception of charismatic gifts and empowerment always occur along with or immediately after the filling in the Holy Spirit must be reminded not to mislead themselves. It must also be noted that any assumption that charismatic gifts cannot be received and exercised without first experiencing baptism in the Holy Spirit—after regeneration—is equally misleading.

Third, according to the biblical evidence, the objectively given charismatic gifts are the treasured theological resources and the most favored functional possessions of Christianity inherited directly from God through his only Son, Jesus Christ. As the Holy Spirit proceeds from God, the gifts, power, and works of the Holy Spirit also spring from God. As the objective manifestation of the Holy Spirit is God's possession, so is the subjective experience that results from his gifts, power, and activities. The Scripture accounts discussed above are clear enough in demonstrating that in biblical times Spirit-charismata manifested only as the divine side of reality, were quite different from the human side, and were never a two-party affair. They were objectively given and received, faithfully experienced, and enabled the practitioners to demonstrate the saving power of the gospel through a supernaturally provided means. Therefore, in biblical times, there was no tension, confusion, or ambiguity related to, or resulting from, the realization and demonstration of Spirit-charismata. The question then is: why have the concept and practice of Spirit-charismata been viewed as points of tensions and church division through the centuries and today? From where have both historical and present tensions and confusions arising about the concept and practice of Spirit-charismata drawn their roots? What is lurking beneath the surface of the tensions and confusions related to the claim and practice of Spirit-charismata? An examination of the historical situations may provide us with possible answers to these and similar questions. This will be pursued in chapters 5 to 10. We now turn our examination to the presence, gifts and works of the Holy Spirit in the founding, organizing, and shaping of the life and ministry of the church at the inception of the church.

CHAPTER 4

The Holy Spirit in Founding, Organization, and Shaping of the Life and Ministry of the Church

WE HAVE CONSIDERED BIBLICAL teachings about the Holy Spirit through examining the Old and New Testament Scriptures. We have seen that the Old Testament primarily identifies the Holy Spirit with God the Creator and attributes to him the manifestations, gifts, power, and activities belonging exclusively to God. Secondly, the Old Testament identifies the Holy Spirit with supernatural gifts, power, activities, renewal, awakening, and inspired movements that involve human subjective experiences as a response to his manifestation and demonstration of his workings. Similarly, the New Testament primarily identifies the Holy Spirit with God and presents him as an independent divine person, distinct from God the Father and the Son within the Godhead, with consciousness, will, a personal sense, and absolute divine authority. We have also seen that the Holy Spirit himself proved his independent personality and operation with absolute authority through both his presence and the role he played in the apostolic missionary movements. Given the post-Pentecost accounts of the New Testament, to repeat what we have already said, the issue of the Holy Spirit's divinity, independent personality, independent operation, and objective and subjective content of manifestation seems to be *incontestable*. Secondly, like the Old Testament, the New Testament identifies the Holy Spirit with supernatural gifts, power, activities, renewal, awakening, and inspired movements that involve human subjective experiences as a response to his manifestation, gifts, and workings.

The findings of these examinations show that although the Bible does not provide us with case-by-case answers to the questions raised or solutions to the problems addressed in this study, it provides us with understanding and insights into the theology, manifestation, gifts, and activities of the Holy Spirit during biblical times. This understanding and insight raise awareness of the deity, independent personality, manifestations, independent authoritative activities, and ways of reception of the Holy Spirit in biblical times. This provides us with clear theological and biblical grounds and guidance for seeking answers and solutions to the subject of this study. With this understanding, then, the next question to be asked is: what role did the Holy Spirit play in founding, organizing, and shaping the life and ministry of the church? The New Testament tells us how the church was founded by the Holy Spirit to continue the Spirit-anointed, Spirit-gifted, Spirit-empowered, and Spirit-guided life and ministry of Jesus in the world. To make this happen, the Holy Spirit played a decisive role in founding the church through *five features as means of salvation* taught and delivered by Jesus and *two ministry methods* with which Jesus served. Here questions are bound to be asked: Which *five features as means of salvation* did Jesus teach about and deliver to the church? With which *two ministry methods* did Jesus serve and how did he set them out for the church to follow? The New Testament tells us that Jesus taught and delivered five divinely designed and divinely destined features as a means of salvation. These are faith in Jesus Christ, holy baptism, holy communion, the word of God, and the gift of the Holy Spirit. The two ministry methods of Jesus, which he served with and set as standard models for the church, are the prophetic gospel proclamation method and the leadership/administration method. This chapter briefly examines each of these features.

4.1. THE FIVE FEATURES JESUS TAUGHT AS DECISIVE MEANS OF SALVATION

Faith: According to the gospel of John, Jesus asserted that believing in him is a decisive means of salvation. He declared that the ultimate purpose of his coming into this world is for those who believe in him to be saved. He declared that God so loved the world and gave his only Son so that whoever believes in him shall be saved and have eternal life (John 3:14–18; 6:40, 47). He asserted that believing in him does not mean believing in him only—Jesus the person—but also believing in God the Father who sent him (John 12:44–45). In contrast to this, said Jesus, those who do not believe in him are those who choose darkness rather than the light that leads them into eternal life (John 3:19). He insisted that while those who believe in him will be saved and inherit eternal life, those who reject him stand under the wrath and judgment of God and will be consumed in their condemnation (John 3:18, 36). These discourses of Jesus affirm that God loves the world with self-giving love and invites people to believe in him through believing in his only Son, Jesus Christ. According to the apostle Paul's witness, even after his ascension and glorification, Jesus revealed himself to Paul on the road to Damascus as an invisible personality and declared to him that those who believed in him are "sanctified by faith in him" (Acts 26:17–18). These discourses of Jesus affirm the saving value of believing in him and that a "treasure" of the life of the new covenant is "committed to faith."[1] Thus, Jesus instituted faith in him as one of the divinely designed, divinely destined, and divinely delivered decisive means of salvation.

Holy Baptism: The Gospel of John tells us that Jesus has constituted holy baptism as one of the decisive and mandatory means for salvation by saying, "No-one can enter the Kingdom of God unless he is born of water and the Spirit" (John 3:1–8). He pointed out that this baptism bears a mysterious substance and power to change and transform the nature of natural man into a spiritual man. He asserted this baptism as the essential, conditional, and primary requirement to be met to be saved and to belong to God's kingdom. While water is the outward visible element in which the candidates are baptized, the Spirit is the inward invisible element in which they are inwardly baptized and united into Christ. Hence, both the outward *visible* water baptism and inward *invisible* Spirit baptism yield the same result: rebirth in the Spirit for a new life, a mystical rebirth of "spiritual seed" that is "begotten *from above*."[2] While external immersion with the element of water symbolizes the death of the fleshly sinful nature, the Holy Spirit baptizes the "soul within" and "enters into the very inmost recesses of the soul."[3] Thereby, the "Spirit seals the soul"

---

1. Cyril of Jerusalem, *Catechetical Lectures* 5.4.13.
2. Beasley-Murray, *John*, 48.
3. Cyril of Jerusalem, *Catechetical Lectures* 17.14.

and the candidate comes up for life "quickened in righteousness."[4] This baptism is acknowledged as a "water-Spirit-death-life-sonship"[5] baptism in which God brings the "dead back to life" and shares the "life of the Trinity" with them.[6] In and through this baptism, the divine life is mystically imparted to the baptized candidate. The candidate, therefore, is given a new mysterious spiritual identity and belongs to the kingdom of God. With this intention, Jesus has instituted water + Spirit baptism as one of the divinely destined and divinely delivered decisive and mandatory means of salvation to be practiced in his church.

Holy Communion/the Lord's Supper: The Gospel of John also tells us that Jesus declared that he is the living bread of life that came down from heaven and that whoever eats this bread will never die but will live forever. This living bread, said Jesus, is "my flesh," given for the life of the world. He asserts, "I tell you the truth, unless you can eat the flesh of the Son of Man and drink his blood, you have no life in you. Whoever eats my flesh and drinks my blood has eternal life." Jesus declared that his life is mystically imparted to those who share in his flesh and blood when he said, "Whoever eats my flesh and drinks my blood, remains in me, and I in him" (John 6:35, 47–58). He is the fulfillment of the "Paschal Lamb . . . whose blood caused the angel of death to pass over the houses of Israel."[7] These assertions of Jesus remind us of the saving value of his flesh and blood, which traditionally came to be known as Holy Communion or the Lord's Supper. Jesus instituted the means of eating his flesh and drinking his blood at the last supper before his crucifixion and stressed that his blood is the blood of the new covenant, which is poured out for the world for the forgiveness of sins (Matt 26:26–28). To partake in his flesh and blood stands as a metaphor for mystical union with him; his constant dwelling in those who are in union with him, and acts as a symbolical affirmation of passing from eternal death into eternal life.[8] Herein lies the mystery of incarnation, Emmanuel, God with us, which is disclosed in Jesus' prayer made towards the conclusion of his earthly ministry (John 17:20–26). Jesus thereby instituted holy communion as one of the divinely designed, divinely destined, and divinely delivered decisive means of salvation to be practiced in his church.

4. Cyril of Jerusalem, *Catechetical Lectures* 3.4.12.
5. Moule, *Holy Spirit*, 33.
6. Beckwith, *Holy Trinity*, 3:233.
7. Weinrich, *John 1:1—7:1*, 594–95.
8. Weinrich, *John 1:1—7:1*, 732–35.

The Word of God: The Gospel of John goes on to tell us that Jesus taught abiding in and keeping his words is a decisive means for salvation. Jesus declared that the "Father loves [him] and has placed everything in his hands" (John 3:34-35). Therefore, all his words and actions are the words and actions of the Father and they fulfil the will and purpose of the Father, rather than his own (John 5:19-24). He declared that the words he spoke during his earthly ministry are "the Spirit and they are life" (John 6:63). For those who hear his words, accept his testimonies, and believe in the Father who sent him, eternal life is given here and now (John 5:19-24). This seems to mean that the "revelation of the Son includes the redemptive action of the Father in and through the Son."[9] This mystery flows from the "completeness of the Son's representation of the Father . . . and the Son's accomplishment of the Father's work."[10] His words and actions, therefore, are accompanied by absolute divine power and authority to give eternal life or to condemn to eternal damnation. Anyone who keeps his words "will never see death" (John 8:51). Accordingly, in his controversial exchange with the Jews, Jesus assured those who had believed in him by saying, "If you hold to my teaching, you are really my disciples" (John 8:31). In contrast to this, said Jesus, those who do not want to hear and hold his word will be judged by that same word (John 12:47-48). He insisted that his words are capable of both saving and condemning. Therefore, for anyone who hears his words but does not keep them, there is a judgment and it is that very word which will judge and condemn him/her at the last day of judgment. Hearing his words and remaining in them, for Jesus, is an integral characteristic of his true followers. When this takes place in the life of the believer, it entails the believers coming to know the truth, i.e., knowledge of the presence and redemptive action of God in Jesus. Those who attain this true knowledge will never see death (John 8:51). Jesus asserted the need to remain in his word and hold fast to it as one of the mandatory requirements for salvation. The proclamation of the words of Jesus to the world, as contained in the gospels, is the sole reason why the church was founded and continues to exist in the world. Thus, Jesus has instituted the word of God as one of the divinely designed, divinely destined, and divinely delivered decisive means of salvation.

---

9. Beasley-Murray, *John*, 55.
10. Beasley-Murray, *John*, 76.

The Gift of the Holy Spirit: Jesus also declared that the Holy Spirit will be given to his followers as the gift of salvation and as a continuation of his saving works. The Holy Spirit is given to the followers of Jesus as God's gift of salvation for the following main purposes:

1. He replaces Jesus and continues Jesus' mission in the world by indwelling, teaching, illumining, comforting, empowering, and guiding believers into all truth in the salvation enterprise (Luke 24:49; John 14:15–17, 26; 16:13).

2. As above-discussed, God has instituted the holy baptism and holy communion as decisive means of salvation, delivered them to the world through his only Son, Jesus Christ, and ever works in and through them towards bringing salvation into sinners' lives. Thus, the Holy Spirit works through these means towards sealing believers' salvation and sanctification.

3. According to the belief and teaching of the apostles, the purpose of the Holy Spirit's indwelling believers is mostly to bring character transformation as evidence of the progressive sanctification of believers' lives. As we shall see, the apostolic teachings emphasized that the indwelling of the Holy Spirit can keep believers' lives in purity and holiness. The indwelling of the Holy Spirit was expected to result in new birth, new creation, and newness which is identified with the kind of life Jesus attained in the resurrection (Rom 8:11; 2 Cor 5:17). The Holy Spirit-filled and indwelt Christians, from the apostles' point of view, are meant to demonstrate a transformed state of moral and ethical behavior by the power and guidance of the Holy Spirit. Attaining the qualities of these characteristics was thought of as "putting off the old Adamic person and putting the new Christly person on" (Eph 4:17–24), "being filled with the Holy Spirit" (Eph 5:18), and bearing fruits of the Holy Spirit (Gal 5:22).

4. As discussed in chapter 3, the coming and reception of the Holy Spirit entails both the objective imparting of the Holy Spirit and the Spirit-initiated subjective experience resulting from the gift endowed and the power imparted along with the Holy Spirit. Biblical evidence affirms that when God imparts the Holy Spirit to believers, his power and charismatic gifts are also imparted along with the impartation of the Holy Spirit. Then his power and charismatic gifts are demonstrated through the experiences of either audibly

uttered or visibly performed sign gifts. Hence, since God's saving purpose for the world continues through the gospel proclamation, the presence, gift, and workings of the Holy Spirit will also continue through the objective and subjective contents of his manifestation.[11]

Considered in the light of these four purposes, the gift, reception, presence, and workings of the Holy Spirit remain the central presupposition of the Christian doctrine of the Holy Spirit in the salvation enterprise. In general, the above-discussed Gospel references assure us that Jesus dogmatized that faith in him, holy baptism, holy communion, the word of God, and reception of the Holy Spirit are an end by themselves for salvation and for attaining eternal life. Hence, these features are theologically originated and destined; christologically introduced and delivered, and pneumatologically applied as decisive means of salvation. When considering how Jesus has laid specific salvific power and mandates on these features, they seem to reveal the entire content of God's heart about what is required for salvation, transformation, and reconciliation with him. When observing how Jesus asserted the saving power and mandates of these features, it seems that salvation is impossible without them. This seems to be the reason the entire content of the early church's life, worship, ministry, and mission were Christ-centered, evangelistic, Pentecostal-charismatic, sacramental, didactic, and apocalyptic. These five features, according to Scripture evidence, are essential, mandatory, and normative for salvation and are paramount parameters of Christian belief, teaching, worship, ministry, and mission. Thus, the church was founded and shaped outright on these decisive features of salvation, through which the world is served and people saved through the two ministry methods with which Jesus served and set as standard ministry models for the church.

---

11. The text under 4.1 is a revised and expanded version of a paper presented at the Global Consultation on Lutheran Identity held by the Lutheran World Federation (LWF) in October 2019, Addis Ababa, and published in the LWF Documentation 63 entitled *We Believe in the Holy Spirit: Global Perspectives on Lutheran Identities*, 2021.

4.2. THE TWO MINISTRY METHODS WITH WHICH JESUS SERVED AND ON WHICH THE CHURCH WAS FOUNDED

The church finds not only its origin in Jesus but also in the methods of his ministry. Indeed the New Testament shows us how the church was founded and organized on the methods of Jesus' ministry. Here there are questions to be asked: What did Jesus' ministry methods look like? How did the Holy Spirit guide the foundation and organization of the church on the methods of Jesus' ministry? Answering these questions requires examining the Scriptures and finding what they tell us about the methods of Jesus' ministry.

4.2.1. General nature of Jesus' ministry

The Scriptures indicate that Jesus was the uniquely anointed divine man to fulfill the entire hope expected from the Old Testament's anointed prophetic, priestly, and kingly ministry offices. Based on the Scriptures' teaching, Christian tradition, in general, classifies Jesus' ministry into these three offices which we shall briefly consider each in turn.

Prophetic Office: The Old Testament's prophetic line anticipated the future, high prophetic figures rooted in the Mosaic prophetic standard (Deut 18:15–22). During his earthly ministry, Jesus was viewed as a great prophet by his contemporaries (Matt 21:46; Luke 7:16; John 9:17). His repeated assertions that he was sent by God to speak his words to the world, clearly demonstrate his belonging to the prophetic line (John 3:44; 5:36–38; 8:25–29, 42–43). Although he did not explicitly call himself a prophet, Jesus seemed not to hesitate to accept the prophetic title as his identification (Matt 13:57; John 4:44). His acceptance of this title can be perceived as evidence of his standing within the Mosaic prophetic line. As presented in the gospels, in his prophetic ministry Jesus stands between God and the world and delivers God's will and call to the world for salvation, reconciliation, and a new relationship with him in the new covenant. Above all else, his prophetic gospel proclamation was accompanied by supernatural power, signs, wonders, miracles, healings, raising the dead, prophecies, revelation, discerning spirits, etc. (Matt 11:2–6; Mark 6:1–3; Luke 4:18–20; 7:11–23). From beginning to end, evidence of a range of miraculous phenomena can be counted in his gospel proclamation which gives firm assurance to the uniqueness of both his Messianic personality and mission (Matt 4:23–25; 8:14–17; 11:2–6; Mark 3:7–11; 6:53–56; Luke 4:31–43). His gospel proclamation was also accompanied by foretelling and forth-telling; outrightly denouncing wickedness without fear or favor; and presenting advocacies, persuasions, encouragements, and rebukes concerning sin and wickedness both in social and religious spheres. After his ascension, the apostles acknowledged that the Old Testament anticipations of the future coming high profile prophet were fulfilled in the person of Jesus (Acts 3:22–24). True it is that in him, the "prophetic Word of God finds its ultimate expression as a truth not only of his teaching but of his very being."[12] Hence, the inheritance of the whole content of Jesus' prophetic ministry characterizes the nature, life, and mission of Christianity as soundly prophetic.

Priestly Office: In the Old Testament, priestly ministry was instituted by God as a mediatorial office and priests were appointed by God as mediators (Exod 28–29). Most importantly, the mediatorial function was embodied in the high priest whose ministry included the offering of sacrifice on the Day of Atonement in the temple holy of holies (Exod 30:10) and the laying of his hands on the scapegoat through which the high priest symbolically place the sins of the people of Israel (Lev 16:20–22). The prophet Isaiah foresaw a suffering and an atoning figure on whom God would lay all the inequities of the world (Isa 53). Isaiah boldly declared that the Lord further willed that the figure would accept pains, bruises, and suffering in silence as a substitutionary sacrifice, just as demonstrated by Jesus' suffering when he was silent before the chief priests and Pontius Pilate (Matt 27:12–14). Christian tradition, therefore, interprets this Isaianic imagery of the substitutionary sacrificial death as the Old Testament's prediction fulfilled in Jesus' suffering on the cross and sacrificial atoning death. Jesus himself affirmed this when he declared that he came into the world to give his life as a ransom for many (Matt 20:28). Jesus repeatedly described his mission in terms of a mediating priest who mediates through self-offering (Matt 26:27–28; Mark 10:45; Luke 22:20; John 10:11, 15; 15:12–13). Thus, Jesus' self-offering and atoning death were understood as the fulfillment of the Old Testament's mediatorial function of the high priest. The apostles understood and declared him as the ultimate reconciler of God and the world through atoning sacrificial death (Eph 2:12–16). He was viewed as the final high priest

---

12. Milne, *Know the Truth*, 191.

in the Old Testament priestly line who offered himself in sacrificial and atoning death as the universal reconciler and savior of the world (Heb 9; 10:10–18) and as the high priest who offered up himself in order to make atonement for the sins of the world (Heb 7:23–27; 9:23–28). His sacrificial self-offering also entails an ongoing intercession and his reconciling ministry extends beyond the once-and-for-all intercession event (Heb 9; 10:10–18). Hence, in his priestly ministry, Jesus stands between God and a sinful world as a mediator and brings about a radical reconciliation and unification (John 17:20–26). He "broke national, religious . . . cultural and sexual barriers by associating with people not usually involved with a Jewish prophet."[13] It was for this purpose that he was incarnated and became a victim of an atoning sacrificial death, as the Lamb of God who takes away the sins of the world (John 1:29). After his ascension and glorification, a new song was heard in the heavenly court celebrating Jesus' atoning sacrificial death with its salvific effects and resulting radical reconciliation and reunification of the peoples everywhere on earth (Rev 5:9–13). Thus, the sacrificial death of Jesus has become the central teaching of the New Testament and has shaped Christian intercessory ministry around emphasizing the purpose, power, and significance of the cross of Christ.

Kingly Office: The Old Testament's anticipation of kingly (regal) terms was rooted in God's promise to David and concerned with his perpetual kingdom (2 Sam 7:16; Ps 89:3, 20–36). This term was attributed to the anticipated messiah in some of the pre- and postexilic prophecies (Isa 9:6–7; 11:1–3; and Zech 9:9–10). The messiah was understood to be the one who would exercise divine rule on earth in the Davidic line and restore peace, order, and justice in the world (Isa 9:1–7; 11:1–3). This messianic theme continues into the New Testament. For example, when the angel announced to Mary her miraculous conception of the "Son of the Most High," he declared that the Son would be the one who fulfils the Old Testament's anticipation and hopes of the Davidic line (Luke 1:32–33). Jesus himself seemed to take up this title when he declared himself to be greater than kings (Matt 12:42) and that he retains universal authority over all (Matt 28:18–20). Jesus also indicated that his future return in glory would be the time at which he will be manifested as king and reign in glory over all (Matt 24:29–31). Peter echoed this conception in his sermon on the day of Pentecost and acknowledged

---

13. Kärkkäinen, *Constructive Christian Theology*, 1:55.

Jesus to be king and Lord over all things (Acts 2:29–36). Paul, too, acknowledged Jesus' kingship and Lordship over all things (Phil 2:9–10; cf. Rev 19:11–21; 21:22–27). From these references it can be noted that Jesus was anointed by the divine Spirit with absolute authority and power to exercise universal authority as the royal ruler (Matt 28:18–20). In his first advent, however, Jesus exercised his power and authority as a humble, serving, leading, teaching, training, self-giving, and liberating servant of God and a close friend of sinners (Matt 13:53–58; Luke 4:31–37). Being shaped in love, mercy, compassion, care, and self-giving love, his use of royal power and authority always demonstrated the opposite of human royal rule. He asserted that the use of power and authority within his community should take the form of a servant-leader like himself (Luke 22:24–27; John 13:2–17). However, he announced that in his second advent he would conversely use his power and authority as an aggressive judging king (Matt 25:31–34). In the light of his future return as the King of kings and Lord of lords, the content, concept, and function of his kingship remain ever active. He, therefore, rules the world "by the Word of the gospel and the power of the Spirit, creating faith in the gospel, putting all opposition to it to shame, assembling believers, and . . . preparing the way for the kingdom of the Father in the world."[14] In general, Jesus introduced to the world a royal rule that had to be realized in the form of servant leadership and he delivered it to the church through his disciples (Matt 20:24–28; John 13:4–17).

In general, when the situation of his earthly life is taken at face value, Jesus appears as neither a prophet, nor a priest, nor a king, but merely as a person, Jesus of Nazareth. When viewed in the light of the content and context of his ministry, however, it becomes evident that his ministry fulfils the threefold ministry offices of the Old Testament. The idea of the threefold office of his ministry, says Wolfart Pannenberg, clearly "expresses the fulfillment and consummation of the old covenant in the history of Jesus by uniting the three most important offices of God's people in the one person."[15] He adds that each of these offices is "characteristic of the human ministry of Jesus that the definitive future of God is already breaking in with him for the world's salvation."[16] It is true that the Old Testament clearly exhibits a history of tradition in the anointing of the priest (Exod 28:41; 29:7; Lev 4:3, 5, 16), anointing of

14. Pannenberg, *Systematic Theology*, 448.
15. Pannenberg, *Systematic Theology*, 446.
16. Pannenberg, *Systematic Theology*, 443.

the prophet (1 Kgs 19:16), and anointing of a King (1 Sam 9:16; 10:1; 24:6; 2 Kgs 9:1–16). The content of these threefold ministry offices always depends on the anointing, empowering, illuminating, and guiding works of the Holy Spirit. In the same way the New Testament exhibits that Jesus was anointed by the Holy Spirit in order to fulfill all the hopes of these three lines of ministry (Luke 4:18–20). Hence, Jesus' ministry, delivered through these three offices, was to be shared with his followers who would represent him, stand in his authority, and extend his mission. All of the three office functions of his ministry were handed over to his followers, who in turn handed them over to the church, which in turn has been carrying it out and will carry it out until his second advent. Bearing this process in mind, Jesus pledged to equip his followers with two major methods of ministry, which comprise all of his ministry offices together and move towards the same purpose and goal, i.e., *mediation, transformation, salvation, reconciliation, and reunification* with the Triune God (John 17:20–23; Rev 5:9–13).[17] Primarily, he pledged to equip them with prophetic gospel proclamation that is accompanied by signs, wonders, miracles, healing, casting out of demonic spirits, raising the dead, etc (Matt 10:5–8; Luke 9:1–6). Secondly, he pledged to equip them with the leadership-administration function which he exercised as a humble serving, teaching, training, and leading servant leader. Each of these methods will briefly be examined here.

4.2.2. How the church was founded on the prophetic-charismatic gospel proclamation method of Jesus' ministry

As noted earlier, Jesus' mission was to be shared with his followers who would represent him in the world, stand in his authority, and act on his behalf. For this purpose, he called a group of twelve people to be with him, trained them, and sent them out to extend his mission (Matt 10:1–8; Luke 9:1–6). Later, at the closure of his earthly ministry, he commissioned them to be his witnesses beginning in Jerusalem to the ends of the earth (Matt 28:18–20; Acts 1:8). In the light of this, Jesus pledged to equip

---

17. Very insightful comments are offered by Kärkkäinen in *Christ and Reconciliation* concerning reconciliation and restoration of peoples' relationships beyond national, cultural, religious, social, and sexual barriers as the church's sole mission in the world (*Constructive Christian Theology*, 1:364–80). See also Kärkkäinen's further emphasis on salvation as union with the Triune God and participation in divine life in *Constructive Christian Theology*, 4:344–35.

them with power and gifts from on high which would be realized in the coming of the Holy Spirit (Luke 24:49; Acts 1:8). His pledges are categorized into two methods of ministry. In the first instance, he pledged to endow them with his prophetic gospel proclamation, which was often accompanied by supernatural power, signs, wonders, miracles, healings, discerning spirits, casting out of demonic spirits, and raising the dead (Matt 10:1–15; Mark 3:14–15; 16:17–18; Luke 9:1–10; 24:49; John 14:12–14). These references point out that Jesus pledged to provide his disciples with all the possible supernatural resources with which he served. During the course of training, he had them exercise this method of ministry when he sent them out to preach, which they tangibly experienced and joyfully reported back to him (Luke 9:1–10). This demonstrates the dynamic continuity between the gospel proclamation of Jesus and that of his disciples. This dynamic continuity most significantly emerged from the day of Pentecost, when the apostles received the gift of the Holy Spirit and were clothed with the promised power from on High. From the day of Pentecost, the gospel proclamation of the apostles was accompanied by signs, wonders, miracles, healings, prophecies, raising the dead, exorcising demonic spirits, and with the confidence of power and authority (Acts 2:43; 3:1–10; 8:5–11; 9:39–41; 14:3–11). All these phenomena were parallel to that of Jesus' gospel proclamation and demonstrations of the dynamic continuity of Jesus' ministry.

In addition to the apostles, the Holy Spirit continued anointing, gifting, empowering, and equipping other believers with the same gifts and power. The book of Acts refers to some individuals as the early church's prophets and miracle workers. For example, Stephen and Philip performed miracles (Acts 6:8; 8:4–6). Agabus (Acts 11:27–30; 21:10–11) and Judas and Silas (Acts 15:32) were prophets. There was a group of prophets at Antioch which also included Paul and Barnabas (Acts 13:1–3) and Philip's four daughters are recorded as being prophetesses (Acts 21:9). From this Scripture evidence, it can be noted that not only the apostles, but many of the early Christians were experiencing the prophetic gospel proclamation content of Jesus' ministry through a variety of gifts. This seems to remind us that the Spirit of prophecy, who anointed, gifted, empowered, and guided Jesus, continued to anoint, gift, empower, equip, and guide the apostles, prophets, teachers, leaders, and miracle workers in the church. This also demonstrates that the church continued living, practicing, and serving the Spirit-anointed, Spirit-gifted, Spirit-empowered, and Spirit-guided life and ministry of Jesus. The church's origin, existence, authority, gifts, ministries, and mission drew their roots from these divine provisions. The apostles called these gifts by the collective name "gifts of grace" or "gifts of the Holy Spirit," which are traditionally called "spiritual gifts." Thus, the church's gospel proclamation accompanied by these gifts and their experience remained as the *Pentecostal-charismatic* nature, life, and function of the church.

In the light of the above accounts and discussion, a few things are worthy of attention. Hereafter, the term *Pentecostal-charismatic* will recur throughout this study. The term *Pentecostal* is used simply for the sake of identification of the supernatural events and practices of participants of the day of Pentecost—the church's birthday. It stands for and refers to the gifts, power, and workings of the Holy Spirit and people's responsive practices of the day of Pentecost. As discussed in chapter 2, the gift of the Holy Spirit on the day of Pentecost entailed both the objective gift (God's gift) and subjective experience (human response through audible/visible charismatic experiences) of the Holy Spirit. In this study, therefore, the term *Pentecostal* refers to both the objective gift and subjective experiential content of the reception of the Holy Spirit on the day of Pentecost. Meanwhile, the term *charismatic* stands for and refers to the gospel proclamation and worship practice which is accompanied by signs, miracles, healings, raising the dead, prophecies, revelation, discerning spirits, casting demonic spirits, etc. For the purpose of this study, both terms are synthesized into a coherent whole as *Pentecostal-charismatic* for the sake of identification and convenience.

Combined from the two terms, the term *Pentecostal-charismatic* in this study refers, primarily, to the objective salvific gift and resulting divinely delivered and divinely initiated subjective experience of the Holy Spirit. Secondly, it refers to the supernaturally gifted, empowered, inspired, and awakened gospel proclamation, worship, and spiritual practice of the church. Thirdly, the term is sometimes applied to the original *Pentecostal-charismatic* nature and function of the church. Fourthly, the term may occasionally refer to those Christians who emphasize these particular categories of teaching, preaching, worship, and spiritual practice. In which sense of these four points the term is used can be understood from the context of a given sentence, paragraph, or section. In this regard, what is worthy of noting is that in this study the term *Pentecostal-charismatic* does not have any relation to and does not make any reference to the Pentecostal and Charismatic Movements (PCMs) which emerged since the turn of the twentieth century. Neither does it refer to contemporary religious groups which designate themselves Pentecostal denominations. Indeed, conversations with and about the PCMs and Pentecostal denominations have a considerable part in this study when the study addresses the contemporary situation of the doctrine of the Holy Spirit in chapters 11 and 12. Even when dealing with the conversation of these movements, usage of the term *Pentecostal-charismatic* will differ from a sense which refers to these movements and Pentecostal denominations.

How the church was founded on the leadership/ administration method of Jesus' ministry

The Gospel accounts show that Jesus pledged to endow his disciples with special power and authority to bind and lose, to lead, to feed, and tend in their ministry (Matt 10:1; 16:18–19; Mark 3:13–15; Luke 10:19; John 20:23; 21:15–17). Concerning losing and binding on earth and in heaven, he pledged to give the disciples the power and authority he retained to "forgive sins" (Matt 9:6) and to "bind evil powers" on earth (Matt 12:28–29). This indicates that Jesus pledged to endow the apostles with an unprecedented and unanticipated pattern of authority on earth. The significance of this can be noted when considering that God had not made such a high promise of power and authority previously, not even to King Solomon, whom he made the only and unparalleled king of knowledge and wisdom on earth at his time (1 Kgs 3:10–13). Jesus also assured his disciples that he who accepts them accepts him; he who rejects them also rejects him; he who hears them hears him (Matt 10:40; Luke 10:16; John 13:20). On the day of final judgment, says Jesus, the extent of judgment to be declared upon Gomorrah and Sodom would be easier than that of those who rejected his messengers (Matt 10:15). This shows that Jesus pledged to his disciples that they would continue his ministry with his ministry methods of absolute power, authority, and leadership. This continuation was demonstrated in the ministry of the apostles who exercised this same power and authority beginning from the day of Pentecost (Acts 5:1–11; 13:8–12). Hence, it may be concluded that in the inception of the church, the apostles combined both *Pentecostal-charismatic* and *leadership-administration* methods in their ministry. Then, the historical transmission of this same leadership function, power, and authority from the apostles to the church had already begun at the time of the apostles.

The leadership/administration—church governance—authority and function entrusted to the apostles soon began to be shared with or even transferred to their immediate successors. In the first instance, this occurred when the apostles felt that they were unable to carry out both the leadership functions and gospel proclamation and they appointed leaders who were perceived to be endowed by the Holy Spirit and who demonstrated special spiritual qualifications (Acts 6). With this election of leaders, a combination of the apostles and some perceptive members from among the young congregations began to carry out the leadership function of the church. Soon varieties of terms and titles such as elders (Acts 14:23; 15:4, 23), bishops/overseers (Acts 20:28), and deacons (Rom 16:1; 1 Tim 3:8–12) began to be given to the elected leaders of local congregations. Bishops, too, began to be appointed and govern the church (Acts 20:28; Phil 1:1; 1 Tim 3:1–7). This Scripture evidence indicates that the Holy Spirit shepherded and governed the church through the elected elders and ordained bishops. This evidence reminds us that the leadership-administration life and function of the church contained both an occasionally elected eldership and ordained bishopric authorities. Elaborating on this case, Paul asserted that God had already instituted the leadership and ordained offices for the church and endowed the church with these gifts of ministry (1 Cor 12:28; Eph 4:11). Although the Jerusalem church might have continued to exercise its overall supervision of other churches, the basic organizational, leadership and pastoral ministry structures continued to be based in the young local churches. The episcopate, presbyters, bishops, deacons, and leaders continued to emerge in all the local churches. The foundation of establishing leadership officials for church governance, setting details of their qualifications, defining their responsibilities, and setting an institutional and organizational form of the church, therefore, was completed during the times of the apostles (1 Tim 3:1–13; Tit 1:5–9; 2:1–6). Thus, *leadership-administration* has remained and continues to be part of the nature, life, and function of the church inherited from God through his only Son, Jesus Christ, and transmitted through the apostles.

4.3. SUMMARY

Given the above accounts and discussion, three features deserve to be underlined in the conclusion of the chapter.

First, the biblical accounts discussed in this chapter tell us that the foundation for the life, function, and mission of the church was laid by the two ministry methods of Jesus. The Holy Spirit guided the foundation and organization of the church on this foundation and shaped its ministry by these two ministry methods. The first method is the anointed prophetic gospel proclamation method, accompanied by signs, wonders, miracle-working, healing, raising the dead, prophetic utterances, discerning spirits, and casting out demonic spirits. Through this method, the church both realizes and preserves the whole content of Jesus' Spirit-anointed, Spirit-gifted, and Spirit-empowered prophetic gospel proclamation. Thus, in reference to the functional nature that this method has taken since the day of Pentecost, it has often been perceived as the *Pentecostal-charismatic* nature of the church's life and function. The second method is the *leadership-administration* method in which the church exercises and preserves Jesus' anointed royal ruler's leadership in a humble servant leadership model. When considering Jesus' pledges to his disciples, it becomes evident that these two ministry methods draw their roots directly from the divine and are delivered to the church as part of God's plan and provision for the church to serve his new covenant community in particular and the larger world as a whole. These two methods of ministry, therefore, can be acknowledged as divinely designed, divinely destined, divinely authorized, divinely delivered gifts, and divinely directed activities of the church. Both methods emanate their theology, authority, legitimacy, and function from God through Christ. They originated from one body, God, to serve one body, God's people, and to remain as two functional faces in one body, the church, through the one Spirit of God. In virtue of their origin from one body, both methods are inextricably connected in the nature, life, and ministry of the church like the two sides of a coin. Their theological and spiritual content, substance, and authority are analogs and are equally significant. They are a dynamic theological and biblical form of the church's nature, life, and ministry. The one church of Christ was founded, organized, shaped, and characterized by these two methods of ministry.

Consequently, the apostles perceived and acknowledged both methods of ministry as the pre-arranged gifts of God to the church and believed that the Holy Spirit operates in the functions of both methods (1 Cor 12:4–11, 28). As both methods are inseparably united in their divine origin, authority, and function, they also inseparably belong to the works of the Holy Spirit in the world through the church. The Holy

Spirit is the one who initiates and conducts the functions of both gifts, endows believers with these gifts, and is active in a variety of workings in the church through these gifts. Both methods, therefore, are equally bearers and demonstrators of the Spirit of sign-charismata and leadership-charismata. The newly emerging congregations of the early church were organized and built upon the model of these two ministry methods. Understandably, Christian tradition adopted a wide range of key study disciplines and practical application strategies of the church's mission to the world. These study disciplines and practical application strategies include features such as Christian worship and liturgy, mission/evangelization, theology and doctrine of holy sacraments, Christian doctrine, hermeneutics, homiletics, Christian education, Christian ethics, spiritual formation, stewardship, Christian leadership, diakonia, etc., However, all these features draw on and emphasize the two basic methods of ministry constituted and delivered to the church by Jesus. Both methods, therefore, are paramount and set the parameters of the ministry of the church of Christ. Thus, this reality can be conceived as the theological, Christological, pneumatological, prophetic, and apostolic living and lasting heritage of the church's nature, life, and function.

Second, when the theological and functional significance of the two methods of ministry are compared and contrasted, it can be evident that their theological significance can be equated, but their functional significance cannot be equated. The *Pentecostal-charismatic* method of ministry has a far-reaching power and purpose for enhancing gospel proclamation through accompanying and validating manifestation of the sign gifts and wonders. When closely observed, *Pentecostal-charismatic* method supersedes in convincing and winning power and impacting results. When and where Pentecostal power and charismatic gifts are objectively manifested and genuinely practised, they manifest a divine power and resulting impact, which bends down the knees of the world's darkness. When the gospel proclamation is accompanied by supernatural sign-gifts, it cuts through the power and resistance of evil realities, disease, deformity, etc. Through this method, the oppressed are freed, the hungry are fed, the sick are healed, new life is given to the dying, the dead are raised, people's lives are inspired, and the new covenant's life and ministry are leavened (Luke 4:18–20). This method has been effective in validating the message of the gospel to the world through audibly uttered and visibly performed charismatic manifestations resulting in the conviction, confession, and conversion of non-believing people. Through this method, the Holy Spirit makes visible the life, power, and mission of Jesus in and to the world. When and where this method is objectively experienced, it contributes to the spiritual, moral, ethical, ecclesiastical, missiological, and social life of the church as well as to the larger world. Furthermore, while the *leadership-administration* method is static and confined to the given local church or denomination, the *Pentecostal-charismatic* method is unconfined. It is dynamic, transdenominational, and always contains a significance that is simultaneously local, global, and universal. This, indeed, is one of the radical, functional departure points of the two methods of the church's life and ministry. Therefore, the church's life and ministry without *Pentecostal-charismatic* gifts and power would, indeed, deny the dynamic which makes Christianity effective and influential in its worldwide mission.

Nevertheless, Jesus did not leave the church only with a prophetic gospel proclamation accompanied by supernatural power and sign-gifts but also provided it with the charismata of leadership, administration, shepherding, pasturing, and caring. While a prophetic gospel proclamation acts with convincing and converting power, the leadership/administration power acts with consolidating, stabilizing, and strengthening power and wisdom. For this purpose, the appointment and authority of the leadership represent structuring, ordering, systematizing, ruling, protecting, and guiding power and ministry of the church. The leadership, therefore, formulates, maintains, and preserves rules, systems, order, peace, orthodoxy, and traditions of the church. It is destined to render the function of church governance, which includes administering the *Pentecostal-charismatic* life and function of the church. It is true that by the gift of *leadership-administration* the Holy Spirit enables the church to discern, authorize, and utilize the *Pentecostal-charismatic* gifts and power. As the manifestations and experiences of the *Pentecostal-charismatic* method often transcend the institutional leadership authorities, structures, rules, and systems, the Holy Spirit intervenes and enables their proper realization through the gift and power of *leadership* ministry. For this purpose, the leadership itself is gifted and illuminated by the Holy Spirit. When the leadership authority is realized in a servanthood heart and mind, then it recognizes and wisely administers the significance of the *Pentecostal-charismatic* life and function of the church. The theological substance of both methods can then be realized meaningfully and edifyingly. The church's life and ministry without leadership, administration, structure, and order, indeed lacks the shape, form, and organized and protected existence of the church. Although its authority is often based on call or selection, depending on a given church body's structure, the leadership/administration function, too, is an objective theological endowment of the church. However, to meaningfully and edifyingly realize the theological and spiritual substance of the two methods, an integrated realization of both methods is indispensable and determinative.

Third, as we have already said, the two methods of ministry are how the initial functional nature of the church was established and organized. Since their origin, both methods are fundamentally complementary, constructive, and belong together. They are always integral and symbiotic. As the appropriation of the *leadership-administration* function is regarded as the appropriation of Christ's authoritative leadership ministry, the appropriation of the *Pentecostal-charismatic* function can also be regarded as the appropriation of Christ's prophetic gospel proclamation accompanied by charismatic gifts of the Holy Spirit. Unless the constituencies have overdue emphases on either of the methods, there is no radical theological departure point between the two methods. Nor is there anything theologically or biblically grounded to favor one of the methods and to neglect or avoid the other. Both methods are meant to be balanced in all theological, doctrinal, worship, and spiritual aspects of the life and function of the church. They should neither be confused nor separated nor subordinated to each other. Rather, they must be recognized, appreciated, and realized together and must equally display the church's dual-functional Christological heritage. For Christianity, both methods are a kind of telos—the final meaning and character of the truth of the church's function. Their integrated realization, therefore, means the teleological end of the church's life and function. An integrated realization of both methods maintains and preserves the church by its original theological, christological, pneumatological, and biblical foundation. Without this integration, each method may lose its proper theological character, substance, and flavor. Where only one of the methods is emphasized and the other is neglected, the original theological and functional nature of the church may be twisted or altered. One method cannot meaningfully, effectively, or edifyingly function in the church without the other. Therefore, each method needs the theological substance of the other to be effective with its dimension.

By integrating both methods in its life and function, the church can examine and differentiate between authentic and inauthentic charismatic experiences and then act by their fruits, deciding whether or not to hold on to them. Meanwhile, it is only in humble submission to one another that the Holy Spirit plays his building up and edifying role through both charismas and both methods can function effectively. Where this submission is exercised in the church, both authorities can accomplish their intended theological objective and receive mutual fulfillment in the submissive service of one another. Only then can the nature of Christianity be realized, experienced, displayed, and preserved under the two methods of ministry equally from Hosanna to Maranatha. Despite this, historical evidence indicates that in practice the equated and integrated use of the two methods depends on the perception and interest of the leadership office bearers. Accordingly, the church has held a biased stance, attributed excessive power and privilege to the *leadership-administration* method, and expressed strict restrictions regarding the *Pentecostal-charismatic* method. This will be considered in more detail in the next chapter.

PART II

The Person, Gifts, and Works of the Holy Spirit in Historical Christian Teaching and Practice from AD 100 to 1900

As indicated in the introduction, part II of the study will engage in a broader exploration of the historical Christian perception, teaching and practice of the person, gifts and works of the Holy Spirit. The examination will begin in the early church and move on to the major church periods: patristic, medieval, Reformation, and post-Reformation periods. Engagement with such a broad historical context may provide reasonable historical practical answers to the questions or solutions to the confusions identified and addressed in this study. The exploration will attempt to raise and answer such questions as: (1) How did the apostles instruct their immediate successors about the presence, gifts, and works of the Holy Spirit in the life and function of the church? (2) What did the presence, gifts, and works of the Holy Spirit look like in the patristic church's perception, teaching, and practice? An exploration of the patristic period will also consider some supplementary questions such as: How did ambiguities, questions, confusions, controversies, and divisions in the doctrine of the Holy Spirit begin in the history of the church? Have there been any overt theological, biblical, or practical reasons for the rise of the ambiguities, questions, confusions, controversies, and divisions over the doctrine of the Holy Spirit? Have there been any evidenced controversial effects where the experience of the gifts and works of the Holy Spirit were incorporated into Christian worship and spiritual practice? And so forth. (3) What did the person, gifts, and works of the Holy Spirit look like in the perception, teaching, and practice of the medieval Western Church and the Reformation and post-Reformation Protestant churches? (4) Why do scholarly evaluations suggest that in the history of Christianity, the Holy Spirit has been treated as the "subordinated," the "Cinderella," the "shy/silent," "dark-sided," and "eclipsed" person of the Trinity? If this has indeed been the case, then to what do these scholarly observations, strange terms, and arguments refer? What happened to the Holy Spirit in the history of Christian belief, teaching, and practice? Thus, the findings of the exploration shall provide us with some form of an overview of the place and role of the Holy Spirit in Christian belief, teaching, and practice through the centuries and some possible historical practical answers to the questions and confusions identified and addressed in this study. This will be examined in chapters 5 to 10.

CHAPTER 5

The Apostolic Transmission and Post-Apostolic Church's Teaching and Practice

We have considered how the Holy Spirit was an architect and guide in the inward life and outward act of the church from its inception; how he guided the foundation and organization of the church, and how the life and ministry of the church were shaped following the two ministry methods of Jesus. In all these activities the Holy Spirit used the apostles as the forefront leaders and ministers of the church. At times the apostles resolved some complicated affairs in agreement with the Holy Spirit (Acts 15). The apostles controlled the leadership and ministry of the church from Pentecost up to the AD 60s as coworkers with the Holy Spirit. As discussed in chapter 4, some perceptive members of the early converts also became involved and experienced both methods of Jesus' ministry as they worked alongside the apostles. Thereby, the historical transmission of the leadership authority and gospel proclamation from the apostles to their successors had already begun at the time of the apostles. In light of this, the question that might be asked here is: what did the place and role of the Holy Spirit look like in the apostolic transmission to their successors and in the early postapostolic church? Search for an answer to this question leads us, primarily, to examination of the nature of the apostolic instructions to their successors about the place and role of the Holy Spirit in the church's life and function.

Secondly, it leads us to examination of the nature of the early postapostolic church's perception, teaching, and practice of the Holy Spirit. This examination in turn leads us to raise such questions as: How did the apostles instruct their successors concerning the presence, reception, gifts, and workings of the Holy Spirit? Was the concept and practice of objective reception and subjective experience of the Holy Spirit an issue of attention in the apostles' ministry and their instruction to their successors? Were the concept and practice of baptism in the Holy Spirit and Spirit-charismata clearly understood, identified, and addressed in their instructions as a matter of worship and spiritual significance? How did they orient or instruct their successors about the *Pentecostal-charismatic* and the *leadership-administration* nature and function of the church? Did they transfer the patterns of dual-faceted ministry entrusted to them to their successors straight away as they were transferred from Jesus to them? What did the early postapostolic and the successive centuries' church's perception and practice toward the reception of the Holy Spirit, Spirit-charismata, and baptism in the Holy Spirit look like? And so on. This chapter examines these features by reviewing the canonical writings of the apostles and a document of the postapostolic period, which is named after the apostles as *Constitutions of the Holy Apostles*. Here a question that might be asked is: how reliable are *Constitutions of the Holy Apostles* to use in academic works such as this one? This can be a valid question. However, this document is intensively reviewed and used for this study on the grounds of the following four reasons:

1. As we shall see in detailed examination here, the *Constitutions* claim to have been written by the apostles and provide a number of pieces of evidence as proof of the apostolic authorship. For example, the *Constitutions* contain many of the experiences of the apostles with Jesus during his earthly ministry and in the intervening days between his resurrection and ascension.[1]

2. The document claims to have been complied and transmitted to the next generations through Clement, who was regarded as the "fellow-apostle" and "faithful and intimate fellow-minister" of the apostles, the "disciple of Paul,"[2] "ordained by the apostle Peter"[3] as the second

---

1. *Constitutions of the Holy Apostles* 2.55, 58; 3.9; 4.12, 14.
2. *Constitutions of the Holy Apostles* 6.8.
3. *Constitutions of the Holy Apostles* 7.46.

bishop of the church of Rome, next to Linus,[4] and who compiled the *Constitutions* in eight books and dedicated it to the ordained leadership of the church.[5] It claims to be the church manual with carefully organized and arranged comprehensive ecclesiastical administrational and liturgical rules, regulations, and orders to meet the needs of the primitive church.

3. The *Constitutions* appear to have been written at the time when the tradition of apostolic succession regarding leadership authority was given a particular place and role in the church and when the church was thoroughly dependent on the teaching and guidance of the ordained leadership as immediate successors of the apostles. In that context, they must have been highly regarded and observed as the essential rule of faith and the life and practice of the church. Within its essential rule of faith, the document contains the perceptions and practices of the primitive church toward the Holy Spirit, his gifts, and workings in the church.

4. Historical evaluations of the status of the *Apostolic Constitutions*, suggest that it was a highly authoritative document of the church up to the end of the seventh century. With the development of new rules and regulations beginning in the fourth century, the power and function of the *Constitutions* had gradually receded. In the Western church, its authority was pushed aside at the end of the seventh century—mostly by the Council of Trullo in 692. However, it is maintained with high regard in the Eastern Church as a lasting authoritative document with the apostolic authority up to the present time.[6] If this suggestion is based on existing reality, then the document must have been of high importance in the church of the first seven centuries, even after the church formed some strong theological and doctrinal rules and regulations which included the canon of Scripture, careful articulations of the Trinitarian doctrine, ecumenical creeds, and similar other relevant rules of faith for the church's life and ministry.

Given these four main reasons, from among many others, it is my conviction that the *Constitutions* provide us with a window into the place

---

4. *Constitutions of the Holy Apostles* 6.8.

5. *Constitutions of the Holy Apostles* 8.47, 84.

6. Clayton, N. Jefford, "Apostolic Constitutions and Canons" in *Anchor Bible Dictionary*, 1:312–13.

and role of the Holy Spirit in the perception, teaching, and practice of the church from the end of the first century into the end of the seventh century.

5.1. HOW DID THE APOSTLES INSTRUCT THEIR IMMEDIATE SUCCESSORS ABOUT THE PERSON, GIFTS, AND WORKS OF THE HOLY SPIRIT IN THE CHURCH?

When the canonized writings of the apostles are examined, the primary clear-cut answer regarding how the apostles instructed their successors about the ways of reception, gifts, and workings of the Holy Spirit is that the apostles did not clearly instruct their successors about this subject. The same answer seems to apply to the associated subquestions: Did they instruct their successors about the concept and practice of baptism in the Holy Spirit? Did they instruct them about the reality and significance of the charismatic gifts of the Holy Spirit? Did they instruct them about the reality of the objective gift and subjective experience of the Holy Spirit? Except for merely providing general information about what had happened in their practices regarding these features, the apostles seem to be silent about them in their canonized writings. Let us briefly examine what their canonized writings contain about these features:

First, as discussed in chapter 1, the apostles indicated in their canonized writings how Jesus taught them about the Holy Spirit in respect of his absolute divinity, independent personality, future coming, permanent indwelling, empowering, and guiding functions. Their writings contain details regarding the reception of the Holy Spirit in and through water baptism; that Christian baptism should be in the name of the Father, of the Son, and of the Holy Spirit; that Jesus promised their imminent baptism in the Holy Spirit; and that the Holy Spirit indwells believers forever. Besides these scant references, the apostles did not provide further information regarding whether Jesus taught them how believers would receive and experience the features at issue here. Nor did they say anything based on their own experiences of these features. There is, therefore, a lack of clarification in the canonized writings of the apostles about the features raised in the questions being discussed here.

Second, regarding when the New Testament accounts of the apostles were written, scholarly speculations suggest that Matthew's gospel was composed sometime between AD 65 and 80;[7] John's gospel between either AD 40 and 70 or between AD 70 and 90;[8] Peter's Epistles between AD 62 and 66;[9] James's Epistle between AD 45 and 62;[10] and John's Epistles between AD 90 and 100.[11] As discussed in chapter 2, these apostles were at the heart of the events at Pentecost in Jerusalem, in Samaria, and in Caesarea. Oddly enough, none of them mentioned any of those experiences as functional or significant in their experiences. There is no direct reference to the Holy Spirit being active among the apostles or among the early congregations as a recognized or wanted divine source of ministry gifts and power. Nor do they mention whether the concept and practice of baptism in the Holy Spirit and the Spirit-charismata were intended to be normative for all Christians of the time. Besides the scant mention of the significance of sacramental baptism, they do not mention anything about what was meant by the experience of baptism in the Holy Spirit at Pentecost, how the received and indwelt Holy Spirit should be experienced by believers, or how believers should identify and differentiate between the objective gift and subjective experience of the Holy Spirit. Nor do they indicate whether those experiences were meant to be continuing Christian experiences until the expected return of Christ. Be it intentionally or unintentionally, the writings of the apostles lack reference to their experiences of baptism in the Holy Spirit at and after Pentecost or their continued experiences of the Spirit-charismata. Accordingly, there is a lack of clarification in the canonical writings of the apostles about the questions raised and the features being discussed here.

Third, the Acts of the Apostles are assumed to have been composed between AD 60 and 65.[12] If this is so, then it reminds us that there was a lapse of thirty-four to thirty-six years between Pentecost and recording of the stories contained in Acts. This entices one to raise the question whether the Holy Spirit's reception experiences at Pentecost, in Samaria, in Caesarea, and in Ephesus were the only incidents that occurred in the ministry of the apostles in the course of those thirty-six years. The book of Acts does not make it clear whether those reception experiences of the Holy Spirit were common among other churches of the time or not.

7. Keener, *Commentary*, 42–44.
8. Weinrich, *John 1:1–7:1*, 31–51.
9. Davids, *First Epistle of Peter*, 9–10. See also Michaels, *1 Peter*, lvii–lviii.
10. Kistemaker, *Epistle of James*, 18.
11. Smalley, *1, 2, 3 John*, xxxii; cf. Schuchard, *1–3 John*, 18.
12. Bruce, *Book of Acts*, 10–11; Kistemaker, *Acts of the Apostles*, 21–22.

Nor does it make clear whether the charismatic manifestations that accompanied the evangelization of the apostles were meant to be normative for all Christians of the time and beyond. Rather, the writer of the book seems to report only the events that had happened in the past with no indications about the future. It can be assumed that since these experiences were a decisive part of the early church's life and evangelization, the author might have taught that they were meant to be normative and to continue until the expected imminent return of Christ. Despite this, however, it can be observed that there is a lack of clear instruction in the book of Acts about the features in the discussion here.

Fourth, Paul, who is exceptional in how he addresses the place and role of the Holy Spirit in empowering his ministry, in uniting believers to Christ, and in the moral purity of the believers, did not instruct his audiences in a clear way about how believers would experience the reception, presence, gifts, and works of the Holy Spirit. As discussed in chapter 3, he taught the Corinthians that the Holy Spirit was a giver of charismata and advised the Ephesians to keep on being filled with the Holy Spirit (Eph 5:18). Since Paul appears to understand the presence, gifts, power, and activities of the Holy Spirit better than the other apostles, his case may entice us to ask the question as to whether the twelve apostles' understanding and experience of the Holy Spirit amounted to the extent we read about in Paul's experience. On the other hand, however, when compared and contrasted to his broader understanding and broader writings, Paul too, did not adequately orient or instruct his audiences in the ways of objective reception and resulting subjective experiences of the Holy Spirit. He did not mention whether what was experienced by him and his audiences in Ephesus (Acts 19:1–6) was a common experience in his missionary movements. Nor did he mention whether such an experience was meant to be a continuous experience for Christians everywhere at that time. His neglect might have resulted not from his negative attitude to these experiences, but it either slipped his notice or was ignored due to his expectation of the imminent return of Christ (1 Cor 7:29).

As discussed in chapter 4, at the outset of the church's formation every radical event related to its foundation, organization, life, and ministry was initiated and guided by the Holy Spirit. This does not, however, appear to be a permanent and common experience of all the young local churches of the time. In their canonized writings, the apostles did not clearly instruct their recipients about how believers would experience the reception, gifts, and works of the Holy Spirit. Nor did they say anything about whether the Holy Spirit who baptized, gifted, empowered, and guided them now and again was necessary for the life and ministry of the present and future church. This seems to indicate that emphasis on the concept and practice of the reception, gifts, and works of the Holy Spirit started to slow down with the apostles' perception and experience of these features. This again seems to be the reason why their writings are lacking clear instruction in the ways of reception and experiences of the Holy Spirit. If this is not the case, they could have encouraged their recipients to retain and experience the reality and significance of these features in the same way they had experienced them. Further, when viewed in the light of the apostles' experiences, as discussed in chapter 3, at the center of the manifestation of the Holy Spirit were both objective gifts and resulting Spirit-initiated subjective experiences. Yet it appears that the apostles had no idea about these features as something significant. While the objective reception of the Holy Spirit might have been thought to continue through sacramental baptism, there was no understanding of the subjective experiential content of manifestations of the Holy Spirit. The same is true regarding the concept and practice of baptism in the Holy Spirit and of the Spirit-charismata.

Thus, in light of the apostolic legacies preserved in their canonized writings, there seems no ground for one to be surprised at the inconsistency in the development of the concept and practice of the reception, presence, gifts, and activities of the Holy Spirit in the church. As their writings left the church with much unclear and unsatisfactory information about the manifestation, reception, baptism, gifts, and workings of the Holy Spirit, there was no authoritative source that provided the church with clear and authoritative answers and solutions to the questions, confusions, and controversies arising concerning the questions raised above and subject in discussion here. This gap seems the reason behind why questions, confusion, and controversies related to the nature, manifestations, gifts, and workings of the Holy Spirit continued in the church before these were settled via authoritative resolutions in the church councils of the fourth century. Thus, the lack of clear instruction in the canonized writings of the apostles can be considered as *one of the root causes* of the historical tensions that arose in reference to the manifestation, reception, gifts, and workings of the Holy Spirit.

In like manner, when the early postapostolic writings are examined on this subject matter, they too appear to contain nothing about the features in discussion here. *Constitutions of the Holy Apostles*, for example, indicate that the church of the postapostolic period developed a tradition of further negligence regarding the place and role of the Holy Spirit in the life, worship, and ministry of the church. The writers of the *Constitutions* attributed only four roles to the Holy Spirit, i.e., comforting, proclaiming, and glorifying Jesus, and standing as a witness at baptism. It was asserted that Christian baptism should be conducted in the name of the Father, of the Son, and of the Holy Spirit. In this assertion, the Holy Spirit was presented as simply a "jointly mentioned witness . . . who testifies."[13] Yet, "witness" of what and "testifies" to what is not made explicit. The writers of the *Constitutions* expressed their belief that the Holy Spirit was the one who worked through all the saints since the beginning of the world, who taught of and was sent by Jesus as the fulfillment of the promise made to the apostles by Jesus, and who is sent to all those who believe in the holy Catholic Church and who "proclaims Only Jesus."[14] The writers of the *Constitutions* believed that in the Catholic Church, "everybody who is baptized remains under the Holy Spirit and the Holy Spirit remains with/in him so long as he does good."[15] The writers asserted that the Holy Spirit is given only through the bishopric laying-on of hands.[16] Besides these scant references, however, there is no further clear instruction in the Constitutions about the ways of reception or place and role of the Holy Spirit in the life and ministry of the church. This seems to indicate that the gap that existed in the canonized writings of the apostles was maintained and preserved by their successors who also continued to turn deaf ears to the place and role of the Holy Spirit in the church's life, worship, ministry, and mission.

5.2. HOW DID THE APOSTLES INSTRUCT THEIR IMMEDIATE SUCCESSORS ABOUT THE PROPHETIC-CHARISMATIC GOSPEL PROCLAMATION METHOD OF THE CHURCH'S LIFE AND MINISTRY?

Again a brief and general answer to the question "how did the apostles instruct their successors about the concept and practice of the Spirit-charismata and charismatic gospel proclamation?" is, in fact, that the apostles

---

13. *Constitutions of the Holy Apostles* 3.17; 7.22, 43.
14. *Constitutions of the Holy Apostles* 3.17; 7.22, 41.
15. *Constitutions of the Holy Apostles* 6.27.
16. *Constitutions of the Holy Apostles* 2.22, 31, 33.

did not clearly instruct their successors about what is meant by "prophetic-charismatic gospel proclamation." Except for Luke merely reporting what had happened in the apostolic evangelization, the canonized writings of the apostles neither encouraged nor discouraged the significance of gospel proclamation accompanied by charismatic manifestations. Let us examine what their canonized writings present about this feature.

First, except for the two mentions of Paul (Rom 12:6–8; 1 Cor 12:4–11), nowhere are the charismatic gifts stated to be sought, prayed for, received, and experienced as pertaining to the life and function of the church. The writings of the apostles present scant evidence even about the apostles' own charismatic experience. For example, the book of Acts reports only two incidents, generalizing that signs, wonders, and miracles were wrought by the apostles (Acts 2:43; 5:12). Meanwhile, from among the twelve apostles, it was only Peter who is specifically identified with the demonstration of these charismata (Acts 3:1–10; 5:12–16; 9:32–43). Besides Peter, Luke associates the apostle John (Acts 3:1–10), Stephen (Acts 6:8), and the evangelist Philip (Acts 8:4–7) with these experiences, each of them on one occasion. However, he associates Paul with large numbers of charismatic phenomena (Acts 14:1–3, 8–12; 19:11–12; 20:7–12; 28:3–6). This may raise a question regarding what happened to the other ten apostles. Were their gospel proclamations never accompanied by charismatic manifestations? Did they perform no miracles, which may be the reason Luke did not associate them with any kind of charismatic events? If they did not perform any miracle, then would it be legitimate to argue that the ten played a very little role in the apostolic missionary movement? And so on. The answer to these questions may, on the one hand, require evidence from primary sources of the apostolic time, while, on the other hand, it cannot be assumed that what is recorded in the Acts of the Apostles contains everything that happened in the apostolic missionary movements. Countless non-recorded charismatic manifestations might have accompanied the apostolic evangelization. And yet, if Luke's report of Peter's and John's demonstration of miraculous charismata was the only one to occur in the whole course of their thirty-six-year ministry, it may lead us to assume that manifestations and experiences of Spirit-charismata were very rare even in the time of the apostles. Furthermore, in addition to mentioning the status of the apostles' charismatic experience, the case of the Corinthian church may provide us with another example. Out of approximately twenty-five churches identified by name in the book of Acts and the Epistles, it was only the Corinthian church that was identified to have been involved in charismatic experiences. What happened to the other churches of the time? Were they not involved in charismatic experiences? If the church in Corinth was the only church of the time involved in the experience of Spirit-charismata, then this may also lead the observer to the assertion that manifestations and experiences of charismata were very rare even in the time of the apostles.

Second, next to his two accounts on charismata (Rom 12:6–8; 1 Cor 12:4–11), Paul asserts prophecy as the most profitable charismata for building up the body of Christ and exhorts the Corinthians to eagerly pursue it (1 Cor 14). He deals with the Corinthian church's case in detail and gives them instructions on the edifying use of the charismata. However, in his other letters, Paul does not indicate whether other congregations of the time were involved in similar charismatic experiences. Except for a single piece of advice to the Thessalonians not to neglect prophecy (1 Thess 5:19), Paul does not extend similar advice to the recipients of his other letters. Nor does he instruct other churches by tracing the problem that had arisen in the church of Corinth concerning the charismatic experience. Hence, besides this evidence, none of the apostles stated that the Spirit-charismata should be sought, prayed for, received or experienced as the divine source for the church's life and function. Neither were they stated as the present possessions of the apostles nor were they meant to be active in the present or future life and function of the church. Neither the apostles nor Luke nor Paul clearly instructed and encouraged their recipients toward the realization and regularization of charismatic experiences. This may lead us to raise questions such as: Why did Peter and John, who seemed to be the leading practitioners of the two methods of Jesus' ministry, not mention in their writings whether charismatic gifts were being experienced in their ministry and in the churches of the time? Why did they not mention whether those experiences were meant to be normative and continuous experiences among Christians of the time and beyond? Answers to these questions may, again, require evidence from the apostles' times, which may, indeed, remain to ask for the moon.

When the New Testament is examined, the experience of the gospel proclamation accompanied by charismatic manifestations does not appear to be consistent and continuous even during the time of the apostles. Rather, charismatic manifestations appear to be quite rare occasions, which are manifested and realized only when and where God wants and wills. This seems to be the reason why neither the apostles nor Luke nor Paul exhorted their recipients to appeal to charismatic gifts as necessary components of the Christian spiritual experience. Luke's intention, when compiling the events contained in the book of Acts, does not seem to be aiming at instructing that charismatic experiences are meant to be normative. Instead, his intention seems to be simply to report on certain conspicuously significant charismatic phenomena within the apostolic missionary movements. Viewed in the light of this enormous gap, the Corinthian church's case, on the one hand, seems to be unique. On the other hand, the Corinthian church was viewed as one of the few churches that had not been identified as having a bishop ordained by the apostles.[17] If this was the case, then it may be assumed that the Corinthian church used the opportunity of the absence of a bishop to become engaged in charismatic experiences, while other churches were denied these experiences by their bishops.

In like manner, when the *Apostolic Constitutions* are examined on this subject, there appears to be just one single positive view about prophecy, while large parts of the *Constitutions* discourage the thought, claim, and practice of charismatic gifts. For example, the writers of the document called the *Teaching of the Twelve Apostles*, traditionally known as the Didache, instructed their audiences to accept and treat the apostles, prophets, and teachers as if they were accepting and treating the Lord. This respective list of apostles, prophets, and teachers seems to correspond to Paul's list, "first of all apostles, second prophets, third teachers, and then workers of miracles" (1 Cor 12:28). Indeed, Paul elsewhere asserted that apostles and prophets were part of the foundation of the church along with Christ (Eph 2:20). He repeated this concept of ranking again in Eph 4:11. This ranking of the three offices, both in Scripture and in the *Constitutions*, as "first," "second," and "third" seems to signify the then perceived importance of these respective offices. Nevertheless, the Didache also attributed supremacy to the prophetic ministry. It instructed its audiences to take every first fruit of their products and give them to the prophets and it enumerated the details of the products from which the firstfruits should be taken. Clarifying the reason for this, the writers of the Didache state that the prophets of the time were regarded as the "High Priests of the believers." The writers warned believers of the time not to "speak against or judge the prophets who speak in the Holy Spirit" because "for every sin shall be forgiven, but this sin shall not be forgiven." The writers also alerted believers to consider the ethics of the

---

17. *Constitutions of the Holy Apostles* 7.4.

prophets and reminded them to discern between true and false prophets according to their ethics.[18] Nevertheless, while the writers of this instruction seem to pay due regard to the prophetic gift, the *Apostolic Constitutions* contained something of a puzzle for the recipients concerning the reception and practice of charismatic gifts.

In general, the *Constitutions* indicate that the church of the postapostolic period developed a tradition in which the realization and practice of charismatic gifts were discouraged. The writers of the *Constitutions* seem to reflect that tradition and promoted a strict restriction on the tendency of claims and experience of the charismatic gifts. Further elaborating on that restrictive tradition, the writers of the *Constitutions* in book 8.1, entitled "On the Diversity of Spiritual Gifts," described how Jesus delivered the "great mystery" of spirituality or "godliness" to the apostles. Clarifying what they meant by the "great mystery of godliness," the writers referred to Jesus' prayer which states, "Now this is eternal life: that they may know you, the only true God, and Jesus Christ whom you have sent" (John 17:3). Referring to this prayer, the writers assert that the great mystery of spirituality or godliness is to know the love of God to the world, manifested in Jesus, and to believe in God through his Son, Jesus Christ. This, as the writers believed, was the main gift of God to the world. Concerning the reception and experience of charismatic gifts, the writers believed that various kinds of gifts are bestowed by God, through Christ. They enumerate some of the charismata, corresponding to the Pauline accounts in Rom 12:6–8 and 1 Cor 12:4–11, and explain that there may be occasions and events when some of these gifts are needed for the sake of unbelievers. In such cases, the writers caution their audiences about two things. First, if any believer is given any of these gifts, then he/she should not exalt himself/herself and should not despise his/her fellow Christians who have not received such gifts. Second, if any believer is given any of these gifts, and if there are no unbelievers around, then the purpose and power of the gift remain "superfluous." In support of this conviction, the writers state that just as the rulers are superfluous where there are no people to be ruled over, so it is with the charismatic gifts where there are no non-believers.[19]

The writers of the *Constitutions* proceed to assert that charismatic gifts are not necessary for believers. In their justification of this conviction,

---

18. *Teaching of the Twelve Apostles* 11.1–12; 13.1–7.
19. *Constitutions of the Holy Apostles* 8.1.

they refer to Jesus' promise that says, "And these signs will accompany those who believe: In my name, they will drive out demons; they will speak in new tongues; they will pick up snakes with their hands; and if they drink deadly poison, it will not hurt them at all; they will place their hands on sick people, and they will get well" (Mark 16:17–18). They then explain that these kinds of gifts were bestowed on the apostles when they were about to preach the gospel. They considered such gifts thereafter to be no longer necessary for believers. They assert that the purpose of these kinds of gifts was only to convince non-believers. To explain what they mean by this, the writers state that when the gospel is preached to non-believers, if they are touched and moved by the power of the preached word and respond in believing in Jesus, then that is all that is desired. But if non-believers are not touched and moved by the preached word and harden their hearts, then the demonstration of charismata may be needed to embarrass, shame, and convict them. According to the writers of the *Constitutions*, therefore, charismatic gifts are needed only for non-believers and not for believers.[20] The writers argue that even non-believers may not be convinced when miraculous charismata are demonstrated. To prove this, they cite two examples from Scripture: first, they refer to Moses's experience and argue that when he performed many kinds of striking signs, wonders, and miracles the Egyptians did not believe in God, but continued in hardening their hearts. Second, they refer to Jesus' ministry arguing that when Jesus performed various kinds of miraculous charismata among Jews, the Jews did not believe in Jesus, but continued in denying him and seeking to kill him. The same, in their belief, is true of the Christian experience, because "signs do not shame all into belief, but only those of a good disposition."[21] Any kind of surprising miraculous phenomenon, therefore, may not convince unbelievers and thus it is vain and futile for believers to think of receiving and practicing such gifts.[22] They further refer to Jesus' discourse such as, "Whoever acknowledges me before men, I will also acknowledge him before my Father in heaven. But whoever disowns me before men, I will disown him before my Father in heaven" (Matt 10:32–33). They, then, assert that if this is so, then there is no need or profit for believers to "cast out demons, or raise the dead, or speak in tongues," but only to believe in God through Jesus. When one believes in Jesus in full assurance, then, he/she is given the best gift of God:

20. *Constitutions of the Holy Apostles* 8.1.
21. *Constitutions of the Holy Apostles* 8.1.
22. *Constitutions of the Holy Apostles* 8.1.

salvation. This gift, in their view, is the best gift that ought to be sought, and when this perfect gift of God is sought and attained, there is no need for signs, wonders, miracles, raising the dead, casting out demons, etc.[23] Thus, herein seems to lie the historically hidden depth of the obstacle of the *Pentecostal-charismatic* form of Christian spiritual experience, as well as the roots of historical tensions regarding the Spirit-charismata within the doctrine of the Holy Spirit.

When considered from the *Constitutions*, it seems evident that the primitive church severely restricted the claim and practice of the Spirit-charismata among believers. There would seem a tendency to either completely ignore the charismatic experience or to remove any attention on anything other than believing in Jesus. It seems that it was by either of these tendencies that the writers of the *Constitutions* put emphasis only on believing in Jesus thereby severely restricting charismatic experiences. The writers' position in this regard, on the one hand, is in absolute agreement with the teachings of Jesus as they emphasize what he emphasized as the decisive means of salvation (John 3:16–18; 6:37–40, 47). Since salvation is possible without receiving and exercising any of the charismatic gifts, this standing of the writers is fundamentally theological, christological, and biblical. Thus, it was fundamentally correct, is fundamentally correct, and it shall remain fundamentally correct. On the other hand, however, there are some puzzling points regarding their avoidance of charismatic experiences among believers. Two things can be considered as examples.

First, in the face of the promise God made to give these gifts of Spirit-charismata to his people along with the gift of his Spirit (Joel 2:28) and declared by the apostles at Pentecost as the promise was fulfilled, those gifts were denied from use in Christian experience. Second, the sign gifts promised by Jesus (Mark 16:17–18) and referred to by the writers in the *Constitutions* were meant to be held and wrought by those who believe in Jesus, not by nonbelievers. When the text says "these signs will accompany those who believe," this can be understood to mean that believers are to be endowed with those sign gifts and that the gifts are meant to be common in believers' faith life and practice. The text here seems to suggest that these gifts are typical means to distinguish faith life from ordinary life, to confirm the credit of believing in Jesus, to confirm the purpose and saving power of the gospel, and to assure of Jesus'

---

23. *Constitutions of the Holy Apostles* 8.1.

assisting of believers with supernatural resources. This seems to be the reason such signs accompanied the apostles' gospel proclamation. Oddly enough, the writers of the *Constitutions* believed that these gifts were not necessary for believers. Despite their acknowledging Jesus' clarification of the significance of believers' endowment with those sign gifts, the writers boldly and blindly denied the claim and experience of these gifts among believers. They seem to be saying, "Jesus promised and delivered these gifts to believers, but we found them not necessary." This conviction seems to have marginalized the charismatic life, power, and attraction of Christianity in the postapostolic church. This highlights that the obstacle of the *Pentecostal-charismatic* form of worship and spirituality took its roots initially in this tradition and continued to influence the church of successive centuries' with a similar perception of these gifts.

Hence, the *Constitutions* are clear enough in demonstrating that the postapostolic church developed a strong restrictionist tradition towards the reception and practice of the Spirit-charismata. It can be assumed that this tradition continued to influence the successors of the writers of the *Constitutions* to emphasize only what their precedents emphasized and to neglect or avoid what they neglected or avoided. Otherwise, it could be illegitimate for their successors to construct and constitute an experience that was textually restricted or even prohibited by their precedents. If this is to be agreed upon, then it is perhaps not surprising if in successive centuries Christians neglected or avoided the *Pentecostal-charismatic* form of worship and spiritual experience because it is not accidental but is referential and reflective of the existing tradition. It is inevitable, therefore, that the legacies of such negligence have played an influential role and have contributed negatively to the overall *Pentecostal-charismatic* life and function of the church through the centuries. In this regard, it seems that a real and serious theological and practical difficulty has been created for the church. Generally, when the nature of the life and ministry that the church inherited from Jesus are compared and contrasted with the rules and regulations constituted by the later church regarding its life and ministry, it becomes evident that what has been thought and practiced by the church up until the end of the nineteenth century is something directly contradictory to the nature, purpose, and function of the church. Had the primitive church not developed, documented, and handed down such restrictionist traditions, surely the nature and quality of Christian spirituality could have been different from what it was up until the end of the nineteenth century. Thus, this historical phenomenon can be considered as *one of the root causes* of tension arising concerning the practice of the Spirit-charismata within the doctrine of the Holy Spirit through the centuries.

5.3. HOW DID THE APOSTLES INSTRUCT THEIR IMMEDIATE SUCCESSORS ABOUT THE LEADERSHIP-ADMINISTRATION METHOD OF THE CHURCH'S LIFE AND MINISTRY?

When the canonized writings of the apostles are examined, we find very scant indications or images of the *leadership-administration* functions of the church. As discussed in chapter 4, we primarily find Jesus' pledge and instruction to the apostles about tending his flock in the ways he would have them tended (John 21:15–17). Later, when churches were planted, elders or leaders were elected, bishops were appointed to oversee the congregations, and Peter reminded those leaders not to exercise power over God's flock (1 Pet 5:1–5). Besides these two references, neither Peter nor other apostles nor Luke offer clear instructions about the *leadership-administration* life and function of the church. It was only Paul who outlined the qualification of those to be elected as elders or leaders of the congregations (1 Tim 3:1–7; Titus 1:5–9). Paul was the one who instructed his congregations to thoroughly submit to their leaders, saying, "Now we ask you, brothers, to respect those . . . who are over you in the Lord. . . . Hold them in the highest regard" (1 Thess 5:12–13) and that "the elders who direct the affairs of the church . . . are worthy of double honor" (1 Tim 5:17). The author of Hebrews also shares Paul's views by saying, "Obey your leaders and submit to their authority" (Heb 13:17). These Scripture references seem to indicate that Paul accorded the authority of the church to the leadership. Other apostles did not offer such strong instructions to their audiences. As pointed out earlier, this may be due to their expectation of the imminent return of Christ and the end of the world. However, it seems that later during the postapostolic times puzzlingly stronger rules were constituted for the leadership-administration function of the church. The *Apostolic Constitutions* show that the *leadership-administration* function of the church shifted from congregationally elected elders to the ordained office of ministry. The appointing of an ordained office or bishops began by referring to the apostles' instruction, which in turn refers to Jesus' instruction to the apostles concerning the appointment of bishops. The *Constitutions*, for example, indicate that during his stay with the apostles in the interim forty days between his resurrection and ascension, Jesus "ordained" the apostles "thirteen in number."[24] Among them was James, who was referred to as "the brother of Christ according to the flesh" and "one appointed bishop of Jerusalem by the Lord himself."[25] The apostles were thereby instructed by Jesus to ordain others and they continued to ordain bishops for the existing congregations.[26]

The *Constitutions* enumerate about thirty-one bishops ordained by the apostles who were entrusted with oversight over the parishes of the time. They were also authorized to run their young churches as successors and representatives of the apostles and were reminded to observe the words and rules of the apostles.[27] This shows that wherever the apostles preached the gospel and planted churches, they appointed bishops as their successors and handed over the *leadership-administration* ministry of the church to them.[28] The *Constitutions* demonstrate that the tradition of ordaining bishops continued beyond the times of the apostles. Some of the listed criteria based on which the candidates of a bishopric should be examined state: "Let him . . . be sober, prudent, decent, firm, stable, not given to wine; no striker, but gentle; not a brawler, not covetous; not a novice, lest, being puffed up with pride."[29] Especially before the gentiles, "Let not a bishop be given to filthy lucre . . . rather suffering than offering injuries; . . . no admirer of rich, nor hater of the poor; no evil-speaker, nor false witness . . . not entangled with the affairs of this life . . . not ambitious; not double-minded, nor double-tongued; . . . not addicted to the heathen festivals; not given to vain deceits; not eager after worldly things, nor a lover of money."[30] The congregations were also instructed to "search diligently all the faults of him who is to be ordained."[31]

Describing the extent of the power and authority of a bishop, the writers of the *Constitutions* state that the bishop is the one who is "set over all men, priests, kings, rulers, fathers, children, teachers"[32] and "exercises

---

24. *Constitutions of the Holy Apostles* 8.46.
25. *Constitutions of the Holy Apostles* 7.46; 8.35.
26. *Constitutions of the Holy Apostles* 8.46.
27. *Constitutions of the Holy Apostles* 7.46.
28. Clement, *First Epistle to the Corinthians* 42.
29. *Constitutions of the Holy Apostles* 8.1.
30. *Constitutions of the Holy Apostles* 2.3.
31. *Constitutions of the Holy Apostles* 2.3.
32. *Constitutions of the Holy Apostles* 2.9, 11.

God's authority" over all classes of people who are meant to submit to him.[33] They express their belief that "God put the church administration into his [bishop's] hands and thought him worthy of so great dignity."[34] They present the bishop as the one who has been given the power and authority to forgive sins and the power of life and death, one who can condemn for eternal death.[35] On account of this, they encourage a bishop by saying, "For to you, O bishop, it is said, 'whatsoever ye shall bind on earth shall be bound in heaven; and whatsoever you loose on earth shall be loosed in heaven.'" They also say, "O bishop, be sensible of the dignity of thy place that as thou hast received the power of binding, so hast thou that of loosing."[36] They add, "Do thou . . . O bishop, judge with authority like God . . . judge as executing judgment for God."[37] According to the conviction of the writers of the *Constitutions*, it is the bishop's privilege to govern overall, but he is subject to no one except God alone. If anybody thinks that the bishop is subject to anybody under him, then that, in the view of the writers, is equivalent to thinking that the head submits to the tail.[38]

In order to draw the attention of the laity to how they should unreservedly honor the bishop, the writers of the *Constitutions* attribute varieties of venerable titles to the bishop. They state that for the laity, the bishop means, "Lord, master, High priest, a teacher from God . . . healing physician . . . Priest . . . Levite . . . prophet, ruler, governor, king, mediator . . . the voice of God . . . the president . . . a teacher next after God . . . earthly god . . . the mouth of God . . . Moses . . . director . . . the one who exercises God's authority over believers"[39] and "the right hand . . . a mother . . . spiritual parent . . . benefactor . . . ambassador . . . regenerator . . . one who endues with the fullness of the Holy Spirit."[40] The writers thereby commanded the laity to fear the bishop as their king, to honor him as their Lord,[41] and to reverence him "as a god."[42] The bishop should, in their view, be revered with all kinds of honor possible and the

---

33. *Constitutions of the Holy Apostles* 2.15–26.
34. *Constitutions of the Holy Apostles* 2.35.
35. *Constitutions of the Holy Apostles* 2.18, 33.
36. *Constitutions of the Holy Apostles* 2.18.
37. *Constitutions of the Holy Apostles* 2.12–13.
38. *Constitutions of the Holy Apostles* 2.14.
39. *Constitutions of the Holy Apostles* 2.15–26.
40. *Constitutions of the Holy Apostles* 2.33.
41. *Constitutions of the Holy Apostles* 3.34.
42. *Constitutions of the Holy Apostles* 2.20, 30.

utmost marks of respect be paid to every distinct order of the bishop.[43] The writers express their belief that God can be loved and honored only through the love and honor given to the bishop.[44] Hearing and obeying the bishop, according to the writers, was hearing and obeying Christ; likewise, rejecting him is as rejecting Christ.[45] They put a question to the laity asking how they can dare to speak or act against the bishop by whom "the Lord gave his Holy Spirit . . . the Lord sends out his sacred voice . . . God adopts them [believers] for his child."[46] Anyone who opposes the bishop in words or deeds, in their view, directly opposes God.[47] The writers conclude by affirming that the bishop attains superior authority from God over all souls and that his authority is beyond that of kings and rulers who exercise power and authority on bodily issues only. The bishop should, therefore, be honored as the Lord himself and be paid more than his precedents and contemporaries.[48] This indicates that the church of the time constituted the bishop as the divinely appointed authority and non-approachable by laity except through the deacon.[49]

In their assertion of the source of the power and authority of their *Constitutions*, the writers appear to act as if they were the twelve apostles. They claimed that their *Constitutions* were divinely provided, divinely delivered, and derived their origin, power, and authority directly from the divine. In their explanation of what they meant by this the writers claimed, firstly, that in the intervening period between his resurrection and ascension, Jesus lived forty days with the apostles and "completed his whole constitution,"[50] which was handed down to them through the apostolic succession. The writers repeatedly refer to Jesus as the "legislator" of their constitution[51] of "every ecclesiastical life."[52] Second, they present their *Constitutions* as "canonical rules" dedicated only to the bishops and not allowed to be published or disclosed in public because of the

---

43. *Constitutions of the Holy Apostles* 2.28, 33.
44. *Constitutions of the Holy Apostles* 2.28.
45. *Constitutions of the Holy Apostles* 2.20.
46. *Constitutions of the Holy Apostles* 2.32, 33.
47. *Constitutions of the Holy Apostles* 2.31, 32.
48. *Constitutions of the Holy Apostles* 2.34.
49. *Constitutions of the Holy Apostles* 2.28.
50. *Constitutions of the Holy Apostles* 8.1.
51. *Constitutions of the Holy Apostles* 3.9; 6.25.
52. *Constitutions of the Holy Apostles* 8.4.

"mysteries" contained in them.[53] The bishops of the time were reminded that they were meant to perform everything in the church following the rules and regulations provided and delivered to them in the *Constitutions*.[54] The bishops were threatened that, if they did not observe the rules and regulations contained in the *Constitutions*, they would be punished, but if they observed all the rules and regulations contained in the *Constitutions*, they would be saved and would have peace in the church.[55] Hence, it is understandable that whether by accident or design, this tradition has sown the seed of institutional dictatorial authority in the church. This tradition also seems to have paved the way for establishing the pride and arrogance of ordained leadership over the church over successive centuries. If this *Constitution* was truly prepared by the theologians and leaders of the church, then the secret of the church's restriction and ignorance of the charismatic experiences for centuries had its roots in this historical event.

5.4. CONTINUED ATTRIBUTION OF ABSOLUTE AUTHORITY TO AND DEPENDENCE ON THE BISHOP

There is evidence that informs us that the tradition of attributing absolute authority to the bishops continued to shape and dominate the thoughts and practices of the churches of the postapostolic period. The congregations continued to situate their schemes and structures in line with the constitutional traditions and continued to be bound to the instructions contained in the *Constitutions*. The entire life of the church was thus meant to be surrendered to the authority of the ordained leadership. The writings of Ignatius appear to constitute a clear example of this. Ignatius wrote short letters to certain congregations sternly warning them to do nothing without the recognition and permission of the bishop. For instance, in his letter to the *Magnesians*, Ignatius commanded the recipients to respect their bishop and to submit to him. He asserted that submitting to the bishops does not mean simply submitting to the visible human, but to God who is behind the appointment of the bishop. He commanded them to submit to the bishops in the light of God's presence and power in and through the bishop. He warned them that if anyone among them

---

53. *Constitutions of the Holy Apostles* 8.47.85.
54. *Constitutions of the Holy Apostles* 8.3.
55. *Constitutions of the Holy Apostles* 8.47.85.

tried to disobey the bishop, that would be the moral equivalent of trying to deceive God.[56] He alerted them saying, "As . . . the Lord did nothing without the Father . . . so neither do ye anything without the bishop." He adds that since the Lord himself does nothing without the Father, quoting Jesus' words, "I can of mine own self do nothing," so should they, "neither presbyter, nor deacon, nor layman, do anything without the bishop."[57]

In his letter to the *Trallians*, headed "Subject to the bishop," Ignatius wrote, "For since ye are subject to the bishop as to Jesus Christ, ye appear to me to live not after the manner of men, but according to Jesus Christ. . . . It is therefore necessary that, as ye indeed do, so without bishop ye should do nothing. . . . It is, therefore, necessary, whatsoever things ye do . . . do nothing without the bishop." He added, "In like manner, let all reverence the deacons, as an appointment of Jesus Christ, and the bishop as Jesus Christ. . . . Apart from this, there is no church."[58] In his letter to the *Philadelphians*, Ignatius wrote, "For when I was among ye, I cried, 'heed to the bishop, and presbyter, and deacons,' the Spirit proclaimed these words to me: Do nothing without the bishop."[59] Similarly, in his letter to the *Ephesians*, Ignatius reminded his recipients to look upon their bishops in the same way as they look upon the Lord himself.[60] In his letter to the *Smyrnaeans*, Ignatius advised the recipients to follow the bishop's direction in everything they do and warned them that not one of them should do anything without the bishop's direction. He alerted them to regard everything that is done under the direction of the bishop as a valid Eucharist. If anyone was to do anything in the church without the bishop's knowledge, then that, said Ignatius, was serving the devil.[61] Ignatius's messages are clear indicators that bishops were already being regarded as someone appointed in the place of Jesus, and therefore respect due to the bishop was almost corresponding to the respect due to Jesus and God the Father.

Similarly, when the church moves from the first century to the second, we see a church that relies upon and refers to the same traditions as tools to defend against emerging heresies and which depends on the power and authority of bishops. The writings of Irenaeus can constitute

56. Ignatius, *Epistle to the Magnesians* 3.1–2.
57. Ignatius, *Epistle to the Magnesians* 7.1–3.
58. Ignatius, *Epistle to the Trallians* 2–3.
59. Ignatius, *Epistle to the Philadelphians* 7.
60. Ignatius, *Epistle to the Ephesians* 6.
61. Ignatius, *Epistle to the Smyrnaeans* 7–9.

an example of this. In his book *Against Heresies*, Irenaeus emphasized the power and authority of bishops and *Constitutions*. First, he strongly acknowledges the apostolic succession of the bishops. He then reminded his audiences that they should consider bishops as instituted by the apostles and successors of the apostles. Defining what he meant by this, Irenaeus stated that it was the apostles who appointed bishops and that the apostles committed the church into their hands to replace themselves and continue its governance in the way the apostles instructed them. Therefore, in his view, bishops were meant to be respected just as the apostles would have been respected.[62] Second, affirming the authoritative status of the *Constitutions*, Irenaeus wrote, "Tradition from the apostles does thus exist in the church and is permanent among us."[63] True knowledge of faith, for Irenaeus, consists of the "ancient constitution of the church" which was being used "throughout the world . . . according to the succession of the bishops." He gave the *Constitutions* equal regard to Scripture and considered it a "lawful and diligent exposition in harmony with the Scriptures."[64] Ignatius's and Irenaeus's accounts give us a glimpse into how churches of the period continued to overemphasize the status of the ordained leadership. This ensures that by referring to and relying on the constitutional affirmation of their authority, bishops continued to play a role in magnifying only the ordained office and leadership function of the church. As time went by, this perception became a strong tradition and led the church to exclusive concentration on the supremacy of *leadership-administration* and pushed the *Pentecostal-charismatic* life and ministry of the church aside.

Paul Tillich observes that in the second generation of Christianity successors of the apostles became more "rational, moralistic, and legalistic." The apostolic succession, too, became the "succession of organizational principle" wherein the prophetic succession was viewed as an "anti-organizational principle." He adds that the attempt made to integrate both the institutional-organizational and prophetic-charismatic succession was "unsuccessful."[65] Yet Tillich does not provide any example of what kind of attempt was made to integrate the institutional-organizational and prophetic-charismatic successions, nor who made such attempts and when. Eddie L. Hyatt affirms Tillich's observation

62. Irenaeus, *Against Heresies* 3.1–3.
63. Irenaeus, *Against Heresies* 3.3, 5.1
64. Irenaeus, *Against Heresies* 4.32.8.
65. Tillich, *History of Christian Thought*, 41.

when he argues that due to the increasingly growing emphasis on the institutional-organizational structure of the church, the responsibility and function of the bishops "evolved into a separate and distinct office with increasing prestige and power."[66] Commenting on the beginning of the church's constitutional, institutional, and organizational development, Rudolf Bultmann insightfully writes that when such decisive works were prepared, the office of church ministry was regarded as "*constitutive of the church*." Consequently, a "monarchical episcopate" was developed in which ordained officials "superseded the Spirit-endowed." Thus, says Bultmann, the "whole church rests upon the office-bearers, whose office is held to go back in uninterrupted succession to the apostles." The "tradition of the gospel proclamation and succession which guarantees its continuity are no longer left . . . to the sway of the Spirit, but are institutionally safe-guarded." This, Bultmann concludes, causes the Spirit to be "bound to the office and is transmitted by a sacramental act, ordination by the laying on of hands."[67] David Allen strengthens Bultmann's observations by stating that, in the second century, the power of the church's life and ministry became completely concentrated in ordained leadership office, was laid in the hands of the bishops, and the church thereby continued to "de-emphasize" the charismatic gifts and workings of the Holy Spirit. Accordingly, says Allen, emphasis on the Holy Spirit's workings in and through charismatic experiences continued to diminish. Consequently, the emphasis on the church as a visible institutional organization continued to move away from the biblical concept of the church's nature.[68] It is evident that the postapostolic church's rules and regulations contained in the *Constitutions* discussed above provided these scholarly observations with tangible historical grounds. The adopters and maintainers of these *Constitutions* seem to have intentionally drafted this monumental tradition and left the church with a monarchical legacy in which unparalleled power and authority are ascribed to the bishops. This tradition seems to have laid down an explicit foundation for an institutional, organizational, structural, and hierarchical church setting a strong hierarchical power apparatus for the church through what it attributed to the bishops.

---

66. Hyatt, *2000 Years*, 24–25.
67. Bultmann, *Theology of the New Testament*, 2:99, 107, 109.
68. Allen, *Unfailing Stream*, 20.

5.5. SUMMARY

Given the accounts and discussion examined above, three points deserve to be drawn out and underlined for concluding the chapter.

First, as discussed in chapters 2 and 3, the canonized writings of the apostles show that at the center of the manifestation of the Holy Spirit were both objective gifts and Spirit-initiated subjective experiences. However, the apostles did not clearly instruct their successors regarding how believers would experience the reception, baptism, gifts, and workings of the Holy Spirit. Nor did they say anything about whether the Holy Spirit who baptized, gifted, empowered, and guided them from time to time was necessary for the life and ministry of the present and future church. The reasons for their silence on this subject matter might be: (1) They thought that every spiritual experience that had begun in their life and ministry would continue as the routine life and practice of the church as long as the church exists in the world. (2) The concept and practice of reception, gifts, and works of the Holy Spirit were not emphasized as such during their days. (3) Their thoughts were entirely occupied with the subject of the immediate return of Christ and the end of the world. Among these three reasons, the most probable, at least in my assumption, could be that of the apostles' expectation of the imminent return of Christ and the end of the world. Their canonized writings show that the apostles were curiously expecting Christ's immediate return and were urging their congregations to prepare for it.

For example, by referring to Jesus' alerting the apostles of his immediate return, Matthew wrote about the imminence of Jesus' return (Matt 10:23; 16:28) and included Jesus' assertion that the current generation of the time would, indeed, not pass away until his return (Matt 24:34). Similarly, referring to Jesus' sayings, Mark writes that the dates were already cut short in months not in years, and the return of Christ would be in the same generation in which Jesus lived during his ministry on earth (Mark 13:20, 30). By tracing these sayings of Jesus, the apostles alerted their recipients to a life of purity in anticipation of the immediate return of Christ. In anticipation of the immediate return of Christ, the idea of believers' being or becoming holy appears to be a dominant subject of the apostles' teaching. In the process of believers' becoming holy, the Holy Spirit was presented, in the teachings of the apostles, as a permanent divine companion by whose indwelling and empowering believers' life can be kept in purity and holiness. As a reflection of their belief that the Holy Spirit enables believers to live a life controlled by the Holy Spirit, the apostles encouraged their audiences to live in purity and holiness. For instance, John reminded his recipients to be alert, waiting for Jesus' imminent return (1 John 2:18) and encouraged them to remain in the anointing, which is the New Testament's imagery of the Holy Spirit, which they received from the "Holy One" (1 John 2:20, 27). In this way, John presented the Holy Spirit as a companion by whose anointing, teaching, and leading believers' lives could be kept in purity, holiness, and watchfulness for Christ's imminent return. Peter alerted the recipients of his letters to live with a blameless mind in their attitudes, actions, and relationships considering that the end of the world is close at the door (1 Pet 4:7, 17; 2 Pet 3:8–15). James referred to the imminence of Christ's return and associated judgment, warning his audiences not to grumble (Jas 5:7–9).

In scores of his messages, Paul alerted the recipients of his letters of the imminent return of Christ and encouraged them to keep in purity and holiness. For example, he exhorted the Romans to live godly lives in line with the coming of the end of the present age and warned them about living a mixed life of spiritual and worldly (Rom 8:12–14; 13:11–12). He alerted the Corinthians that the time was becoming increasingly short and warned them also about living a mixed life (1 Cor 10:21; 1 Cor 7:29–31). He warns the Galatians of comprising two groups of Christians, spiritual and carnal, and against living a mixed Christian life at the end time (Gal 3:1–5). Alongside these warnings, Paul presents the Holy Spirit as the divine companion, by whose indwelling and power the believers' life can be kept in purity and holiness (Rom 8:5–11; 1 Cor 3:16–17; 6:9–11, 15–20; 2 Cor 6:16). He reminds his recipients that the indwelling of the Holy Spirit must result in new birth and new creation (2 Cor 5:17), and a newness that is identified with the kind of life Jesus attained in the resurrection (Rom 8:11). In this sense, the Holy Spirit-indwelt Christians are meant to exhibit a transformed state of moral and ethical behavior by the power of the Holy Spirit. This moral and ethical purity, according to Paul, was supplemented by the Holy Spirit as he indwelt believers and gave them the power to overcome sinful inclinations (Rom 6:6–13; Gal 5:24). Attaining the qualities of these characteristics was thought of as being "filled with Spirit" (Eph 5:18), bearing the "fruit of the Spirit" (Gal 5:22), and "putting off the old Adamic person and putting the new Christly person on" (Eph 4:17–24).

Paul repeatedly asserted that the Holy Spirit enables Christians to experience the moral character of Christ. To be baptized into Christ and be filled with the Holy Spirit, for Paul, means to be equally holy in moral and ethical behavior. In view of this, he sternly advised his audiences to resolve to "present themselves as a holy and living sacrifice to God" (Rom 12:1–4) and to regard themselves as the holy temple of the Holy Spirit and a holy bride of the holy Lord, Jesus Christ (1 Cor 6:12–20). It was well known that in the Old Testament tradition, the temple was a building set apart from common use for a special and holy purpose. Paul, therefore, uses the imagery of the temple's holiness to illustrate that Holy Spirit-indwelt Christians are set apart for godly life and are holy. This, as perceived by Paul, means acquiring the spiritual qualities essential to the Christian life, in which the Holy Spirit works in them and transforms their lives into Christlikeness (Rom 6:5–11). He expressed this in these terms: "If the root [Jesus] is holy, so are the branches" (Rom 11:16). Accordingly, believers of the time were urged and encouraged to pursue a life of purity as quickly as they could before Christ's return, to be ready so that their body, spirit, and soul are prepared to stand sound and blameless at the coming of Christ (1 Thess 3:11–13; 5:23), and to be fit for the glory they would share in his return (Heb 12:1–9). Thus, the moral and ethical purity of believers, by the indwelling, teaching, anointing, and empowering of the Holy Spirit was viewed, by the apostles, as a primary characteristic of the believers' present life which would reach its climax in the return of Christ and at which time all the benefits of their salvation were to be consummated.

These apostolic teachings seem to draw their roots from Jesus' teachings outlined in Matt 5–7 regarding the new moral and ethical life of godly people. As outlined in these chapters, godly people are meant to live in line with the ethics and character of the new kingdom of God. The teachings of these chapters alert their audiences that the new kingdom of God demands clear moral and ethical purity and that belonging to the kingdom of God and moral purity are like two sides of the same coin—they cannot be separated. Jesus also declared that the new life of the kingdom of God would be initiated by the Holy Spirit (John 3:8). In this regard, it seems that the apostles followed the same line as Jesus. Their messages, as analyzed here, demonstrate the conviction of the apostles that the Holy Spirit does not only bring salvation, charismatic gifts, and empowerment but also enables believers to live the life of salvation reality—a moral and ethical purity. As discussed in chapter 4, this conviction and teaching of the apostles affirms the character formation role of the Holy Spirit in Christian life. Hence, the apostolic call for Christian life purity and holiness comes in reference to the permanent indwelling and continuous power supply of the Holy Spirit. Believers' reception of the Holy Spirit, therefore, was expected to result in and be demonstrated in distinct moral and ethical life, which from the apostles' point of view, can only be attained by the Holy Spirit's indwelling, ongoing renewal, empowering and guiding toward the kind of faith life such that believers' moral-ethical life becomes a reflection of the ethical character of the kingdom of God. Thus, given these apostolic accounts, a couple of points seem to require particular attention.

On the one hand, it appears to be explicit that the thoughts, actions, and teachings of the apostles were preoccupied and dominated by the imminent return of Christ. If Jesus' alerting of the apostles to his immediate return as recorded by Matthew (10:23; 16:28) and Mark (13:20, 30) was based on the existing reality, then the apostles' expectation of his immediate return, alerting their audiences for preparation of it, and being shortsighted toward the fate of history may not be a matter of surprise. The event of the day of Pentecost in particular could be said to provide a clear example of this. According to the Scriptures, it was between his resurrection and ascension that Jesus promised the apostles that they would be baptized with the Holy Spirit and clothed with power in just "a few days" after his departure (Luke 24:49; Acts 1:5–8). The promise was fulfilled within a lapse of ten days after his ascension. When they saw how quickly the promise of their baptism with the Holy Spirit was fulfilled, the apostles might have thought that the promise of his immediate return would also be fulfilled in the same manner, i.e., as quickly as possible. This subject seems to have severely influenced their overall thoughts and actions. This in turn seems to be the reason why their canonized writings appear to be simply focused on the end of the age rather than containing significant predictive teachings for the future of the church. On the other hand, the apostles associated the Holy Spirit only with salvific acts, moral and ethical transformation, purity, and the holiness of believers' lives, but never with ongoing realization and practice of charismatic gifts. This might indicate their ignorance of the concept and practice of charismatic gifts for both the present and future life of the church. If this were not so, given the valuable contributions of the charismatic gifts in their gospel proclamation, it is unlikely that the apostles would intentionally ignore the reception and practice of the charismatic gifts. Whatever the reason may be, the lack of clear instruction in the apostolic canonized writings can be considered as *one of the root causes* of the historical tensions relating to the practice of the Spirit-charismata within the doctrine of the Holy Spirit.

Nevertheless, there is a question that should be asked in this regard: does the lack of apostolic emphasis on the subjective experiential content of the Holy Spirit's manifestation and significance of the charismatic gifts necessarily mean the absence of these features in Christian practice? The answer to this question is no! Not at all! The reason for this negative answer is that the apostles were neither the initiators of the objective gift and subjective experience of the Holy Spirit nor dispensers of the charismatic gifts. Initiating the objective gift of the Holy Spirit and endowing believers with charismatic gifts was, is, and will forever remain the possession and prerogative of God. The apostles were only the receivers and practitioners of these divine possessions like any other believer of their time. Their lack of emphasis on these features, for one or another reason, does not necessarily mean the absence of these features in the Christian experience. As believers' experiences are not the choices, interests, or feelings of the apostles, but the divine reality they experienced in their days, it is up to each believer to either long for, seek, pray for, receive, and realize or ignore these gifts.

Second, as can be seen through the window of the *Apostolic Constitutions*, the postapostolic church laid down an explicit foundation for an institutional, organizational, structural, and hierarchical church and set a strong hierarchical power apparatus for the church through what is attributed to the bishops in it. As discussed in chapter 4, Jesus pledged to equip the apostles with special power and authority so that they may continue his authoritative ministry, on behalf of him and represent him. As he commissioned them to go throughout the world and preach the good news, he pledged to equip them with special power and authority to tend, feed, lead, and protect his flock from wolves and to bind and lose evil realities, powers, actions, thoughts, etc. in authority. He thereby appeared to endow them with an unprecedented and unanticipated pattern of power and authority on earth. Further, he pledged that whoever hears and obeys the words of the apostles hears and obeys him, and whoever rejects their words also rejects him. He assured them that on the day of final judgment, the extent of judgment to be declared upon Sodom and Gomorrah would be easier than that on those who reject the words of his messengers (Matt 10:15). This biblical evidence reminds us that as the apostles were commissioned to go through the world and preach the gospel of Jesus Christ as his successors, they were also girded with unprecedented and unparalleled power and authority. Thus, as we have seen the apostles in turn ordained and authorized the bishops with the same power and authority as their successors.

The writers of the *Constitutions* testify, as discussed above, that the apostles appointed bishops and authorized them as their successors to run their young churches with apostolic authority. They then reminded the bishops to strictly observe the words and rules of the apostles. Tracing this tradition, the church of the postapostolic period adopted and developed a tradition in which it attributed to the bishops a kind of power and authority that paralleled Jesus' power and authority in heaven and on earth. By referring to and relying on the apostolic succession tradition, bishops were viewed and ranked as the highest divinely appointed officials of the church such that no power on earth remains above them. This seems to be where the tradition of the dogmatization of the power and authority of the ordained office of the church drew its roots. The bishops were privileged to exercise unparalleled power and authority over the church. Their power and authority were dogmatized in a way they may not be questioned, resisted, or objected to, but only submitted to. In the meantime, the laity was sternly instructed to regard everything the bishops said or did as part of divine revelation and divine law. It is, therefore, obvious that for this kind of highly privileged leadership, all those who do not submit to it and do not agree with it are always considered to be wrong and thus deserve due measure.

Furthermore, the writers of the *Constitutions* seem to imagine that their *Constitutions* were legislated and completed by Jesus. Such a pretension could persuade the recipients to think that the setting up of rules, regulations, norms, and criteria according to which the church's life and ministry were to be shaped, maintained, regulated, and preserved was completed by Jesus and handed over to the church through the apostles. In turn, such a perception regards the *Constitutions* as part of the primary revelation. In the course of time, this tradition led the ordained office bearers to claim that their authority was derived directly from God through Christ and transmitted through the apostles. It is conceivable that any word said, any deed performed, or any judgment made or a measure taken in the church by such constitutionally instituted and backed authorities could undoubtedly be regarded as divinely approved. In light of this, it would be no surprise if any single rule or regulation contained in the *Constitutions* was considered as a divine heritage to the extent that it became a manipulative, authoritarian instrument for the ordained leadership. Thus, no doubt may remain that successive ordained leaders of the church, well grounded in this tradition, led the church to the extreme institutive, constitutive, authoritative, and regulative organizational direction by making a clear division between the institutional governmental and Pentecostal-charismatic life and functions of the church. The most troubling feature of the scenario is that this hierarchy-centered tradition was adopted at a time when the church had not developed a structure but was thoroughly dependent on the teaching and guidance of the ordained leadership as successors of the apostles. In that context, therefore, the *Constitutions* at stake here must have been highly regarded and enthusiastically observed as the true and essential rule of faith and the life and practice of the church.

Consequently, the church of the centuries intervening between the fourth quarter of the first century and the end of the seventh century must have been guided by these *Constitutions*. Particularly when considering the writings of Irenaeus, as presented above, it can be assumed that the church of the period was protecting itself from emerging heresies by using or referring to these *Constitutions* as the only tools. As presented above, with the development of new rules, regulations, systems, and orders in the church, the power and function of the *Constitutions* have gradually been pushed aside in the Western church. Hence, it is perceivable that the historical institutional organizational form of the church must have drawn its roots from and benefited from this human hierarchy-centered constitutional tradition first established in the primitive church. In the meantime, the tradition of apostolic succession regarding ordained leadership power and authority was given a particular place and role in the church. Yet, as the institutional hierarchical form of Christianity continued, the content of the *Constitutions* never died out and has continued throughout the history of the church and is evident even in present times. It may, therefore, come as no surprise if such overprivileged authority obscured any tendency for the church to depend on the presence, gifts, power, and workings of the Holy Spirit.

Third, the church of the postapostolic period ironically developed the view that charismatic gifts are not necessary for believers. The *Constitutions* contain the belief that when one believes in Jesus in full assurance, then he/she is given the best gift of God: salvation. When this gift of God is sought and attained, there is no need to seek out or demonstrate the charismata of signs, wonders, miracles, healing the sick, raising the dead, casting out demons, etc. It was thereby emphasized that God encounters believers and speaks to them only in and through the bishop. This tradition led the church towards drawing a clear line of demarcation between *leadership-administration* and the *Pentecostal-charismatic* nature and functions of the church. As time went by, this division led believers into *two distinct Christian views* on the doctrine of the Holy Spirit: the institutional organizational view, which emphasizes objective reception and doctrinal belief of the Holy Spirit, and the Pentecostal-charismatic view, which strives to add the subjective experience of the Holy Spirit to the doctrinal belief. The institutional church held the entire power and authority of the church's life and ministry and avoided the *Pentecostal-charismatic* form of spirituality within the life of the church. In the meantime, the place and role of the Holy Spirit in Christian teaching and practice continued to be marginalized. This historical tradition can, therefore, be considered as *one of the root causes* of tensions concerning the Spirit-charismata within the doctrine of the Holy Spirit. Insightfully elaborating on this tradition, Veli-Matti Kärkkäinen argues that tensions between "Spirit/Charisma" and "institution" wherein "charisma versus institution" has been one of the "perennial problems of Christianity."[69] This would indeed appear to be the case. As we shall see in chapter 7, when the *Pentecostal-charismatic* form of worship and spiritual experience became emphasized through the Montanist movement, perennial tension between the two distinct views on the doctrine of the Holy Spirit became embedded and has continued until the present day. In the light of this brief consideration of the place and role of the Holy Spirit in the apostolic transmission and postapostolic church's teaching and practice, we will now turn our examination to the church of the patristic period.

---

69. Kärkkäinen, *Toward a Pneumatological Theology*, 111–12.

CHAPTER 6

The Patristic Period Church's Teaching and Practice

WE HAVE CONSIDERED HOW the apostolic canonized writings did not emphasize the gifts and workings of the Holy Spirit in the life and function of the church. We have also considered how the postapostolic church adopted and developed a clear demarcation between upholding the *leadership-administration* function and rejecting the *Pentecostal-charismatic* life and function of the church. With this in mind, there is a question to be asked here: Was the postapostolic church's emphasis on the *leadership-administration* function the only cause of the church of successive centuries pushing aside its *Pentecostal-charismatic* life and function? Was there anything else that caused question, confusion, or controversy regarding the presence and role of the Holy Spirit in the life and function of the church? This chapter attempts to explore the historical situations of the patristic period's church and develop some reasonable answers to these questions. The exploration considers historical evidence which indicates that other problems began to emerge and challenge the church's doctrine of the Holy Spirit beginning in the early second century. According to this evidence, those problems led the church of the period to further emphasize and depend on the *leadership-administration* function and ordained leadership power and authority and to push the *Pentecostal-charismatic* function further aside. From this evidence, some suggest that various kinds of competing religious movements emerged with varying religious interests and challenged the patristic church's belief, teaching, and practice of the Holy Spirit. Some suggest that the church intentionally continued to emphasize only Christology and to neglect the role of the Holy Spirit in its teaching and spiritual experience. Some suggest that Constantine's conversion to Christianity and his favor towards the church caused an unanticipated lacking of interest in the experience of the presence, gifts, power, and workings of the Holy Spirit. Others also suggest that the question, confusion, and controversy of the doctrine of the Holy Spirit soon shifted from the practice of the gifts and workings of the Holy Spirit to the nature of the Holy Spirit. This chapter will explore each of these perspectives in order to see a glimpse of the nature of the overall doctrine of the Holy Spirit in the belief, teaching, and practice of the patristic period's church.

6.1. EMERGENCE AND INFLUENCE OF THE COMPETING RELIGIOUS MOVEMENTS

Historical accounts indicate that beginning early in the second century, there were different kinds of competing religious movements that challenged the church. Larry Christenson, for example, suggests that the early church was faced with the problem of maintaining order and orthodoxy as a result of the challenges of different competing religious movements. He states that developing and strengthening institutional power and authority was a pressing need of the time in order to deal with the challenges of the impositions of those movements. Accordingly, rigid orders and rules were developed and rigid measures continued to be taken against those movements. Therefore, concludes Christenson, the clergy were given sole and final authority over the church's life, worship, and function.[1] Here the question is: to which religious movements does Christenson refer? Well, he might have referred to many kinds of movements driven by the spirit of the time. For the purpose of this study, however, it suffices to mention only a few closely related to the study subject. Historical accounts indicate that Gnosticism was one of the foremost movements competing with Christianity in the second century.

Irenaeus, for example, in his *Against Heresies*, pointed out that in the early stage of Christianity, the Gnostic movement emerged with different groups spreading various teachings about the Holy Spirit which contradicted Christian beliefs and teachings. He stated that different groups of Gnostics taught different beliefs about the Holy Spirit. One

1. Christenson, *Welcome Holy Spirit*, 296–97.

group declared the Holy Spirit to be sent by a kind of "Archangel, who stands by the side of God." Another group declared the Holy Spirit to be a creature, born at some specific time or "begotten from the Father's and Son's relation." The latter group, in particular, according to Irenaeus, considered the Holy Spirit to be the "first woman" in creation, and the "mother of the living."[2] In accord with Irenaeus, Bultmann points out that the Gnostic movement combined itself with Christianity by adopting some of the thoughts and experiences of Christianity. He states that "because of the far-reaching relatedness" between Christianity and Gnosticism, the Gnostic movement was a "competitor of the most serious and dangerous" sort for Christianity. The movement emphasized knowing of "one's world-foreignness, the heavenly origin of one's life and the way of redemption out of this world—*that is the definite knowledge: the Gnosis*," which gives the movement its designation and identification. This sort of knowledge "gives the Gnostic *his consciousness of superiority to the world.*" Bultmann continues by stating that Gnostics believed that once such knowledge is attained, an individual is on the road to becoming a Gnostic in whom the "spark of heavenly light is alive." That Gnostic was believed to then be the "spiritual man," the "pneumatic" in whom the Spirit dwelt and can demonstrate that knowledge "either by asceticism" or by a "meditative contemplation which culminates in ecstasy." Such a Gnostic was believed even to demonstrate the "power of the Spirit . . . by miraculous deeds." In such and similar ways Gnostics adopted and mixed up Christian pneumatic elements with Gnostic "heavenly light elements." With this conviction, teaching, and experience, concludes Bultmann, the Gnostic movement "crept into Christian congregations" and penetrated them through the Gnostic "Spirit-enthusiasts."[3]

The same sort of observation is offered by S. M. Horton. He observes that in the early stage of the second century a Christian Gnostic movement began to teach that salvation was not through the work of and faith in Christ but through "higher knowledge attained through the gifts of the Holy Spirit" in which the Holy Spirit works only on the "moral nature of human." He states Gnostics believed that individuals who attained such special knowledge were then given the gifts of the Holy Spirit. Such people were recognized, by Gnostics, as the people of the Spirit and his gifts. Horton states that the church's resistance to the Gnostic Christians'

---

2. Irenaeus, *Against Heresies* 1.29.4; 30.1–2.
3. Bultmann, *Theology of the New Testament*, 1:164–67.

pneumatic conviction, teaching, and experience led it into a deeper "fear and suspicion of anyone who claimed special knowledge or new revelation." Thus, as a measure of the church's resistance to this movement, the place and roles of ordained office and prophetic ministry were formally separated. Horton asserts that this case, more than anything else, influenced the second-century church to intentionally diminish the place and role of prophets in the church and to place more power and authority on bishops. Consequently, they conclude, the "institutional church allowed the charismata to die." As a result of this, the prophetic ministry came to "centre in sectarian movements."[4]

Affirming these observations, Berkhof suggests that some enthusiastic movements such as Montanism emphasized the presence and workings of the Holy Spirit through the *Pentecostal-charismatic* form of worship and spiritual experience. Such movements seemed to the institutional church to loosen the ties between the Holy Spirit and Christ, between Scripture and the Holy Spirit as well as the ties between the institutional life of the church and the Holy Spirit. The institutional church, therefore, resisted, restricted, and even rejected the tendencies of such competing movements.[5] In its battle against the challenges of such movements, says Christenson, the early church continued to become increasingly suspicious of the concept and practice of the gifts and workings of the Holy Spirit. Hence, the institutional structure continued to be perceived as a defender and provider of sustainability and permanence, while awakening religious movements were viewed in negative and hostile terms as illegitimate and competitive to the institution, and eventually destructive.[6] Earle E. Cairns affirms this observation by suggesting that the need for maintaining the peace and health of the church led the early church to the "centralization of power." Accordingly, the bishops continued to be regarded as the "guarantors of the orthodox doctrine of the church" and in the course of time this provided the bishops with the opportunity to build their power and authority.[7] Hence, beginning from the late second century, the most prominent charismatic experience was in the circle of fringe groups such as Christian Gnostics and the Montanists.[8]

4. S. M. Horton, "The Holy Spirit, Doctrine . . . " in Dictionary of Pentecostal and Charismatic Movements, ed. by. Burgess and McGee *Dictionary*, 411, 418–20.

5. Berkhof, *Doctrine of the Holy Spirit*, 11.

6. Christenson, *Welcome Holy Spirit*, 299.

7. Cairns, *Christianity Through the Centuries*, 150.

8. Burgess, "The Holy Spirit, Doctrine of the Ancient Fathers" in Dictionary of

In light of these accounts, two points appear worthy of attention. First, in the early patristic church, different religious movements were practicing charismatic spirituality in one form or another. The defense against those movements led the church toward diminishing the tendency of the claim and practice of the presence, gifts, power, and workings of the Holy Spirit. Added to the existing tradition of the church, which overemphasized the power and authority of the ordained leadership and restricted the *Pentecostal-charismatic* life and function of the church, defending newly emerging competitive movements could be said to send the situation out of the frying pan and into the fire. Any kind of measure or mechanism to defend against those movements could have the potential to act as a mask to internally suppress any charismatic tendency. Second, these historical events indicate that tensions arising concerning the concept and practice of the gifts and workings of the Holy Spirit explicitly began with the influence of those movements and the church's response to them. Thus, this historical situation can be considered as *one of the root causes* of the church's historical negligence of the place and role of the Holy Spirit through *Pentecostal-charismatic* form of worship and spiritual experience.

6.2. EMPHASIS ON CHRISTOLOGY AT THE EXPENSE OF PNEUMATOLOGY

Scholarly observations indicate that there were other kinds of religious views and experiences that had considerable influence on the early church's belief, teaching, and practice of the Holy Spirit. Burgess, for example, observe that in their struggle to defend the church from Roman pagan attacks the church fathers, especially those regarded as apologists, gave priority, both in their teaching and writings, to "conceptualize and interpret Christian theology with the tools of classical philosophy." Accordingly, the church fathers were concerned with "Christology—especially Logos theology" and continued to emphasize Christology, giving little attention to the theology of the Holy Spirit.[9] Berkhof adds to this by suggesting that in the early theology of the church, Christology was itself recognized as thoroughly pneumatic. In addition, the concept of "Logos-Christology" emerged, which was a popular philosophical concept of the

---

Pentecostal and Charismatic Movements, *Dictionary*, 417.

9. Burgess, "The Holy Spirit, Doctrine of the Ancient Fathers" in *Dictionary*, 418.

time, beginning in the middle of the second century. Christian apologetics of the time, therefore, as Berkhof notes, used this popular philosophical concept as a tool for two purposes: firstly, to defend their Christological doctrine from heresies and, secondly, to win the attention of intellectual contemporaries to Christ. As a result, concludes Berkhof, the concept of a "pneumatological approach to Christology died away" and was replaced by "Logos-Christology."[10] Similarly, Moltmann suggests that for the institutional church, the history of "Christ is thoroughly pneumatological" and that the Holy Spirit is the "divine subject of the history of Jesus." For that reason, the institutional church believed that "Jesus is present in the church through the Holy Spirit," and that this "pneumatological Christology" was thought to lead the church into "Charismatic ecclesiology." In this sense, says Moltmann, Christian faith experience of the history of Christ is understood to be the presence and work of the Holy Spirit, and the church is understood to be the "object of faith in Christ" alone. Thus, the church continued to stress that pneumatic Christology is realistic only when it is developed into the Trinitarian theology of the cross.[11]

Further strengthening on these evaluations Moule suggests that the patristic church's formulation of the Christian understanding of the Holy Spirit was largely derived from and dependent on the formulation of the church's understanding of Christology.[12] Ray S. Anderson affirms these observations by stating that the church took up incarnation and redemptive theology by putting more emphasis on Christology and Christ-centered theology, while the *Pentecostal-charismatic* aspect, as praxis of the Holy Spirit, lost its place in the life of the church. The interaction of the objective revealed truth and subjective spiritual praxis of the Holy Spirit was thereby cast aside. Anderson considers this to be an "institutional embodiment" of Christ in contrast to the *Pentecostal-charismatic* presence through the praxis of the Holy Spirit.[13] These scholarly observations indicate that most of the interest and attention of the institutional church focused on the importance of Christology at the expense of pneumatology. This may also indicate that as the church attempted to address the significance of salvation theology through Christology, the understanding, interpretation, and application of the presence, gifts, and workings

---

10. Berkhof, *Doctrine of the Holy Spirit*, 20.
11. Moltmann, *Church in the Power of the Spirit*, 36–37.
12. Moule, *Holy Spirit*, 43.
13. Anderson, *Shape of Practical Theology*, 319–21.

of the Holy Spirit continued to be neglected in the church's teaching, and practice.

6.3. EFFECTS OF EMPEROR CONSTANTINE'S FAVOR TOWARDS CHRISTIANITY

Some scholarly evaluations suggest that Constantine's conversion to and favor towards Christianity in the early fourth century played a significant role in the church's negligence in forming a dependency on the gifts, power, and workings of the Holy Spirit. Paul E. Pierson, for example, suggests that there has been a saying in the history of the church: "The Holy Spirit died early in the fourth century when Constantine became a Christian, and only rose from the dead in the sixteenth."[14] Hyatt affirms this when he suggests that the "final blow to the charismatic character of the church would come with the conversion of Constantine and the church's acquisition of earthly affluence and power."[15] David Allen strengthens this argument by stating that when Constantine came to power, he favored Christianity unreservedly such that his favor towards Christianity included the giving of one of the imperial palaces to the pope, as well as extensive lands in central Italy. The notion of establishing papacy in authority as the apostle Peter's successor began in Constantine's time and within his unreserved and undeserved favor to the church. From then on the pope was regarded as the head of the church on earth. All these practices, as Allen observes, were additional forces for the church's ongoing upholding of the power and authority of the office of ordained leadership and ongoing lack of interest in the Holy Spirit's gifts, power, and workings in the church's life and ministry.[16] The questions that might then be asked in this regard are: What effect did Constantine's conversion and favors towards Christianity have on the church's doctrine of the Holy Spirit? How did his conversion and favor towards the church contribute to the church's negligence of the experience of the presence, gifts, and workings of the Holy Spirit? It is important to explore these questions and find some possible answers by consulting some of the patristic period's accounts. Hence, Eusebius (ca. 260–339), who was regarded as a respected historian of the patristic period for his church history accounts, seems

---

14. Pierson, *Dynamics of Christian Mission*, 129.
15. Hyatt, *2000 Years*, 30.
16. Allen, *Unfailing Stream*, 33–34.

to be the best reliable source of detailed accounts of Constantine's life, conversion to and favor towards Christianity.

In his account of the *Life of Constantine*, Eusebius describes the death of Emperor Constantius and the declaration of his son Constantine as the emperor by the military forces. After his ascent to power Constantine intended to engage in war with Maxentius and to free the Romans from his "tyrannous oppression."[17] In his curiosity about winning the war, Constantine "needed some more powerful aid than his military forces could afford him." Accordingly, he "sought Divine assistance" and engaged in the enquiry concerning "on what God he might rely for protection and assistance."[18] He then engaged in "earnest prayer and supplication" that the Supreme God might reveal himself, talk to him, and support him in the difficulties at hand. While he was "praying with fervent entreaty," says Eusebius, "a most miraculous sign appeared to him from heaven." Referring to Constantine's own witness Eusebius records how God showed him a "Vision of a Cross of Light in the Heavens at Mid-day" above the sun and an inscription "Conquer By This"[19] While he was pondering how to interpret and appropriate the message of the vision, Eusebius notes, later that night God showed him another further assuring vision whereby Christ appeared to him in a night vision with the same sign and "commanded him to make a likeness of that sign . . . and to use it as a safeguard in all engagements with his enemies."[20] Struck with amazement at the message, Constantine made a symbol of the cross, which included the first two letters of Christ's name, X and P in Greek, where the letter P is intersected by the letter X in its center. Eusebius states that Constantine "constantly made use of this sign of salvation as a safeguard against every adverse and hostile power, and commanded that others similar to it should be carried at the head of all his armies."[21]

Eusebius continues to describe how Constantine continued to ponder and enquire about what was "intended by the sign of the vision he had seen" and who the person was appeared in the vision telling him to make a likeness of the symbol he had seen in the vision. He then looked for help from those whom he thought were well "acquainted with the mysteries" of such things—perhaps Christians. The people whom he contacted and

17. Eusebius, *Life of Constantine* 1.26.
18. Eusebius, *Life of Constantine* 1.27.
19. Eusebius, *Life of Constantine* 1.28.
20. Eusebius, *Life of Constantine* 1.29.
21. Eusebius, *Life of Constantine* 1.31.

consulted about the case, as Eusebius notes, explained to him that the person he had seen in his vision was "the only begotten Son of the one and only God" and all the "accounts of his incarnation" and that the sign he had seen was the symbol of the cross of Christ—"the symbol of immortality and the trophy of that victory over death." The people advised him to read the Scriptures and find out more about the reality of the redemptive works and saving power of the cross of Christ. Comparing the nature of the symbol he had seen in the vision with the explanation given about the cross, Constantine assured himself that it was indeed God who had "imparted to him" those divine mysteries. Thereupon he determined to read the Scriptures, worship God with all devotion, and unreservedly favor Christianity. Subsequently, he made some of the ordained officers of the church, perhaps those who interpreted his vision, his friends and counselors. Well convinced and assured of the divine offer of assisting him, Constantine hastened to encounter his rival, Maxentius, and to quench his threat to the Romans once and for all.[22] Therefore, states Eusebius, assuming the "Supreme God as his patron," Christ as his "preserver and aid" and setting the symbol of the Cross "in front of his soldiers and bodyguard," Constantine marched into battle against his rival. As told to him through the sign and the inscription "Conquer By This," the battle was easily advanced and he defeated his rival with "ease at the first assault."[23] Eusebius acknowledges that particular war to be a war "under divine direction," divine aid, and divine protection.[24] Constantine, for his part, acknowledged God as the "Author of his victory"[25] and continued to declare the name of God as "the Supreme Saviour."[26] On account of his devotion to worshiping God and his commitment to supporting Christianity, he was viewed as "the friend of God."[27]

Having succeeded in winning the marvelous victory over his rival, says Eusebius, Constantine headed for Rome to celebrate his trophy. He entered the city in "triumph" and was received by "countless multitudes" with "acclamations and abounding joy . . . as deliverer, preserver, and benefactor."[28] He explained to the public that the mystery of his victory

22. Eusebius, *Life of Constantine* 1.32.
23. Eusebius, *Life of Constantine* 1.37.
24. Eusebius, *Life of Constantine* 1.38.
25. Eusebius, *Life of Constantine* 1.39.
26. Eusebius, *Life of Constantine* 2.6.
27. Eusebius, *Life of Constantine* 1.52.
28. Eusebius, *Life of Constantine* 1.39.

lay within the power of the cross of Christ and ordered the symbol of the cross to be "engraved in indelible characters" and set at the center of the city as the symbol of the "safeguard of the Roman government and of the entire empire." He ordered that the following inscription be engraved at the bottom of the set symbol of the cross: "By virtue of this salutary sign . . . I have preserved and liberated your city from the yoke of tyranny. I have also set at liberty the Roman senate and people, and restored them to their ancient distinction and splendor."[29] He assured the Romans that his victory was the victory of the cross of Christ and boldly proclaimed the saving power and act of the cross to the Romans. When celebrating their freedom from the "pressure of a bitter and tyrannical domination," of Maxentius, the Romans seemed, according to Eusebius, to "enjoy purer rays of light and to be born again into a fresh and new life." Not only the Romans, says Eusebius, but also "all the nations," particularly those which had been set free from the impositions of Maxentius's domination, praised Constantine as victorious and declared that he had "appeared by the grace of God as a general blessing to humankind."[30] Eusebius expresses his feelings by saying that he couldn't express in words all the "indescribable wonders" God had done for and through Constantine.[31]

Constantine's commitment to and favor towards Christianity, according to Eusebius, began with two major actions. First, he made ordained officers of the church, bishops, his "friends" and "counselors."[32] He regarded them as those "consecrated to the service of God," "distinguished them with the highest possible respect and honour," and showed them all possible favor in "deed and word," and thus made them his "companions in travel, believing that he whose servants they were would thus help him."[33] He honored them as those consecrated servants of God, the most trustful guardians of the soul, and thus made them his constant companions. They were "constantly with him and about his person," standing at his side and supporting him with constant prayers. Eusebius asserts that earnest supplications to God and reliance on God, as well as the symbol of the cross, the salutary sign, and bishops' companionship never departed Constantine throughout the intervening years between his conversion

---

29. Eusebius, *Life of Constantine* 1.40.
30. Eusebius, *Life of Constantine* 1.41.
31. Eusebius, *Life of Constantine* 1.47.
32. Eusebius, *Life of Constantine* 1.32.
33. Eusebius, *Life of Constantine* 1.42.

and the last moment of his rule.³⁴ Second, Constantine declared unreserved freedom for Christians, which included "freedom of access to the imperial palaces."³⁵ He also gave some of his "private resources costly benefactions to the churches... both enlarging and heightening the sacred edifices and embellishing the august sanctuaries of the church with abundant offerings."³⁶ As a demonstration of his "peculiar care over the church," Constantine at times became involved in convening synods of the bishops and shared in their deliberations.³⁷ These accounts inform us that Constantine wholeheartedly committed to worshiping God and unreservedly favor the church.

Some contemporary scholarships, however, argue that Constantine's favor for both the church and bishops resulted in the unbridled growth of formalism which continued to quench the tendency of depending on the gifts, power, and workings of the Holy Spirit. For instance, Cairns suggests that with Constantine's unreserved favor towards the church, the bishop of Rome came to be regarded as the first among many equal bishops of the time and began to "exercise authority both in religious and political affairs." Added to the already existing tradition of Petrine power and authority theory in Rome, Constantine's favor toward both the bishops and the church further enforced the church's dependence on the ordained leadership. This idea was developed into the tradition that Peter's key, which symbolizes divinely sanctioned authority, was handed over to his successor, the bishop of Rome, whereupon the bishops of Rome declared the "See of Rome" as the "Apostolic See" and thus claimed "universal supremacy over all other leading clerics" of the church.³⁸ Charles E. Hummel strengthens Cairns's observation by suggesting that all the Christian ministry charismata were understood to have been held by the clergy. All kinds of church ministry, which originally were to be performed by all members of the body, were put under the control of the ordained officers of the church. This situation, as Hummel notes, had been reenforced further by the time of Constantine, under whom the church was "highly organized; socially and politically empowered; and whose prestige gave the church ecclesiastical, social and political success." Thereupon, says Hummel, the church became a "bastion of the political

---

34. Eusebius, *Life of Constantine* 2.4, 12.
35. Eusebius, *Life of Constantine* 1.52.
36. Eusebius, *Life of Constantine* 1.42.
37. Eusebius, *Life of Constantine* 1.44.
38. Cairns, *Christianity Through the Centuries*, 151.

status quo." Thus, he concludes, the early church model of *Pentecostal-charismatic* Christianity was not compatible with such a highly privileged institutional, organizational, political, structural, and hierarchical church.[39] Consequently, ecclesiastical attention to the gifts and workings of the Holy Spirit, as Burgess as Burgess notes, continued to diminish along with the prophetic aspect of the church's life and ministry such that the church's awareness of the place and role of the Holy Spirit was almost lost in the church. Burgess adds that this resulted from the "institutionalization process in which Spirit *charismata* came to be localized in the office of the bishop" and were "reserved for exceptional Christians, such as those who were to be martyred, those who became confessors, and ascetics."[40] In general, Constantine's favor toward the church was understood to have brought "relaxation" in the church whereupon it continued to be "powerful, carnal, and worldly."[41]

If these scholarly observations are based on the existing reality, then two points may be drawn. On the one hand, in the light of Eusebius's witness regarding the life of Constantine, it might be unfair to argue that Constantine's favor to the church as a whole and to the individual bishops contributed to the church's negligence of the place and role of the Holy Spirit. Nevertheless, it may not be denied that by depending on his unreserved favor ordained officers of the church could lead the church to relax through ill motives. This relaxation may have enabled the church to further empower its human hierarchy and further expose itself to carnality. The whole scenario could suggest that such continued emphasis on human hierarchies was an additional force for the church's extreme dependence on human authority, which resulted in an extreme ongoing lack of interest in the claim of the Spirit-gifted, Spirit-empowered, Spirit-awakened, and Spirit-initiated pattern of the church's life, experience, and function. On the other hand, Rome's claim of Peter's key had already been well recognized and an accepted tradition of the church since apostolic times. Evidence indicates that Rome owed its exceptional historic position in the church to the actions of the first-century emperors' "sack of Jerusalem and two executions of key early Christian figures, the Apostles Peter and Paul, in Rome."[42]

---

39. Hummel, *Fire in the Fireplace*, 79–80.
40. Burgess, "The Holy Spirit, Doctrine of the Ancient Fathers" in *Dictionary*, 417.
41. Congar, *I Believe*, 1:69.
42. MacCulloch, *History of Christianity*, 110.

Early church documentation shows that there was a belief among the early Christians in Rome that acknowledges Peter and Paul to be "the two great lights," which God made for the church of Rome in particular and the universal church as a whole. It was believed that God united those "two great lights" in a way no power on earth could separate—from each other and from believers in Rome. This documented tradition holds that these apostles were sentenced to death and killed by the Roman Empire on the same day. While they were being taken to the execution point, according to the documentation, Paul was beheaded on the road, and a little while later Peter was "hanged head downwards."[43] By affirming this tradition, Irenaeus wrote that a very great and universally recognized church was founded in Rome by the "two most glorious apostles, Peter and Paul." He asserted that it was a matter of necessity that every church founded in the world at that time must agree with the church in Rome because of its "pre-eminent authority." He declared that the particular authority of the church in Rome came from Peter and Paul through Clement, the second bishop of Rome next to Linus, who had direct personal contact with Peter and Paul. In the time of Irenaeus, that special authority was strongly claimed by the church of Rome.[44] Eusebius, too, affirms this tradition, by citing from many of the earliest primary sources, that the story of the murder of Peter and Paul was by the same sentence, on the same day, and at the same place in Rome.[45] He states that Peter, in particular, was viewed by the early believers in Rome as the "strongest and greatest of the apostles," a "noble commander of God," and was regarded even as a "god." Accordingly, his "statue" was "erected" during the early years of Christianity in Rome.[46] Consequently, it was believed that their blood, their key, and their divinely endowed authority remained in Rome. Thus, these accounts point out that Rome's claim of the handing over of Peter's key and his divinely sanctioned authority to the successive bishop(s) was already a well-recognized and accepted tradition of the church at the time. This case, therefore, seems by no means to be associated with Constantine's favor towards the church or individual bishops. Constantine's favor towards the church or individual bishops might nevertheless be assumed as an additional force to the ongoing extreme dependence on bishops, which may have led to the ongoing lack of interest in dependence on

---

43. *Acts of the Holy Apostles Peter and Paul*, 477, 484–85.
44. Irenaeus, *Against Heresies* 3.3.
45. Eusebius, *Church History* 2.25.
46. Eusebius, *Church History* 2.14.

the presence, gifts, and workings of the Holy Spirit in the church. Added to these cases was the growing controversy over the nature of the Holy Spirit that emerged in the fourth century and forced the church to hold the second council in 381.

6.4. QUESTIONS, CONTROVERSIES, AND DISPUTES OVER THE NATURE OF THE HOLY SPIRIT

Historical evidence indicates that in addition to the existing ambiguities and tensions regarding the place and role of the Holy Spirit in the life and function of the church, questions and controversy related to the nature of the Holy Spirit emerged as a crucial challenge to the patristic church and its theology. Scholars examined the features that incited doubts, question, and controversy on the nature of the Holy Spirit that suggested that the church before the fourth century never dared to proclaim the Holy Spirit God on a *homoousios* level.[47] They suggest that such reservation was due to a lack of clear and strong sanction of the status of the Holy Spirit in Scripture. The early church, therefore, was confused and unable to develop a settled doctrine of the Holy Spirit. Accordingly, even some of the prominent writers of the period were hesitant to speak openly about the Holy Spirit as God.[48] For example, Burgess suggests that Justin Martyr's definition of the nature of Godhead has been argued to be "indeterminate and tended to introduce subordinationism" by placing the Son below the Father and the Holy Spirit below the Father and the Son. He adds that this subordinationist tendency was repeated in Origen's writing, which was denounced by the church in both the Nicene and Constantinople councils.[49] In accord with this, Kärkkäinen suggests that the early church had a "grave difficulties" in trying to figure out what exactly the nature and role of the Holy Spirit look like. Discussing the early church's "continued confusion and struggle" towards establishing the full deity of the Holy Spirit, Kärkkäinen states that even Origen, one of the ablest church fathers of time, "continued to encounter tremendous difficulties." He provides an example for this by referring to Origen's confusion on the idea of

---

47. Badcock, *Light of Truth*, 55.
48. McGrath, *Christian Theology*, 243.
49. Burgess, "The Holy Spirit, Doctrine of the Ancient Fathers" in *Dictionary*, 418–20.

the procession of the Holy Spirit from the Logos and his explanation of the idea of the "created nature of the Holy Spirit."[50]

Strengthening these observations, Louis Berkhof suggests that although many contradicting opinions about the deity of the Holy Spirit were being expressed and heard in different parts of the church, it was not a great issue of controversy for the church until some time after the Nicene Council. He states that as the Nicene Creed contains only the indefinite statement "And we believe in the Holy Spirit," some educated members of the church continued to investigate the teaching of the Bible on the issue and continued to express their questions, doubts, and confusions regarding the nature of the Holy Spirit.[51] Such educated members' questions, doubts, and confusions, says Alister E. McGrath, were brought to light in the final statement of the doctrine of the Holy Spirit formulated at Constantinople in 381, which defines the Holy Spirit as "the Lord and giver of life, who proceeds from the Father, and is worshiped and glorified with the Father and the Son." This statement, according to McGrath, does not clearly identify the Holy Spirit as God, but it simply declares him as the "Lord and life-giver, proceeding from the Father, object of the same worship and the same glory with the Father and the Son."[52] Such lack of clear identification of the deity of the Holy Spirit aroused suspicions, questions and confusions, in many parts of the church, and resulting controversy continued until it was settled at Constantinople in 381.[53]

According to the evidence, controversy over the nature of the Holy Spirit emerged openly from the Arian influence. The major point of the controversy was the suggestion that Scripture clearly indicates the inferiority of the Holy Spirit to the Father and Son.[54] When Arianism was denounced at Nicaea in 325, Arians were expelled from the Roman Empire. Some of them reorganized themselves into a different phase of Arianism under the leadership of Macedonius, after whom the movement was later named. They rejected the deity of the Holy Spirit and taught that he is the greatest of creatures and a "mere personal power or influence."[55] Neither the person nor the work of the Holy Spirit, in Macedonians' view, was

---

50. Kärkkäinen, *Christian Understandings of the Trinity*, 95 and 109 in particular, and 95–113 in general.

    51. Berkof, *History of Christian Doctrines*, 90.

    52. McGrath, *Christian Theology*, 243.

    53. Thomas, *Holy Spirit*, 85–86.

    54. Berkof, *History of Christian Doctrines*, 90–91.

    55. Horton, "The Holy Spirit, Doctrine . . ." in *Dictionary*, 411.

to be regarded as having the status of divine nature.[56] They spread their views, notes Tixeront, into different parts of the church and produced adherents of their beliefs in the years 360 to 380. During this period, according to Tixeront, about four consecutive councils were held in Rome, in the years 369, 376, 377, and 380, in order to respond to the teaching of the Macedonians. Those councils reviewed the Nicene Council's resolutions, strengthened the church's position on the divinity of the Holy Spirit, and denounced the Macedonians. Tixeront adds that two similar councils held in Alexandria in the years 362 and 373 also subscribed to the resolutions of the councils in Rome and denounced the Macedonians. A similar council was held in Antioch in 379. Nevertheless, concludes Tixeront, Macedonians continued to spread their views and influence the church.[57] In order to prove whether these contemporary scholarly observations and suggestions are based on the existing reality, we need to examine some of the reliable accounts from the patristic period.

Athanasius, bishop of Alexandria (ca. 296–373), was one of the first reliable church fathers to confront issues of the controversy over the nature of the Holy Spirit. In his letters to Serapion *On the Holy Spirit* he documented the nature of the controversy and the questions raised by Macedonians. In these letters, Athanasius responds to the teaching of the Macedonians who fought against the Holy Spirit and whom he calls *Tropikoi*. He states that these heretics emerged from among the former adherents of Arianism who later withdrew from this belief and accepted the church's position. Sadly, says Athanasius, they later "set their mind against the Holy Spirit" and declared him to be a "creature," "one of the ministering spirits," and "different from the angels only in degree."[58] He considers them to be instruments through whom the devil played the role of his "madness" to "disparage the Holy Spirit" and to exhibit "blasphemy against the Holy Trinity" through their "heterodoxy and diabolical presupposition."[59] He considers them to have been "deceived" through a "certain mode of exegesis"[60] and criticizes them for rupturing the Trinity by "reducing him down" to the level of the creature and "mixing him up" with the creaturely world, which is "different in kind and foreign" to the

---

56. McGrath, *Christian Theology*, 243. See also *Seven Ecumenical Councils*, 172–73.
57. Tixeront, *History of Dogmas*, 2:59–62. See also *Seven Ecumenical Councils*, 172–73.
58. Athanasius, *On the Holy Spirit* 1.1.2.
59. Athanasius, *On the Holy Spirit* 1.1.3–4.
60. Athanasius, *On the Holy Spirit* 1.2.2.

nature of the Holy Trinity.⁶¹ Their thoughts against the Holy Spirit, in the view of Athanasius, amount to "dividing and dissolving the Trinity."⁶²

Referring to Jesus' saying, "whoever blasphemes against the Holy Spirit has no forgiveness either in this age or in the age to come," Athanasius asks the opponents, "Where did you find a pretext" from Scripture for "your audacious thought" against the Holy Spirit that does not consider this biblical sanction? Even when teaching against the Son, the Arians "found a pretext for their own heresy in what he said." He then asks Macedonians, "What teaching of the Arians have you countenanced?" and, "What mode of exegesis is responsible for this great error of yours?"⁶³ "Tell me," says Athanasius, "have you found any passage in the Divine Scriptures where the Holy Spirit is called 'spirit' without qualification, without being modified with either 'of God' or 'of the Father' or 'of Christ' or 'of the Son' . . . or 'the Spirit' . . . or without the very term 'the Holy Spirit' or 'Paraclete' or 'of Truth'?"⁶⁴ He goes on to cite biblical texts from which the Macedonians drew their teaching against the equal ranking of the Holy Spirit with the Father and Son and argues that their heresy was based on their particular "mode of exegesis" and "misinterpretation" of the texts. He criticizes the mode of their exegesis as a fallacious equivalent of the former Valentinian heresy,⁶⁵ and their bringing the Holy Spirit "down to the level of angels," and "ranking the angels with the Trinity" as an "irrational audacity."⁶⁶

Athanasius then goes on to declare that wherever the Holy Spirit is mentioned in Scripture, there is no ambiguity about his divinity. To prove this, he conducts an intensive exploration of Scripture from Genesis to Revelation and provides evidence that Scripture consistently shows that the Holy Spirit is not the creature but the divinity of Godhead. He draws his conclusion from Matt 28:19–20 and asserts that the Trinity is "holy and perfect, confessed in Father, and Son, and Holy Spirit," and that this confession is the foundation of the "Catholic Church's faith" and "proclamation under heaven."⁶⁷ The Holy Spirit, therefore, is "glorified together

---

61. Athanasius, *On the Holy Spirit* 1.2.3.
62. Athanasius, *On the Holy Spirit* 1.2.5.
63. Athanasius, *On the Holy Spirit* 1.3.1–2.
64. Athanasius, *On the Holy Spirit* 1.4.1.
65. Athanasius, *On the Holy Spirit* 1.10.4–5.
66. Athanasius, *On the Holy Spirit* 1.10.6—11.1.
67. Athanasius, *On the Holy Spirit* 1.28.2–4.

with the Father and Son" and "acknowledged as God."[68] He asserts that true worshipers worship the Father, Son, and Holy Spirit because the Holy Spirit is inseparable from the Son, as the Son is inseparable from the Father, thus the "perfection of the Holy Trinity, which is one indivisible Trinity."[69] In light of this biblical reality, concludes Athanasius, those who classify the three persons of the Holy Trinity in different ranks are repeating the evil thoughts of the Pharisees who ascribed the work of the Holy Spirit to Beelzebul which incurs the punishment that has no forgiveness either in this age or in the age to come.[70]

Gregory of Nazianzus (ca. 325–390) in his *Fifth Theological Oration: On the Holy Spirit* reports that the understanding of the believers of his day varied regarding the nature of the Holy Spirit. He describes that some conceived the Holy Spirit as an "Activity," some as a "Creature," some as "God," and some were even "uncertain what to call him." From those who were "uncertain what to call him," some expressed their feeling that "Scripture . . . did not make the matter clear either way." Accordingly, they "neither worship him nor treat him with dishonour, but take up a neutral position, or rather a very miserable one." Even from those who conceived the Holy Spirit to be God, some were "orthodox in mind only, while others venture to be so with the lips only." Still others ventured to "measure Deity" by separating the three persons of the Trinity. Such doubtful people, says Gregory, made one of the persons "infinite both in essence and power," the second in "power but not in essence" and the third "circumscribed in both."[71] He states that some of those opposed to the church's doctrine of the Holy Spirit would confront him and his groups asking, "What have you to say about the Holy Ghost? From whence are you bringing in upon us this strange God, of Whom Scripture is silent?" He states that even those who agreed with the church regarding the doctrine of the Son were involved in the disputation of the nature of the Holy Spirit.[72]

Gregory reports further that the disputers raised other questions such as, "Who in ancient or modern times ever worshipped the Spirit? Whoever prayed to him? Where is it written that we ought to worship him, or to pray to him, and whence have you derived this tenet of

68. Athanasius, *On the Holy Spirit* 1.31.2.
69. Athanasius, *On the Holy Spirit* 1.33.3–4.
70. Athanasius, *On the Holy Spirit* 1.33.6.
71. Gregory of Nazianzus, *On the Holy Spirit* 5.5.
72. Gregory of Nazianzus, *On the Holy Spirit* 5.1.

yours?"⁷³ Explaining the multitude of questions raised and how bitter the disputations against the Holy Spirit were, and how this was imposing on him and his allies, Gregory states that the case was tedious to discuss and resolve. He then says this: "We ourselves being worn out by the multitude of their questions are something of the same condition with men who have lost their appetite" by taking more of a "particular kind of food" and then "shrink from all food." In the same manner, "we . . . have an aversion from all discussions."⁷⁴ The "subject of the Holy Spirit," for Gregory, presented itself as a "special difficulty." Despite this tedious condition, declares Gregory, "we refute their objections to the utmost of our power" because "we have so much confidence in the Deity of the Spirit Whom we adore."⁷⁵

Gregory proceeds to respond to the disputers by saying that since the Holy Spirit "proceeds from the Father," he is not a "Creature" and since he is not "Begotten" he is not "Son." Since he is between the "Unbegotten and the Begotten" God, he is thoroughly "God." What differentiates between the three persons of the Godhead, according to Gregory, is only the "difference of manifestation" which in turn has caused the "difference of their Names." The distinction of the three persons of the Godhead, may, for Gregory, be conceived and preserved in the "One nature and dignity of the Godhead," because the "Three are One in Godhead and the One Three in Properties."⁷⁶ He then asks questions: "What then? Is the Holy Spirit God?" He answers "Most certainly" the Holy Spirit is God. If so, he asks again, is "he Consubstantial?" He answers, "Yes, if he is God."⁷⁷ Tracing this conclusion, Gregory delivers a strong message to the disputers saying, "Rank no part of the Trinity with thyself . . . cut not off from either the One and equally august Nature."⁷⁸ He then declares, "To us, there is One God, for the Godhead is One" because "one is not more and another is less God; nor is one before and another after; nor are They divided in will or parted in power" and are "undivided" and "inseparable" Godhead. He adds, "We conceive Three Persons in Whom the Godhead dwells" and those "Who timelessly and with equal glory have

---

73. Gregory of Nazianzus, *On the Holy Spirit* 5.12.
74. Gregory of Nazianzus, *On the Holy Spirit* 5.2.
75. Gregory of Nazianzus, *On the Holy Spirit* 5.3.
76. Gregory of Nazianzus, *On the Holy Spirit* 5.8–9.
77. Gregory of Nazianzus, *On the Holy Spirit* 5.10.
78. Gregory of Nazianzus, *On the Holy Spirit* 5.12.

their Being."⁷⁹ He asserts that the Holy Spirit is "God," an "object of adoration" to be "worshipped," and "glorified, reckoned with the Father and the Son." We, therefore, Gregory concludes, "worship God the Father, God the Son, and God the Holy Ghost, Three Persons, One Godhead, undivided in honour ... glory ... substance."⁸⁰

Gregory of Nyssa (ca. 331–395), a fellow Cappadocian with Gregory of Nazianzus, in his *On the Holy Spirit: Against the Followers of Macedonius* recounts how the Macedonians "accused" them of confessing the Holy Spirit as of the "same rank" and an "exact identity" with the Father and the Son.⁸¹ Their opponents believed and taught that the Holy Spirit:

- ← is a stranger to any vital communion with the Father and the Son;
- ← is inferior to, and less than the two in power, glory, dignity, and in everything that is ascribed to deity in word or thought;
- ← does not have equal honor with the other two;
- ← possesses partial power to fulfil; partial activities assigned to him.⁸²

Citing one of the major questions the Macedonians raised over and over again, Gregory writes,

> We [Macedonians] have been taught by Scripture that the Father is the Creator, and in the same way that it was through the Son that all things were made; but God's word tells us nothing of this kind about the Holy Spirit; and how then can it be right to place the Holy Spirit in a position of equal dignity with One Who has displayed such magnificence of power through the Creation?⁸³

Gregory then goes on to answer the disputers' question by saying, "We say nothing different from that which Scripture says." Drawing intensive evidence from Scripture, he declares that the Holy Spirit is "absolutely Divine," "Omnipotent," "glorious," "eternal," "grandeur of his Being," "Divine in Essence," and "transcendent."⁸⁴ He asserts that neither did God make the universe "through the Son as needing any help, nor does the Only-begotten God work all things by the Holy Spirit as having

---

79. Gregory of Nazianzus, *On the Holy Spirit* 5.14.
80. Gregory of Nazianzus, *On the Holy Spirit* 5.28–29.
81. Gregory of Nyssa, *On the Holy Spirit*, 315.
82. Gregory of Nyssa, *On the Holy Spirit*, 316.
83. Gregory of Nyssa, *On the Holy Spirit*, 319.
84. Gregory of Nyssa, *On the Holy Spirit*, 316–17.

a power that comes short of his design, but the fountain of power is the Father and the power of the Father is the Son, and the spirit of that power is the Holy Spirit." Creation in its entire visible and invisible extent, in Gregory's belief, is the perfect work of that "One Divine Power," of the Father, the Son, and the Holy Spirit. He adds, "Nature, which came into existence by creation" is the "design of the Father, advancing through the Son, and completed in the Holy Spirit."[85] Further, says Gregory, when delivering the Great Commission to his disciples, Jesus "joins the Father, the Son and the Holy Spirit." This union of the three persons is "continual." For it was not joined for an occasional purpose as if it was meant to be separated on other occasions, but ever remains an "inseparable union" in everything attributed to the Godhead.[86] The Holy Spirit, therefore, asserts Gregory, cannot be separated from any divine activity carried out by the Father and the Son. Thus, the "identity of operation in Father, Son, and Holy Spirit" clearly shows the "undistinguishable character of their substance." This "community of substance" and "community of the attributes," for Gregory, clearly affirms the "Godhead of the Holy Spirit." As the identity, substance, and attributes of the three persons of the Godhead are one, the "operation of the Father, the Son, and the Holy Spirit is one." Therefore, concludes Gregory, "any diversity" cannot be made in the nature of the three persons of the "Godhead" which is defined as the "Holy Trinity."[87] Thus, the true "Christian is marked by his belief in Father, Son, and Holy Ghost."[88]

Basil of Caesarea (ca. 329–379), a brother to Gregory of Nyssa, friend of Gregory of Nazianzus, and the oldest of the Cappadocian fathers,[89] in his treatise *On the Spirit*, responds to the teaching of the group he considers to be "opponents," "adversaries," and a "band of... enemies." He states that these opponents rejected the equal status of the Holy Spirit with the Father and the Son and declared that "it is not permissible . . . for the Holy Spirit to be ranked with the Father and Son, on account of the difference of his nature and the inferiority of his dignity."[90] The opponents asserted that the "Spirit is not to be ranked along with the Father and the Son, but under the Son and the Father; not coordinated, but subordinated;

---

85. Gregory of Nyssa, *On the Holy Spirit*, 320.
86. Gregory of Nyssa, *On the Holy Spirit*, 327.
87. Gregory of Nyssa, *On the Holy Spirit*, 329.
88. Gregory of Nyssa, *On the Holy Spirit*, 321.
89. Basil of Caesarea, *Oration on the Spirit* 29.74.
90. Basil, *Oration on the Spirit* 10.24.

not connumerated, but subnumerated."[91] He considers them as "blasphemers of the Spirit"[92] who "set at naught their own confessions."[93] Drawing from Matt 28:18–20, Basil proceeds to declare the true theology and doctrine of the Holy Spirit and assert that Jesus has delivered a necessary and saving doctrine that the Holy Spirit is to be ranked with the Father.[94] When delivering the formula of "the Father, the Son, and the Holy Ghost," says Basil, Jesus did not rank the three persons of the Godhead into "First, Second, and Third" but he declared employing one and equal "holy names."[95] This fundamental doctrine of salvation, for Basil, is established through the Father, the Son, and the Holy Ghost. He declares that as they, Basil and his allies, were baptized in the name "of the Father and of the Son and of the Holy Ghost," they believe in "the Father and the Son and the Holy Ghost."[96] Basil further asserts that in the creation process, the Father is the "original cause," the Son is the "creative cause," and the Holy Spirit is the "perfecting cause" of all things that are created.[97] In every conception, therefore, the Holy Spirit, according to Basil, is *"inseparable from the Father and the Son, alike in the creation of the perceptible objects, in the dispensation of human affairs, and in the judgment to come."*[98] He declares that there is "One God and Father," "one Only-begotten," the Son, and "one Holy Ghost." Therefore, "we [Basil and his allies] believe and proclaim" each of the "hypostases singly"[99] and that Christians should never "shrink" from believing that "doctrine," which was "preserved by unbroken sequence,"[100] primarily revealed in the creation process and later established and delivered to the church through the Great Commission.

These reliable patristic accounts are clear enough to display that the Holy Spirit's nature was controversial for some Christians in the patristic period. For some, the Holy Spirit was not God but one of the entities

---

91. Basil, *Oration on the Spirit* 6.13.
92. Basil, *Oration on the Spirit* 30.79.
93. Basil, *Oration on the Spirit* 10.25.
94. Basil, *Oration on the Spirit* 18.44.
95. Basil, *Oration on the Spirit* 12.28.
96. Basil, *Oration on the Spirit* 16.38.
97. Basil, *Oration on the Spirit* 16.
98. Basil, *Oration on the Spirit* 18.44.
99. Basil, *Oration on the Spirit* 30.79.
100. Basil, *Oration on the Spirit* 30.79. See also a similar opinion offered by Cyril of Jerusalem, *Catechetical Lectures* 16 and 17.

which came into being through the Son. For some, he was an angel superior in rank to other angels. For others, he was just a ministering Spirit, utterly different from the Father and the Son in substance. For others still, he was neither God nor part of creation, but rather a middling being who was somewhere between the Godhead and creatures. Some still considered him as merely a divine force. Even among those who believed the Holy Spirit to be God, some distinguished degrees of divinity within the Trinity, mostly by making the Holy Spirit inferior to the Father and the Son. Some refrained from committing to any belief that declares the Holy Spirit is God. Others boldly proclaimed that the Holy Spirit is God. However, the church fathers of the period, mostly those cited here, secured a fundamental biblical basis for the church's belief and teaching as well as for the future formulation of the doctrine of the Holy Spirit. While each of them takes a slightly different emphasis and analysis, they all hold a common understanding and position towards the doctrine of the Holy Spirit. They provided the church of the period with clearly annotated theological and biblical evidence on which the church could safely ground its response to the controversies raised and comfortably teach its members, particularly those who had internal questions about the nature of the Holy Spirit. With this in mind, the question to be asked is: what was the response of the wider church to the Macedonians' controversy over the nature of the Holy Spirit?

6.5. THE WIDER CHURCH'S RESPONSE TO THOSE IN DISPUTE

As already presented, the dispute over the nature of the Holy Spirit divided the church of the patristic period into two camps, i.e., the disputants on the one side and the wider church on the other side, which drew the attention of the emperor of Rome. Like Constantine during the Arian controversy regarding the Son's relation to the Father at Nicaea in 325, in 381 Emperor Theodosius I called a church council in Constantinople to settle the controversy by common consensus. Evaluations of the council suggest that this particular council was "not intended to be an Ecumenical Council at all" but was just a "local gathering of only one hundred and fifty bishops" and that "no diocese of the West" attended it either by "representation or in the person of its bishop; neither the see of Rome nor any other see." It was simply a regional council wherein 150 bishops of the

Eastern churches assembled. It was declared of the council: "The Bishops out of different provinces assembled by the grace of God in Constantinople, on the summons of the most religious Emperor Theodosius."[101] Among them were prominent church fathers such as Gregory of Nazianzus, Gregory of Nyssa, Meletius of Antioch, and Cyril of Jerusalem. From among those church fathers Meletius of Antioch was assigned to preside over the council. Unfortunately, Bishop Meletius died during the session and the meeting was adjourned to attend his funeral. When the meeting resumed Gregory of Nazianzus was elected to replace the late Meletius and preside over the meeting.[102] The evidence further indicates that the meeting strictly dealt with, condemned, and anathematized not only the Macedonians but also that of Eunomians, Marcellians, Sabellians, Photinians, and Apollinarians.[103]

Discussing particularly the case of the Macedonians, Leo Donald Davis suggests that in addition to the 150 bishops of the Eastern churches, "thirty-six Macedonian . . . bishops attended the early sessions" of the council. The council "attempted to conciliate the Macedonian faction on the basis of a creed embodying the faith of Nicaea." The council asked the Macedonians to abjure their error in its attempt to conciliate them. However, the Macedonians insisted on maintaining their views and withdrew.[104] The council nevertheless proceeded with its deliberations and prepared a declaration of the church's position towards the doctrine of the Holy Spirit. The council approved the Nicene Creed, which contains the statement "And we believe in the Holy Spirit" and added the following statement to clarify the status of the Holy Spirit: "The Lord and Giver-of-Life, who proceeds from the Father, who with the Father and the Son together is worshipped and glorified, who spoke by the prophets."[105] This indicates that in its declaration the council attributed to the Holy Spirit the divine title "Lord," the divine function of "giving life," and worship equal to that rendered to the Father and Son. Having settled the position of the church towards the doctrine of the Holy Spirit with this declaration, the council stipulated certain conditions by which the church would accept individuals who would confess their heresy and turn to orthodoxy. The condition says, "We receive [them] upon their giving a

---

101. *Seven Ecumenical Councils*, 162–63, 172.
102. *Seven Ecumenical Councils*, 162–63.
103. *Seven Ecumenical Councils*, 172.
104. Davis, *First Seven Ecumenical Councils*, 119, 122
105. *Seven Ecumenical Councils*, 163.

written renunciation [of their heresy] anathematize every heresy which is not following the Holy, Catholic, and Apostolic Church of God." When the supposed heretics agreed to do this, they would then be "sealed or anointed with the holy oil upon their forehead, eyes, nostrils, mouth, and ears," which the church would declare to be "the seal of the gift of the Holy Spirit."[106] Thus, the sought-after agreement was reached on the doctrine of the Holy Spirit.

It was affirmed that since the full divinity of the Holy Spirit was declared, he must be "*homoousios* [of the same substance] with the Father and the Son distinguished from them by his procession."[107] After the second council, "The full divinity and consubstantiality of the Spirit with the Father and the Son was soon the consensual teaching of the entire church."[108] Thus, it was in the "Nicene-Constantinopolitan Creed of 381" that the Holy Spirit must be "worshipped and glorified" along with the Father and the Son was sanctioned.[109] Hence, the identity and identicality of the substance of the Father, the Son, and the Holy Spirit were formulated into a strong theological and doctrinal position and the doctrine of Christianity's Trinitarian theology was officially formulated. Thereupon, Christian theology has confessed the doctrine of the immanent Trinity, i.e., three persons having identical beings and authority in one Godhead.[110] This doctrine has thus been historically viewed as settling the questions, doubts, and controversy over the nature of the Holy Spirit. Nevertheless, evidence shows that controversies related to the doctrine of the Holy Spirit continued to arise from time to time and challenged the church, within the Western church in particular, which led to the adoption of the *filioque* clause (see chapter 8).

6.6. SUMMARY

Given these accounts and discussion, two points can be drawn in the conclusion of the chapter.

---

106. *Seven Ecumenical Councils*, 185.
107. Elowsky, *We Believe*, 236.
108. Elowsky, *We Believe*, 235.
109. Elowsky, *We Believe*, 246.
110. Badcock, *Light of Truth*, 54–55. See also Kärkkäinen, *Constructive Christian Theology*, 2:250–71, wherein he analyzes wonderfully how Christian belief in the Triune God and its doctrine of the Trinity is impressively unique.

First, when viewed in light of the historical accounts analyzed above, the doctrine of the Holy Spirit was an issue of ambiguities, questions, controversy, and divisions until the last quarter of the fourth century. The causes were sometimes related to the place and role of the Holy Spirit in the life and function of the church, mostly through subjective experiences, and sometimes to his essence, authority, independent personality, independent function, and relationship with the Father and the Son. There are, therefore, some questions to be asked in this respect. For example, what caused all those ambiguities, questions, confusions, and controversies about the nature, manifestation, gifts, and workings of the Holy Spirit? Does Scripture contain explicit answers or solutions to those ambiguities, questions, confusions, and controversies? Three factors may be presented as the most probable answers to these questions:

(1) As discussed in the first four chapters, Scripture contains clear themes, indications, and images of the divinity, independent personality, manifestations, gifts, and independent operations of the Holy Spirit. It also contains clear teaching about the objective gift and subjective experiential contents of the Holy Spirit's manifestation. Despite this, as discussed in chapter 5, Scripture, in general, does not teach deeply about the overall place, role, and authoritative activities of the Holy Spirit. Especially in comparison to what it teaches about the Father and the Son, Scripture does not contain similar strong teaching and sanction about the Holy Spirit. Accordingly, it does not provide a fully developed doctrine of the Holy Spirit that answers certain academic, intellectual, or practical questions. Furthermore, it does not sanction the place and role of the Holy Spirit in Christian belief, teaching, and practice.

(2) Scripture does not explicitly teach about the ways of objective reception or subjective experience of the Holy Spirit through the reception of verbally uttered or visibly performed charismatic gifts. As discussed in chapter 5, Scripture does not clearly set out the nature of the reception, gifts, and workings of the Holy Spirit or the ways these are experienced. This lack of an authoritative source containing clear-cut authoritative answers and solutions to respond to and settle the ambiguities and controversies related to the doctrine of the Holy Spirit and resulting gaps appear to have left the church of the period in ambiguity and confusion about how to develop definitive answers and explicit solution to the subject matter.

(3) As discussed in chapter 5, the church of the postapostolic period adopted and developed a tradition in which it clearly restricted the role

of the Holy Spirit in the church's life and function, and strictly restricted believers from attaining the charismatic gifts of the Holy Spirit. This tradition continued to influence the church throughout the successive generations.

Thus, the roots of the early church's ambiguities, questions, confusions, and controversies over the nature, reception, gifts, and workings of the Holy Spirit seem to be drawn both from the divine side and the human side. From the divine side, it is notable that God does not usually make clear everything that humans want to *know* about his nature and actions. He does not reveal to humans everything that is in his mind about the status of each person of the Trinity. However, he has revealed what he considers to be sufficient for salvation, reconciliation, and unification with him. From the human side, for those who consider this gap from an academic point of view, Scripture offers no clear-cut answer regarding how to perceive, interpret, and act with the mystery of the particularity, independence, reception, gifts, and workings of the Holy Spirit. In particular, the more academics struggle with how to understand, interpret, and clarify biblical texts such as John 16:13–15, the more the gap in understanding the status of the Holy Spirit will be. Thus, the gap created and drawn from these root causes may never be fully resolved and thus remains insoluble. Viewed in the light of this insoluble gap, what the second council of the church attributed to the Holy Spirit was fundamentally right, is fundamentally right, and shall remain fundamentally right. The second council's statement contains all that can be said or done about the Holy Spirit following the biblical teaching. Therefore, it answers all questions and resolves all confusion about the Holy Spirit in a very simple, clear, and general way. It deserves due respect and attention. What could have been done otherwise? Standing firm and remaining bound by it is the only valuable solution.

Second, it seems that beginning from the second council's formulation of the church's position towards the Holy Spirit, the Holy Spirit became only an object of faith. This position, in principle, seems to assume the reception of the Holy Spirit through sacramental baptism. Since the matter of objective gift and subjective experience of the Holy Spirit was not part of the controversies at issue here, the council addressed and emphasized only the doctrinal belief of the Holy Spirit. Accounts of the council indicate that it addressed the issues of the Montanist movement and declared it to be a heretic sect.[111] Even when doing this, it seems that the council never raised the issue of the gifts and workings of the Holy Spirit in the life, worship, ministry, and mission of the church. Following the second council's position, nor did the institutional church consider the issue of the place and role of the Holy Spirit in the life of the church which would be experienced through his gifts and workings. Rather, the institutional church continued to emphasize the doctrinal belief and avoid the subjective experience of the Holy Spirit in, with, and through a charismatic form of worship and spiritual experience. This played a decisive role in dividing objective doctrinal belief and subjective experience of the Holy Spirit and in obscuring the place and role of the Holy Spirit in the life and function of the church, which has continued through the centuries to the present day. Hence, this historical event can be considered as *one of the root causes* that has caused tensions between doctrinal belief and subjective experience of the Holy Spirit in the history of Christianity. This then raises the question: what happened to the subjective experience of the Holy Spirit, through the charismatic form of worship and spiritual experience in those interim periods between AD 100 and 500? To this, we will now turn our examination.

---

111. *Seven Ecumenical Councils*, 186.

CHAPTER 7

The Emergence of Tension and Division over the Experience of the Presence, Gifts, and Works of the Holy Spirit

THE PREVIOUS CHAPTER REMINDED us about three particular features: (1) how doubts, question, confusion, and controversy of the nature of the Holy Spirit challenged the patristic church; (2) how the second council of the patristic church formulated the doctrine of the Holy Spirit; and (3) how the institutional tradition continued in quenching the experience of the presence, gifts and works of the Holy Spirit. The fear of competing religious movements, in particular, pushed the church toward further restriction of the *Pentecostal-charismatic* form of religious experience. Different kinds of defense mechanisms used by the church authorities to overcome those movements acted as a mask to suppress internal tendencies of a *Pentecostal-charismatic* form of worship and spiritual experience. Accordingly, the *Pentecostal-charismatic* nature of the church's life and function continued to be pushed aside. Despite this, there are historical accounts that indicate that despite the growing institutional formalism along with increasingly oppressive structures, experience of the presence, gifts, and works of the Holy Spirit through *Pentecostal-charismatic* form of worship and spirituality did not disappear from the church of the patristic period. Evidence preserved from the patristic church indicates that there were individuals and groups with a *Pentecostal-charismatic* voice who rose up from time to time and emphasized charismatic spirituality. This chapter will examine historical accounts related to the continued experience of the presence, gifts and works of the Holy Spirit through *Pentecostal-charismatic* form of worship in the church of the patristic period and provide some examples of this.

7.1. EMPHASIS AND EXPERIENCE OF CHARISMATIC GIFTS IN THE PATRISTIC CHURCH

In the second century, Justin Martyr (ca. 100–166) witnessed that charismatic experience was evident in the church of his time. In his *Dialogue with Trypho* he states that many believers were receiving the gifts of the Holy Spirit such gifts as healing, prophecy, exorcism, and foreknowledge. Justin explains how the risen and ascended Lord Jesus was imparting all these gifts to those who believed in him, to each one as he reckoned deserved which gift. He affirms that the prophetic ministries of the old times were transferred to believers of his days, and were given to men and women who demonstrated them effectively.[1] In his *Second Apology*, Justin testifies that many Christians throughout the world were exorcising demonic spirits by the name of Jesus. Demonic spirits which were resisting other exorcists, those who were using various traditional means, were being easily exorcised by the name of Jesus. Justin asserts that different kinds of physical healings were taking place by the name of Jesus and that Jesus, who healed people from different kinds of sicknesses during the time of his earthly ministry, was healing many sick people in many churches.[2]

Irenaeus (ca. 115–200) testified that all kinds of miraculous charismata were present in the church of his day. In *Against Heresies*, he reports that those he considered truly disciples of Christ were given gifts of the Holy Spirit and were performing miracles in the name of Jesus. Those who received the gifts were serving "according to the gift which each one has received from him [Jesus]," and in such a manner, their service promoted the "welfare of others." He states that some were given authority over demonic spirits and were driving them out and those who had been freed from the demonic spirits believed in Jesus and joined the church. Some believers, says Irenaeus, were given foreknowledge of things to come, visions, and prophecy while others were given the gifts of healing and raising the dead. He attests that there were people who had been raised from the dead and then continued in church membership

---

1. Justin Martyr, *Dialogue with Trypho* 39, 82, 89.
2. Justin Martyr, *Second Apology* 6.

for many years. Expressing his surprise at the multiplicity of charismatic phenomena, Irenaeus asks a question, "And what shall I more say?" and then concludes, "It is not possible to name the number of the gifts which the church, throughout the whole world, has received from God, in the name of Jesus."[3] Elsewhere Irenaeus refers to the ministry of the apostles and expresses his admiration for how their ministry was accompanied by authoritative speeches in different languages and manifestations of different sign charismata. He then writes, "In like manner, we do hear many brethren in the church, who possess prophetic gifts, and who through the Spirit speak all kinds of languages." He adds that some of those gifted believers were "bringing to light hidden things for the benefit of all" and that those believers, being partakers of the Spirit, were given deeper spiritual insight to the extent that they "declare the mysteries of God."[4]

Tertullian (ca. 150–230) in his *Treatise on the Soul* reports that God's grace impressed the church by giving continuous revelations and that many believers were endowed with charismata of prophecy, revelation, vision, and speaking in tongues. He attests to a prophetess whose gift surprised him and his peers stating that her visions, revelations, and ecstatic experiences were quite authentic. He recognizes her special gift of reading what is hidden in people's hearts and minds and then revealing it. He expresses his special evaluation of her gifts of "mysterious communication with the Spirit, angels," and at times with the Lord Jesus. Regarding how the church viewed and treated those given the gift of the Holy Spirit, Tertullian states that the church directed them to report for examination and counseling to take appropriate care toward the authentic realization of the gifts and to avoid mere illusions.[5] In his treatise *Against Marcion*, Tertullian attests that all the sign and wonder charismata were forthcoming without any difficulty and that the church was realizing them in agreement, according to the rules of Christ, the Holy Spirit, and the apostles.[6] Tertullian's account, in particular, indicates that all the charismata presented in the New Testament were being manifested and realized by Christians of his day and that individuals endowed with the gifts were advised first to consult the leadership, before pronouncing the messages to congregations. In this way, the church could verify whether the claimed gifts were genuinely from the Holy Spirit and exert control over mere

---

3. Irenaeus, *Against Heresies* 2.32.
4. Irenaeus, *Against Heresies* 5.6.
5. Tertullian, *Treatise on the Soul* 2.9.
6. Tertullian, *Against Marcion* 5.8.

sentimental experiences. This, in a sense, seems to be an important move in enabling the church to recognize and realize the gifts of the Holy Spirit in accordance with biblical instruction (Matt 7:20–23).

Nevertheless, historical accounts indicate that the Montanist movement emerged in the second half of the second century in reaction to the church for not realizing charismatic gifts and devotional spirituality. This, on the one hand, seems to contradict and conflict with the witnesses of the above accounts of the church fathers. On the other hand, it leads us to raise questions such as: When and how did the Montanist movement emerge? What did it emphasize? What was its departure point from the wider church? In order to answer these questions, some historical accounts of the movement are examined in the following discussion.

7.2. EMERGENCE, EXPANSION, AND INFLUENCE OF THE MONTANIST MOVEMENT

Tillich suggests that there was a "fear of spiritual movements" in the church of the patristic period, particularly as "Gnostics had claimed to have the Spirit." Therefore, assuming that different kinds of "disruptive elements" may enter the church in the name of the Spirit, the church was "afraid of the Spirit." Accordingly, says Tillich, "The Spirit was suppressed by the organized church" and the church was "unable to understand the prophetic Spirit anymore." He adds that the Montanist movement consequently emerged as a "reaction of the Spirit against the developing order."[7] Similarly, Thomas suggests that the subject of the Holy Spirit came to the church's attention more prominently through the Montanist movement. He states that the period in which the Montanist movement emerged was a "non-reflective period" regarding the church's doctrine of the Holy Spirit. It was during that "non-reflective period" that the Montanists emerged and connected the Holy Spirit with subjective experience, charismatic gifts, and Spirit-inspired devotional worship and deep spiritual life. The original impetus of the movement, says Thomas, was a reaction against the church in favor of the recognition of the gifts, power, and activities of the Holy Spirit in a church that was tending to become "too rigid in its intellectual conception and ecclesiastical organization."[8] Dunn affirms these observations by suggesting that the church of the period continued

---

7. Tillich, *History of Christian Thought*, 40.
8. Thomas, *Holy Spirit*, 80–82.

to strengthen legalism, order, and hierarchical authority. Thereby the issue of the Holy Spirit's functional role became more and more confined within the church "until the church stood above the Holy Spirit." To all intents and purposes of the church, says Dunn, the Holy Spirit became "property of the church, with the gifts tied to and determined by a ritual act, and church authority." Dunn affirms that the Montanists emerged in reaction against the church's stance when the Holy Spirit became "more the object of faith and less the subject of experience," and when the claim of inspiration by the Holy Spirit became more an issue that was "suspect by the institution."[9] In its reaction against this stance of the church, the movement became a rigorous challenge to the structured church.[10] These observations may lead us to ask questions as to when, where, and how the Montanist movement emerged and what the emphasis of its adherents looked like.

Historical accounts indicate that the Montanist movement emerged in Asia Minor, Phrygia, in the second half of the second century.[11] The movement drew its name from its founder Montanus, who was a convert from paganism and who began to speak in tongues and prophesy from the moment of his conversion baptism.[12] He became "priest of a church called Cybele" and began to prophesy in about 155.[13] He claimed to have been gifted and inspired by the Holy Spirit and began experiencing manifestations of charismata and inspiring many followers.[14] Hyatt attests that Montanus was concerned about the "growing formalism in the church and increasing moral laxity among its members." As a result of his concern, says Hyatt, Montanus began to advocate for the intervention of the gifts and workings of the Holy Spirit in the church. He stressed that the qualifying factor for Christian ministry was not an appointment of ecclesiastical office but possession of the gifts of the Holy Spirit. He also stressed the importance of moral purity in the Christian lifestyle.[15] Following Montanus's teachings, the movement reacted against the growing formalism in the church, the power abuse of the bishops, the dying

---

9. Dunn, *Baptism in the Holy Spirit*, 224.

10. Hamilton, *Charismatic Movement*, 65.

11. Burgess, *Ancient Christian Traditions*, 49. See also Cook, *Routledge Companion to Christian History*, 5–11.

12. Allen, *Unfailing Stream*, 18.

13. Burgess, "The Holy Spirit, Doctrine of: The Ancient Fathers" in *Dictionary*, 419.

14. Hamilton, *Charismatic Movement*, 65.

15. Hyatt, *2000 Years*, 26–27.

spirituality of the church,[16] as well as the spiritual insufficiency of the hierarchy.[17] Montanus and his adherents emphasized strong asceticism, strict practice of penance, and free charismatic experiences[18] and they practised strict fasting, prayer, and charismatic gifts such as prophecy, speaking in tongues, visions, healing, exorcism, and revelations.[19] They also insisted on moral purity in anticipation of the imminent end of the world, emphasized the significance of charismatic spirituality to keep oneself unspoiled by the world, and exalted charismatic spirituality at the expense of institutional offices and officers.[20]

Evaluations testify that on account of authentic miracles wrought by the Montanists people were persuaded to commit themselves to the movement[21] As the movement continued in attracting people and "received more and more favorably," it also "spread so rapidly"[22] throughout Asia Minor, Europe, and North Africa and impacted the institutional church.[23] The influence of the movement divided the church when some believers thought that the prophecies of the Montanists were of the divine, while others thought that they were diabolic.[24] Thiselton suggests that the movement influenced not only the laity but also prominent church fathers such as Tertullian. He states that Tertullian viewed the prophecy of the Montanists as an "authentic call to a lax church which was obsessed with the formal office" but he did not actually "hold every tenet of the movement but was attracted by its emphasis on the immediacy of the Holy Spirit, its rigor asceticism, and its separation from the world, along with its indifference to 'order' in the church." Thiselton adds that Tertullian's own rigorous attitude on "Christian thought and life, tending toward asceticism" and his "interest in eschatology" might have attracted him to the movement. Yet, says Thiselton, Tertullian "did not convert to Montanism, but saw it largely as representing what he earlier stood for."[25] Congar suggests that Tertullian was "increasingly drawn to-

16. Middlemiss, *Interpreting Charismatic Experience*, 2.
17. Bouyer, "Some Charismatic Movements," 119.
18. Hagglund, *History of Theology*, 57.
19. Anderson, *Introduction to Pentecostalism*, 20–21.
20. Berkhof, *History of Christian Doctrines*, 54–55.
21. Allen, *Unfailing Stream*, 18.
22. Congar, *I Believe*, 1:66.
23. Hyatt, *2000 Years*, 27.
24. Chadwick, *Early Church*, 52.
25. Thiselton, *Holy Spirit*, 179–81.

wards Montanism finding an answer to the reasons which had at first deterred him from a church in which women prophesied."[26] It is alleged that the movement attracted not only Tertullian but also the bishop of Rome.[27] Discussing how the movement attracted the bishop of Rome, Kilian McDonnell and George T. Montague state that the bishop of Rome of the time acted in favor of the movement and "bestowed his peace" on the churches troubled by division caused by the movement through his "letters of peace." They state that "the Pope could not have given his peace" if he did not know that prophecies of the Montanists were "within the bounds of orthodoxy."[28] However, despite its immense attractions and contributions to believers' spiritual renewal, the influence of the movement caused a serious crisis of divisions in the wider church.[29]

7.3. THE RESPONSE OF THE WIDER CHURCH TO THE MONTANIST MOVEMENT

As a result of the above-mentioned divisions that arose across the churches, the wider church held regional councils in the last quarter of the second century to respond to the influence of the movement. After the Jerusalem council of the first century (Acts 15), as McDonnell and Montague note, it was to respond to the Montanism that councils of the church were held during the last quarter of the second century. They add that "neither the threat of Gnosticism, nor Marcionism had ever pressed the church into calling councils" but Montanism, being a real threat to the institution, pressed the church to call regional councils[30] which censured Montanus as heretical.[31] The first regional council was called in 177 and denounced the Montanists.[32] Those councils, says Allen, denounced not only the Montanists but also their own church members who adhered to the movement such that many were forced to undergo an exorcism on the assumption that they were possessed by demonic spirits.[33] In

---

26. Congar, *I Believe*, 1:66.
27. Gulley, *Systematic Theology*, 528.
28. McDonnell and Montague, *Christian Initiation*, 118.
29. Congar, *I Believe*, 1:66.
30. McDonnell and Montague, *Christian Initiation*, 118.
31. Hyatt, *2000 Years*, 27.
32. Congar, *I Believe*, 1:66.
33. Allen, *Unfailing Stream*, 19.

considering the movement as a threat to the institution, the hierarchies of the church advocated for its rejection and became chief enemies of the movement.[34] Hence, official condemnation of the movement began before the year 200 by Asian local synodical councils.[35] In light of these accounts, questions might be asked such as: Why did the church consider the Montanists to be heretical? What was the theological and practical departure of the Montanists from the wider church? How and by what components did the movement become a threat to the church? Answering these questions with reliable answers requires examining reliable accounts of the patristic period.

Eusebius in the fifth book of his *Church History* recorded the perceived weaknesses of Montanus the person, and of the movement. He writes,

> The enemy of God's church, who is emphatically a hater of good and a lover of evil, and Leaves untried no manner of craft against men, was again active in causing strange heresies to spring up against the church. For some persons, like venomous reptiles, crawled over Asia and Phrygia, boasting that Montanus was the Paraclete, and that the women that followed him, Priscilla and Maximilla, were prophetesses of Montanus.[36]

In chapter 16 of the same book, Eusebius writes this by citing primary sources:

> A recent convert, Montanus by name, through his unquenchable desire for leadership, gave the adversary opportunity against him. And he became beside himself, and being suddenly in a sort of frenzy and ecstasy, he raved, and began to babble and utter strange things, prophesying in a manner contrary to the constant custom of the church handed down by tradition from the beginning. . . . And he stirred up besides two women, and filled them with the false spirit, so that they talked wildly and unreasonably and strangely.[37]

Eusebius writes, by citing the primary source, that some of the audiences of Montanus's prophetic utterances examined the nature of his prophecy and they felt that his prophecy was false and profane. The

---

34. Cox, *Fire from Heaven*, 90.
35. McDonnell and Montague, *Christian Initiation*, 119.
36. Eusebius, *Church History* 5.14.
37. Eusebius, *Church History* 5.16.

examiners of his prophecy considered Montanus as if he was possessed by demonic spirits and they rebuked him as a heretic. However, says Eusebius, Montanus exerted influence on other believers among whom he stirred up two women, Priscilla and Maximilla, with his prophetic experience. Eusebius criticizes them for prophesying in a "wildly and unreasonably and strangely" manner. He presents Maximilla's prophecy, in which she prophesied war and anarchy that was expected for thirteen years, as an instance of unfulfilled prophecies of the Montanists.[38] The thirteen years might have been the intervening years between the date the woman uttered the prophecy and the time when the story was recorded. In chapter 18 of his book, again citing from the primary source, Eusebius generalizes some of the perceived ethical weaknesses of Montanus and his adherents. He states that they were criticized for forbidding marriage;,setting strict orders for fasting and prayer, and receiving money from the "rich," "poor," "orphans," and "widows." They were further criticized for "dyeing hair," "lending money on usury," receiving gifts of "gold," "silver," "costly garments," being "delighted in ornaments," "boasting," and for being "puffed up" in vain elation by a false spirit. They declared two small Phrygian towns, "Pepuza and Tymion," as the new Jerusalem of gathering people there at the imminent end of the world.[39] Eusebius presents these features as observed ethical weaknesses in the Montanist experiences. Besides these, his account does not identify and point out other fundamental heretical characteristics of the Montanists on theological, doctrinal, and canonical grounds.

Cyril of Jerusalem (ca. 315–387) in his *Catechetical Lectures* 16 refers to the Montanists as "Cataphrygians." He considers Montanus the "ringleader in evil" who was "out of his mind" and "dared to say that he was himself the Holy Ghost." He argues that Montanus was filled with "uncleanness and lasciviousness" and criticizes him for practicing "inhuman cruelty" such as "cutting the throats of wretched little children, and chopping them up into unholy food, for the purpose of their so-called mysteries." On account of these acts, says Cyril, Montanus was "condemned by an irrevocable sentence."[40] Basil of Caesarea declares the Montanists to be plainly heretical because they applied the title of the Paraclete to Montanus and Priscilla, which is a "shameful blasphemy" against the Holy Spirit. Therefore, they were condemned for their

38. Eusebius, *Church History* 5.16.
39. Eusebius, *Church History* 5.18.
40. Cyril of Jerusalem, *Catechetical Lectures* 16.8.

"unlawful" and "shameful" application of the title of the Paraclete to humans and they are "liable to eternal damnation, inasmuch as blasphemy against the Holy Spirit admits of no forgiveness."[41] Hippolytus, in his *Refutation of All Heresies*, considers the Montanists "more heretical in nature" and "victims of error . . . by wretched women called . . . Priscilla and Maximilla" whom the movement presumed to be prophetesses. He criticizes the Montanists for magnifying the two women more than the apostles and for not heeding those who were viewed as "competent to decide." Against the church, says Hippolytus, the Montanists introduced the "novelties of fasts . . . feasts . . . meals of parched food."[42] Yet, Hippolytus does not indicate which of the movement's taught or practice was heretical in content and on what ground. Gregory of Nazianzus in his *Oration 33, Against Arians*, refers to Montanus as a heretic without giving any further explanation about the heretic content of his practices.[43] Thus, the finalized repudiation of the Montanists, according to Hyatt, came from the Second Council of the church convened at Constantinople in 381, which declared that Montanists were to be regarded as "pagans."[44]

In contrast to these patristic church fathers' accounts, modern scholarly evaluations suggest that as the character of the movement was "not universally the same,"[45] its evaluations, too, "vary dramatically."[46] This, indeed, seems to be the case because different evaluations offer different accounts of the characteristics of the movement. Some evaluations suggest that a number of the features referred to as the heretical character of the movement were not sufficiently convincing. Thiselton, for example, suggests that the main problem the church had with the Montanists was the "extravagant and exclusivist claims of the New Prophecy."[47] More than anything else, says Robert H. Culpepper, it was the Montanists' claim they had "access to a continuing revelation that was distasteful to the church" and that their claim seemed to "undermine the authority of the bishops."[48] Others suggest that many strong Christian characteristics of Montanus the person and the movement as a whole have been noted. Hippolytus,

41. Basil of Caesarea, *Letter* 188.1.
42. Hippolytus, *Refutation of All Heresies* 8.12.
43. Gregory of Nazianzus, *Against Arians* 16.
44. Hyatt, *2000 Years*, 28.
45. McDonnell and Montague, *Christian Initiation*, 119.
46. Thiselton, *Holy Spirit*, 180.
47. Thiselton, *Holy Spirit*, 179.
48. Culpepper, *Evaluating the Charismatic Movement*, 40.

for instance, attests that the Montanists agreed with the church regarding the doctrine of God, creation, Christ, and many other teachings that are contained in the Gospels.[49] It was also attested of Montanus the person that he was "orthodox in his faith, accepting all the books of the canon and ... the rules of faith"; that he was "distinguished in working authentic signs and miracles" and that even some of his adversaries admitted that "his life and doctrine were holy and blameless."[50] It was also attested of the movement that besides its "reaction against formalism and bureaucracy in the church,"[51] it was "solid orthodox" in its whole belief, teaching, and practice. It accepted and advocated all the rules of faith held by the wider church and was highly appreciated for its orthodox position against the teachings of Gnosticism.[52] It did not accept any "unorthodox teaching" regarding the doctrine of "creation" or the "nature of Christ" and was in utter agreement with the church in other matters of dogma.[53] It was also attested that the attitude of the Montanists towards codes of ethics, the organization of ministry, commitment to the extent of martyrdom, and eschatological thinking were doctrinally healthy and utterly Christian.[54] These attested qualities of orthodox Christian standing could have been characterized as the moral excellence of Montanus the person and his constituencies. This factor alone might rule out the legitimacy of questioning the authority and authenticity of Montanus the person and faith practice of the movement. In the light of these accounts, the question that might be asked is: if these attestations were based on the genuine evaluations of the existing reality, and if the Montanists had this quality of orthodox Christian standing, then what was the theological, doctrinal, and canonical departure of the movement from the wider church? In order to answer this and similar questions, further light will be shed on the subject matter below but before doing that we will examine the effects of the repudiation of the Montanist spirituality on the wider church's worship life and overall spiritual status.

---

49. Hippolytus, *Refutation of All Heresies* 8.12.
50. Hyatt, *2000 Years*, 26.
51. Thiselton, *Holy Spirit*, 179.
52. Berkhof, *History of Christian Doctrines*, 54–55.
53. McDonnell and Montague, *Christian Initiation*, 169.
54. Kydd, *Charismatic Gifts*, 31.

7.4. EFFECTS OF THE REPUDIATION OF MONTANISM ON THE SPIRITUAL STATUS OF THE CHURCH

Different evaluations of the effects of the church's repudiation of the Montanist spirituality offer many negative results that occurred in the worship and spiritual life of the church. Two of the negative results are presented here as examples.

First, evaluations suggest that the church's repudiation of Montanist spirituality became crucial grounds for the further development of the well-ordered and strengthened institutional and hierarchical church. Allen, for example, observes that after the repudiation of Montanism the church continued to grow "structurally fat; physically and organizationally comfortable" but increasingly "impoverished in genuine spiritual power" and the whole Christianization continued as "superficial and cosmetic." As evidence of the increasing spiritual nominalism of the church, says Allen, some traditional "pagan festivals" were adopted as "Christian festivals" such as the feasts of Christmas and Easter, with only minor ceremonial changes, a traditional "mother goddess" was "metamorphosed into Mary," and even the image of Jupiter was replaced by the image of St. Peter. Conversely, charismatic experiences were regarded as "symptoms of heresy and witchcraft" to the extent that claims of such experiences sometimes led the claimants to a "trial and to burning at the stake."[55] Strengthening Allen's observation, Hyatt argues that following the repudiation of the Montanist spirituality, the institutional church granted limitless power and authority to the bishops. As a result, the bishops of the period strengthened the process of institutionalization further and deeper, whereupon the churches of the time came "under control of a single individual for whom the title 'bishop' was reserved exclusively." Consequently, concludes Hyatt, the bishops were regarded as the "possessors and guarantors of the apostolic doctrine; possessors of charisma virtues; and possessors of the sole right and authority from God to act on earth on his behalf.[56] Tillich identifies four points to demonstrate the effects of the church's rejection of the Montanists: (1) The canon of Scripture was strengthened against any possibility of new revelation.

---

55. Allen, *Unfailing Stream*, 25–26, 29. Hermann Sasse offers a detailed account concerning how the Marian cult was the Christian replacement for the cults of the female deities that played many great roles in the life of pagan people. See Sasse, *Letters to Lutheran Pastors*, 1:368–82.

56. Hyatt, *2000 Years*, 30.

(2) The institutional hierarchy was further strengthened and confirmed against the prophetic Spirit. (3) The teaching and expectation of the end time became less significant than it had been in the apostolic time. (4) Unreserved laxity grew up in the church as the teaching of strict Christian discipline was lost along with the Montanists.[57] In the repudiation of Montanism, Christenson notes, the church's conservatism continued to gain a stronghold and the church continued moving into ascendancy over *Pentecostal-charismatic* elements of the church's life and ministry.[58] The church's rejection and repudiation of Montanism thereby became crucial grounds for the development of a well-ordered and strengthened institutional, organizational, structural, and hierarchical church.[59]

Second, evaluations suggest that the church's repudiation of Montanist spirituality became crucial grounds for further suppression and quenching of any similar spiritual tendencies within the institutional church which continued for centuries.[60] As the church hierarchies continued to be anxious to avoid sectarian forms of such movements, they declined to integrate *Pentecostal-charismatic* forms of spiritual experiences into the life of the church. This remained the basic reaction of the church authorities to movements with similar tendencies throughout the history of the church.[61] Consequently, the issues of gifts and workings of the Holy Spirit in and through *Pentecostal-charismatic* forms of spiritual experiences were associated with "fiery zeal and zest." All subsequent revivalist tendencies were then viewed as a matter of offense to the institution and its structure.[62] It is alleged that after it repudiated Montanist spirituality, Christianity never really recovered its spiritual balance.[63] If these evaluations and arguments are to be agreed upon, then it can be argued that the Montanists' reaction against formalism, nominalism, and hierarchical power abuse only succeeded in speeding and strengthening them, as well as strengthening older formal and structural trends. It seems that in thinking to make the church better, the Montanists made it worse. Despite this, there is evidence that reminds us that despite the church's rejection of *Pentecostal-charismatic* forms of spiritual experiences as the

---

57. Tillich, *History of Christian Thought*, 41.
58. Christenson, *Welcome Holy Spirit*, 297.
59. Hamilton, *Charismatic Movement*, 65.
60. Anderson, *Introduction to Pentecostalism*, 20.
61. Bouyer, *Some Charismatic Movements*, 114.
62. Moule, *Holy Spirit*, 2.
63. McDonnell, *Baptism in the Holy Spirit*, 44.

sole experience of the Montanists, tangible, genuine, and effective charismatic experience remained in the patristic period's church.

7.5. GENUINE CHARISMATIC EXPERIENCE IN THE PATRISTIC PERIOD CHURCH

Evaluations of the fate of the charismatic experiences in the church during the patristic period offer two main conclusions. First, they suggest that Montanists continued to thrive in different parts of the church and became stronger and stricter after their repudiation even after the death of Montanus. Despite the church's continued repudiations, says Hyatt, the Montanists continued to set up their own ecclesiastical structures and systems with their deacons and bishops, continued to thrive in various places to gain favorable acceptance, and continued to influence the wider church.[64] Despite suffering from severe continued persecution by the institutional church, the movement remained strong and survived until the sixth century, when its adherents were finally "exterminated under Justinian,"[65] and had a definite lasting influence on the church's doctrine of the Holy Spirit.[66] Second, evaluations indicate that despite the church's continued suppression of any tendency towards charismatic experience, there was an ongoing, genuine, and effective charismatic experience within the church of the patristic period. A few examples are presented here.

In the third century, Origen of Alexandria (ca. 185–254) viewed charismatic experiences as evidence of the validating power of Christ in worship and mission. In the first book of his *Against Celsus*, he comments on the apostolic experience of the multiple aspects of the Holy Spirit's manifestations, gifts, and power. He then attests that all those experiences were in evidence in the church of his time. He refers to the apostles' gospel proclamation, which was accompanied by signs and wonders, and which prevailed in easily attracting audiences. He then affirms that those gifts were preserved for the church's proclamation and were in evidence during his time. Origen also states that believers of his time were endowed with different gifts of the Holy Spirit: some "expel evil spirits," some "perform many cures," and some "foresee events to come." All do

---

64. Hyatt, *2000 Years*, 28.
65. Burgess, "The Holy Spirit, Doctrine of: The Ancient Fathers" in *Dictionary*, 419.
66. Thomas, *Holy Spirit*, 81.

this "according to the will of the Logos."⁶⁷ In book 2, Origen asserts that prophecies and miracles were occurring to a more remarkable extent than had been seen or reported previously.⁶⁸

In the fourth century, Hilary (ca. 291–371), in the second book of his *On the Trinity*, discusses Pauline accounts of the gifts of the Holy Spirit. He comments on the Trinitarian nature of the charismatic gifts and underlines the involvement of all three persons of the Trinity in the giving of such gifts. Yet he acknowledges that it is the Holy Spirit who both distributes the gifts and works through them. He discusses in great depth the purpose, function, power, and results of the gifts of the Holy Spirit and states that the gifts were being given to the church to "illuminate feeble minds and weak faith" in order to comprehend the mystery of the "incarnation and will of God." After extended discussion on the function, power and effects of the gifts, Hilary concludes, "I cannot conceive what doubt can remain, after so clear a definition of his origin, his action, and his powers." By "his origin, his action, and his power," Hilary seems to refer to the origin, power, and action of the Holy Spirit. He goes on to alert his readers that "unless appropriated" of the gifts of the Holy Spirit, the "soul of man will have the innate faculty of apprehending God" but remain "destitute of the light of knowledge." The gifts of the Holy Spirit, for Hilary, are the "light of our minds and the sun of our souls." In exhorting his audiences to seek and receive these gifts, Hilary considers that the gifts are "given to each according to the measure of his willingness to receive." He concludes by stating "the more earnest the desires to earn them, the richer are the stores of the Holy Spirit."⁶⁹ In book 8, Hilary discusses the Pauline accounts of the charismata. Once again asserting the purpose, function, power, and results of the charismata, he emphasizes that the gifts of the Holy Spirit are the "church's agents of ministry" and that "God has ordained them." In his admiration, Hilary says, "How truly is the manifestation of the Spirit seen in the bestowal of such useful gifts" and "how rare and hard to attain are such spiritual gifts!"⁷⁰

In the fifth century, Augustine of Hippo (ca. 354–430), observed an incredible number of charismatic experiences in the church. In *City of God*, book 22, he lists great numbers of miracles related to healing, exorcism and the raising of the dead. He affirms that the miraculous

---

67. Origen, *Against Celsus* 1.2.46.
68. Origen, *Against Celsus* 2.8.
69. Hilary, *On the Trinity* 2:33–35.
70. Hilary, *On the Trinity* 8:33–35.

works of God never ceased, even when the world largely believed in Christ and churches were built on a large scale. The world's continued belief in Christ, he observes, was not a result of the persuasion of human preachers but the result of divine power being manifested through different kinds of miracles. He declares that the churches of Carthage, Hippo, Calama, and Milan were some of the places recognized for miraculous charismata. He also names bishops, presbyters, and lay members, both men and women, who were recognized for leading prayers of healing. He states that the miracles were wrought most often in the name of Jesus, sometimes by prayer, sometimes through sacraments and at other times through the relics of the saints such as Stephen the martyr. He claims that some of the healing miracles occurred in his presence when he too was among those kneeling for prayers of healing. When more impressive miracles occurred in his absence, Augustine would call witnesses and hear testimony from the lips of those who attended the events. Expressing his motivation to leave written documents of the miraculous deeds of his days, he states, "For when I saw, in our own times, frequent signs of the presence of the divine powers similar to those which had been given of old, I desired that narratives might be written, judging that the multitude should not remain ignorant of these things."[71] He adds that the number of miracles had been so great that it was tedious to speak about them all. Regarding the multiplicity of the miraculous and his inability to record them all, he writes,

> What am I to do? I am so pressed by the promise of finishing this work, that I cannot record all the miracles I know; and doubtless several of our adherents, when they read what I have narrated, will regret that I have omitted so many which they, as well as I, certainly know.... I beg these persons to excuse me, and to consider how long it would take me to relate all those miracles, which the necessity of finishing the work I have undertaken forces me to omit.[72]

Augustine affirms that of the many miracles of which he had had close knowledge, a number were selected and published for public recitations. When he wrote this part of his work the number of published miracles amounted to seventy. He adds, "Even now ... many miracles are wrought, the same God who wrought we read of still performing

---

71. Augustine, *City of God* 22.8.
72. Augustine, *City of God* 22.8.

them, by whom he will and as he will." He concludes by stating that if all the miraculous phenomena of his days were collected and written down, "they would fill many volumes."[73]

7.6. SUMMARY

Given the above accounts and discussions, three points deserve to be identified and underlined at the conclusion of the chapter.

First, the accounts and discussions presented above are clear enough to tell us that the charismatic gifts were genuinely and effectively experienced in the church of the patristic period, despite the institutional church's resistance to them. As discussed in chapter 6, the church of the patristic period was influenced by different kinds of competing religious movements that emphasized charismatic spirituality in different forms. The defense against those movements led the church toward diminishing the tendency of the claim and practice of the presence, gifts, and workings of the Holy Spirit through the *Pentecostal-charismatic* form of worship and spiritual experience. Any kind of measure or mechanism to defend against those movements could have the potential to act as a mask to internally suppress charismatic tendencies. Added to the influence of those competing religious movements, the Montanist movement emerged in Asia Minor, Phrygia, in the second half of the second century. Despite the church's suppression of charismatic experiences as a measure of defending against those movements, as well as its rejection and repudiation of the Montanists' charismatic spirituality, the charismatic gifts and their genuine experience were in existence in the church during the patristic period. The records of reliable church fathers, from Irenaeus to Augustine, assure us that the gifts and works of the Holy Spirit did not depart from the church throughout the four hundred years of the patristic period. Charismatic experiences of the period may have been impacted by various institutional factors such as increasingly established traditions and norms that integrated secular social issues into the church. However, the cessation of the charismatic gifts and workings of the Holy Spirit in the church of the period is neither documented nor justifiable.

Second, the reason the church labeled the Montanist spiritual experience heretical remains somewhat ambiguous. In this regard, two features seem worthy of attention:

---

73. Augustine, *City of God* 22.8.

(1) It seems that the wider church of the time clearly observed something defective in the religious practice of the Montanists. Otherwise such prominent church fathers of the period as Eusebius, Cyril, Basil, Hippolytus, and Gregory may not have engaged in such a bitter criticism of both the person of Montanus and of the movement as a whole and deemed them heretical. The writings these church fathers, however, appear to be lacking in convincing evidence of the fundamental heretical characteristics of the Montanists on theological, doctrinal, and canonical grounds. Most of the features they attributed to both the person Montanus and the movement as a whole appear to be simply ordinary ethical issues. For example, practices which Eusebius lists such as frenzy, ecstasy, babbling, and prophesying in a strange manner may not be sufficient grounds to label the movement "heretical." These are normal worship experiences, though sometimes viewed as exaggerated, enthusiastic, and emotional. Similarly, Hippolytus writes that the Montanists were blamed for introducing the novelties of fasts, feasts, and meals of parched foods against the church, for magnifying Priscilla and Maximilla more than the apostles, and for not heeding those who were viewed as competent to decide. If these features were the only perceived weaknesses of the Montanists, then these features cannot by any means be considered basic theological, doctrinal, or canonical rationale for the church's labeling of the movement as heretical. Nor can such experiences send a shock wave through the church to the extent that it should label the movement heretical and eventually repudiate it. Cyril and Basil, on the other hand, reported something of a shock. Cyril writes that Montanus "dared to say that he was himself the Holy Ghost." Basil writes that the Montanists "applied the title of the Paraclete to Montanus and Priscilla." If this was genuinely the case, then this could have been clearly identified and addressed by the church fathers, consulted here, unanimously. In contrast to Cyril's and Basil's point, there is evidence from the patristic period which indicates that Montanus claimed to be inspired by the Holy Spirit in a "peculiar way" and began to prophesy.[74]

When observed from these differing accounts, it seems that there were no objectively examined, clearly identified, and commonly agreed-upon heretical features of the Montanist movement. Most of the features these accounts attribute to the person Montanus and the movement as a whole are simply ordinary ethical issues, disparaging words, and

---

74. *Seven Ecumenical Councils*, 186.

criticism. None of them has identified and addressed which of the Montanists' teaching or practice could be considered heretical and on what grounds. From a genuine Christian perspective, therefore, it seems that no convincing heretical characteristic of the Montanists has been identified and addressed in the accounts of the church fathers consulted above. Hence, it seems to remain a bizarre mystery regarding where to place the theological, doctrinal, canonical, or logical grounds for the church's rejection of the Montanists as heretical. One might simply agree with scholars who argue that although they did not find tangible and convincing fault in the content of Montanist spiritual practices, bishops of the institutional church simply accused them of delivering their prophecies in a "frenzy and ecstatic"[75] way and that they became "chief antagonists" of the movement.[76]

(2) The historical accounts consulted here indicate that any historical evidence left behind from the beliefs, claims, and experiences of the Montanists, is known only through the institutional church, which was, of course, the "ecclesiastical enemy" of the movement.[77] Although documentaries on Montanist prophecies are thought to have been compiled, including Tertullian's seven books on ecstatic prophecy, these sources were sought out and destroyed by the church authorities following its repudiation of the movement.[78] Affirming this supposition, Hippolytus reports that Montanists had an "infinite number of books" of which the "majority" were viewed as "silly" and "overrun with delusion" and that believers of the wider church were instructed not to give attention to the Montanist writings.[79] If this was the case, then it would be difficult to draw an accurate conclusion regarding who is right and who is wrong in this conflict. If they had been preserved Tertullian's writings, in particular, might indeed have been written from a balanced point of view and could have been used as a reliable source to identify the rights and wrongs of the teachings and practices of the Montanists. However, his writings also were sought out and destroyed by the opponents of the movement. It could, therefore, be argued that if the church hierarchies of the time had honestly found the Montanists to be running in the wrong direction of Christian belief, teaching, and practice they could have identified and

75. Hyatt, *2000 Years*, 26.
76. McDonnell and Montague, *Christian Initiation*, 168.
77. Allen, *Unfailing Stream*, 20; and cf. p. 46.
78. Burgess, "The Holy Spirit, Doctrine of: The Ancient Fathers" in *Dictionary*, 419.
79. Hippolytus, *Refutation of All Heresies* 8.12.

recorded the heretical profile of the movement instead of simply reinforcing that everything about the movement was heretical. Hence, there seems no clear evidence of a theological, doctrinal, or canonical basis for the church's labelling of the movement as heretical and the eventual rejection of it. This perhaps demonstrates that the church leadership of the time was effective at voting collectively to protect its own power and prestige but signally poor at discerning between genuine objective facts, mere pretension, or even heretical teachings of the movement and to account it.

Third, we have noted that the church of the post-apostolic period had drawn a clear demarcation between the *leadership-administration* and *Pentecostal-charismatic* nature and functions of the church. This division created a concept of *two distinct Christian views* on the doctrine of the Holy Spirit. Our discussion in the current chapter has attempted to make it clear that this concept became evident when the church experienced intense tension caused by the Montanist movement. Given this, it can be justifiably concluded that tensions between the institutional-organizational and Pentecostal-charismatic forms of the church's life and function formally began with the church's response to the Montanist movement. This became the time when the church took the first and most extreme formal measure to push aside the experience of the gifts and workings of the Holy Spirit through the *Pentecostal-charismatic* form of worship and spiritual experience. The two contradicting and conflicting views of the doctrine of the Holy Spirit, of the institutional church and charismatic groups, formally took root in this historical event. Consequently, this historical event became the *major root cause* of tensions in relation to the Spirit-charismata within the doctrine of the Holy Spirit in the history of the church.

From this time on, the institutional church has continued to emphasize the Holy Spirit as an objective gift of God to believers, given in sacramental baptism, and doctrinal belief of the Holy Spirit as an object of faith. It continued to view subjective experience of the Holy Spirit as a threat to the church and has thus avoided it. Consequently, the institutional church has limited itself to structured and fixed worship experiences and rejected claims of fresh reception, gifting, empowering, and workings of the Holy Spirit. Traditionally, therefore, the institutional church has been understood and defined as the "established, organized and stabled form of the church with definite and defined structures and orders"[80] which emphasizes "organization at the expense of the life and freedom of the Spirit."[81] For this reason, the institutional church was identified with the routinization of certain structured and formalized patterns of worship practice, which lack fresh charismatic vitality.[82] Hence, it has been viewed as "objectivist" or "objectivism" as opposed to "subjectivism" and its objectivism is understood to be found in "sacramentalism, creedalism, and ecclesiasticalism, in which the confession of faith and the church is made the final criterion for life and thought."[83] Thus, the institutional church has continued to maintain orthodox faith in the finished and closed revelation and with an imbalance between its *leadership-administration* and *Pentecostal-charismatic* nature, life, and functions.

Charismatic groups or individuals have also continued to experience the gifts and workings of the Holy Spirit as a periphery experience and have continued to emerge from time to time, often in the shadows. In virtue of its emphasis on the subjective experience of the Holy Spirit, the charismatic group has traditionally been viewed as "subjectivist" or "subjectivism" as opposed to "objectivism,"[84] referred to as a "subjectivist face of Christianity" and viewed as the "threat to the institutional objectivity."[85] Thus, as Kärkkäinen insightfully observes, to repeat what we have already said, since the repudiation of the Montanist movement tensions between "Spirit/Charisma" and "institution" wherein "charisma versus institution" have become "one of the perennial problems of Christianity."[86] Since the institutional church, which has held the entire authority and power of the life and ministry of the church, has continued to avoid the charismatic form of spirituality beginning in that historical event, Kärkkäinen's observation seems surely right and valid. Maintaining this tradition, the church hierarchies of every century have left an impact on their successors with their rejectionist convictions and views on the charismatic experience, as well as the subjective experience of the Holy Spirit. However, the church's repudiation of the Montanist spiritual

---

80. Berkhof, *Doctrine of the Holy Spirit*, 60.
81. Hyatt, *2000 Years*, 24.
82. O'Brein, *Corpus Dictionary*, 402.
83. Bloesch, *Theology of Word*, 131.
84. Bloesch, *Theology of Word and Spirit*, 131. See also Kärkkäinen, *Toward a Pneumatological Theology*, 11, 13, 30.
85. Berkhof, *Doctrine of the Holy Spirit*, 24.
86. Kärkkäinen, *Toward a Pneumatological Theology*, 111–12.

experience and continued avoidance of the charismatic experience does not necessarily mean refuting the source of charismatic gifts or discarding the *Pentecostal-charismatic* nature and content of Christianity. As long as God and God alone is its possessor and dispenser, it was in existence, it is in existence, and it will be in existence acting fully in God's plan and initiation only when and where God wants and wills. Thus, with these two contradicting and conflicting views of the presence, gifts, and workings of the Holy Spirit, the church moved from the patristic period to the medieval period. To this, we will now turn our examination.

CHAPTER 8

Medieval Western Church's Teaching and Practice

WE HAVE SEEN THAT beginning with the second council's formulation of the church's doctrine of the Holy Spirit, the Holy Spirit became part of the confessional statement of the church. The confessions held only doctrinal belief of the Holy Spirit as "the Lord . . . Giver of Life" and "worthy of worship" that is rendered to the Father and Son and did not consider the gifts and workings of the Holy Spirit in and through subjective experience as a significant practice of the church. Accordingly, the church of successive centuries continued to maintain the doctrinal belief of the Holy Spirit through these confessions and did not consider a need to integrate the subjective experience of the Holy Spirit in its faith practice. When the church moved from the patristic period to the medieval period, we find some evidence that suggests the medieval period was viewed as a period of "long drought" in the history of the church.[1] The term "long drought" seems to refer to the complete absence of subjective experience of the Holy Spirit in which the church may practice a Spirit-gifted, Spirit-empowered, Spirit-inspired, and Spirit-initiated charismatic form of spirituality due to the domination of the "growing institutionalization" and "spiritual decline" of the church of the time.[2] If this is so, it may lead us to ask: how and why did the charismatic form of spirituality disappear from the medieval church's life and function to the extent that the period

---

1. Allen, *Unfailing Stream*, 32.
2. Poewe, *Charismatic Christianity*, 124, 126.

was perceived to be a "long drought"? There seem to be three pointers that lead us on the path to finding possible answers to this question.

Firstly, when viewed through the window of the historical accounts and discussions in chapters 5, 6, and 7, the church of the medieval period had three obvious theological and historical reasons for avoiding charismatic forms of religious experiences: continued emphasis on the authority of the ordained leadership; maintaining and preserving the patristic church's repudiation of the Montanist movement; and the church's adherence to the second council's doctrine of the Holy Spirit, which promoted doctrinal belief and ignored subjective experience. Secondly, some accounts suggest that the Western church of the medieval period intentionally neglected the place and role of the Holy Spirit in "liturgy, spirituality, creedal statements, and theology."[3] Evidence indicates that the medieval Western church not only neglected the gifts and works of the Holy Spirit but also adopted substitutes by which it replaced the place and role of the Holy Spirit in the church. For example, it's alleged that the medieval Western church "replaced the Holy Spirit and let him be overshadowed by the pope, the Virgin Mary, and the cult of the Blessed Sacrament."[4] Thirdly, the medieval Western church also attributed all the Christian ministry charismata to the sacred images or icons of the saints, through which believers expected to receive the gifts, power, and works of the Holy Spirit.[5]

This evidence, then, leads us to also question how the place and role of the Holy Spirit came to be substituted by the pope, Mary, the cult of sacraments, and sacred images or icons of saints. This chapter will examine possible reasons for this. The chapter will briefly examine such major features as: (1) How the place and role of the Holy Spirit in Christian belief, teaching, and practice was replaced by the papacy, Mary, and sacred images or icons of saints. (2) Whether the church of the medieval period completely excluded the teaching and practice of the Holy Spirit in its faith practices. (3) Whether the gifts and workings of the Holy Spirit completely disappeared from the church's life and ministry. (4) What the overall nature of the belief, teaching, and practice of the church of the period looked like. In this respect, there are two things worthy of attention, i.e., hereafter our examination will not consider the issue of the cult of the Eucharistic sacraments but will focus on other features mentioned

3. Dreyer, *Holy Power*, 13.
4. Congar, *I Believe*, 1:160.
5. Davis, *First Seven Ecumenical Councils*, 290–95.

above, and it will focus only on the Western church's belief, teaching, and practice of the Holy Spirit.

8.1. HOW THE PAPACY, MARY, AND SACRED IMAGES SUBSTITUTED THE GIFTS AND WORKS OF THE HOLY SPIRIT IN MEDIEVAL WESTERN CHURCH

How the Papacy substituted the gifts and works of the Holy Spirit

To understand how the papacy substituted the Holy Spirit, his gifts, and works in the medieval Western church, it is important to first briefly examine the rise of the papacy. Allen, for instance, suggests that the notion of establishing the papacy in authority as Peter's successor began in about AD 254. Meanwhile, in reference to Peter's presumed ministry as the first bishop of Rome, the primacy of Rome also became established. Allen states that the notion of establishing the papacy continued to be strengthened when Stephen, the bishop of Rome, settled the dispute between himself and Cyprian, the bishop of Carthage, concerning the efficacy of sacraments. From then on, says Allen, Stephen began to claim that he sat in Peter's chair in Rome, with Peter's key of divinely endowed authority. Therefore, he, Stephen, alone should attain and exercise supreme authority over all important matters of the church. In addition to this, continues Allen, Emperor Constantine's unreserved favor for Christianity included the "giving of one of the imperial palaces to the pope" and "extensive lands in central Italy." Following his favor, notes Allen, the "Bishop of Rome . . . lived in the palace . . . both as symbolic and prophetic." From then on the "Pope came increasingly to be regarded as the Head of the Church" on earth. Even when Constantine built a new capital in the East, as Allen observes, the "position and prestige of the See of Rome were greatly enhanced in the West."[6] Allen's evaluation provides us with some insight into how Rome's claim to be the chief of the universal church and the papacy's claim of absolute authority over the church began and how it continued to be enhanced in the medieval Church. Elaborating on Allen's suggestion, Cairns suggests that the tradition of the apostolic succession of the bishop of Rome and the "primacy of the Roman See" was officially recognized by the second council at Constantinople in 381. The second council's official recognition of the supremacy of the bishop of Rome, as

---

6. Allen, *Unfailing Stream*, 33–34.

Cairns notes, provided the bishop of Rome with the opportunity to be regarded as a "supreme court on all spiritual and ecclesiastical affairs" and what he decreed continued to be regarded as the "law for all."[7]

Cairns goes on to describe how the designation of the papacy had begun with Leo I, bishop of Rome from 440 to 461, who often used the title *"papas"* from which the word "pope" was derived. He states that Leo I declared that any appeal from the "church courts of bishops" on any ecclesiastical issue should be brought to him, that what he decided should be regarded as the final decision, and that other bishops should not look for any court to appeal beyond his court. By that declaration, says Cairns, Leo I paved the way for the future designation of the papacy, even though he was not entitled "pope." The first bishop to be entitled "pope," according to Cairns, was Gelasius I who was enthroned from 492 to 496. To support this, Cairns cites this statement from the document he claims was written by Gelasius I in 492: "God gave both sacred and royal power to the pope and the king. Because the pope had to account to God for the king at the judgment, the sacred power of the pope was more important than the royal power" and rulers should "submit to the pope."[8] Cairns adds that the consecration of Gregory I as bishop of Rome in 590 "ushered in a new era of power for the church in the West."[9] Cairns considers this event a "landmark" in the transition of the church's history from ancient to medieval. He concludes that Gregory I "made the church power in politics" and laid a foundation for the "sacramental hierarchical system of the institutionalized church of the Medieval Ages." These trends became known as the symbol of the church's institutional cultures dominated by popes.[10]

Similarly, Gunther Gassmann and Scott Hendrix suggest that the local and national councils of the medieval Western church also promoted absolute authority and infallibility of the pope and of his decrees. Those councils promoted rulings that required the laity's absolute submission to the papacy, and those rulings and papal decrees gradually became part of the church's body of law and formed part of the church's law called "canon law."[11] In this way, says Christenson, the Western church continued to stand "under the standard of the papacy's universal rule" and the

---

7. Cairns, *Christianity Through the Centuries*, 151.
8. Cairns, *Christianity Through the Centuries*, 152.
9. Cairns, *Christianity Through the Centuries*, 159.
10. Cairns, *Christianity Through the Centuries*, 162–63.
11. Gassmann and Hendrix, *Fortress Introduction*, 48.

papacy for its part continued to claim and enjoy absolute power and the "highest respect as possessor of supreme authority." Consequently, the pope was believed to establish "infallible" and "unalterable rules of faith" and the canon laws issued by the pope were regarded as "divine law." Thereby, concludes Christenson, all charismatic gifts and workings of the Holy Spirit were attributed to the pope, and charisms of the Spirit were "eclipsed" by "canon laws" and the authority of the pope.[12] Tillich affirms these observations by stating that in the medieval Western church, the "freedom of the Spirit was limited by canon law," that the church insisted on applying only the "Christocentric criterion to all Christian piety," and that the application of this criterion was regarded as a particular "prerogative of the pope as the vicar of Christ."[13] More detailed accounts of the place and role of the papacy are offered by Congar.

In his book *I Believe in the Holy Spirit*, Congar presents some examples of how the Western church substituted the place and role of the Holy Spirit with other features. In volume 1, under subtopics entitled "Forgetting the Holy Spirit" and "Substitutes for the Holy Spirit," Congar cites evidence from primary sources, which in turn were cited from the medieval church's confessional statements, that indicate the Western church's excessive devotion to the "Eucharist, the Pope and the Virgin Mary" to the extent that these substituted the place of and obscured the role of the Holy Spirit:

> There are three sanctuaries: the crib, the tabernacle, and the Vatican. There are three (he says "a word is missing here"): "God, Jesus Christ, and the Pope. [There are] three incarnations of our Lord—in Mary's womb, in the Eucharist, and in the Pope. There are three main gifts that God has given us [Catholic believers]: the Pope, the most holy Virgin and the Eucharistic sacrifice.[14]

> The Catholic church is one with a unity that is visible and perfect throughout the whole world and among all peoples, with a unity, the beginning, the root and the indefectible source of which is the supreme authority and the "excellent principality" of blessed Peter, the prince of the apostles and of his successors in the Roman throne.[15]

---

12. Christenson, *Welcome Holy Spirit*, 297.
13. Tillich, *Systematic Theology*, 3:149.
14. Congar, *I Believe*, 1:61.
15. Congar, *I Believe*, 1:162.

> Together with those sacred sources (Scripture and tradition), God has given to his church a living magisterium to throw light on and explain those matters that are contained in the deposit of faith only in an obscure and so to speak implicit manner.[16]

> The one who made the church unique also made it one ... one body one spirit ... For this reason, Jesus Christ established in the church a living authentic and permanent magisterium that he provided with his own power and instructed with the spirit of truth.[17]

Congar expresses his admiration at how excessive devotion was made to the popes to the extent that it "borders on idolatry."[18] He asserts that the Pope, Mary, and the Eucharist were regarded as the best links by which the church was established, maintained, and in living communion with God. These features, Congar concludes, substituted the place and role of the Holy Spirit in the church's life and function.[19] Congar's account seems to clearly indicate how the medieval Western church developed confessional statements that intentionally excluded the Holy Spirit from its structure, life, and ministry. If this was indeed the case, then the church not only set aside the intention of subjective experience but also the objective creedal belief in the Holy Spirit itself seems to be impossibly remote from the church's thoughts and practices.

Hendrikus Berkhof sheds further light on this when he suggests that it was believed that bishops were instituted by the Holy Spirit with the authority to forgive sins and that the Holy Spirit "works in the inferior members of the church through the ministry of the superior ones." Any practice individual believers intend to engage in with the Holy Spirit was "swallowed up by their relation to the ecclesiastical institution." Accordingly, says Berkhof, any strong stress on the deeper spiritual experience was viewed as a "detriment to the church's hierarchical structure." Berkhof continues to describe that it was believed and taught that the primary work of the Holy Spirit is the "creation and preservation of sacramental and hierarchical structure and that an individual believer is fully dependent on that structure for his/her participation in the works of the Holy Spirit." The Holy Spirit, Berkhof notes, was perceived and presented only

---

16. Congar, *I Believe*, 1:162.
17. Congar, *I Believe*, 1:162.
18. Congar, *I Believe*, 1:163.
19. Congar, *I Believe*, 1:160–61.

as a hidden worker in the church while the church hierarchies were presented as the visible workers and rulers of the church. These two means were regarded as the "means by and through which Christ is active in the church."[20] In this way, all the Christian ministry charismata were localized in the office of the bishop and were "identified in a new way with the institutional life" of the church and thus "no longer is there tension between institution and charism."[21] Tracing these and similar notions, say Duquoc and Floristan, the papacy of the period built itself into absolute power to such an extent that no secular or religious power could shake it and all the power and rights of the church ministry were preserved for itself so as to interpret and apply all the ecclesiastical affairs from its own point of view. Such prestigious authoritarian hierarchy continued to treat the charismatic experiences as a threat to the institution.[22]

Thus, the medieval Western church's ignorance of the presence, gifts, and works of the Holy Spirit is attributed to the rise of successive bureaucratic hierarchies that pushed out charismatically gifted people from the church in the interest of maintaining formalistic structures and their own power.[23] Consequently, the gifts and works of the Holy Spirit became obscured by the institutional structures, sacramental practice, leadership, and pastoral offices.[24] Furthermore, the accounts cited here clearly indicate how the papacy held all the ecclesiastical power and rights. Hence, it can be assumed that such a privileged papacy could interpret and rule over all the ecclesiastical affairs from their own perspective and with their interests in mind. Accordingly, the church of the time was led in a direction that maintained and preserved the power and authority of human hierarchies and treated the charismatic form of spirituality as a threat to the institution. Indeed this should come as no surprise at least for two reasons: firstly, this position of the church, as discussed in chapter 5, was an extension and preservation of the constitutional tradition of the postapostolic church, which encouraged the ordained leadership to claim and exercise unparalleled authority on earth. Secondly, it was a formally established means to suppress the charismatic voice that may arise within the church and criticize the ordained leadership for power abuse and corruption. Hence, it would seem that the life and function of the medieval

20. Berkhof, *Doctrine of Holy Spirit*, 43–44.
21. McDonnell and Montague, *Christian Initiation*, 256.
22. Duquoc and Floristan, *Charisms in the Church*, 5–6.
23. Deer, *Surprised By the Power*, 78.
24. Anderson, *Shape of Practical Theology*, 320.

Western church reverted back to the Jewish Pharisaic tradition which was dominated by the prestige and interests of individual hypocritical hierarchies (Matt 23; Luke 11:37–52).

How Mary substituted the gifts and works of the Holy Spirit

Historical evaluations indicate that among the many notable features adopted by the medieval Western church's practice was the cult of Mary. For example, Cairns describes that the veneration of Mary began to acquire special attention in the patristic period and spread rapidly. He presents some features that contributed to this: (1) Certain patterns of interpretation of the Scriptures and the mass of miracles that were associated with Mary in the apocryphal gospels created a greater reverence for Mary. (2) Church fathers such as Tertullian, Jerome, and Augustine attributed veneration to Mary and ascribed perpetual veneration to her. (3) Based on the declaration of the Council at Ephesus, what at first was mere "acknowledgment of her as the mother of Christ, was soon turned into a belief in her intercessory power." Accordingly, notes Cairns, in the middle of the fifth century Mary was placed almost at the "head of all other saints" and various kinds of festivals associated with her veneration began to spring up. For example, says Cairns, in the sixth century Emperor Justinian asked for Mary's intercession on behalf of his empire. Such conviction was expanded among other Christian emperors and largely contributed to giving Mary a "unique position in the worship." Consequently, concludes Cairns, Mary was given a unique position in the worship and liturgical structures of the medieval church.[25] Burgess suggests that since the Council of Ephesus in 431, the status of Mary was conceived differently, because the Council declared Mary to be "bearer of God," *Theotokos*, instead of "bearer of the human Jesus," *Christotokos*. Following the declaration of the Council at Ephesus, the place and role of the Holy Spirit in the church were gradually replaced by Mary in medieval popular piety. Burgess asserts that only in the Eastern church did the Holy Spirit remain an "object of piety" but was never to be regarded as important for Christian piety in the Western church.[26]

Strengthening these assertions, Tixeront suggests that following the Ephesus Council's definition of Mary's status, her divine maternity was

25. Cairns, *Christianity Through the Centuries*, 153–54.
26. Burgess, "Holy Spirit" in *Encyclopaedia*, 244.

used as a "password to the extension of her veneration." The conviction and advocacy of her perfection from hereditary sin and her retention of stainless virginity have continued to prevail. Since the Ephesus Council Mary was "exalted above the apostles and the angels and believed to be a mediator between heaven and earth." Consequently, says Tixernot, churches, chapels, and different buildings were erected in her memory and her name. Feasts in her honor such as the annunciation, conception, and nativity were identified, fixed on certain dates and named after her. Hymns continued to be composed and sung in her memory and for her glory. Amidst all these, says Tixeront, the concept that the "earth no longer holds the body of the blessed virgin" emerged and spread. This, along with the concept of her "perpetual virginity," held a special attraction for the public and "added value to her veneration." Thus, she was regarded as a "holy creature" and attributed due submission.[27]

The nature of the belief regarding the special deep bond that existed between Mary and the Holy Spirit is recounted more precisely by Congar. He states that Mary was regarded as the first recipient of God's grace to bring Christ to the world through the operation of the Holy Spirit. He quotes this from the primary source of the time: "All grace that is communicated to this world comes to us by a threefold movement" and is "dispensed according to a very perfect order from God in Christ; from Christ in the Virgin, and from the Virgin in [believers]."[28] This happens, notes Congar, due to the belief that Mary has a certain "authority over the procession of the Holy Spirit" to the extent that no creature has ever received the grace of any virtue from God. He states that it was believed that "there is a deep relationship between Mary and the Holy Spirit" which derives from the mystery of salvation which is connected to the "operation of the Holy Spirit during the course of the conception of Jesus in Mary's womb." Accordingly, says Congar, she was viewed as the first to be given a place and to be associated with God's action in the Spirit as well as being regarded as the "soul of the church" which, according to the gospels, is the title applied to the Holy Spirit (John 6:63). As a result of this belief, concludes Congar, Mary has been attributed the titles and functions of comforter, advocate, and defender of believers and given a role that should belong to the Holy Spirit.[29] Evaluations also indicate

27. Tixeront. *History of Dogmas*, 3:255-57. See also his *History of Dogmas*, 2:192-93; cf. pp. 2:330-31.

28. Congar, *I Believe*, 1:163-64.

29. Congar, *I Believe*, 1:163-64.

that not only in the medieval period but also at present time there are many Catholics, even among elite theologians, who believe and declare that Mary gives to them the gifts of the Holy Spirit such as speaking in tongues.[30] It was believed that the best way to achieve unity with the Holy Spirit and to benefit from his gifts and works is unity with Mary.[31] Thus, every place and role attributed to the Holy Spirit by Protestants has been attributed, by Catholics, to Mary.[32] From this evidence, it can be noted that Mary, who was indeed significant as an object of divine grace and power by being chosen as the vessel for the incarnation, was later given extraordinary theological and spiritual significance by the church beginning in the patristic period and continuing to the present. While every role she played in the incarnation and salvation process can be neither denied nor refuted, what was attributed to her by the medieval Western church seems to be remote from Christian theology, doctrine, and the canonical core messages of salvation.

How the sacred images/icons substituted the gifts and works of the Holy Spirit

Evaluations indicate that the medieval church also attributed the place and role of the Holy Spirit to sacred images. Tixeront, for instance, describes how the use of sacred images was well established in almost all the churches of the first three centuries. He states that images of Mary, Jesus, the Cross of Jesus, and the apostles Peter and Paul were specially recognized as part of the church's religious practice and their veneration became universal in the fourth and fifth centuries.[33] Tixeront describes that it was believed and advocated that when the image of the cross was presented and adored at public events, it was accompanied by miraculous manifestations. On account of this belief, the concept of regarding the images of the cross and Mary as not made by human hands but "of miraculous origin as gifts of God" was adopted and grew in popularity. Above all else, notes Tixeront, an image of Jesus was believed to have been sent directly by Jesus himself to Abgar, king of Edessa, and that the image saved the city of Edessa from the "attacks of Chosroes." The popularity

30. MacArthur, *Charismatic Chaos*, 17.
31. Clement, *Pentecost or Pretense?*, 15; cf. pp. 123–24.
32. Congar, *I Believe*, 1:64.
33. Tixeront, *History of Dogmas*, 3:427–28.

of this event gave further impetus to the veneration of the sacred images and increased their use in Christian spiritual practices. Because of the alleged event in Edessa, says Tixeront, the image of Jesus became established in the written doctrine of the church. Thereby fixing images in the churches and on the walls of homes, kissing them, prostrating before them, and expecting supernatural miraculous phenomena through them became part of the fervent religious experience of the medieval Western church. Tixeront cites this statement from an early medieval document that indicates how Christians of the time emphasized veneration of the images: "Whoever fears God, therefore, honours, venerates, and adores Christ... and the representation of his cross and the image of his saints." On account of this belief, concludes Tixeront, believers were encouraged to owe, venerate, and pray to his/her own "guardian angel" through the sacred images. Thus, "superstitious tendencies" emerged and developed in the church.[34]

John of Damascus (ca. 674–749) reported a clear example of how the medieval church emphasized the worship of the image of the Cross by stating that an image of the Cross was regarded as the "shield and weapon against and trophy over the devil." Describing the church's justification of the reason why an image of the cross was to be worshiped, John states that it is the "resurrection of those lying in death... support of the standing... staff of the weak... road of the Flock... safe conduct of the earnest... perfection of those that press forwards... salvation of soul and body... aversion of all things evil... patron of all things good... taking away of sin... plant of resurrection and the tree of eternal life."[35] John asserts that although made up of a tree, the image of the cross, on which Jesus has offered himself as a sacrifice for the sake of the world, is sanctified by contact with the body and blood of Christ. Therefore, says John, "we worship the image of the precious and life-giving Cross" because by worshipping the image of the cross "we are not worshiping and honouring the tree but the One who is imaged and typified in it." To worship a visible image of the cross of Christ, in John's view, means

---

34. Tixeront, *History of Dogmas*, 3:257; cf. pp. 3:432–37. Martin Luther the reformer claimed to have read the story of an Edessa event. He claimed to have noted that the city of Edessa was besieged by powerful Persian king. Considering that the city could not hold out that war alone, the bishop of Edessa prayed to God, made the sign of the cross, and went to the war with the cross. Luther noted that "God sent a wonderful host of great flies and gnats, which filled the enemy's horses' eyes, and dispersed the whole army." See Luther, *Luther's Table Talk*, 65.

35. John of Damascus, *Exposition of the Orthodox Faith*, 80.

to "worship Christ himself" because wherever the sign of the cross is, there also will Christ be. Worshiping the image of the cross, therefore, does not mean worshiping the material of which the image of the cross is made, but it is worshiping Christ whose suffering and sacrificial death are symbolized by the visible image of the cross.[36]

Davis provides a further detailed account of how sacred images were worshiped and how the gifts and works of the Holy Spirit were attributed to and expected through the images. Seven features, out of many, can be identified from Davis's account concerning the presumed significance of the sacred images and are summarized below (with some emphasis added.

- **Memorial significance:** The images reminded the practitioners about the Christian values of the figured persons or items.

- **Devotional significance:** The images were believed to draw the attention of the worshiper and direct him/her to look beyond what is visible. The worshiper can contemplate the transcendent, invisible God, his power, and his action through the given sacred image. The invisible power and act are manifested in the visible image—the image that ensures the imminence of the invisible reality. When the worshipers burn incense and bow down before the images, the images incite, inspire, and animate their worship atmosphere and create an incitement for spiritual nurture and nourishment.

- **Didactic significance:** The images were believed to bear impressive and attractive qualities so that they could easily depict the reality of the supernatural power of the figure they represent. Therefore, they were regarded as the means or instruments of illustrative and elaborative instruction.

- **Doctrinal significance:** The images were considered to depict the mystery and doctrine of God's love revealed in the incarnation, crucifixion, and aims and objectives of Christ's suffering on the cross. Accordingly, they were regarded as an integral part of the church's fundamental doctrine of God.

- **Charismatic significance:** The images of the cross and Mary, in particular, were placed on the sick. They were believed to cure the sick, exorcise demonic spirits, and perform miracles. It was alleged, for example, that when Mary's image was put on a dry water well

---

36. John of Damascus, *Exposition of the Orthodox Faith*, 80, 88.

and prayed for, the well instantly streamed water. Such phenomena raised the confidence of the practitioners in the images.

- **Economic significance:** The practitioners would carry images of the cross and Mary and move around the villages and towns to raise funds—begging in the name of Jesus and Mary. It was believed that people were touched and moved by the figures they saw in the image and offered money in far greater amounts than they would otherwise have done.

- **Defensive significance:** Images of the cross and Mary were believed to bear special power and were believed to be able to protect people during times of anxiety or to protect nations during war or similar national calamity. Accordingly, they were carried before the military and before kings during times of national war just as the Ark of the Covenant was carried into battle by the Israelites.

Davis further asserts that such beliefs and practices significantly raised the theological, spiritual, social, economic, and political meaning and value of the sacred images. He adds that even Gregory the Great considered the images as a signal "means of leading the illiterate to the knowledge of the truths of faith." Therefore, the images were regarded as "links to the realities of the spiritual world offering them help and protection." Accordingly, images became "objects of private devotions." Thus, the Holy Spirit, dwelling in the real figure of the image, overshadows his/her image and incarnates miraculous power and deeds.[37] MacCulloch strengthens these accounts by saying that it was believed that whenever people wanted to communicate with God or felt that God was calling or talking to them, they could easily "reach God through icons" and that such belief became both "the salvation and the strength of icons."[38]

These accounts provide us with a window to see how the practice of sacred images gradually evolved from mere images to sacramental status. It can be noted from the Scriptures that it was God who primarily introduced the concept of making visible images of invisible transcendent beings. For example, firstly, while God is invisible and transcendent, he created visible humans in his image and after his likeness (Gen 1:26). In this process God is the prototype, who is imaged in a structured and

---

37. Davis, *First Seven Ecumenical Councils*, 290–300.
38. MacCulloch, *History of Christianity*, 442, 445.

visible personality in humankind and the human is the derivative that is obtained. Secondly, God instructed Moses to make visible images of invisible heavenly creatures such as cherubim exactly like the pattern of the creature he showed him on the mountain and to put them in and around the tabernacle—the early Old Testament worship place (Exod 25:9, 18, 40; 26:30–31). In light of these biblical references, it may be assumed that God may work through any possible external means to communicate with his people whenever and wherever he wants and wills. Yet, God did not instruct Moses that those images should be considered as elements of an object lesson for the worshipers. However, as can be seen from the New Testament and the history of the early church, as discussed in chapters 1 to 4, God can come closer, gift, empower, and work through the Holy Spirit in ways far beyond such ordinary visible and tangible physical items. Oddly enough, the medieval Western church shifted its entire attention to these physical items while neglecting the actual presence, gifts, power, and workings of the Holy Spirit. Thus, the only factor the medieval Western church did discuss about the Holy Spirit was the issue of double procession through the doctrine of *filioque*—the doctrine that the Holy Spirit proceeds from both the Father and the Son.

8.2. THE WESTERN CHURCH'S ADOPTION OF THE DOCTRINE OF *FILIOQUE*

Evaluations of the aftermath of the second council's formulation of the doctrine of the Holy Spirit suggest that the formulation did not adequately settle the controversies about the relationship between the Son and the Holy Spirit. It was, therefore, followed by different critiques and accusations against the council for imposing on the church a pneumatic concept that appears not to be well substantiated by Scripture. Berkhof for example, identifies three features on which critics of the council based their points. Firstly, that the consubstantiality of the Holy Spirit with the Father was not clearly defined. Secondly, the relation of the Holy Spirit to the other two persons was not clearly defined. Thirdly, the phrase "who proceeds from the Father" neither affirms nor denies his procession from the Son. For such critics, as Berkhof notes, the second council's formulation of the doctrine of the Holy Spirit creates a clear gap between the essence and the equality of the Father and Son. It was to refute such continuous critiques that the third council, held at Toledo in 589, added the controversial doctrine *filioque* clause to the creed and led to the Western church's insistence on the doctrine of the double procession of the Holy Spirit.[39] Similarly, Burgess states that as the issue of the relationship between the Son and the Holy Spirit was left unresolved at the second council, controversies continued to emerge from different groups such as Arians and Priscillians, and continued to challenge the church. To address such challenges, the Western church developed what came to be known as the *filioque* doctrine, which in Latin means "and the Son" and through which the church continued to strengthen its position of the double procession of the Holy Spirit.[40]

Congar elaborates on this in his discussion of how the Priscillians emerged at the end of the fourth century, with a view that combined the persons of the Trinity in the single person of God, and Arians emerged at the beginning of the fifth century with their view that regarded the Holy Spirit as a creature. Congar describes how these two heresies continued to challenge the church's Trinitarian doctrine and how the regional and national councils of the Western church responded to these heresies by developing faith statements that asserted the concept of *filioque*. The concept of *filioque*, says Congar, was strengthened by the council of Toledo in 589, which declared that the Holy Spirit proceeds from the Father and the Son and that he is of the same substance as them. The council further affirmed the "consubstantiality of the Spirit with the Father and the Son" and thus denounced both heresies.[41] Hence, the conviction that the Holy Spirit proceeds from the Father *and the Son* was given the status of doctrinal definition through insertion into the creed. Throughout the subsequent five hundred years, says Badcock, *filioque* was used in liturgy and was strongly defended as doctrine by the Western church and was inserted into the Western version of the Nicene Creed by papal authority in 1014. The insertion resulted in a further schism between the Western and Eastern churches in 1054 and remains a matter of real division between the two churches to date.[42] Despite the insertion, this doctrinal position has been viewed as a "partial culprit, blamed for obscuring the fullness of the Spirit's distinctive role."[43] In light of this evidence, it can be noted that,

39. Berkhof, *History of Christian Doctrines*, 90–91.
40. Burgess, "The Holy Spirit, Doctrine of: The Medieval Churches" in *Dictionary*, 432–433.
41. Congar, *I Believe*, 3:51–52.
42. Badcock, *Light of Truth*, 75, 81.
43. Dreyer, *Holy Power*, 13.

although the doctrinal position of his double procession was strengthened, the place and role of the Holy Spirit in the church's life and functions was beyond the thought and practice of the medieval Western church.

8.3. OTHER NONBIBLICAL TRADITIONS THAT FURTHER OBSCURED THE GIFTS AND WORKS OF THE HOLY SPIRIT

Historical accounts indicate that the medieval Western church adopted some nonbiblical traditions such as the doctrine of purgatory, indulgence trade, penance, prayer to saints and angels, and prayer for the dead. The doctrine of purgatory and trade of indulgences, in particular, were considered as the major abusive practices of the church and were attacked by theologians of the time, eventually leading to the quest for Reformation.[44] According to the confessional statements of the reformers, purgatory is a supposed middle state, with a time limit, between heaven and hell, but with a promise of an eventual entrance into heaven as a result of an indulgence purchase.[45] MacCulloch elaborates on this by stating that the medieval Western church believed and practiced that it was possible to do a good work for one's salvation during the period of his/her soul's stay in purgatory in order to earn a reduction in the number of years spent there. An indulgence, therefore, was a treasury of merit purchased by the living friends or families to help the souls of the dead in order to shorten the time the dead were supposed to spend in purgatory doing penance. However, some theologians of the time, concludes MacCulloch, reacted against the indulgence merit claiming that every assumption behind the indulgence system was contradictory to the biblical teaching of justification by the grace of God through faith.[46] Martin Brecht points out that indulgence was considered to exemplify the four chief activities of grace: complete remission of all sins; entitling people to receive a confessional letter from the church for repeated absolutions; allowing the dead members, those assumed to be in purgatory, to participate in the life and ministry of the church, and providing the dead who are

---

44. *Apology of the Augsburg Confession* 12.13–16, 24, 26, 118, in Tappert, *Book of Concord*.

45. *Apology of the Augsburg Confession* 12.13–16, 24, 26, 118.

46. MacCulloch, *Reformation*, 14–15. See also Beckwith, "Purgatory," 549.

still in purgatory with the possibility of entering eternal life. Brecht cites a popular saying of the time, "As soon as the coin in the coffer rings, the soul from purgatory springs."[47]

However, leaders of the Reformation movement ridiculed and criticized this practice of the church. For example, Martin Luther in his *Ninety-Five Theses* cites this popular conviction and saying of the time, "as soon as the money clinks into the money chest, the soul flies out of purgatory." This seems to say that when the living purchase indulgences for the dead thought to be in purgatory and put the money in the money chest, the soul of the dead immediately transfers into eternal life. Luther ridiculed the practice saying, "It is certain that when money clinks in the money chest, greed and avarice can be increased; but when the church intercedes, the result is in the hands of God alone."[48] On account of these features, the liturgy and worship of the period became impossibly remote and unable to satisfy the spiritual needs of believers, which eventually led them toward the Reformation movement. Beginning from the twelfth century, many theologians and laity alike continued to object to worship abuses and the spiritual decline of the church. The sixteenth-century reformers, therefore, were not the first group to criticize and challenge the church for worship abuses and spiritual decline.[49] Further defining the church's spiritual status of the period, Richard F. Lovelace states that it was a period in which many were longing for and looking forward to the outbreak of a time of spiritual renewal in which the spiritually declining church would be revived. It was a period of growing monastic movements in reaction to the spiritual decline of the church. Many theologians, most of whom came from monasteries, says Lovelace, continued to attack the church's position over the doctrine of purgatory, the trade of indulgences, the cult of saints, and relics, and for keeping believers away from Scripture. Therefore, when the Reformation broke through in the early sixteenth century, declares Lovelace, it was viewed as a spiritual renewal movement for the entire church.[50]

Supporting Lovelace's observation, Pierson suggests that many Christians of the period were longing for reform: some for administrative reform, some for moral and ethical reform, and some for spiritual

---

47. Brecht, *Road to Reformation*, 191–92.
48. Martin Luther, Theses 27 and 28 in *Ninety-Five Theses*, 57.
49. MacCulloch, *Reformation*, 122–23.
50. Lovelace, *Dynamics of Spiritual Life*, 32–35.

reform. Side by side with the administrative corruption, says Pierson, "sexual immorality was flagrant" from the grassroots up to the "papal court." Amidst that situation, some of well-educated theologians began to critically study Scripture anew and to search what it teaches concerning the spiritual and moral nature of the church. Those theologians, notes Pierson, discovered that the existing religious practice of the church fell far short of Christian spirituality and that the church was entangled with nonbiblical traditions. Thus, the discovery of the need for reformation emerged from a renewed reading of Scripture, which resulted in the reformers' emphasis on and call for "salvation by grace alone through faith alone." The greatest virtue of the Reformation theology, concludes Pierson, was its "rediscovery and emphasis on the gospel of grace."[51] Luther, in particular, who was regarded as the architect of the Reformation movement, passionately argued that the church of his days had "cast itself adrift from the New Testament" in both "its doctrine and its practice." In his work *The Babylonian Captivity of the Christian Church*, to which McGrath refers, Luther argues that the "gospel had become captive to the institutional church" and that the church had "imprisoned the gospel in complex systems," hierarchies, sacraments, and nonbiblical traditions. While the church, in Luther's view, was meant to be the servant of the gospel, it had become the master of the gospel.[52] Accordingly, reformers focused on the "bringing together of the Word of God and the individual [believers] that had never happened before and can never be undone."[53]

These accounts indicate how the medieval Western church shifted its attention to different kinds of nonbiblical means to access divine gifts, power, intervention, protection, and provision. Indeed, all of these human developments can be viewed as obscuring and eclipsing the distinctive gifts and works of the Holy Spirit in and through the diversity of charismatic gifts. This may also indicate how the church of the period potentially kept itself away from the gifts and works of the Holy Spirit as well as avoiding charismatic forms of spirituality. In light of this, there

51. Pierson, *Dynamics of Christian Mission*, 129–35.

52. McGrath, *Historical Theology*, 164. See also Luther's severe argument in *Babylonian Captivity* (LW 36), 11–125, where argued the absolute authority and right of the pope to interpret Scripture. Read also Luther's position against the pope's absolute authority in *Treatise on Christian Liberty* (*The Freedom of a Christian*) (LW 31), 334–76, wherein he asserted that "a Christian is a perfectly free lord of all, subject to none. A Christian is a perfectly dutiful servant of all, subject to all."

53. Berkhof, *Doctrine of the Holy Spirit*, 66.

is a question that must be asked: What happened to the experience of the gifts and workings of the Holy Spirit amidst all these complexities of the medieval church's religious life and practice? Did these experiences completely disappear from the spiritual experience of the church or individual believer? Some evidence suggests that the gifts and works of the Holy Spirit did not completely disappear in the medieval Western church. They were in existence and experienced albeit very rarely and quite sporadically. If this is so, how and where were they experienced? This will be briefly explored in the next and final section of the chapter.

8.4. WANING EXISTENCE OF THE GIFTS OF THE HOLY SPIRIT IN THE MEDIEVAL CHURCH

Despite the obscuring features of the place and role of the Holy Spirit's workings in the medieval Western church's religious practice discussed above, there is evidence indicating a waning but continuous charismatic experience in the church of the period. Although most often confined to certain groups such as those in monasteries and certain devoted individuals, the range of charismatic experiences did not entirely cease from the Christian experience. In the sixth century, for example, Gregory the Great (ca. 540–604) in his *Dialogues* reported continued charismatic experiences in his day and recorded various kinds of miracles, healing, and prophecies. For example, in the first book of his *Dialogues* Gregory reports that a powerful fire threatening a city with destruction was put under control; a massive rock rolled away from a field of vegetables; a glass lamp that was broken into pieces was miraculously put back together into a whole and intact lamp as if it had not broken at all; an empty jar was filled with oil in the course of prayer; a little wooden jar of wine continued to refill with wine when the wine was finished; and dead were raised before burial.[54] In book 2 Gregory reports that two pieces of a broken tray were joined again as if the tray had never cracked and the tray hung at the entrance of the church as a testament to the miracle; an iron axe was recovered from the bottom of a lake and made to float on the water; a monk walked on water; a huge and heavy rock lost weight and was picked up as easily as if it was a small piece of a stone; prophecy was uttered and its message instantly fulfilled; flour was miraculously provided during a time of famine and starvation; leprosy was cured; an empty oil cask was

---

54. Gregory the Great, *Dialogues*, 20–50.

filled; insanity was cured; and money was miraculously discovered.[55] In book 3 Gregory reports that a river flooding its banks and surrounding farm fields was given a command by prayer and then receded; another river rising above the height of the city walls and inundating the whole city was commanded to stand still in front of the church door; the dead were raised before and after burial; sick people were healed; the blind received sight; and demonic spirits were exorcised. Gregory points out that most of these miraculous events happened through the prayers of bishops such as Boniface, Fortunatus, Marcellinus, and Abbot Benedict and that the manifestation of such miracles had a positive effect on the conversion of pagans and the deepening of faith.[56] Gregory's accounts show the sporadic occurrence of charismatic experiences until the end of the sixth century.

There are, nevertheless, scholarly evaluations that suggest that charismatic experiences continued beyond the sixth century. Their findings report a sporadic continuation of charismatic experiences from the repudiation of Montanists until the breakthrough of the Reformation movement. Scholars who have explored this case have tried to establish their case based on primary sources from the medieval period's history of the church and to substantiate their conclusions with documentary warrants. The following list of evidence is presented here as a sample of the examples they offer. The Venerable Bede (673–735) reported the existence of a remarkable ministry of healing, exorcism, raising the dead, and prophetic utterances.[57] Symeon the New Theologian (949–1022) experienced speaking in tongues, seeing visions, and focused his ministry on the Holy Spirit's baptism.[58] Hildegard of Bingen (1098–179) performed numerous miracles, prophecies, speaking and interpretation of tongues, and singing in tongues.[59] It was attested that Hildegard was a "visionary and prophetic" woman of the time.[60] Francis of Assisi (1181–226), the founder of the Franciscan order, performed several prophecies, healings,

---

55. Gregory the Great, *Dialogues*, 56–108.
56. Gregory the Great, *Dialogues*, 145–85.
57. Cartledge, *Encountering the Spirit*, 39.
58. Anderson, *Introduction to Pentecostalism*, 22.
59. Burgess and Van Der Mass, *New International Dictionary*, 1:234.
60. Thiselton, *Holy Spirit*, 235–36.

and miracles.[61] The sermons of Thomas Aquinas (1225–74) were understood to be frequently accompanied by miraculous manifestations.[62]

However, Aquinas for his part did not indicate if this was the case in his ministry. He rather expressed his belief in supernatural gifts beyond the captivity of nature to give and beyond the merit of the people to whom they are given. After explaining the list of charismata in 1 Cor 12:8–10, Aquinas asserted that these gifts transcend reason and are required by the church to lead one another in divine matters. He declared that the gifts of healing and speaking in tongues would lead people to faith in a special way. Physical healing in particular, he asserts, should be distinguished from the general working of miracles because when a person acquires bodily health through the power of faith it leads a person to faith in a special way. Therefore, such gifts should be "regarded as free graces of a special kind."[63] Similarly, Gregory of Palamas (1296–359) reported that the gifts of healing, speaking, and interpretation of tongues and many miracles took place during his days.[64] Vincent Firrer's (1350–419) ministry was accompanied by miracles, healings, and raising the dead.[65] Others, such as Gertrude of Helfta (1256–301), Birgitta of Sweden (1302–73), Catherine of Siena (1347–80), Julian of Norwich (1342–416), and Margery of Kempe (1373–433) are reported to have played significant roles as prophets, healers, speakers in tongues, and founders of worship orders with a charismatic spirituality.[66] While these are some examples of individuals who demonstrated charismatic experiences, Jeff Doles affirms that there were many others and that "miracles, signs, wonders, healing, and prophecies" continued in the church throughout the Middle Ages.[67]

These scholarly findings and suggestions indicate that experiences of varieties of the gifts of the Holy Spirit have continued through the centuries and across church history. They were exercised by believers, albeit sporadically, and continued until the breakthrough of the Reformation in the early sixteenth century. Despite its subjection to institutional rejection and suppression, a charismatic form of spirituality was held to be part of the Christian experience through individuals or groups whether

---

61. Burgess, *Medieval Roman Catholic*, 74–75.
62. Burgess and Van Der Mass, *New International Dictionary*, 1:235.
63. Thomas Aquinas, *On Nature and Grace*, 168–72.
64. Anderson, *Introduction to Pentecostalism*, 22.
65. Burgess and Van Der Mass, *New International Dictionary*, 1:235.
66. Burgess, *Medieval Roman Catholic*, 87–88.
67. Jeff Doles, *Miracles and the Manifestations*, 101–23.

to a greater or lesser degree. Individual believers or groups might have demonstrated these experiences in ways and means not recognized by the institutional church such as secretly in underground fellowships or house churches, in private homes, or monasteries. In general, given all the discussions and historical accounts presented thus far, it would appear that subjective experience of the Holy Spirit continued through the centuries in unbroken continuity from the time of the apostles up until the Reformation, recurring here and there through individuals or groups as a kind of on-again-off-again experience. With this in mind, we will now turn our examination to the place and role of the Holy Spirit in the Reformation and post-Reformation period Protestantism.

CHAPTER 9

The Reformation and Post-Reformation Protestant Churches' Teaching and Practice

WE HAVE CONSIDERED HOW the medieval period was viewed as the period of a growing reaction against the spiritual decline of the church. Many Christians of the period were longing for a time of spiritual renewal, both for individual believers and for the church as a whole. When the Reformation occurred in the early sixteenth century, it was viewed as a movement of spiritual renewal. However, evaluations of the early nature of the Reformation movement suggest that the movement did not adequately address all the expected aspects of spiritual renewal and thus caused division among the staunch leaders of the movement. Certain aspect of the division was related to the Holy Spirit, his gifts and works in the church. Therefore, this chapter examines the nature of the teaching and practice of the Holy Spirit in the Reformation and post-Reformation Protestant churches. The examination focuses on three major features: (1) the theological and spiritual issues targeted by the Reformation movement; (2) the Holy Spirit in the teaching and practices of the mainstream Protestant Reformation and its influence on successive Protestant churches; and (3) the Holy Spirit in the teaching and practice of the Radical Reformation and its influence on successive movements. Here it must be noted that the mainstream Protestant Reformation is represented by Martin Luther, John Calvin, and Ulrich Zwingli, who have also come to be known as the "magisterial reformers." The Radical Reformation is represented by Andreas B. Karlstadt and Thomas Muentzer, who are also known as "Anabaptists." Here noting worth is that the Reformation tradition churches are mostly targeted churches for this study. Therefore, hereafter the discussion of the chapter will focus only on the Reformation tradition churches and will exclude the Catholic Church.

9.1. PRIMARY THEOLOGICAL TARGET OF THE REFORMATION MOVEMENT

We have stated that the Reformation was not simply a movement of reaction against existing theological and spiritual traditions of the church, but of real spiritual hunger and concern for bringing together Scripture and believers. As we shall see here, the Reformation movement indeed succeeded in satisfying some of that spiritual hunger which included bringing together Scripture and believers. The movement also succeeded in removing nonbiblical traditions adopted by the medieval Catholic Church as part of the church's religious practice. Yet it was criticized by some of its constituencies for continuing to adhere to some of the medieval Catholic Church's worship and liturgical traditions and for not adequately addressing the deeper spiritual renewal long sought after. Confessional statements of the Reformation period constitute some examples of this. For example, confessional statements indicate that during the course of controversial exchanges with their Catholic opponents, the reformers declared that their evangelical churches dissented from the Catholic Church in no article of faith or tradition that had been passed down through the centuries, but simply omitted a small number of features which they thought to have exposed abuses by the church or were contrary to the intent of the canons.[1] The reformers insisted that they were not reacting against the church on any of the fundamental articles of faith and that they actually observed many of its standard traditions and practices. They insisted that they were not dissenting from the church on any fundamental practice of faith. Rather, they strongly pledged to keep

1. *Augsburg Confession* 22. All of the Lutheran Confessional statements with its ten major texts are compiled in Tappert, *Book of Concord*: the three ancient ecumenical creeds; the *Augsburg Confession*; the *Apology of the Augsburg Confession*; the *Smalcald Articles*; *Treatise on the Power and Primacy of the Pope*; the *Small Catechism*; the *Large Catechism*, and the *Formula of Concord*, which contains the *Epitome* and *Solid Declarations*. These confessions are assumed to contain all the basic and authoritative theological, doctrinal, and worship, and liturgical teachings and practices of the Evangelical Lutheran Churches.

all the biblical traditions and faith articles of the church in order to foster harmony with the entire Christendom.[2]

The reformers further insisted that they had introduced nothing new in their teaching or rites which had not existed in the church from ancient times, nor had they made changes to the public ceremonies of the mass, except for a few unnecessary masses held as a result of abuses.[3] They insisted that the old mass, which had formerly been observed in the Catholic Church, had been preserved and performed among the Reformation churches in its proper order. They boldly declared that they were glad to realize and preserve all the traditions established in the church because those traditions, in their view, were useful and promoted tranquillity. They pledged to interpret and apply all the church traditions only in an evangelical way. Accordingly, the reformers blamed their opponents for falsely accusing them of abolishing church traditions such as the mass. In reality, they had not abolished them, but retained and preserved almost all of the customary ceremonies, including the mass, and celebrated them with the greatest reverence.[4] The reformers also insisted that nothing should be changed from the accustomed rites, but that all the accustomed rites and orders of the church should be preserved so that harmony would be fostered.[5] They claimed that they were even more faithful to the canon and old traditions of the church such as conducting the public liturgy in its usual state and cherishing and preserving all the ordinances for the sake of tranquillity.[6]

Luther's writings also strongly affirm this position of the reformers. Particularly concerning the structures of liturgy and worship, Luther declared he had no intention of forming a new evangelical worship order. Rather, he wished to use and preserve the worship service which was being used by the Catholic Church of the time. Luther declared that Christian worship everywhere drew its roots from the worship services of the early church. However, these have, as he observed, been abused, perverted, and corrupted by hypocritical spiritual hierarchies. He asserted that they, the reformers, did not intend to abolish the traditional worship order on account of such abuses, but they aimed to correct the abuses, mostly those which had silenced and replaced the word of God, and to

2. *Augsburg Confession* 22. Cf. *Apology of the Augsburg Confession* 15.36–39, 50–51.
3. *Augsburg Confession* 24.40.
4. *Augsburg Confession* 14.1, 34, 35, and 40.
5. *Apology of the Augsburg Confession* 15.50–51.
6. *Apology of the Augsburg Confession* 7; 8.33; 15.38–39.

restore the church's worship to its proper original order and disciplined evangelical use.⁷ Here a question to be asked is: to what does Luther refer when he says that the worship service, which draws its roots from the worship services of the early church, has been abused, perverted, and corrupted? It is obvious that he was referring to the nonbiblical traditions that the reformers and their allies had been attacking for years.⁸ Nonbiblical traditions such as the doctrine of purgatory, indulgence trade, papal infallibility, prayer to saints and angels, prayer for the dead, and authority centered within the church and its hierarchies, which the reformers altogether viewed as "additions to and distortions of the Christian faith."⁹

The confessional statements declare that the reformers especially criticized the trade of indulgence and the doctrine of purgatory for being extensions of the doctrine of the devil,¹⁰ demonic businesses against the doctrine of justification by faith alone,¹¹ and the instruments of imposition of the devil's yoke on people in order to promote distrust in God and lead the sinners astray from God's promise to give grace and salvation through faith alone.¹² They viewed such practices as shameful, scandalous, and accursed abuses promoted to obscure people from God's grace and the gift of faith.¹³ Against these practices, the reformers asserted that traditions instituted by men to propitiate God and earn grace are thoroughly contrary to the teaching and power of the gospel and thinking to merit forgiveness by the indulgences of erroneous and ungodly action. They then declared that there is only one propitiation sacrifice that perfectly reconciles man with God and merits true forgiveness, i.e., the death of Jesus Christ. To access this sacrifice, Scripture should be released from such encumbrances, and the path should be cleared for all people to freely access it.¹⁴ Above all else, they emphasized that the chief purpose of

---

7. Luther, *Lectures on Liturgy and Hymns* (LW 53), 11–19. See also Lull, *Basic Theological Teaching*, 445–46.

8. *Augsburg Confession* 24.

9. *The Augsburg Confession* 21; 24; 26.4–6; and 28. See also *Apology of the Augsburg Confession* 12.13–16; *Smalcald Article* 2.12–15; McGrath, *Reformation Thought*, 20, 30; Lull, *Basic Theological Teaching*, 445–46; MacCulloch, *Reformation*, 11–15; and Dunn, *Baptism in the Holy Spirit*, 225.

10. *Augsburg Confession* 28.49.

11. *Apology of the Augsburg Confession* 12.15.

12. *Apology of the Augsburg Confession* 12.167; 28.8.

13. *The Smalcald Articles* 2:12–14; cf. *Augsburg Confession* 26.4.

14. *Apology of the Augsburg Confession* 15.3–4, 11; 24.22. See also Oyer, *Lutheran Reformers*, 114.

all faith practices was to teach people only what they need to know about the saving work of Christ, the forgiveness of sins, and the justifying grace of God through faith in Christ.[15] The reformers emphasized the exclusiveness of Scripture alone, faith alone, and grace alone. Luther's question "How can I find a gracious God?," in particular, and his answer "by faith alone" gave prominence to the doctrine of justification by faith.[16] The doctrine of justification by faith, the doctrine "with and by which the church stands and without which it falls"[17] has been regarded as the chief article of grace, faith, and salvation. It was also viewed as the doctrine on which individual believers could "stand or fall."[18] This doctrine was regarded as an essential norm and served as the principal criterion of true belief, teaching, and practice in Reformation theology.[19] Thus, reformers, Luther in particular, asserted that faith in Christ is the only means in and through which God delivers his objective saving gracious acts to the world.[20] It was on this ground that reformers emphasized objective salvation, overlooked the idea of subjective effort to achieve salvation, and rejected any boasting of self-effort in the Christian salvation enterprise.[21] This doctrine caused many subsequent adherents of Reformation theology to hold the person of Luther and his prolific theological writings in high regard.

This evidence reminds us that the reformers did not seek to become a new church in their religious practices, but wished to remain one body within the Catholic Church. Besides reacting against the stated nonbiblical traditions, they did not intend to make significant changes to the worship and liturgical traditions of the existing Catholic Church. The reformers accepted and extended all the longstanding worship traditions of the church, making revisions only where they thought the pure teaching of Scripture was at stake. They approved faithful realization and preservation of the Catholic Church's traditional worship and liturgical orders along with a strong emphasis on faith with authority centered in Scripture, which came to mean putting all the weight of Christianity on faith and Scripture. The call to return to biblical sources of faith teachings

---

15. *Augsburg Confession* 24.3.
16. McGrath, *Historical Theology*, 167.
17. Sproul, *Faith Alone*, 67–68.
18. Sproul, *Faith Alone*, 70.
19. *Apology of the Augsburg Confession* 4.86, 132–35, 292–95.
20. Althaus, *Theology of Martin Luther*, 211–20.
21. *Augsburg Confession* 20.

and practices remained a distinctive characteristic of the Reformation movement and theology.[22] Accordingly, says Dunn, "Where Catholics fastened on to the objectivity of the sacraments," the Reformers "fastened on to the objectivity of the Bible."[23] If this was the case, then the question to be raised is: how far did the Reformation movement go in reforming worship and spiritual practices and how far did it succeed in meeting the spiritual hunger of its adherents?

9.2. THE REFORMERS' POSITION REGARDING REFORMING THE WORSHIP AND LITURGY

As discussed above, at its inception the Reformation movement was viewed as a profound movement of renewal, which began with an intense zeal for spiritual revival. Nonetheless, evaluations suggest that it was soon criticized for not fulfilling the expected revival and renewal hopes in practical application. For instance, McGrath suggests that Luther was viewed as a popular charismatic reformer as his reform program emphasized the exclusiveness and authority of Scripture, marked the revival of the theology of forgiveness of sin and justification by faith, and opened the way for a new social and religious order in Europe. However, says McGrath, his reform program was also criticized for being much more conservative and obstinate, which is why it met with considerably less success than expected.[24] Here a question must be asked: what does it mean to say that Luther's reform program was more conservative and obstinate? Martin Brecht provides us with a possible answer to this question. He suggests that on account of his devotion to the existing traditional worship and liturgical orders, Luther boldly approved this existing traditional worship and liturgical order, i.e., the Latin mass, *Formula Missae*, and insisted that it should be used and preserved. Even when Luther drafted a new liturgical draft, his German mass, *Deutsche Messe* of 1525, says Brecht, he did not create a new worship order but merely shortened the orders of the traditional worship, which he thought to be too long, too legalistic, and strayed from the content of Scripture. Luther's liturgical draft, says Brecht, was utterly conservative and followed all the worship orders of

---

22. Badcock, *Light of Truth*, 96.
23. Dunn, *Baptism in the Holy Spirit*, 225.
24. McGrath, *Reformation Thought*, 7.

the traditional liturgy but was adapted only to meet the needs of German-speaking worshipers.[25]

Brecht proceeds to suggest that Luther's rigid and obstinate conservative attitude towards reform disappointed some of his colleagues and caused the emergence of radical reformers and their separation from the magisterial reformers. He states that the radical reformers criticized Luther for confining the reform program to the traditional worship framework and preventing it from achieving the anticipated spiritual fruits of worship renewal. As Brecht notes, this disappointed some of Luther's colleagues, i.e., those who later followed Muntzer and Karlstadt, one of Luther's closest friends at the beginning of the Reformation. This disappointment led to the birth and growth of the Radical Reformation. Consequently, the Radical Reformation, which meant "reforming further and deeper," emerged at the early stages of the Reformation movement.[26] A similar observation is offered by Allen, who argues that the chief leaders of the Reformation movement did not go far enough in reforming and reviving worship and spiritual experiences. Rather, they firmly held on to some of the views and stands of the Catholic Church authorities, who viewed the church as a visible organization rather than a Spirit-gifted and Spirit-guided spiritual body of believers. Thus, says Allen, the reformers established a kind of "official organizational church" which can be understood as the "Protestant initiation of Catholic structure." Thereby, Allen notes, most of the Reformation movement's energies, hopes, and promises dissipated quickly in different kinds of quarrels and divisions. Their great Reformation, therefore, concludes Allen, remains in reality *"the Arrested Reformation."*[27] Hence, it was in reaction against the "mechanical sacramentalism of extreme Catholicism and the dead biblicist orthodoxy of extreme Protestantism" that the radicals shifted the focus of their attention to the *"experience"* of the gifts and works of the Holy Spirit.[28]

When considering these accounts it can be noted that magisterial reformers did not emphasize the role of the Holy Spirit, usually realized through the subjective experience, in their programme of revival and renewal. As discussed in chapter 1, it is biblically substantiated that God always brings spiritual renewal and transformation through the gifts,

25. Brecht, *Shaping and Defining the Reformation*, 254–57, 275.
26. This reference is paraphrased from Brecht, *Shaping and Defining the Reformation*, 137, 148, 158, 161, 256, and 258.
27. Allen, *Unfailing Stream*, 63–64.
28. Dunn, *Baptism in the Holy Spirit*, 225.

power, and activities of the Holy Spirit. However, the magisterial reformers seem not to have paid attention to this as a significant aspect of their reform movement. Consequently, despite its emphasis on the absolute authority of Scripture, the issue of the subjective experience of the Holy Spirit did not "return to prominence" and was still "hardly to be experienced apart from the Bible" in Reformation theology.[29] Thus, the lack of emphasis on the significance of the gifts, power, and workings of the Holy Spirit in Christian worship and spiritual experience led the Reformation movement to split and caused the birth of what became known as the Radical Reformation.

9.3. THE RISE OF THE RADICAL REFORMATION

As stated above, the Radical Reformation movement arose as a reaction against the reform stand of the magisterial reformers. As Brecht notes, the radicals criticized the magisterial reformers for not going far enough in reforming the spiritual status of their churches. Brecht states that because of Luther's high regard for the conventional form of worship, the radicals rejected his liturgical drafts. They criticized mostly Luther for preventing the reform movement from achieving the anticipated spiritual changes. They viewed Luther as a papist, who having once strongly attacked the papacy for worships abuses, was now reverting back to that same worship program. Indeed, says Brecht, the radical reformers criticized Luther more strongly than Luther criticized the papacy and accused him of being a false teacher and unfaithful servant of God who perverted the teaching of Scripture. Against all the reform and the worship program of Luther, notes Brecht, the radicals wanted to go further and deeper in order to penetrate the long-standing spiritual longing of the believers. They declared that the teaching of Scripture should be combined with mystical experiences. Accordingly, concludes Brecht, they began to advocate for free and spontaneous forms of worship, appealing for new revelations, prophetic messages, and personal experience of receiving such things directly from God through personal communication.[30] The radical reformers continued by believing, practicing, and advocating the possibility of receiving the gifts of the Holy Spirit without the preached word and

---

29. Dunn, *Baptism in the Holy Spirit*, 225.

30. For this reference, see Brecht, *Shaping and Defining the Reformation*, 137, 148, 158, 161, 256, and 258.

emphasizing that God illuminates, converts, saves, justifies, and draws people to himself through the gifts and works of the Holy Spirit without any external means.[31]

Similarly, Carter Lindberg suggests that the radical reformers criticized the magisterial reformers for laying undue emphasis upon Scripture alone and avoiding the experience of the gifts and workings of the Holy Spirit beyond Scripture. He states that the radicals criticized Luther, in particular, for emphasizing only the dead letter of Scripture and elevating the sacraments and thus blocking the gifts and works of the Holy Spirit. The radicals declared that Scripture alone is not enough to teach believers and that the true word of God does not come only from the written letter but also directly from God through the "inner voice." Accordingly, says Lindberg, the radicals asserted that believers had to be taught and encouraged to experience the gifts of divine revelation through the "inner light of the Holy Spirit." He adds that they insisted on what they called the *"inward clear voice of God,"* i.e. the voice in which God speaks to people through the Holy Spirit, rather than through external means. As Lindberg notes, this *"inward voice of God,"* for radical reformers, was not connected with Scripture or the sacraments, but comes directly from God to the human heart through the gifts and works of the Holy Spirit. The radical reformers, in general, says Lindberg, asserted that believers must experience new revelations through dreams, visions, prophecy, and the inner light of the Holy Spirit through direct communication with God, but not through Scripture alone.[32] The radicals thereby adopted free worship experiences such as dancing, speaking in tongues, and other spontaneous verbal movements.[33] Their worship was accompanied by ecstatic movements, prophecy, physical healing, and miracles.[34] In this way, the radicals claimed to be able to recover and revive the worship, spirituality, and ministry of the early church with all its original purity, gifts, power, and freedom without compromising any of the church's current structural worship orders.[35] This evidence indicates that the radical reformers' view of the presence, gifts and works of the Holy Spirit was directly opposed to that of the magisterial reformers.

31. *Augsburg Confession* 5.4; cf. *Formula of Concord, Epitome* 2.13 and *Solid Declaration* 2.4.
32. Lindberg, *Third Reformation?*, 61–62, 83, and 104.
33. Littell, *Origins of Sectarian Protestantism*, 2 and 19.
34. Oyer, *Lutheran Reformers*, 67.
35. Hyatt, *2000 Years*, 79–80.

9.4. THE RESPONSE OF MAGISTERIAL REFORMERS TO THE RADICAL REFORMERS' REFORM STRATEGY

Historical accounts indicate that the magisterial reformers engaged in a bitter controversy with the radical reformers and responded to their reform strategy with fiery words and attacks, which are reflected in their confessional statements as well as their other theological writings. The magisterial reformers' confessional statements, for instance, indicate that they criticized the radical reformers as fanatic enthusiasts who believed and advocated that God draws people to himself, illuminates, justifies, and saves them without hearing the preached word and without the holy sacraments.[36] The magisterial reformers viewed the radicals as those who did not want to read or hear the preached word or to take the holy sacraments, but to idly sit in expectation of the manifestation and illumination of the Holy Spirit and to wait until God poured his gifts into them without external means.[37] They criticized the radicals for striving to adopt a "self-chosen spirituality,"[38] for throwing themselves on their own piety and holiness under the pretext of the guidance of the Holy Spirit, and for establishing a "self-elected service of God" without the word.[39] They regarded them as a sect with false teaching, which called upon the name of the Lord as a cover for their devilish teaching and practice, as wicked fanatical robbers who allowed error and schism to creep into the church, and as arrogant spiritualists who twisted Scripture according to their enthusiastic desires.[40] They further described them as blind fanatics behind whom lurked a "sneaky, seditious devil" who liked to "snatch the crown from the rulers and trample it underfoot" and to "pervert and nullify all God's works and ordinances."[41] The magisterial reformers equated the radicals with Satan and the serpent who led Adam away from the word of God to enthusiastic spiritualization and temptation. Their spiritual enthusiasm, according to the magisterial view, was a passion instilled in

---

36. *Formula of Concord, Solid Declaration* 2.80.

37. *Apology of the Augsburg Confession* 13.13; *Formula of Concord, Epitome* 2.13; *Solid Declaration* 2.4, 46.

38. *Formula of Concord, Epitome* 12.5.

39. *Formula of Concord, Solid Declaration* 6.20.

40. *Apology of the Augsburg Confession* 9.2; 21.43; cf. *Large Catechism* 3.47; 4.62–63; *Smalcald Articles* 3.8; and *Solid Declaration* 7.29.

41. *Large Catechism* 4.61–62.

humankind by the devil and the source of heresy and temptation.[42] These strong and fiery sayings are also clearly reflected in the personal writings of Luther and Calvin.

Luther's biblical commentaries indicate that he strongly condemned the radicals for being false prophets, led by a satanic spirit, and instruments through which Satan attacks the gospel.[43] In his commentary on Isa 35:5–6, "The eyes of the blind will be opened . . . the ears of the deaf will hear . . . the lame will leap . . . the mute tongue will shout in joy," Luther stated that such signs and miracles were necessary only as a witness to the Jews who should have recognized the gospel. Since the gospel had spread and was known to all the world at that time, such signs and miracles were no longer needed in Christian ministry and belonged forever to the past.[44] In his commentary on John 14:12, 30–31, "He who believes in me will do what I have been doing. . . . He will even do greater things than these," Luther commented that in the early Christian experience, God caused visible miracles to foster faith in the gospel but when this was no longer necessary, God stopped those miracles. He asserted that God no longer wanted to defeat the works of the devil through the might of signs and miracles but by gospel proclamation, obedience, humility, and submission.[45] He declared that since there are no new revelations, the Holy Spirit does not speak or act outside the written word. The whole activity of the Holy Spirit remained dependent on the word. He advised his adherents not to delude themselves by imagining that God speaks to his people in any way outside the preached word. He believed that the Holy Spirit kindles in the believers' hearts only the preached word and brings or speaks nothing besides that word. Claiming any personal communication with or immediate response from the Holy Spirit, in his view, is a product of the fanciful imagination of enthusiastic sectarians. Therefore, when believers pray for the gifts and workings of the Holy Spirit, they must pray only in terms of accompanying and kindling the preached word in their hearts. He asserted that since the word is the only unconditional means to access the gifts and activities of the Holy Spirit and the Holy Spirit is given to no one and does nothing without the preached word, believers should not delude themselves by hoping and expecting immediate acts from the Holy Spirit. God, in Luther's belief,

---

42. *Smalcald Articles* 3.8.
43. Luther, *Lectures on Church and Ministry* (LW 40), 110; see also pp. 144–47.
44. Luther, *Lectures on Isaiah 1–39* (LW 16), 302; cf. p. 168.
45. Luther, *Sermons on the Gospel of John 14–16* (LW 24), 79; cf. p. 192.

has determined to give the invisible gifts of the Holy Spirit to no one without the visible instruments, i.e., the preached word and holy sacraments.[46] Any worship experience that intends to have an experience apart from Christ alone and Scripture alone should, in Luther's view, be considered the invention of the devil and the activity of sectarians inspired by Satanic spirits.[47] A similar opinion was offered by John Calvin.

Calvin, who later became a chief leader of the Reformed wing of Protestantism, in his *Institute of Christian Religion*, declared that the "Holy Spirit is recognized in his agreement with scripture." He says that anyone who wants to know about the Holy Spirit, his gifts, and works, and who wants to benefit from his activities must read and listen to Scripture because God has joined his written word and his Spirit in a unique mutual bond. He stated that "Word and Spirit belong inseparably together" and declared that the word is the instrument by which God dispenses the illumination of the Holy Spirit to believers. In the past, says Calvin, God dispensed the word by the power of the Holy Spirit and has sent his Spirit to complete his work by the "efficacious confirmation of the Word." Therefore, the Holy Spirit is the "Author of the Scriptures" and yet is "himself to be subject to Scripture." Calvin insisted that it is only through the written word of God that believers can recognize the image, nature, gifts, and activities of the Holy Spirit and can benefit from his gifts and activities. As the work of the Holy Spirit, in Calvin's view, is not to invent a new revelation but to seal believers' minds with the preached word, any claim of receiving the gifts of the Holy Spirit apart from the preached word should be treated as a "vanity and a lie." He insisted that only when the word is given proper honor and value can the Holy Spirit exercise his gifts and working only through the word does not cause any affront to the essence and personality of the Holy Spirit. In line with this fact, Calvin concludes, that the "fanatics" of his days were "*wrongly appealing to the Holy Spirit*" to act outside the word.[48]

Commenting on the issue of claiming an ongoing manifestation of signs, miracles, and healing, Calvin wrote that in the early church, miracles were dispensed when the apostles laid their hands on people and prayed for them. These signs were quite fitting for the proclamation

---

46. *Smalcald Articles* 8.3–5 and 9–10. See also Luther, *Lectures on Church and Ministry* (LW 40), 146; *Luther's Table Talk*, 141–42; and Lohse, *Martin Luther's Theology*, 235–39.

47. *Smalcald Articles* 8.10. See also Luther, *Sermon on The Mount* (LW 21), 55.

48. Calvin, *Institute of Christian Religion* 1.9.1–3.

of the gospel at its beginning. Such previously unheard and unseen extraordinary signs and miracles, in Calvin's view, were required in order to magnify the power of the gospel message at its inception. Such experiences, he believed, had lasted only a short period, only during the period of the apostles' ministry, and had ceased with the end of the ministry of the apostles. Therefore, when God withdrew such extraordinary signs and miracles from the church, in Calvin's conviction, he preserved the magnificence of preaching the gospel. Drawing on this conviction Calvin argued that the radicals of his days, who were advocating the reality and significance of those signs and miracles and claiming them here and now, were "gripped by error . . . carried away with frenzy" and "miserable folk willingly prefer to wander to their doom."[49] This indicates that against the teaching of the radical reformers, the magisterial reformers emphasized the external means of the word over the gifts and works of the Holy Spirit.

Magisterial reformers emphasized that all the significance and function of the signs and miracles of God are replaced by and preserved in the word of God and the holy sacraments.[50] Therefore, the Holy Spirit is "given through the Word"[51] and works only in, with, and through the preached word and the holy sacraments.[52] For magisterial reformers, the Holy Spirit is present in order to assist the preached word and to help people in the course of conversion as an effect of the power of the preached word.[53] The Holy Spirit, in their view, "does not effect conversion without means." In order to effect conversion the Holy Spirit "employs the preaching and the hearing of the Word."[54] The Holy Spirit, therefore, is present to reveal the preached Word, to illumine and to kindle the hearts of the audiences.[55] The word is the office, work, and ministry of the Holy Spirit,[56] and the Holy Spirit can be "efficacious only through the Word."[57] All activities of the Holy Spirit, for the magisterial reformers, are "hidden

---

49. Calvin, *Institute of Christian Religion* 4.19.6; cf. 1.9.1–2.

50. *Apology of the Augsburg Confession* 13.20–21.

51. *Augsburg Confession* 18.3.

52. *Apology of the Augsburg Confession* 24.70; cf. *Formula of Concord, Solid Declaration* 2.52, 54, 65, 71.

53. *Formula of Concord, Epitome* 2.4–5.

54. *Formula of Concord, Epitome* 2.4 .

55. *Large Catechism* 2.42–44; cf. *Epitome* 2.5.

56. *Formula of Concord, Solid Declaration* 2.56; 11.29.

57. *Formula of Concord, Solid Declaration* 2.56.

in the Word"[58] because the word "contains and conveys all the fullness of God."[59] Therefore, it is the word that gives the Holy Spirit and the saving power of God.[60] The magisterial reformers asserted that God gives the Holy Spirit to his people only in and through the written, published, and preached word so that the Holy Spirit may offer and apply the treasure of salvation.[61] Therefore, only the ministry of the word should be extolled with every possible praise, taught in its purity, cherished, treasured, and given the highest possible praise in the church as well as in the life of an individual believer.[62] Accordingly, believers were advised to hold the conviction that God does not deal directly with his people and gives no one his Spirit except through external instruments and that whatever is attributed to the Holy Spirit apart from the external instruments should be treated as of the devil.[63] In general, magisterial reformers roundly condemned the radicals as fanatical schismatics and approved their persecution and execution. Luther in particular, as Brecht notes, viewed the radicals as instruments of the devil, sowing his evil seeds of false teachings and practices. The seeds the radicals sowed through their teaching and practice appear, for Luther, deceptively impressive and attractive but lead their practitioners astray. The enthusiastic practices of the radicals were not only heretical but were also criminal offenses and they should, therefore, be imprisoned, expelled from the country, or even executed.[64] Accordingly, many of the radicals suffered terribly at the hands of Protestants just as the charismatics had suffered at the hands of the medieval Catholic Church.[65] These accounts are clear enough in signaling how the magisterial reformers engaged in bitter controversy with the radicals and responded to their reform strategy with fiery words and attacks.

It can also be noted from these accounts, without any prejudices, that the harsh reactions of the two leading reformers, Luther and Calvin, against the radicals' emphasis on the experience of the gifts and works of the Holy Spirit appear to have been a driving force behind their reflections on their deeper understanding of the presence, gifts, and works

58. *Formula of Concord, Solid Declaration* 2.56.
59. *Large Catechism* 4.17.
60. *Formula of Concord, Solid Declaration* 11.29.
61. *Large Catechism* 2.38.
62. *Apology of the Augsburg Confession* 4.67, 73; 13:13; cf. *Large Catechism* 3.47–48.
63. *Smalcald Articles* 3.8.
64. Brecht, *Road to Reformation*, 37–39.
65. Allen, *Unfailing Stream*, 61, 63.

of the Holy Spirit in Christian teaching and practice. Viewed through the window of Luther's and Calvin's accounts, it appears that any faith teaching and practice, which might include the claim and experience of the subjective experience of the Holy Spirit, which is not clearly stated in the magisterial reformers' teaching, practice, and writings, would be considered heretical and duly reacted against.[66] Consequently, what Luther and Calvin rejected and excluded from their teaching, practice, and writings have continued to be rejected and excluded from the teaching, practice, and writings of their successors. Shedding further light on this, Badcock suggests that Reformation pneumatology is one that was carved out among controversies with radical reformers on one side and Catholic opponents on the other. It was these twin controversies that formed the background for the pneumatology of the magisterial reformers. As a reflection on those twin controversies, the magisterial reformers excluded any tendency towards the subjective experience of the Holy Spirit in their worship practices. Subsequently, says Badcock, this conviction has continued to influence the theological traditions of most mainline Protestants in pushing subjective experience of the Holy Spirit to the periphery of their theology and practice. In the same way, this tradition has continued to subordinate the Holy Spirit to the written word.[67] While Badcock's latter point may be indeed the case, in reality, Lutherans do not subordinate the Holy Spirit to Scripture. Emphasizing the gifts and works of the Holy Spirit through Scripture and means of grace does not necessarily mean subordinating the Holy Spirit to these features. However, the general implication is that the magisterial reformers' controversial exchange with the two camps impacted on their theology and doctrine of the Holy Spirit. Their reaction against the teaching and practice of the radical reformers, in particular, seems to have significantly contributed to the magisterial reformers' deeper theology of the Holy Spirit. Their position has also continued to influence the views of their successors, who have continued to maintain and preserve those elements maintained and preserved by the magisterial reformers and to reject what those reformers rejected from their teaching and practice. This stance has continued to shape the theology and practice of the Holy Spirit in most Protestant churches to the present day and is reflected in the writings of several

---

66. *Formula of Concord, Solid Declaration* 12.6–7.
67. Badcock, *Light of Truth*, 91–94.

adherents to the magisterial reformers' theological tradition of which we will consider a few examples below.

9.5. HOW THE MAGISTERIAL REFORMERS' POSITION CONTINUED TO INFLUENCE THEIR SUCCESSORS

As discussed above, the magisterial reformers associated the claimants and advocates of the subjective experience of the Holy Spirit with the nature and activities of the devil, referring to them as serpents, murderers, fanatics, and heretical sects. Therefore, it would be quite challenging for their successors to break away from that legacy and integrate the subjective experience of the Holy Spirit into their structured and standard worship order. There are nevertheless some accounts that indicate that the spiritual status of subsequent Reformation tradition churches was criticized and attacked for being nominal. Evaluations of the worship and spiritual status of the Reformation tradition churches suggest that the second half of the sixteenth century was a period of "self-identification," "theological consolidation," and "doctrinal emphasis" for all the newly established Protestant churches. For example, McGrath observes that at this time the Reformation tradition churches were under pressure to clearly define and demonstrate how their theological and doctrinal position compared and contrasted with that of their Catholic opponents and Protestant colleagues. In order to respond to such pressure, the Protestant churches felt that the rapid formulation of their theological and doctrinal position was the best way of defining the boundaries of their theological and doctrinal similarities and differences with other groups. Accordingly, says McGrath, a new form of academic theology began within each group, and each group strived to demonstrate the rationality of its theology, doctrine, and systems. Consequently, the academics of each group concentrated on defining and defending their theological and doctrinal identity at an academic level. Similarly, says McGrath, theologians and writers of each group continued to produce systematic presentations of their theology and doctrine in the face of intense opposition from each other. As a result of such theological pressures and concentrations of self-identification, the second half of the sixteenth century came to be known as the period of "doctrinal emphasis," "theological consolidation," and "orthodoxy." Following the directions and rules of those academic works and their orthodoxy, concludes McGrath, a "new emphasis came to be placed upon the public status of scripture within the church" and that the "expository sermon, the biblical commentary, and works of biblical theology came to be characteristic" of Reformation tradition churches.[68]

Strengthening McGrath's observation, MacCulloch suggests that post-Reformation Protestant churches became very good at "replacing the all-embracing medieval Western Church at the public expression." He states that Protestants of the time "had settled down into dogmatic patterns dependent on public community worship" and "rejected monasteries, solitary religious life, and devotional confraternities" and thus became "less effective in becoming an expression of devotional reflection or meditation." With the lack of such devotional expression in their churches, says MacCulloch, many of the Protestant church members were induced to listen to the radical preachers and to read devotional literature from the Jesuit writings. As time passed, concludes MacCulloch, such a lack of interest in devotional spirituality on the side of mainstream Protestants caused both the rise of the "Further Reformation" movement in the "Reformed Netherlands" and that of the Pietist movement in "Lutheran Germany."[69] Further elaborating on these observations, David W. Buschart suggests that in the seventeenth century well-strengthened "orthodoxy" and "scholasticism" emerged particularly in Lutheran churches. He states that the "scholastic dogmatic theologians" of the Lutheran churches "sought to preserve and advance Lutheranism's doctrinal gain of the sixteenth century in elaborate, rationally sophisticated theological works." Buschart highlights some of the sophisticated scholastic theological works which included a "nine-volume of *Loci Theologici*" and a "twelve-volume of *Systema Locorum Theologicorum*." While these and similar scholastic theological works of the time were highly regarded for maintaining orthodox Lutheran teaching, as Buschart observes, in the latter part of the seventeenth century the Pietist movement emerged in reaction to this rationalistic scholastic theology and the resulting rigid conservative worship practices.[70]

A similar observation is offered by C. P. Williams who suggests that the post-Reformation period was marked as the period of "confessional orthodoxy in which a distinctive Protestant scholasticism emerged," which was "heavily intellectualized" like its "Catholic counterpart."[71] Such

68. McGrath, *Historical Theology*, 168–71.
69. MacCulloch, *Reformation*, 699.
70. Buschart, *Exploring Protestant Traditions*, 35.
71. Williams, "Protestantism," 540.

"rigid academic theology" and its "dogmatic rigidity" resulted in "rigid traditionalism"[72] whereby "disturbing doctrinal aridity and moral laxness" became evident to the extent that an urgent "second Reformation" was tended to.[73] This situation prevailed mostly in Lutheran churches and later became fertile ground for the birth and growth of the Pietist movement as a reaction against the "arid rationalism and barren orthodoxy" and "dead creedal assent" of the Lutheran churches.[74] The movement began by calling upon Lutherans to be "less concerned with doctrinal details and more concerned with living Christian life, less concerned with winning theological battles and more concerned with studying the Bible and demonstrating Christian charity."[75] The movement heavily emphasized the "balancing act of both drawing on adventurous devotional mystical sources" and "doctrinal patterns dependent on public community worship."[76] In light of these accounts, two main points may be considered: *first*, the tendency towards the subjective experience of the Holy Spirit for devotional spiritual life was no longer possible in mainstream Protestant Churches of the post-Reformation period; and, *second*, the worship and spiritual life status of the post-Reformation Protestant Churches seems to have been led straight back to the status of the medieval Catholic Church from which they had broken away at the turn of the century. Accordingly, the worship and spiritual status of mainstream Protestants were continuously challenged and impacted by different kinds of revivalist movements. We will examine only two of these movements to constitute examples, i.e., Pietism and Methodism.

Pietist movement

As seen above, evaluations of the rise of the Pietist movement suggest that it was a movement of spiritual renewal that emerged within Lutheranism in the late seventeenth century in reaction against "rigid academic theology," "dogmatic rigidity," and "rigid traditionalism" in the worship and spiritual practice of the Lutheran churches.[77] It reacted against "arid

72. Zahl, "Reformation Pessimism," 81.
73. Leonard and Crainshaw, *Encyclopedia of Religious Controversies*, 2:599.
74. McGrath, *Historical Theology*, 175.
75. Buschart, *Exploring Protestant Traditions*, 35.
76. MacCulloch, *Reformation*, 699.
77. Zahl, "Reformation Pessimism," 81. See also Zahl's discussion in his *Pneumatology and Theology of the Cross*; MacCulloch, *History of Christianity*, 741; and Rahner and

rationalism and barren orthodoxy," "dead creedal assent of Protestant orthodoxy," and emphasized that a "reformation of doctrine must always be accompanied by a reformation of life" through experiential faith.[78] Against the "doctrinal aridity and moral laxness among Protestants" the movement "aimed at a Second Reformation" and called for a "reform of individuals, the church, and the broader society."[79] The movement asserted that "true church cannot be defined by its confessional and dogmatic stances" but by its fidelity to "inner-life" through new birth by the Holy Spirit.[80] It asserted that the personal experience of the pious is the basis of certainty for religious knowledge. To attain such knowledge, one must have a "personal experience of illumination of the Holy Spirit," which characterizes an "inner transformation of regenerate believers."[81] In reference to its commitment to devotional worship and faith life, the movement was acknowledged as an "intimately devotional renewal movement" that emphasized the "inner encounter with the divine"[82] and as an entire "Protestant evangelical awakening."[83] The movement emphasized "ecstatic experiences and visions," yielded a "series of prophets," and had "many parallels with later Pentecostalism."[84] Its worship and spiritual practices were accompanied by signs, miracles, and healings. Accordingly, it was acknowledged as one of the most significant Charismatic movements in the history of Christianity[85] and was appreciated for making many important contributions to the whole of Christianity in that it "developed new methods of theological education, . . . inspired many moral reforms, . . . [and]gave birth to the revivalism prominent in . . . Protestantism." Above all else, the missionary efforts of the Western churches in the nineteenth and twentieth centuries were rooted in the influence of the Pietist movement. In reference to this contribution, the movement was acknowledged to be an "international and inter-confessional Protestant movement" in the seventeenth and eighteenth centuries, with continuing

---

Vorgrimler, *Theological Dictionary*, 389.

    78. McGrath, *Historical Theology*, 175.

    79. Leonard and Crainshaw, *Encyclopedia of Religious Controversies*, 2:599.

    80. P. D. Hocken, "European Pentecostalism" in Dictionary of Pentecostal and Charismatic Movements, *Dictionary*, 279.

    81. Hagglund, *History of Theology*, 325–29.

    82. MacCulloch, *Reformation*, 665.

    83. Zahl, "Reformation Pessimism," 81.

    84. Thiselton, *Holy Spirit*, 276–78.

    85. Hyatt, *2000 Years*, 95–96.

impact in the nineteenth and twentieth centuries[86] until the birth of twentieth-century Pentecostalism.[87] Historical accounts further suggest that not only those of the Pietist movement in Lutheran Germany but also some believers within British Anglicanism became dissatisfied with their church's negligence of devotional worship and personal spiritual experience which led to the rise of the revivalist movement that came to be known as Methodist movement.

Methodist movement

Evaluations of the rise and growth of the Methodist movement suggest that one of the most remarkable results of the Pietist movement was the birth and growth of eighteenth-century Methodism. Methodism was viewed as the best channel through which the Pietist movement extended its influence into the Pentecostal movement of the twentieth century.[88] Historians recognize John Wesley (1703–91) as the founder of the Methodist movement, who was born, brought up, and taught within Anglicanism.[89] He was a "High Church Anglican Priest,"[90] "ordained in 1728 at the age of twenty-five,"[91] who lived and died an Anglican.[92] On account of his passion for "deep religious devotion," he became a member of the "Holy Club at Oxford University,"[93] along with his brother Charles, which was formed for the purpose of deepening of personal faith life, attaining devotional spirituality, and encouraging others to do the same. Wesley's views were influenced by the "Puritans' stress on moral earnestness and their insistence on single-minded purity in devotion."[94] The Moravians too "sensitized [him] to the inner workings of the Holy Spirit and the importance of fervent personal religious experience."[95] In general, he

86. Leonard and Crainshaw, *Encyclopedia of Religious Controversies*, 2:600–601.

87. D. D. Bundy, "European Pietist Roots of Pentecostalism" in Dictionary of Pentecostal and Charismatic Movements. See also Bundy in *New International Dictionary*, 610–612. Dictionary, 279–80. See also Bundy, "European Pietist Roots," 610–12.

88. Bundy, "European Pietist Roots of Pentecostalism" in *Dictionary*, 279-289.

89. Buschart, *Exploring Protestant Traditions*, 173.

90. MacCulloch, *Reformation*, 700.

91. Hyatt, *2000 Years*, 101.

92. Allen, *Unfailing Stream*, 74.

93. Buschart, *Exploring Protestant Traditions*, 173.

94. Buschart, *Exploring Protestant Traditions*, 174.

95. Buschart, *Exploring Protestant Traditions*, 174.

was influenced by the genuine piety of "Puritanism, Moravians, and Pietism"[96] and thus inspired to go further in the practice of deep spiritual formation.[97] Accordingly, he "organized the first Methodist society" in England in 1738.[98]

The term "Methodist" was originally used by some who "ridiculed the Holy Club's rigorous effort" of attaining devotional spirituality but Wesley later adopted the term to refer to believers who live by the "method of life set forth in the Bible."[99] As such, the term "Methodism" drew its roots from the movement's emphasis on a "methodical approach to seek and encounter God."[100] Wesley also emphasized "second baptism," "holiness," and "perfection," which eventually developed into the doctrine of "entire sanctification."[101] He claimed that God endowed him and his followers with spiritual gifts which enabled them to attain a mystical union with God without any sacramental mediation.[102] His gospel proclamation was said to be accompanied by different kinds of miraculous manifestations, including physical healing and physical movements such as falling on the ground, trembling, roaring, laughing, and crying.[103] The movement was credited for impacting the morality of the entire nation in the country of its birth and growth.[104] From this evidence, it can be noted that the Methodist movement of the eighteenth century observably practiced the gifts and works of the Holy Spirit and thus influenced Anglicanism. Nevertheless, observations indicate that over the course of time even Methodism lost its original passion for deep religious experience after the mid-to-late nineteenth century, which in turn led to the rise of the Holiness movement.

Historical accounts indicate that in the second half of the nineteenth century a separate movement known as the Holiness movement emerged within Methodism in reaction against a "growing formality of Methodist

---

96. Buschart, *Exploring Protestant Traditions*, 174. See MacCulloch, *Reformation*, 700.
97. Dayton, *Theological Roots*, 117–19.
98. Buschart, *Exploring Protestant Traditions*, 174.
99. Buschart, *Exploring Protestant Traditions*, 173.
100. Hyatt, *2000 Years*, 101.
101. Ferm, *Readings*, 413–14.
102. Clement, *Pentecost or Pretense?*, 36.
103. Hyatt, *2000 Years*, 102.
104. Allen, *Unfailing Stream*, 77.

worship ... and liberal theology."[105] Initiators of the movement viewed Methodism as becoming negligent of its original piety and adopting the more common Protestant view of the progressive sanctification of the Christian life.[106] Accordingly, claimants of the movement started with a renewed emphasis on personal experience of faith, moral discipline, sanctification, and perfection.[107] They emphasized a "separate conscious religious experience," a "complete cleansing from sin," and "living with a purity of motives" resulting in a "second blessing" and an "entire sanctification." The core belief, teaching, and experience held by the Holiness movement later became the core teaching, belief, and experience of the Pentecostal movement. Accordingly, in the early twentieth century, both the Holiness and Pentecostal movements continued in parallel to influence other churches with the same worship and spiritual experience.[108] These accounts indicate that concerns over devotional worship, deep religious experience, and a Christian lifestyle continued among the Reformation tradition churches through the nineteenth and twentieth centuries. The same issue that caused the birth and growth of the Radical Reformation continued to cause divisions and split at various times among mainstream Protestants and led to the birth and growth of different revivalist movements.

The story of Pietism and Methodism, in particular, shows that post-Reformation Protestants were continuously challenged by many different revivalist movements concerning devotional worship and deep spiritual experiences. As these two movements contributed to the birth and growth of other movements with similar religious views and emphases, mainstream Protestants have experienced continuous theological, worship, and spiritual experiential shifts in many places from the seventeenth century into the nineteenth century. There seems no account that would indicate whether there were any compromises or modifications in relation to worship and spiritual experience in the majority of mainstream Protestants as a result of the influence of the revivalist movements. There are, however, numerous accounts that indicate that there was substantial and abiding theological, liturgical, and organizational continuity within mainstream Protestant churches and that the magisterial reformers' legacy remained plausible, powerful, and actively continued through

---

105. Leonard and Crainshaw, *Encyclopedia of Religious Controversies*, 1:364.
106. Ledrele, *Treasures Old and New*, 16.
107. Anderson, *Introduction to Pentecostalism*, 27.
108. Leonard and Crainshaw, *Encyclopedia of Religious Controversies*, 1:364–65.

successive centuries. The magisterial reformers' theological and liturgical stance have continued in influencing and shaping successive Protestant churches' theology and doctrine of the Holy Spirit and worship practice even to the present time. Historical accounts affirm that those who subsequently adhered to the theology and practice of the magisterial reformers held the view that the promotion of charismatic piety could subvert the historic Reformation theology of salvation and justification by grace through faith alone, and viewed subjective experiences of the Holy Spirit as a threat to Scriptural and creedal authority.[109] Accordingly, all personal claims regarding the direct experience of the gifts and works of the Holy Spirit were viewed by them as detrimental to Reformation theology and practice.[110] As a result of the influence of these views, successive Protestant churches did not recognize the practice of the gifts and workings of the Holy Spirit as a significant part of faith practices. Rather, they continued to emphasize the real presence of the Holy Spirit only in the preached word and to claim "where the Word is, the Spirit also is." Berkhof refers to Lutheran churches as models of these emphases and asserts that Lutherans strongly maintained the view that the working of the Holy Spirit occurs only "through and together with the Word" and their religious experience continued to be bound to the traditionalist institutional stance.[111] While Berkhof's observation could be considered as based on the existing reality, this has been the case not only with Lutherans but with many other Protestant churches whose theology and worship are also rooted in the Reformation tradition. This is expressly reflected in the writings of some twentieth-century Protestant theologians, who adhere to the magisterial reformers' theological position. The following are presented as examples.

Barth argued that there is fundamentally nothing that can be said about the Holy Spirit and his works except that he is the "power in which Jesus attests himself effectively" and that he is the only "awakening . . . quickening and enlightening" power.[112] He asserted that the Holy Spirit is "no other than the presence and action of Jesus Christ" and is the "power in which Christ is alive among [believers] and makes them his witness." For Barth it is by this power that Jesus enables believers to live in "His presence, in attentiveness to his action, in discipleship as those who

---

109. Lindberg, *Pietist Theologians*, 86.
110. Lindberg, *Third Reformation?*, I.
111. Berkhof, *Doctrine of the Holy Spirit*, 66.
112. Barth, *Church Dogmatics* 4/1:648–49.

belong to him." The Holy Spirit, therefore, in Barth's view, is the power by whose operation Jesus "allows, commands and empowers" believers. Thus, Barth concludes, the Holy Spirit, who makes "Christians Christians is the power of the revelation of Jesus Christ . . . and is self-revelation of the man Jesus"[113] and thus he "cannot be separated from the Word and his power is not a power different from that of the Word, but the power that lives in and by the Word."[114] Similarly, Brunner suggests that the "operation of the Holy Spirit is necessary for the Word about Christ to become the Word of Christ for us, and for the Word of Christ to become the Word of God." The primary and decisive activity of the Holy Spirit, therefore, in Brunner's view, is making Christ present and known to believers.[115] Hence, successors of the magisterial reformers have adopted the view that says, "We should so centre our work on Christocentric preaching, trinitarian Baptism, apostolic teaching, social service, sacramental worship, and evangelical prayer meetings that our parishes will be filled with the Holy Spirit and moved by the challenge of the world mission."[116] Conforming to this, Brecht writes that if any renewal of worship pattern and spiritual practice is sought, then renewal must be made primarily in the belief that Jesus Christ is actively present in worship to save and renew believers and to help and enable them to encounter God the Father. He asserts that where there is awareness of the dynamic presence of Christ in Christian worship and a belief of encounter with that dynamic presence, therein worship is everything it can be, it should be and it must be. For Brecht, it is only Christ's dynamic presence that radically changes and transforms the worshipers' lives into one of God's very own.[117] A similar view was also offered by Clement.

Clement believes that any church which expounds Scripture as the true Word of God and rightly applies this word to its people stands on the right path of dealing successfully with their spiritual questions. In such a church, believers who feel a lack of spiritual vitality in themselves are those "missing the life-giving power of the Holy Spirit" which comes through the word and sacraments. The word, which is "the heavenly manna," in Clement's view, is the only "source of spiritual vitality for heart and spirit." He asserts that it is only when believers sense that

113. Barth, *Church Dogmatics*, 4/2:322–23.
114. Karl Barth, *Church Dogmatics*, 1/1:150.
115. Brunner, *Christian Doctrine of the Church*, 3:12.
116. Bruner, "Of Water and the Spirit," 58.
117. Brecht, *Road to Reformation*, 26–27, 57.

they are not properly fed the word of God in their own church that they are driven to seek spiritual fulfillment elsewhere and search for answers to their questions of spiritual hunger. In such instances churches must be reminded of their failure in helping their members remain close to the word and sacraments through which alone the true feeling of the presence and power of the Holy Spirit can come to them. Any spiritual hunger, says Clement, can never be overcome by engaging in subjective experience, but only through the written and preached word of God and the sacraments. He insists that Christian spiritual hunger can be met and spiritual maturity achieved only by the long process of spiritual growth—growth that can be achieved only through the word and sacraments. He concludes that it is only through these means that the Holy Spirit works and produces a fully sanctified and matured Christian life.[118] Therefore, any movement of spiritual renewal, in his view, must begin from the pulpit wherein the renewing message of God is delivered through the law and the gospel. Every act of any desired spiritual renewal, for Clement, lies in the word, and through that word, the Holy Spirit acts to bring about spiritual renewal. He concludes by saying, "God does not promise spiritual renewal through super-religious experience. . . . Instead he promises spiritual renewal through the Christian's steady, serious, prayerful, and thoughtful use of his Word, the Bible."[119] Taddeus D. Horgan offers a similar observation when he suggests that the gifts and activities of the Holy Spirit, for mainstream Protestants, are not limited to certain patterns of the Spirit manifestations. Rather, all pastoral activities, oversight, direction, sacramental, ordained ministries, etc. are important channels for the presence and workings of the Holy Spirit. Horgan considers that it is in and through these acts the Holy Spirit works towards making the church holy and making believers into charismatic spirituals. Mostly it is in and through the seven sacraments, the acts that are believed to communicate the grace of God, that believers can be nourished, renewed, transformed, and empowered through the works of the Holy Spirit. Protestants emphasize, as Horgan notes, that faithful experience of these channels of grace enables a fuller and deeper understanding of the presence, gifts, and activities of the Holy Spirit.[120] In virtue of this belief,

---

118. Clement, *Pentecost or Pretense?*, 131–33; cf. pp 136–37.

119. Clement, *Pentecost or Pretense?*, 226–28. See also Badcock, *Light of Truth*, 94, and Gerberding, *Way of Salvation*, 97–101. See also Opsahl, *Holy Spirit*, 239–40; Brunner and Hordern, *Holy Spirit*, 50–58.

120. Horgan, "Biblical Basis and Guidelines," 26.

says Moltmann, in most Reformation tradition churches, the Holy Spirit was "bound for mediating grace" and to the preaching of the church and believers' personal experience of the Holy Spirit as "their own personal charismatic endowment," was understood as "unholy and enthusiastic" or even as offensively fanatical.[121]

These accounts are just examples of the dominant conception and practices of the majority of mainstream Protestant churches. From these accounts, it can be noted that the majority of mainstream Protestants continued to maintain what the magisterial reformers maintained and to reject what they rejected. It would seem that most mainstream Protestants have strictly held this conviction until the mid-twentieth century when the Charismatic movement began to introduce the gifts and workings of the Holy Spirit in, with, and through subjective experience. In general observation, it was not until the mid-twentieth century that it was possible to claim and experience the subjective experience of the Holy Spirit in the post-Reformation mainstream Protestant churches. Thus, it can be noted that the sixteenth-century church reformers and their successors did not play a significant role in reviving the subjective experience of the Holy Spirit, but the radical wing of reformers and their successors did.

9.6. HOW THE RADICAL REFORMERS' POSITION CONTINUED TO INFLUENCE THEIR SUCCESSORS

As mentioned above, the radical wing of Protestantism played an important role in reviving the concept and practice of the subjective experience of the Holy Spirit. Interestingly, it seems that no account indicates that the radical reformers tended to deny the presence and working of the Holy Spirit in, with, and through the written and preached word and the sacraments. Even the accounts of their opponents, some of which have been considered in the current chapter, do not suggest that the radical reformers tended to perceive the Holy Spirit apart from objective reception and doctrinal belief. Neither did they deny either the authority of Scripture or the doctrine of justification by grace through faith in Christ. Unlike the magisterial reformers, however, they attempted to revive the place and role of the Holy Spirit in the life and function of the church beyond external means. Although they and their successors were marginalized and continued to survive as a peripheral movement, the conviction

---

121. Moltmann, *Spirit of Life*, 2.

and experience of the radical reformers continued to influence individuals and groups within mainstream Protestantism and produced some movements with similar convictions and practices from the Reformation up to the turn of the twentieth century. Their convictions of attaining, living, and serving Spirit-gifted, Spirit-illumined, Spirit-empowered, and Spirit-inspired devotional worship and charismatic form of spirituality continued to influence as many people as possible.

In virtue of this conviction, the successors of the radical reformers reacted against an overemphasis on rigid academic theology, confessional orthodoxy, and a conservative evangelicalism of Protestantism. For example, Mennonites were influenced by the radical reformers and became their immediate descendants. They continued the radicals' legacy through their charismatic influence on succeeding generations[122] and have remained strictly faithful to their "Anabaptist roots" until the present day.[123] Quakers advocate an "inner word" or "inner voice" of God which is given directly to the human heart through the Holy Spirit.[124] They emphasize that believers can experience "personal inner light" and directly communicate with God without any need for external worship. For Quakers, says Congar, true worship does not take place in churches and Scripture cannot be regarded as the Christian norm. Instead, the Holy Spirit reveals himself in the "inner light and baptizes with true baptism." They emphasize "inner prayer in sitting silently" and wait on a word from God through revelation whereby one of the participants who might be inspired by the Holy Spirit breaks the silence and speaks the revealed word to the congregation.[125] Several religious groups such as Hutterite Brethren and Amish Mennonites also belong to the Radical Reformation.[126] These religious groups will not be considered further here. However, in general, it seems that the influence of the radical reformers' conviction and practice of devotional worship and subjective experience of the Holy Spirit produced many like-minded revivalist movements into the twentieth century. The twentieth-century Pentecostal movement emerged as a result of the continued influence of and as a real and final offshoot of the Radical Reformation.

---

122. Hyatt, *2000 Years*, 84–85.
123. Balmer, *Encyclopaedia of Evangelicalism*, 447.
124. Burgess, "Quakers (Society of Friends)," 1014.
125. Congar, *I Believe*, 1:142.
126. Buschart, *Exploring Protestant Tradition*, 59; cf. pp. 66–68.

9.7. SUMMARY

In closing the chapter, three points deserve particular consideration with regard to the Reformation theological tradition in light of the above accounts and discussion.

Firstly, if the magisterial reformers emphasized salvation by faith alone, grace alone, Scripture alone, and the sacraments as the means for the workings of the Holy Spirit, did they deviate from biblical teaching? If they did emphasize these features, is this not utterly in agreement with Jesus' teaching and deeds? As discussed in chapter 4, it is obvious that Christianity in its entirety is rooted in five divinely appointed and divinely delivered means of salvation, i.e., faith in Christ, holy baptism, holy communion, the word of God, and the gift of the Holy Spirit. The gospel accounts indicate that Jesus asserted these features as an end in themselves for salvation and for attaining eternal life. The Holy Spirit, in particular, is God's unique gift to believers to indwell, gift, empower, and guide them into all truth in the salvation process. Since God has instituted these features as essential means of salvation and works in and through them towards bringing salvation, the Holy Spirit also works through them as he works only what God works. According to the gospels, salvation is impossible without these features. It seems that God has laid specific salvific power and mandates on these features. When the entire New Testament is examined, it seems that salvation is possible without receiving and experiencing charismatic gifts, but not without these essential features. The Gospel accounts assert that faith in Christ, holy baptism, holy communion, and the word of God are essential and normative for salvation, Christian theology, doctrine, life, and practice. These features form the basis of Christian salvation and make salvation the settled possession of a believer. They are paramount parameters for Christian belief, teaching, practice, and mission. Their theological and salvific significance is enduring and lasting from Hosanna to Maranatha. Thus, by asserting the centrality of these features for the church's life and practice, the reformers were able to give proper theological and functional place and role to these features. By the same token, what the reformers attributed to the Holy Spirit in relation to these features was theologically correct, christologically correct, pneumatologically correct, soteriologically correct, and ever remains thus. Their position in this regard, at least in my opinion, was fundamentally right, is fundamentally right, and shall remain fundamentally right. It answers all questions and resolves all confusion about salvation and Christian practice. Thus, once again we must acknowledge, in agreement with Luther, that "here we Christians stand!" Despite these fundamental facts, it cannot then be refuted that the controversial exchange of the magisterial reformers with the radical reformers, their defecting colleagues, on the issues of the gifts and workings of the Holy Spirit, has played a significant role in forming the background for the development of their understanding, interpretation, and application of the presence, gifts, and works of the Holy Spirit in Christian teaching and practice.

Secondly, if the magisterial reformers did not emphasize the subjective experience of the Holy Spirit, which includes "inward-voice of God," does that mean they entirely reacted against the presence, gifts, and working of the Holy Spirit in faith experience? Can it be imagined that they lived and acted without realizing the gifts, power, and guidance of the Holy Spirit? If Luther, for example, was not gifted, empowered, illumined, and guided by the Holy Spirit, could he have the power and encouragement to start the Reformation movement from Wittenberg, one of the famous theological institutions of the time in Europe? If the Holy Spirit, who has been the architect of renewal, reformation, and transformation from the inception of creation, had not enlightened Luther on the way toward the Reformation and renewal of the church, could his reform ambition have succeeded in becoming such an effective and prevalent movement? If the Holy Spirit, who inspired and guided the writing of the Scriptures, had not spoken directly to Luther through the inner voice towards the rediscovery of the secret of salvation by God's grace through faith in Christ, could Luther's reform movement have been favorable and influential as it no doubt was? The short answer to these questions, I believe, is: no, not at all! Luther did not simply throw himself into the risk of the reform movement which acted against his powerful church—the church that was burning theologians at the stake, such as John Hus, who intended to reform the church. Rather, he was clear enough in understanding what is meant by gift, inner light, empowerment, and guidance of the Holy Spirit. These features, for Luther, are meant not only for some audibly uttered and visibly performed charismatic gifts but also to enlighten and lead to the truth as revealed in the Scriptures. It is this that caused him to be the ever confident conqueror for the entire Reformation vision and movement. If the "inward voice" of the Holy Spirit is meant to be sought after, attained, and acted upon to serve God, save others, and build up the church, then surely Luther's story sets an example. From a genuine Christian point of view, his was a genuine realization and experience of the "inward voice" of the Holy Spirit.

Thirdly, in light of the above accounts and discussion, it may be argued that, despite Protestantism having many positive things to say about the strengths of the magisterial reformers' theological convictions, teachings, practices, and prolific written legacies, their doctrine of the Holy Spirit employed apparent negligence towards the presence, gifts, and works of the Holy Spirit in the church beyond the external means. It would nevertheless be difficult to criticize them on this case, because, on the one hand, their mother church had ignored the experiential aspect of the Holy Spirit for centuries. Therefore, they might have been unsure about how to adapt and experience this. On the other hand, they might have opposed the radical reformers' extreme claim and practice of the Holy Spirit. Be that as it may, another extreme emerged when successors of the magisterial reformers continued to emphasize what the magisterial reformers emphasized and to reject what they rejected. This led most mainstream Protestant churches to the perception that integrating the subjective experience of the Holy Spirit into their teaching and practice could be the moral equivalent of defecting to the radical reformers' theology and practice. As a result, the claim of, and experience of, the presence, gifts, and workings of the Holy Spirit and the resulting charismatic spirituality was no longer possible in mainstream Protestant churches until the mid-twentieth century when the Charismatic movement began to introduce to their congregations these. This lack of attention to the experience of the Holy Spirit in mainstream Protestantism led churches to periodically break away and caused the birth and growth of the revivalist movements which held views mostly similar to those of the radical reformers. One of such movements was the Pentecostal movement which emerged in the early twentieth century as a result of the continued influence of the Radical Reformation. Through the influence of this Radical Reformation offshoot movement, the subjective experience of the Holy Spirit has become somehow a common experience of Christendom. This will be briefly discussed in chapters 11 and 12.

CHAPTER 10

The Overall Image of the Christian Teaching and Practice of the Person, Gifts, and Works of the Holy Spirit from AD 100 to 1900

In the introduction, I mentioned that some scholars, those who have critically examined the place and role of the Holy Spirit in Christian belief, teaching, and practice through the centuries, have argued that the Holy Spirit was a neglected member of the Trinity. I indicated that some of these scholars have argue that the doctrine of the Holy Spirit "belongs to the uncompleted doctrines of the church." Some have argue that historically the Holy Spirit was treated as the "eclipsed," "subordinated," the "shy/silent member of the Trinity," etc. Others argue that the Holy Spirit was treated as the "stepchild of theology," the "Cinderella of the Trinity," and the "dark side of the moon" in Trinitarian councils. These strange scholarly terms and designations of the place and role of the Holy Spirit in the church have raised questions in my mind such as: What do these scholarly terms and designations refer to? Does this mean that the church lacked interest in the person, presence, gifts, and workings of the Holy Spirit? If this was indeed the case, then what factors led the church to the ignoring of the Holy Spirit to the extent that he was treated as the Cinderella, the stepchild, the shy member of the Trinity, \ the dark side of theology, etc.? A search for answers to these questions played a role in prompting this study and in leading to the writing of this book. After exploring the place and role of the Holy Spirit in Christian belief, teaching, and practice from the apostolic times up to the end of the nineteenth century these questions are answered albeit in part. This chapter will briefly summarize the findings of the overall images of the historical Christian perception, teaching, and practice of the presence, gifts, and works of the Holy Spirit discussed in chapters 5 to 9.

10.1. OVERALL IMAGES OF THE PLACE AND ROLE OF THE HOLY SPIRIT FROM A. D. 100 TO 1900

Historical accounts examined and discussed in chapters 5 to 9 are clear enough in demonstrating two things. *First*, they demonstrate that the Holy Spirit is believed in and worshiped as the divine and understood and described as ever present in Christian theological tradition since Pentecost of the first century. *Second*, they demonstrate that the presence, gifts, and workings of the Holy Spirit were mostly ignored in Christian perception, teaching, and practice. As discussed in those chapters, there have been some biblical and historical practical reasons behind the identified ignorance. To summarize what we have already discussed in those chapters, the following points suffice as examples:

1. The biblical accounts discussed in chapters 1 to 3 clearly show that manifestations of the Holy Spirit often entailed both the objective impartation and subjective experiential content of the Holy Spirit in equal measure. As discussed in chapters 2 and 3, biblical accounts indicate that in biblical times the coming of the Holy Spirit sometimes equally entailed both objective manifestation of divine reality and subjective experience of the gifts, power and works of the Holy Spirit. When God imparted the Holy Spirit to his people, his gracious charismatic gifts and power were also imparted along with the impartation of the Holy Spirit. There was both objective imparting of the Holy Spirit from the divine side and subjective experiential movement from the people's side, which resulted from the gift endowed and the power imparted along with the Holy Spirit. The subjective experiences of the Holy Spirit, which were manifested in audible or visible charismatic experiences, were divinely destined, divinely delivered, Spirit-initiated, theologically objective, and practically genuine. The New Testament, however, does not strictly instruct its audiences in a clear way regarding how to realize and preserve subjective experiential content of reception of the Holy

Spirit as a necessary part of Christian teaching and practice. The New Testament's silence would, therefore, appear to have created a gap of instruction for the views of either claiming or ignoring the subjective experience of the Holy Spirit.

2. The church of the postapostolic period, as discussed in chapter 5, developed a hierarchical mindset that formally declared that the Spirit-charismata should not be sought and experienced among believers. This tradition persisted in strictly restricting the subjective experience of the Holy Spirit through audibly uttered and visibly performed charismatic gifts. This restrictionist tradition took a stronghold and led the ordained leadership of successive centuries to avoid a *Pentecostal-charismatic* form of spiritual experience within the institutional life of the church. This tradition continued in obscuring the place and role of the Holy Spirit in the church's teaching and practice.

3. In the church of the early second century, as discussed in chapter 6, many competing religious movements claimed to practice the gifts and workings of the Holy Spirit in one form or another. Defense against the teachings and practices of those competing movements led the early patristic church toward further restriction of any tendency to claim the gifts and workings of the Holy Spirit. Any kind of measure taken to defend those movements acted as a mask to internally weaken the thought and practice of the gifts and workings of the Holy Spirit.

4. The worst and deadliest scenario of the church's ignoring of the reception, gifts, and workings of the Holy Spirit came along with the emergence of the Montanist movement and the church's repudiation of it. As discussed in chapter 7, it was the wider church's repudiation of the Montanists' *Pentecostal-charismatic* form of worship and spiritual practice that marked the beginning of a course of events that severely affected the church's belief, teaching, and practice of the subjective experiential content of the Holy Spirit and created tensions between the institutional and charismatic forms of Christian perception, teaching, worship, and practice. This was the time when the church took formal measures to push aside belief in, and claims of, the presence, gifts, and workings of the Holy Spirit through subjective experience. These historical events led the church to the two contradicting and conflicting views of the doctrine

of the Holy Spirit, i.e., those of institutional-organizational, on the one hand, and of Pentecostal-charismatic views on the other. From then on the institutional church continued to closely associate the Holy Spirit with emotional and enthusiastic subjective experience and strictly avoided such experiences. Through the veil of avoiding such enthusiastic subjective experiences, the church continued to ignore the place and role of the Holy Spirit in its teaching, worship and spiritual practices for centuries.

5. The second council's formulation of the doctrine of the Holy Spirit emphasized doctrinal belief in the Holy Spirit and ignored the issue of his gifts and workings through subjective experience. As discussed in chapter 6, the second council's formulation of the doctrine of the Holy Spirit played a decisive role both in settling the church's doctrine of the Holy Spirit and in clearly dividing objective doctrinal belief and subjective experience of the Holy Spirit. Through the veil of maintaining the patristic church's repudiation of the Montanist spirituality and the second council's formulation of the doctrinal belief of the Holy Spirit, the medieval church further ignored the role of the Holy Spirit in and through subjective experience.

6. The medieval Western church developed the practice of nonbiblical traditions by which it replaced the place and role of the Holy Spirit and obscured the Holy Spirit from the church's teachings, worship, and spiritual practices. As discussed in chapter 8, not only subjective experience but also the concept of objective reception and doctrinal belief of the Holy Spirit appears to have been thoroughly ignored in the medieval Western church's thoughts and practices. According to the accounts consulted in chapter 8, indeed, the medieval Western church excluded not only the gifts and workings of the Holy Spirit but also excluded him from confessional statements. In this period of church history, the church's rejection of Montanist spirituality resulted in the church's complete omission of the Holy Spirit in confessions, teachings, and worship practices. Consequently, the entire teaching, worship, and spiritual practice of the church moved away from Spirit-gifted, Spirit-empowered, Spirit-inspired, and Spirit-initiated worship and spiritual practice and prioritized organizational structure and human hierarchy dominated practice.

7. In line with the church's long-standing doctrine of the Holy Spirit, the sixteenth-century church reformers also failed to emphasize the

subjective experience of the Holy Spirit as part of their central theological teaching and spiritual practice. As discussed in chapter 9, the lack of emphasis on the subjective experience of the Holy Spirit resulted in division among the leading reformers and caused the birth and growth of the Radical Reformation. Even though there are many positive things to say about the strengths of the magisterial reformers' theological convictions, teachings, practices, and prolific written legacies, their pneumatology employed negligence toward the subjective experience of the Holy Spirit.

8. The theological tradition of successors to the magisterial reformers continued to maintain what the magisterial reformers maintained and reject what they rejected. This stance led most mainstream Protestant churches to the perception that integrating the subjective experience of the Holy Spirit into their theological teaching and spiritual practice might be considered the moral equivalent of defecting to the radical reformers' theological tradition. Accordingly, the claim and experience of subjective experience of the Holy Spirit and resulting charismatic spirituality was impossible in mainstream Protestant churches until the mid-twentieth century when the Charismatic movement began to introduce to their congregations the workings of the Holy Spirit in, with, and through subjective experience. This lack of attention to the subjective experience of the Holy Spirit in mainstream Protestantism led churches to periodically break away and caused the birth and growth of revivalist movements which held views mostly similar to those of the radical reformers.

As a result of these major features, the working of the Holy Spirit in and through the *Pentecostal-charismatic* aspect of the church's life and function was subjected to the institutional church's severe rejection and suppression. Taken together, these features might indeed have played a role in contributing to obscure the distinctive place and role of the Holy Spirit in the life and function of the church. Viewed through the windows of these features, it can be noted that in the history of the church the Holy Spirit was often ignored member of the Trinity from Christian teaching, worship, and spiritual practices. In the light of these features, it can be neither denied nor refuted that there was a grave imbalance between the institutional-organizational and Pentecostal-charismatic life and function of the church which in turn exposed the institutional church to the unintentional ignoring of the place and role of the Holy Spirit. Hence, this historical negligence of the place and role of the Holy Spirit in the life and function of the church resulted in the emergence of two different views: The first view argues that the Holy Spirit was neglected to the extent he was considered as "the Cinderella of the Trinity." The second view argues that manifestation of the Spirit-charismata had ceased in the postapostolic life and function of the church. This view has traditionally been viewed as the "cessationist view." These two different views will be briefly examined as follows.

10.2. THE VIEW THAT ARGUES THAT HISTORICALLY THE HOLY SPIRIT WAS NEGLECTED PERSON OF THE TRINITY.

Some scholars who have critically examined the place and role of the Holy Spirit in Christian belief, teaching, and practice through the centuries have argued that the Holy Spirit was a neglected member of the Trinity. A few of their arguments are presented here as examples. Elizabeth A. Dreyer, in her book entitled *Holy Power, Holy Presence: Rediscovering Medieval Metaphor for the Holy Spirit*, under sub-topic "Neglect of the Spirit," argues that the Western church has often been criticized for neglecting the Holy Spirit in its theology and practices. Citing from many different primary sources that criticize the medieval Western church's theology of the Holy Spirit, Elizabeth writes that the Holy Spirit was viewed as "personally amorphous, faceless, forgotten, upstaged, ethereal and vacant, unclear, and invisible." She adds that he was also viewed as "ambiguous, reticent, obscure, neglected, groping, [and] abstract."[1] Brunner argues that in church history "less than justice" has been done to the "dynamic operation of the Holy Spirit" and that the Holy Spirit and his operations have held a "much less important place than in the New Testament witness to the Holy Spirit."[2] Traditionally, argues Brick Bradford, the Holy Spirit has been regarded as the "stepchild of theology" and that the "dynamism of the Spirit has been a bugbear for theologians."[3] Similarly, Cartledge argues that the Holy Spirit has traditionally been "seriously subordinated to the other two persons of the Trinity; to the

---

1. Dreyer, *Holy Power*, 13.
2. Brunner, *Christian Doctrine of the Church*, 3:15.
3. Bradford, *Releasing the Power*, 18

institutional order; to ministerial orders; and sacraments" such that the Holy Spirit's "significance for both theological practices and Christian life has been eclipsed."[4] Amos Yong argues that the Holy Spirit was made the "shy or silent member of the Trinity" whose role has been "marginalized" in Christian thoughts, practice, and academic theological works.[5] On account of such negligence, says McGrath, the Holy Spirit has traditionally been made the "Cinderella of the Trinity." Explaining what he means by "Cinderella of the Trinity," McGrath states that while the other two persons of the Trinity may have gone to the "theological ball; the Holy Spirit was left behind every time."[6] Accordingly, say Burgess and McGee, the Holy Spirit has traditionally been the "neglected member of the Trinity" and was treated as if he were a "mere influence of little importance" such that he became "the dark side of the moon."[7] Surely, says Dale F. Bruner, the Holy Spirit was "the great neglected person of the Godhead" and is "really the shy member of the Trinity."[8] Here the question that might be considered is: are these strange and unusual scholarly terms and designations regarding the status of the historical place and role of the Holy Spirit correct?

Whether these strange and unusual scholarly terms and designations regarding the historical situation of the person, gifts, and works of the Holy Spirit are literally right or not, there are sufficient grounds to acknowledge their terms and designations to be justifiable and valid. Given the historical practical situations discussed in chapters 5 to 9, it can be noted that there was indeed a grave imbalance between the institutional life of the church and the realization of the presence, gifts, and workings of the Holy Spirit through Spirit-initiated subjective experience. As repeatedly mentioned in previous chapters, the entire teaching, worship, and spiritual life of the church continued to move from a Spirit-gifted, Spirit-empowered, Spirit-inspired, Spirit-initiated, and Spirit-awakened worship and spiritual practice into an institutional-organizational and human hierarchy dominated life and practice. Consequently, the entire nature of the church's theological teaching and spiritual practice became

---

4. Cartledge, *Encountering the Spirit*, 15.

5. Yong, "Ruach," 183. See also Bruner and Hordern, *Holy Spirit*, 16; Bergmann, "Revisioning Pneumatology," 183–87, wherein Bergmann expresses his impression of how the Holy Spirit was "reduced and marginalized" in the history of the Church.

6. McGrath, *Christian Theology*, 240.

7. Horton, "Holy Spirit" in *Dictionary*, 410.

8. Bruner, "Shy Member of the Trinity," 16.

"practical-minded, this-worldly, and authoritarian."[9] Hence, close observation and critical examination of this historical reality led scholars such as those cited above to coin these unusual terms and designations to interpret, express, and display the story of the place and role of the Holy Spirit in a comprehensible manner. Viewed in this way, the scholars' coining of terms such as "eclipsed," "subordinated," "silenced member," "stepchild," "Cinderella," and "dark side of the moon" in the church's Trinitarian teaching and practice is reflective of and referential to the church's ignoring of the presence and role of the Holy Spirit for most of its history. The scholars' strange terms and designations are, therefore, surely based on the reality that existed through the centuries and are thus valid and valuable insofar as they reflect that reality.

10.3. THE CESSATIONIST VIEW

The church's negligence of the manifest connection of the Holy Spirit with charismata and experience of the resultant audibly uttered and visibly performed charismatic gifts has caused the rise of the cessationist view of charismatic gifts of the Holy Spirit. We have noted in chapters 1 to 3 that Scripture recounts that in biblical times the coming of the Holy Spirit mostly entailed two features equally: the objective manifestation of divine reality and subjective experience of the presence, gifts, power, and workings of the Holy Spirit. Expression of reception of the Holy Spirit, his gifts, and his moving power took place only through the expression of the Spirit-initiated, audibly uttered, and visibly performed charismatic experiences. The manifestation of audibly uttered and visibly performed charismata, therefore, acted in biblical times as the means of believers' expression of the reception of the Holy Spirit as well as Spirit-delivered and Spirit-initiated subjective experience. However, except for clear indications of the Holy Spirit's manifest connections with audible and visible charismatic gifts and resultant Spirit-initiated subjective experience, the New Testament neither encourages nor discourages continued realization and regularization of the Spirit-charismata. When the New Testament books are examined it becomes evident that none of their writers wrote firmly that Spirit-charismata were meant to be sought, prayed for, received, and experienced as mandatory components of the life and function of the church.

9. Culpepper, *Evaluating the Charismatic Movement*, 40.

In addition to the lack of strict sanction in Scripture, the postapostolic church adopted and developed a hierarchical mindset that declared that Spirit-charismata should not be sought or experienced among believers. This tradition was further strengthened when the church rejected and condemned Montanist charismatic spirituality. Thereafter, on the pretext of protecting itself from a sectarian form of spirituality, the church continued to firmly push charismatic experience aside. Accordingly, subjective experience of the biblical times did not continue in the life and function of the church for centuries. We have considered some of the main biblical and historical practical reasons for why the perception and practice of charismata did not continue and why it contributed to tensions, conflicts, and controversies within the doctrine of the Holy Spirit. In the course of time, this stance contributed to the church's ignoring of the Holy Spirit in confessions, theological teachings, and spiritual practices. It is as a result of all these features that the Holy Spirit's working in and through charismatic gifts was subject to the institutional church's thorough rejection and suppression. Consequently, this tradition resulted in the emergence of those scholars who held a view advocating that charismatic gifts of the Holy Spirit were a decadent theological tradition and, therefore, in the postapostolic life and function of the church charismata ceased. It was this view that became known as the "cessationist view."

Proponents of this view present two reasons to justify why they think charismatic gifts of the Holy Spirit were ceased in the post-apostolic life and function of the church.

The first reason was the temporary and foundational nature of the charismatic gifts. Cessationists argue that the apostles received charismatic gifts because they were a special group as revelatory agents of God. These gifts, however, ceased when the time of the apostles came to an end. Among scholars who take a cessationist view is Benjamin B. Warfield. In his book entitled *Counterfeit Miracles*, under the sub-topic "The Cessation of the Charismata," Warfield discusses charismatic gifts in detail and considers a question: "How long did this state of things continue?" In response to this question, he argues that the existence and function of the charismatic gifts were confined only to the apostolic ministry and not intended to direct the extension of the church thereafter. He asserts that charismatic gifts were "distinctively the authentication of the Apostles" and that these gifts were "part of the credentials of the Apostles as the authoritative agents of God in founding the church." Their function, therefore, in his view, "confined them to distinctively the Apostolic church, and they necessarily passed away with it." At the beginning of the foundation of the church, according to Warfield, "God was pleased to accompany it with a miraculous power," but after the church was founded God purposely ceased that power and left the church to be "maintained by ordinary ways." To support his argument, Warfield adduces other sources that argue that charismatic gifts "continued for a while in the post-Apostolic period, and only slowly died out like a light fading away by increasing distance from its source." In agreement with this source, Warfield asserts that the "rich manifestations of spiritual gifts present in the Apostolic Church, gradually grew less through the succeeding centuries until they finally dwindled by the end of the third century." He states that the cessation of charismata was particularly dated to the time of Constantine, when "Christianity came to be established by the civil power." Being delivered and protected from all the dangers of persecution, "under the protection of the greatest power on earth," that is the protection of Constantine, Warfield notes that the church was no longer in want of the charismatic gifts. Therefore, concludes Warfield, there is no reason to expect the apostolic miracle-working to continue for successive centuries.[10]

An analogous argument is offered by John F. MacArthur, Jr. In his book entitled *Charismatic Chaos*, MacArthur argues that the apostles had a non-transferable unique commission to reveal doctrine and establish the church. He argues that the apostles' "names are unique; their office is unique; their ministry is unique; the miracles they did are unique. [They] were . . . a special breed; they had no successors" and the "age of the apostles and what they did is forever in the past." "After the martyrdom of Stephen," says MacArthur, "no miracle was performed and recorded." The miracles of the apostolic age, in MacArthur's view, were not to be the pattern for Christians of succeeding generations. Therefore, concludes MacArthur, there is no need and no mandate for Christians beyond the apostolic age to expect or to perform miracles, except the mandate to study and obey the written and preserved word of God.[11] Further strengthening these arguments, Richard B. Gaffin, Jr. argues that anyone dealing with the New Testament is bound to recognize the temporary and foundational character of the apostolic ministry. Gaffin suggests that the "once-for-all foundational work of Christ" that is "consummated in his

---

10. Warfield, *Counterfeit Miracles*, 3–7.
11. MacArthur, *Charismatic Chaos*, 150–52.

death and resurrection," was joined by the "once-for-all witnesses" of the apostles. The apostles, therefore, had a "foundational, that is a temporary, non-continuing function in the church's history." He asserts that by God's design the apostolic charismatic ministry "pass out of its life, along with the apostles." Therefore, claiming a continuance of the apostolic charismatic experiences into subsequent generations of the church, in Gaffin's view, would "create tensions with the closed and finished character of the canon"[12] of Scripture. Offering a conclusive statement to the cessationist arguments, John Metcalfe writes,

> Just as the manna ceased, the pillar of cloud and fire departed, the water from the Rock which followed them withdrew, having fulfilled their purpose when Israel entered into the land, so it is with us, in terms of apostolic signs, since we have entered by so great salvation into the rest that remains for the people of God, being baptized into one body in one Spirit our signs—the signs of the *new* covenant—likewise having reached the satisfactory conclusion of their abundant witness.[13]

Metcalfe then asks "what remains?" He answers by drawing from Eph 4:4–6 and asserting that what remains is the word of God, one body and one Spirit, One Lord, one faith, one baptism; One God and the Father of all. Having fulfilled their destined purpose of the time, the generation of the apostles and the signs of the apostles have ceased. Therefore, any pursuit of the apostolic signs and wonders, in Metcalfe's view, simply diverts attention from the one and the main thing needed—i.e., Scripture—to the futile things.[14] Similar strong cessationist arguments are offered by such scholars as Samuel E. Waldron and Douglas Judisch.[15]

The second reason for the ceasing of the charismatic gifts, for the cessationists, is the completion of the New Testament canon. Cessationists argue that any miraculous and revelational charismata were bestowed on the apostles to advocate will of God before the canon of Scripture was completed after which these gifts ceased. Asserting this notion, MacArthur argues that "just as the close of the Old Testament canon was followed by silence, so the close of the New Testament canon has been followed by the utter absence of new revelational charismata

---

12. Gaffin, *Perspectives on Pentecost*, 89–100.
13. Metcalfe, *Gifts and Baptism of the Spirit*, 40–41.
14. Metcalfe, *Gifts and Baptism of the Spirit*, 40–41.
15. Waldron, *To Be Continued?*, 38–43; Judisch, *Evaluation of Claims*, 80–83.

in any form." Since the canon of Scripture was completed, MacArthur declares, *"no genuine revival or orthodox movement has ever been led by people whose authority is based in any way on private revelations from God."* Therefore, concludes MacArthur, it is incorrect to claim that the miraculous and revelational charismata should be the norm beyond the apostolic age.[16] After the close of the canon of Scripture, says Warfield, the "one gospel suffices for all lands and all peoples and all times, by so much does the miraculous attestation of that one single gospel suffice for all lands and all times, and no further miracles are to be expected in connection to it." Warfield asserts that after the canon of Scripture was completed, "God the Holy Spirit has made it his subsequent work, not to introduce new and unneeded revelation into the world, but to diffuse this one complete revelation through the world and to bring mankind into the saving knowledge of it." Through this one gospel, notes Warfield, God has given to the world "one organically complete revelation, adapted to all, sufficient for all, provided for all, and from this one completed revelation he requires each to draw his whole spiritual sustenance." Therefore, concludes Warfield, the miraculous working of God, "cannot be expected to continue, and in point of fact does not continue, after the revelation of which it is the accompaniment has been completed."[17] The next revelation to be expected, in the view of the cessationists, is the exalted Lord's immediate appearance in judgment. Until then the "governing principle is 'the Spirit with the word': the Spirit working in a convincing and illuminating fashion the foundational, apostolic tradition or deposit" which is the completed, closed and finished character of the canon.[18] From these accounts, it can be noted that the time of the completion of the New Testament canon, which is traditionally recognized to have been at the Council of Carthage in 397, was the point of departure for the charismatic gifts of the Holy Spirit from the church.

10.4. SUMMARY

In light of the above accounts and discussions, two main points can be drawn in the conclusion of the chapter.

---

16. MacArthur, *Charismatic Chaos*, 72, 86 (emphasis original); cf. pp. 123–24.
17. Warfield, *Counterfeit Miracles*, 26–27.
18. Gaffin, *Perspectives on Pentecost*, 112–13.

First, in light of the biblical and historical factors presented above, the cessationists' view, on the one hand, appears to be rationalistic. The lack of Scriptural dogmatization of the continued realization and regularization of the charismatic gifts can lead people to views such as those of the cessationists. As the Scriptures neither encourage nor discourage the continued realization of the charismatic gifts, it might indeed be difficult to emphasize those features where the Scriptures seem silent. Since the Scriptures do not dogmatize the continued realization of the charismatic gifts in the same way they dogmatize faith in Christ, holy baptism, holy communion, and abiding in the word of God, the notion of charismatic experience could be subject to views which both ignore and claim this. This could indeed be one of the main reasons why many prominent evangelical theologians could feel afraid of or draw back from emphasizing the continued realization of charismatic experiences. As we shall see, a change relating to emphasis on the continued realization of the charismatic gifts has come about only since the 1970s when the Charismatic movement emerged, expanded, and impacted all the Christian denominations indiscriminately. Viewed in light of all these biblical and historical situations, the cessationists' perception and interpretation cannot be criticized as mere groundless fantasy. On the other hand, however, the cessationist position can not be favored over other perspectives of the New Testament's teaching. Four particular reasons can be suggested in this regard:

(1) When viewed in the overall context of the realized kingdom of God, no segment of the apostolic gifts, ministry, and mission can be declared ceased. True it is that the age of the apostles ended, but that does not mean their gifts, ministry, and mission also ended or ceased. Nothing that is related to the realized and yet-to-come kingdom of God, begun with Jesus' ministry and transmitted to the church through the ministry of the apostles, ended at any point. Rather, everything that began with Jesus' ministry and transmitted to the church continues to the destined end at the perfection of the eternal state, consequent upon Christ's return. As the church is apostolic in its entire content, mission, and quality, Christian theology should rather affirm that the mission of the apostles had, has, and will have proper successors and will continue to the end of the present age. Through the apostolic ministry gifts of different varieties of charismata, God enables the church to progress toward the complete realization of the eschatological goals of consummate spiritual maturity. While it is true that the mission and ministry of the apostles were

foundational, the charismatic gifts the apostles realized and with which they served were meant for the entire church of Christ as an expression and assurance of salvation, and for the entire period from Hosanna to Maranatha. As the charismatic gifts are broadly connected to the apostles through the context of the life and ministry of the realized kingdom of God, but not narrowly to the age and ministry of the apostles only, they will persist until the end of this age.

(2) The charismatic gifts of the Holy Spirit were not intended only for the writing and canonization process of Scripture, as the cessationists maintained. Therefore, their function cannot come to an end with the closure of the canon of Scripture. While it cannot be denied that God speaks through Scripture, he also speaks and works through charismata beyond Scripture through individuals whom he counts deserving to be given charismatic gifts. As discussed in chapters 3 and 4, the gospel message and the church's mission are always divine power and action-oriented. The striking power and action of God are still revealed and enacted through the manifestation, realization, and practice of the gifts and works of the Holy Spirit. The canonization of Scripture, therefore, does not set a boundary for God nor make him remote transcendent. Nor is the church living on the planet closed off from God's intervention nor is it using the Scriptures closed off from the affirming gifts, power, and action of God. The cessationists' argument in this regard, therefore, can be viewed as alien to the entire context of the church's life and practice of the realized kingdom of God that lasts from Hosanna to Maranatha, and thus their view and argument are pointless.

(3) As already noted previously, the church's lack of interest in charismatic gifts does not necessarily mean the absence of the charismatic gifts and charismatic content of Christian spiritual experience. The church's lack of interest in, or even restriction of, the workings of the Holy Spirit in, with, and through the Spirit-charismata, for whatever reason, does not necessarily mean that the restriction of these gifts came from the giver's side. It was rather only receivers and practitioners who have restricted these through their documented rules and regulations of restriction. Neither does this mean that Christians who long for, seek, and pray for these gifts disappear from the church. When viewed from theological, biblical, and historical practical perspectives, the experiences relating to the reception of the Holy Spirit and Spirit-charismata came as God's manifestation and communication to renew, transform, gift, empower, equip, and guide his church. Therefore, initiating the reception of

the Holy Spirit and dispensing charismatic gifts was, is, and will forever remain the possession and prerogative of the Triune God. As long as God communicates with his people not only through the ordained leadership but also individually, he continuously endows individual believers with these gifts whenever and wherever he targets specific salvation acts or in response to specific spiritual hunger. From a human side, no one has been given the authority to dispense or prohibit these divine possessions and gifts. Neither the apostles nor the church nor the ordained leadership were the initiators of the reception of the Holy Spirit and dispensers of the charismatic gifts. Since Christians do not experience the choices, interests, or feelings of the apostles or successive ordained leadership but the divine gifts of the divinely initiated mission of the church, it is up to the beneficiaries to long for, to seek, to pray for, to receive and realize, or to ignore these gifts. While what the church of earlier centuries said or did in its context may not be criticized from the perspectives of a contemporary mindset, its persistent restriction of the experience of the Spirit-charismata among believers has been pointless and is impossible to concede from theological and biblical standpoints. Thus, the cessationists must be reminded about this reality.

(4) Above all else, the evidence presented in chapters 3 to 9 presents examples of the weakened but continued existence of charismatic experiences in the church through the centuries. To summarize some of the conclusions drawn from the evidence in earlier chapters:

> A. This study has attempted to carefully examine whether there are any theological or biblical grounds for charismatic experiences becoming a pattern of tension within the doctrine of the Holy Spirit but no such reasons were found. As discussed in chapter 3, in biblical times Spirit-endowed and Spirit-initiated charismata were experienced only as the divine side of reality and as Spirit-endowed and Spirit-initiated experiences. Therefore, it would appear that there was no tension, confusion, or ambiguity related to or resulting from the realization and experiences of Spirit-charismata.
>
> B. The study has also attempted to carefully examine if there have been any proven detrimental effects when and where charismatic experiences were incorporated into worship through the history of the church, but found no evidence that indicates this. For example, charismatic gifts were in existence in the

church during the patristic period. As discussed in chapter 7, the records of reliable church fathers, from Irenaeus to Augustine, assure us that the charismatic gifts did not depart from the church throughout the four hundred years of the patristic period. Even the accounts of those church fathers, who gave an account of some defective practices and ethical issues in the Montanist movement, did not indicate clearly identified detrimental effects of the charismatic experiences.

C. Despite the institutional church's persistent rejection and suppression of charismatic experience, as discussed in chapter 8, this was still evident in almost every century of the medieval period through both individuals and groups of Christians who experienced it in ways not recognized by the institutional church.

D. During the Reformation, the radical wing of Protestantism played an important role in reviving the realization of charismatic gifts. As discussed in chapter 9, radical reformers emphasized that believers must experience the charismatic gifts of revelations, dreams, visions, prophecy, and the inner light of the Holy Spirit through direct communication with God. They also adopted a worship experience accompanied by ecstatic movements, speaking in tongues, prophecy, physical healing, and miracles. Despite the successors of the radical reformers being marginalized, they continued as a peripheral movement, and their conviction and experience continued to influence and attract individuals and groups within mainstream Protestantism. Thus, their influence produced several movements with similar convictions and practices from the Reformation up to the turn of the twentieth century when the Pentecostal movement emerged as a result of the continued influence of the Radical Reformation. Through the influence of the Pentecostal movement, the charismatic experience began to become a common experience of entire Christendom.

E. There is evidence from accounts of contemporary charismatic experience. As will be discussed in chapter 12, the contemporary live experience of the charismatic gifts among many traditionalist denominations is not only a theological trophy of twentieth-century Pentecostal and Charismatic Movements (PCMs) but is also an indication of the nature of the ongoing gifts and works of the Holy Spirit. The spectacular audibly uttered and visibly performed charismatic manifestations that have been taking place within different Christian denominations since the 1970s are clear theological and practical evidence of the continued existence of the charismatic gifts in the church. The divine power and action manifested through the visible charismata such as physical healing and miracles, in particular, have been evidencing and affirming to the world what God's care and protection for his people look like. This practically observable current situation assures us that Charismatic gifts are not a decadent treasury and tradition of Christianity, as cessationists assume, but are enduring afresh.

Viewed through the lens of these historical and contemporary continuations of charismatic experiences, albeit as a sporadic and on-again-off-again phenomenon, the theological, genealogical, historical, and practical link between currently claimed charismatic experiences and those held and experienced by prophets, Jesus, apostles, and the early church would appear to be evident and convincing. This again, as stated already, reminds us that objectively given and subjectively experienced, Holy Spirit-initiated charismatic gifts are the treasured theological resources and the best functional possessions of Christianity inherited from Christ. This reality also reminds us that it is up to the beneficiaries to long for, seek, pray for, receive, and realize charismatic gifts for their spiritual life and ministry or to ignore them. Hence, viewed from the perspective of this theological, biblical, historical, and current practical fact, it would appear that the cessationists' position, which assumes that the purpose and mission of the apostolic charismatic gifts ended with the close of the age of the apostles and that the apostles have no successors, may not be favored. The cessationsts' argument in this regard, therefore, can be regarded as one that considers charismatic gifts and their experiences from a institutional-organizational ecclesiastical mindset and is a view that is merely prejudiced, institutionalist, traditionalist, conservative, and thus, pointless.

Second, one aspect that cannot be refuted is the notion that the office of ordained leadership has always held the power that decides all the ups and downs of the church's life and functions. Accordingly, in every century of the church, the equations of the leadership-administration and Pentecostal-charismatic function of the church depended on the perceptions or interests of the bearers of the leadership office. It is also understandable that the life, function, and mission of the church are always a common business of both God and wicked, frail, and finite humankind. Scripture testifies that beginning from the time of Moses God was calling and appointing priests, prophets, and leaders as his mouthpiece or contact persons in the process of delivering his purpose for his people. Jesus' earthly ministry, as discussed in chapter 4, fulfilled these threefold Old Testament offices of ministry. Thus, the ministry of Jesus, as delivered through these threefold offices of ministry, was also meant to be shared with his followers. It was for this purpose that Jesus called a group of twelve people to be with him, to be trained in the model of his ministry methods, and to be sent out to extend his mission to the world. Later, at the end of his earthly ministry and before his exaltation, Jesus commissioned them to go throughout the world, to be his witnesses, and handed over to them his ministry models. In turn, his messengers handed those ministry models over to the church, which is meant to carry out Jesus' mission in the world until his expected second coming. Through this process, the church was founded on two methods of Jesus' ministry: the *leadership-administration* and *prophetic-charismatic gospel proclamation* methods.

In the inception of the church, the apostles combined both of these methods of Jesus' ministry. As can be seen from Acts 6, the leadership-administration function soon began to be transmitted to some Spirit-touched perceptive people from among the early converts. In this way, the early congregations began to exercise the church's leadership-administration function. Scripture testifies that varieties of terms and titles such as elder, deacon, episcopate/bishop, overseer, etc. soon began to be given to the elected or ordained leaders of local congregations. Those appointees were regarded, by the apostles, as worthy of double honor (1 Tim 5:17; Heb 13:17). Congregations of the time were instructed to completely submit to their elected/ordained leaders and to respect them in the highest regard (1 Thess 5:12–13). This biblical evidence reminds us that during the apostolic ministry, sound authority was accorded to the church's *leadership-administration* office, and congregations of the time were strongly reminded to submit to their authority. As discussed in chapter 5, in the churches of the postapostolic periods the understanding, interpretation, and application of these apostolic instructions were developed into a strong hierarchical tradition and took a very different authoritarian nature.

The postapostolic church, as discussed in chapter 5, established an explicit foundation for an institutional, organizational, and hierarchical church, and set a strong hierarchical power framework for the church through what it attributed to the ordained leadership. As documented in the *Constitutions of the Holy Apostles*, there is evidence that the apostles ordained bishops and authorized them to run their young churches with apostolic authority, as immediate successors of the apostles, and reminded them to strictly observe the words and rules of the apostles. Tracing this tradition, the ancient church then adopted and developed a tradition by which it attributed to the bishops a kind of power and authority that paralleled Jesus' power and authority in heaven and on earth. The power and authority of the bishops then were dogmatized in the way they should not be questioned, resisted, or opposed, but rather only submitted to. The laity of the time was also strictly instructed to regard everything the bishops said or did as part of divine law. By referring to, and relying on, the tradition of apostolic succession, bishops were ranked as the highest divinely appointed officials of the church such that no power on earth remained above them. In subsequent centuries the understanding, interpretation, and application of the biblical themes of leadership authority most often depended on the individuals who assumed an ordained leadership position. Such glorious authoritarianism, similar to that of the Pharisees of Jesus' times, was well developed in the church, albeit in a different language and under a different mask and title, through the centuries.

This authoritarian hierarchical tradition took on a special image and reached its climax in the medieval Western church through the appointment of the papacy and attributing a rigid, dictatorial, and infallible authoritarian leadership status to it. Drawing from the papacy's authority, leadership bureaucracy has always been an inevitable institutional fact of the Western church's life and function through the centuries, although not always in the form of the papacy. In almost every period of church history, it was such authoritarian human hierarchies who saw themselves as better off, who thought they knew better, and who considered affairs beneath their dignity. Accordingly, traditions, rules, systems, orders, procedures, etc. of the church have continued to easily fall into the trap resulting from such kinds of individual authoritarian leaders' views, choices, or interests. From the turn of the fifth century, in particular, the church acknowledged the finished and closed revelation of the divine and the finished and closed canon of Scripture. Yet, the ordained leadership continued to create or devise its own version of the rules and orders of the divine, by imitating those of the divine and then imposing these on the church as well as on individual believers. It uses certain words from Scripture to cover its views, interests, and impositions with a spiritual concept but internally exerts its own privileges. Consequently, the balance of the church's life and ministry continued to tilt towards the one single view of those authoritarian hierarchies' choices or interests. Since these highly privileged authoritarian hierarchies obscured the place and role of the Holy Spirit in the church, there were always ambiguities, questions, confusions, and tensions in the church, mostly concerning the realization of the gifts and workings of the Holy Spirit through charismatic experiences.

As a result of this dominant hierarchical tradition, for centuries Christianity has struggled to evangelize the world with a mission movement devoid of the gifts and workings of the Holy Spirit. As mentioned earlier, although there were certain individuals as well as groups of Christians in every century who experienced the gifts and workings of the Holy Spirit in ways not recognized by institutional hierarchies, there was explicit avoidance of this experience in the church. Even since the Reformation, although it does not claim the pattern of the medieval church's papacy, modern Protestantism, too, has been experiencing dictatorial hierarchy in a different name, under a different mask and title. Such dictatorial and bureaucratic hierarchies have always been reluctant to accept the gifts and workings of the Holy Spirit through charismatic experiences and are resistant to them. In the meantime, tensions and divisions between the institutional bureaucratic hierarchies and charismatic groups through the centuries have become evident. Consequently, New Testament Christianity and historical Christianity followed parallel but separate lines up to the 1970s when the Charismatic movement emerged and impacted this long-standing parallelism. Hence, in light of this, it can be noted how flawed human bureaucratic hierarchies' interests, choices, and privileges have been imperiling authentic divine gifts of Christian spiritual life through the Spirit-initiated subjective experience of the Holy Spirit. Nevertheless, since the turn of the twentieth century, it has been demonstrated that this dictatorial hierarchical leadership power tradition has been strongly challenged through the increasingly emergent prophetic-charismatic voice of the PCMs. The next two chapters will attempt to further elaborate on this observation through an examination of the effects of the twentieth-century PCMs.

PART III

The Person, Gifts, and Works of the Holy Spirit in Contemporary Christian Teaching and Practice

IN THE PREVIOUS TWO major parts of the book, we have examined the biblical teaching and historical practical situations surrounding the doctrine of the Holy Spirit. In this third and last part of the book, we will examine the nature of contemporary Christian perception, teaching, and practice of the doctrine of the Holy Spirit. To accomplish this, there are some pertinent questions to be considered. For example: What does contemporary Christendom's doctrine of the Holy Spirit look like? Are there differences between the former and contemporary Christendom's perception, teaching, and practice of the presence, gifts, and works of the Holy Spirit? If there are differences, where did these changes come from and how have they come about? What do contemporary scholarly observations and evaluations from different theological traditions and geographical territories suggest about the nature of the contemporary doctrine of the Holy Spirit? And so on. As we shall see, scholars from different theological traditions and geographical backgrounds are in agreement that there is a remarkable difference between the former and contemporary Christians' perception, teaching, and practice of the presence, gifts, and works of the Holy Spirit. They suggest that contemporary Christian perception, teaching, and practice of the presence, gifts, and works of the Holy Spirit are influenced by the Pentecostal and Charismatic Movements (PCMs) that emerged in the twentieth century. As a result of such influence, the church's traditional perception, teaching and practice of the entire doctrine of the Holy Spirit is changed.

Examining the evaluations, observations, findings and proposals the scholars may help to identify examples and to draw on these to develop possible answers to the questions and solutions to the confusions prompted this study. This part of the book will deal with this case. The examination of this part will focus on three major features. First, it examines when, where, and how the PCMs emerged and what theological, biblical, and spiritual features they emphasized. Second, it examines how PCMs expanded and influenced the traditional Christian perception, teaching, and practice of the presence, gifts, and works of the Holy Spirit and how the perceived change has come about. Third, it will draw together all the issues raised and discussed in the study and conclude with a summary and personal reflection. This will focus mostly on features such as the theological and practical lessons that might be learned from the biblical teaching about the doctrine of the Holy Spirit, lessons that might be learned from historical practical situations, and issues that might be proposed for future consideration concerning how to treat or deal with the mysteries of the presence, gifts, and works of the Holy Spirit in the church as a whole and individual believers' life in particular.

CHAPTER 11

The Rise, Emphases, and Expansion of the Pentecostal and Charismatic Movements

TO ACCOMPLISH THE PURPOSE of the third part of the study presented above, this chapter examines the rise, emphasis, and expansion of the Pentecostal and Charismatic Movements (PCMs) and how they influenced the established churches' traditional teaching and practice of the presence, gifts, and works of the Holy Spirit and how their influence brought about changes. This will be done by reviewing scholarly observations, evaluations, and suggestions from different theological traditions and geographical territories.

11.1. THE RISE AND GROWTH OF THE PENTECOSTAL MOVEMENT

The rise, emphasis, designation, and expansion of the twentieth-century Pentecostal movement have been recounted in many writings such as personal testimonies, seminar presentations, devotional books, and standard academic works. Indeed, many dignified scholarly works on American, European, African, Asian, Latin American, and Australian Pentecostalism can be listed. One detailed account of the movement can be found in Allan H. Anderson's two volumes, *An Introduction to Pentecostalism* and *Spreading Fires*. He provides us with insight into the origin, expansion, and recent developments of the movement. A similar detailed account of the movement is provided by Murray W. Dempster, Byron D. Klaus, and Douglas Petersen in *The Globalization of Pentecostalism; A Religion Made to Travel*. The most distinguished and comprehensive source of accounts regarding the worldwide Pentecostal and Charismatic Movements, however, is *The New International Dictionary of Pentecostal and Charismatic Movements*, edited by Stanley M. Burgess and Eduard M. Van Der Maas. These accounts propose similar dates and places for the rise of the Pentecostal movement. A few sources, however, suggest differing dates and locations for the rise of the movement. Mentioning a few of them will suffice here to build a background for this study.

In his brief evaluation of the rise of the twentieth-century Pentecostal movement, Thiselton dates the rise of the movement to June 1901. He writes that Charles F. Parham (1873–1929) founded the Bible School in Topeka, Kansas, where he taught five main courses: "gospel of justification, sanctification, Spirit baptism, divine healing, and the imminence of the return of Christ." He states that Parham "believed that new healings and miracles would follow a period of dryness [and] looked for the latter rain of a new Pentecost." He then asserts this regarding Parham: "In June 1901 his hope and experience passed to one of his students . . . and then to half of the student body." Thiselton thus affirms June 1901 as the starting time of the twentieth-century Pentecostal movement.[1] However, this view seems to be little supported by others and appears to stand alone as the date of rise for the Pentecostal movement.

Contrary to Thiselton's view, Allen suggests that the Pentecostal movement began, primarily, in Cherokee County, North Carolina, in the summer of 1896, with an event where about 130 people claimed to have been baptized in the Holy Spirit and spoke in tongues. Allen describes how different kinds of miracles were wrought at the event, including physical healings, and that the Church of God, one of the Pentecostal denominations, is the fruit of that movement. Unfortunately, that movement, says Allen, was persecuted by the established local churches, had difficulties in expanding, and was confined only to the North Carolina and Tennessee area. Allen then suggests that the second historical Pentecostal movement occurred in Bethel Bible School, Topeka, Kansas, in January 1901. He associates the rise of the movement with Charles F. Parham, stating that Parham was a preacher of *Pentecostal-charismatic* Christianity at the time and founder of the Bethel Bible School in Topeka.

---

1. Thiselton, *Short Guide*, 137–38.

The core issue of the Bible School's teaching, discussion, and prayer, says Allen, was the "Second Blessing," in which the experience of baptism in the Holy Spirit was enthusiastically anticipated. That anticipation was realized on New Year's Day of 1901, when one of the students, Agnes Ozman, claimed to have been baptized in the Holy Spirit and spoke in tongues. Other students of the school soon had similar experiences. From then on, affirms Allen, all doubts about baptism in the Holy Spirit, along with speaking in tongues as its initial evidence, were "swept away." Thereafter, Parham and his Spirit-baptized students continued to preach about their experience and to persuade others to commit themselves to the same experience. Thousands of believers yielded to that preaching and the majority of them received Spirit baptism and spoke in tongues. Consequently, concludes Allen, the emphasis on Spirit baptism and speaking in tongues became a standard doctrine of the movement and resulting denominations.[2] Cartledge supports Allen's account by connecting the movement to Charles F. Parham, the Bethel Bible School, and by dating it to 1901. He states that Parham and his Bible School students were praying incessantly for baptism in the Holy Spirit, which they received on New Year's Day of 1901. Beginning with that particular phenomenon, says Cartledge, within a short period of time Parham and his students experienced Spirit baptism. Hence, that very day and that very moment have been recognized as the historical moment of the rise of the twentieth-century Pentecostal movement.[3]

Leonard and Crainshaw also suggest that Parham strictly guided his Bible School students to study Acts 2 and to discover that speaking in different tongues is the initial evidence of the baptism in the Holy Spirit. They state that the language Agnes Ozman spoke on January 1, 1901, was "Chinese" and following that event "twelve others claimed to speak in other languages." Leonard and Cairnshaw, however, do not confirm January 1, 1901, as the beginning date of the movement. They rather lean to the Azusa Street revival movement in Los Angeles, which started on April 9, 1906, as the authentic beginning day of twentieth-century Pentecostalism.[4] Cartledge objects to this, however, arguing that the Azusa Street Pentecostal movement in April 1906 emerged as the influence of the Bethel Bible School movement of 1901. He states that the Azusa Street movement came about through William Seymour, who was a leader of the Azusa

2. Allen, *Unfailing Stream*, 102–8.
3. Cartledge, *Encountering the Spirit*, 21–23.
4. Leonard and Crainshaw, *Encyclopedia of Religious Controversies*, 1:364–365.

Street movement but had previously been a "care-taker of the Bethel Bible School" when the movement began in January 1901 and was allowed by Parham to attend his teachings about Spirit baptism during class lectures. Seymour, therefore, was one of the recipients of Parham's teaching about Spirit baptism and was already involved in the experience. Seymour then moved to Los Angeles and organized a prayer group at 214 North Bonnie Brae Street, which later moved to Azusa Street. Cartledge asserts that the Bethel Bible School Pentecostal movement of 1901 was the source of the movement in Los Angeles which started on April 9, 1906.[5] Gary B. McGee concurs with Cartledge stating that the Bethel Bible School event in January 1901 placed "theological and missiological stamps on Pentecostalism that have endured and created a movement" and later became to be known as "Classical Pentecostalism."[6] Many scholarly evaluations agree with these accounts and affirm that the movement initially began in Bethel Bible School, in 1901, and then later in Azusa Street, Los Angeles, in 1906.

The emphasis and designation of the Pentecostal movement

According to the evaluations, the movement was designated "Pentecostal" on account of its emphasis on the possibility of continuous experience of the day of Pentecost. Steven J. Land, for instance, suggests that in its inception the movement was viewed as "the answer to the earnest prayers of thousands of believers who through global networks of personal association, periodicals, camp meetings, etc. prayed for a renewal of Pentecost." In the experience of the movement "Pentecost has surely come" with all the evidence demonstrated on the day of the first Pentecost. Accordingly, says Land, claimants of the movement believed that "God was restoring the apostolic faith and power for the end times through signs and wonders."[7] In the experience of the movement, McGee observes, "The long quest for the full restoration of the Spirit's power had finally produced the most unusual phenomenon of all: the divine bestowment of unlearned languages."[8] Hence, the designation of the movement, says Dunn, draws its roots from the belief and claims of the experience of the 120 people on the Day of Pentecost. He states that "Pentecostal" means to

5. Cartledge, *Encountering the Spirit*, 22.
6. McGee, *Miracles*, 90.
7. Land, *Pentecostal Spirituality*, 4–6.
8. McGee, *Miracles*, 76.

be filled with the Holy Spirit and to speak in tongues in the same manner as those 120 people experienced on the day of Pentecost in Jerusalem. The event of the day of Pentecost, concludes Dunn, does not only give Pentecostals their designation but it also provides them with the "distinctive . . . most precious doctrine" of Spirit baptism, affords them the "key to a full Christian life and witness," speaks to them of their "most treasured experiences of Christ," and enables them to express their "deepest devotion and praise."[9]

Dunn proceeds to describe how the accounts of the apostles' experiences at Pentecost (Acts 2) and of the Samaritans' experience of receiving the Holy Spirit (Acts 8) are the two key passages that provide Pentecostals with strong biblical grounds for the doctrine of subsequence. Consequently, says Dunn, Pentecostals refer, primarily, to the passage in Acts 2 and emphasize that the experience of the Day of Pentecost should be a continuing Christian experience. They believe that the 120 who were baptized in the Holy Spirit at Pentecost were already saved Christians and their experience at Pentecost was not their conversion or the beginning of faith life but was a second experience distinct from their conversion and salvation. This second experience was instead one of empowerment and reception of charismatic gifts for both life and ministry. Thus, says Dunn, Pentecostals believe and advocate that the second reception experience of the Holy Spirit on the Day of Pentecost provides a pattern for all Christian experiences thereafter. In other words, just as those who were already saved and regenerated were baptized in the Holy Spirit at Pentecost, so should all regenerated Christians of all generations be baptized in the Holy Spirit after conversion and regeneration. Dunn adds that the prooftexts normally cited by Pentecostals concerning the already saved and regenerated state of the 120 are Luke 10:20; John 13:10; 15:3, 16; and 20:22. These texts are drawn on by Pentecostals as evidence that disciples were already saved, regenerated, spirit-breathed, and certified Christians before their strange experience at Pentecost. What happened to them at Pentecost, from the viewpoint of Pentecostals, concludes Dunn, was a second experience, i.e., the reception of the Holy Spirit for further experience of spiritual maturity, empowerment, and reception of the charismatic gifts for life and ministry.[10]

---

9. Dunn, *Baptism in the Spirit*, 38.

10. Dunn, *Baptism in the Spirit*, 52–54. See also Gause, "Issues in Pentecostalism," 107–9.

Elaborating further on Dunn's comments, Frank, D. Macchia, suggests that the Samaritans' case of Acts 8 is used by Pentecostals as the biblical warrant to draw their understanding, interpretation, and application to the doctrine of baptism in the Holy Spirit as subsequent empowerment to conversion. He states that Acts 8 is a "classical text" for Pentecostals to which they refer in support of their belief in and claim of baptism in the Holy Spirit as a "doctrine of subsequence" and "subsequent to the salvific categories of conversion and sanctification." What this means is that the Pentecostals put "conversion and sanctification" in one category as the first stage and baptism in the Holy Spirit as a "second stage" entry into the blessings of the Holy Spirit. Thus, the "conversion and sanctification" plus "Spirit baptism" together, for Pentecostals, yield a doctrine of "two-stage blessing." He says that although some Pentecostal theologians do not emphasize the doctrine of subsequence, a large majority of Pentecostals still embrace this as "distinctively classical Pentecostal." Therefore, baptism in the Holy Spirit for Pentecostals, concludes Macchia, is an experience of "enhanced power and openness to extraordinary gifts of the Spirit."[11] In his paraphrasing of other sources on the Pentecostal theology of subsequence, Robert P. Menzies states that Spirit baptism for Pentecostals is a "subsequent empowerment experience to conversion." The doctrine of subsequence, therefore, "articulates a conviction crucial to Pentecostal theology and practice" as well as a "continued sense of expectation and effectiveness in mission."[12] Strengthening these suggestions, Macchia asserts that when one thinks about Pentecostal theology, what usually comes to mind is the "doctrine of the baptism in the Holy Spirit as an experience of empowerment." The doctrine of Spirit baptism for empowerment is a "crown jewel" doctrine of Pentecostal theology and is the "*power* of God for enhancing worship and service and overcoming obstacles to the life of faith . . . with aid of powerful manifestations and gifts of the Holy Spirit." Macchia adds that "Spirit baptism as an empowerment for gifted witness became the hallmark of the movement" and that the movement was viewed as entirely "Spirit baptism centred" in its theology and practice.[13] Thus, baptism in the Holy Spirit was considered the "reason for the existence of Pentecostalism."[14]

---

11. Frank, D. Macchia, "Baptism in the Holy Spirit" in *Encyclopaedia*, 53–54.
12. Menzies, *Empowered for Witness*, 236.
13. Macchia, *Kingdom and the Power*, 109–10; cf. pp. 112, 121.
14. Clement, *Pentecost or Pretense?*, 87.

These scholarly evaluations indicate that the movement was designated "Pentecostal" due to its emphasis on the normative continuation of the experience of the day of Pentecost among Christians of all ages and times. Concerning the emphasis and commitment of the movement, evaluations suggest that the movement began as a reaction against "creedal emphasis" and "religious status quo" and to protest against "man-made Creeds" and the "coldness" of traditional conservative evangelical worship.[15] The movement emphasized the belief that baptism in the Holy Spirit is an indispensable part of Christian life and experience; that the church's worship should be accompanied by continuous manifestations of the gifts of the Holy Spirit; and that all the charismatic gifts listed in Scripture are to be restored, come alive, and be given new expression in all Christian worship and spiritual experiences.[16] The movement generated new concepts of Christian spiritual experiences, a new age of the power of Pentecost, and the finding of better answers to moral, ethical, and spiritual questions by leading people to the experience of the fullness, power, and charismatic gifts of the Holy Spirit.[17]

Expansion of the Pentecostal movement

Evaluations of the nature of the movement suggest that before the rise of the Charismatic movement in the 1960s, the Pentecostal movement did not expand as quickly as such. Challenges such as "lack of finances," "biting opposition,"[18] and "racial, theological, and social controversies"[19] were encountered and derailed the growth and expansion of the movement in its early stages. Due to various challenges encountered the movement, Parham himself was "distracted by other interests" and did not continue as a missionary of the movement.[20] Estrelda Y. Alexander supports this perspective by stating that the Pentecostal movement was not successful before the rise of the Charismatic movement as such. Apart from formally established Pentecostal churches, the movement was embraced only by college and university students as well as local underground prayer groups within

---

15. Cox, *Fire from Heaven*, 14–17. See also Cox, "Spirits of Globalization."
16. Bruner, *Theology of the Holy Spirit*, 132–33.
17. Synan, *Aspects of Pentecostal Charismatic Origins*, 58–59.
18. McGee, *Miracles*, 90–91.
19. Land, *Pentecostal Spirituality*, 9.
20. McGee, *Miracles*, 90–91.

Protestant churches. However, says Alexander, within a short time after the Charismatic movement began in the 1960s, it took hold in churches that had not been touched by the Pentecostal movement. He concludes that it was through "Charismatic Christianity" or "Neo-Pentecostals" that the Pentecostal movement grew and by the end of the twentieth century had influenced millions.[21] However, some sources acknowledge the movement was "made to travel" and was steadily growing and expanding from its very beginning and has "flowered multi-million religious enterprises" worldwide.[22] Among many reasons proposed for the movement's ongoing growth and increasing influence, is that its emphasis on the gifts and workings of the Holy Spirit through Pentecostal-charismatic form of worship and spiritual experience attracts people everywhere and that through the Charismatic movement, its teachings and experiences are being transmitted and practiced in established churches across the world.[23]

11.2. THE RISE AND GROWTH OF THE CHARISMATIC MOVEMENT

Evaluations of the beginning of the Charismatic movement seem to agree that there was no single founder of the Charismatic movement like Parham was for the Pentecostal movement. Nor does it have a single event that clearly marks its beginning.[24] The origins of the Charismatic movement, says Peter D. Hocken, were more diverse than that of the Pentecostal movement because, in the rise of the Charismatic movement, there were many paths through which believers were led to the experience of baptism in the Holy Spirit. Hocken asserts that there has never been a clearly noted charismatic equivalent of Bethel Bible School in 1901 or Azusa Street of Los Angeles in 1906.[25] Burgess and McGee suggest that the Charismatic movement emerged as a "distinct movement of the Holy Spirit" when some leaders and teachers of established churches became convinced by the Pentecostals' teaching and experience of baptism in the Holy Spirit. Such people moved towards renewal of the entirety of

---

21. Alexander, *Black Fire*, 342–43.
22. Kalu, *African Pentecostalism*, 11.
23. Poewe, *Charismatic Christianity*, 105. See also Land, *Pentecostal Spirituality*, 9–11.
24. Koenig, *Charismata*, 15.
25. Hocken, "Charismatic Movement," 515–17.

church life rather than renewing certain traditionally neglected charismatic gifts.[26] Yong suggests that the Charismatic movement emerged in mainstream churches in the 1950s, '60s, and '70s at the time when the "Pentecostal experience of the Spirit had ceased to be a unifying force for Christians." Yong notes that it was the time when the "power of the Spirit to bring people together from diverse branches of Christendom was being resisted by the various human-made boundaries that had emerged in Pentecostal churches over the course of a generation." In reaction to this, says Yong, charismatics of mainline churches began to recognize the "ecumenical potential of the experience of the Spirit" and to emphasize that the "vitality imparted to the Christian faith by the Pentecostal outpouring was a common experience that cut across creedal, denominational, liturgical, traditional, and theological/doctrinal lines."[27]

In contrast to these suggestions, however, Cartledge suggests that there were certain identifiable founders of the Charismatic movement. He divides the story of the beginning of the Charismatic movement between Britain and America. He suggests that in Britain the Charismatic movement started in the house church movement of the 1960s when Michael Harper claimed a personal experience of baptism in the Holy Spirit. He states that after the claim of baptism in the Holy Spirit, Harper felt that he was being forced by the Holy Spirit to leave his ministry at All Souls Church in London and form a charismatic renewal church. Harper eventually proceeded with the idea and went on to found the renewal movement trust called "Fountain Trust." Beginning in 1965, says Cartledge, the Fountain Trust published and disseminated magazines and pamphlets on issues relating to charismatic renewal and promoted the idea of Charismatic movement across the country. Cartledge proceeds to explain how the Charismatic movement began in America. He states that the movement began in America in 1959/1960 when Dennis Bennet, an Episcopalian church minister in California, experienced baptism in the Holy Spirit evidenced by speaking in tongues. Cartledge suggests that, like Harper, Bennet also felt that he was being called by the Holy Spirit to leave his church and ministry and join the charismatic renewal movement which Bennet eventually did. Thus, concludes Cartledge, the Charismatic movement rose out of these two simple beginnings and grew to the extent that it became a

---

26. Hocken, "Charismatic Movement" in *Dictionary*, 215.
27. Yong, "Pentecostalism and Ecumenism," 219.

source and power of influence on both the established Protestant Churches and the Roman Catholic Church of the time.[28]

Anderson, however, objects to Cartledge's conclusions regarding the leading events for the rise of the Charismatic movement and considers Cartledge's accounts to be the "culminations" rather than the "commencements" of the movement. He suggests that there were other historical events before the 1960s that helped change the attitude of many in the established churches toward Pentecostal experiences and eventually led to the development of the Charismatic movement. He presents three different historical events that he considers to have played a pivotal role in the rise of the Charismatic movement. He asserts:

1. The rise of Pentecostal movement in Europe in the early twentieth century was a "Charismatic and ecumenical movement in the mainline churches." He presents some events leading to the rise of the movement across Europe, North America, Asia, South America, and Africa in the years from 1907 to the 1940s.

2. The acceptance of white Pentecostal denominations into the "National Association of Evangelicals in 1943 signaled the beginning of the thawing of the relationships between Pentecostals and Evangelical Churches" in America.

3. Independent evangelists, who were not affiliated with any Pentecostal denomination and were conducting healing ministries, played a significant role in expanding the charismatic perspective outside the Pentecostal Churches. Here he attests that "remarkable healings and miracles" were wrought in the ministries of those independent evangelists.

Some of those charismatic events, says Anderson, were transmitted on national television programs and brought the message of healing and miracles into the homes of the public. Added to the magazines and pamphlets distributed by these independent evangelists, these events played a significant role in attracting public attention to the Charismatic movement in many churches. Anderson concludes that it was on this fertile ground that the 1960s events took root and became leading factors in the rise and expansion of the movement.[29] His latter point is view as a key

---

28. Cartledge, *Encountering the Spirit*, 23. See also Synan, *Century of the Holy Spirit*, 151–200.

29. Anderson, *Introduction to Pentecostalism*, 158–59.

feature in regard to the rise of the Charismatic movement in the 1940s and the 1950s.[30] While these observations may remain valid, many scholars agree that the 1960s events, as presented above, were the significant points in the rise of the Charismatic movement.[31]

Emphasis, designation, and commitment of the Charismatic movement

Evaluations suggest that the Charismatic movement was designated "Neo-Pentecostalism" in its inception because it was viewed as the "Second Wave of the classical Pentecostalism."[32] It was designated "Neo-Pentecostal" simply for the sake of recognition, identification, and naming it in its own independent name.[33] For others, it was designated "Neo-Pentecostal" because it was viewed as the "Protestant version of Pentecostalism."[34] For others still, the designation "Neo-Pentecostal" was related to the movement's emphasis on the Pentecostals' experience of Spirit baptism and charismatic gifts,[35] and its adoption of religious expressions held by classical Pentecostalism.[36] The term Neo-Pentecostal, according to Koenig, was coined by journalists in order to identify the charismatics of the established churches who became involved in the movement but remained in their churches. Such people, notes Koenig, attempted to interpret and apply their Pentecostal experiences within their own churches' theological framework and thereby preferred to be recognized as "Charismatics" rather than "Pentecostals."[37] Hocken takes a similar view and suggest that the Charismatic movement is the new occurrence of the experience of baptism in the Holy Spirit and can, therefore, be considered as a "new phase of the Pentecostal movement" with

30. Lederle, *Theology with Spirit*, 91.

31. Hayford and Moore, *Charismatic Century*, 189–94. See also Hocken, "Charismatic Movement," 477–88; Alexander, *Black Fire*, 342–45; and Thiselton, *Holy Spirit*, 366–69.

32. Christenson, *Welcome Holy Spirit*, 82. See also Synan, *Spirit-Empowered Christianity*, 58–59.

33. Synan, *Century of the Holy Spirit*, 151.

34. Sullivan, *Charisms and Charismatic Renewal*, 55.

35. Christenson, *Charismatic Renewal Among Lutherans*, 33.

36. McDonnell, *Charismatic Renewal and the Churches*, 42.

37. Koenig, *Charismata*, 15–16. See also Synan, *Spirit-Empowered Christianity*, 58–59.

only a slight distinction. Since charismatics emphasize the experience of baptism and gifts of the Holy Spirit, the Charismatic movement, for Hocken is clearly rooted in a Pentecostal type of spirituality. Despite this connection, Hocken concludes, the Charismatic movement differs from the Pentecostal movement in doctrinal affiliation and religious practices.[38] Cartledge suggests that in its beginnings, the Charismatic movement emphasized the Pentecostal idea of speaking in tongues as the initial evidence of Spirit baptism. However, later charismatics objected to this idea and continued to consider speaking in tongues as one of the gifts of grace that may or may not be given.[39] Despite its difference in theological perception and explanation of the experience, the Charismatic movement is entirely grounded in the same religious experience as Pentecostalism concerning baptism in the Holy Spirit and charismatic gifts.[40] In the observation of the emphases and practices of the PCMs, says Clement, there is no Pentecostal or charismatic who does not emphasize baptism in the Holy Spirit and charismatic gifts. The experience of charismata and baptism of the Holy Spirit is what both movements have in common.[41] Thus, the very terms "Pentecostal" and "charismatic" are sometimes "applied in a rather bewildering range of senses."[42] If these accounts are based on the existing reality, then this may lead us to conclude that the Charismatic movement was developed from the nature of Pentecostalism into an independent charismatic nature.[43]

Accounts that evaluate the nature of the Charismatic movement suggest that one of the wisdom of the movement is that believers of established denominations who are involved in charismatic experience are encouraged to remain in their churches. They do not intend to introduce any new doctrine but introduce believers to a new way of spiritual experience within their churches' theological traditions and spiritual practices.[44] All the concern of the movement is not to react against any of the traditional systems of the established churches but to revive the long-neglected charismatic gifts and restore the charismatic life and ministry

---

38. Hocken, "Charismatic Movement" in *Dictionary*, 130-131.
39. Cartledge, *Encountering the Spirit*, 78.
40. Pomerville, *Third Force in Missions*, 11.
41. Clement, *Pentecost or Pretense?*, 90; cf. p. 111.
42. Heron, *Holy Spirit*, 132.
43. Dunn, *Ministry and The Ministry*, 82.
44. Clement, *Pentecost or Pretense?*, 122–23.

of Christianity.[45] In all its principles the movement does not intend to protest against institutional structures. It neither neglects nor despises the sacramental rites of churches nor urges rapid changes in institutional structures. Rather, it merely introduces the vitality of the charismatic experience and aims to infuse it through a renewed and empowered devotional worship experience.[46] The movement does not inspire a systematic attitude of flight from established churches nor does it intend to reformulate the doctrine of the Holy Spirit.[47] Instead, it strives to engage believers in a renewed experience of the charismatic gifts of the Holy Spirit.[48] It emphasizes the reality and presence of God in worship, takes seriously the manifestations of charismatic gifts, encourages the deeper study of the Bible and prayer in an intensified way, demonstrates the special quality of faith centered on the gifts and power of the Holy Spirit, and encourages the exchanging and spreading of gifts amongst one another across denominational borders as a demonstration of the activities of the Holy Spirit.[49] It also emphasizes a new release of praise with distinctive characteristics of worship, which removes the dependency on traditional liturgical resources and breaks new ground in all worship and spiritual practice.[50] Thus, the sole commitment of the movement is regarded as deepening spirituality regardless of religious background.

As it is not tied to any specific denomination but embraces all denominations and peoples across the world, the movement is viewed as transdenominational, transconfessional, and a new kind of ecumenical movement that touches the whole of Christendom with charismatic effects, reawakens a new interest in the theology of the Holy Spirit, and restores the Pentecostal-charismatic nature of Christianity's life and ministry.[51] It is viewed as a movement penetrating "right across denominational and cultural norms" by sharing a new experience and life in the Holy Spirit and has touched heartfelt spiritual needs where denominational dogmas appear unable to reach.[52] It has had its greatest impact

---

45. Heron, *Holy Spirit*, 132.
46. Congar, *I Believe*, 2:152.
47. Duquoc and Floriston, *Charisms in the Church*, 32–33.
48. Christenson, *Charismatic Renewal Among Lutherans*, 33–34.
49. Welker, *God the Spirit*, 11–13.
50. Smail et al., *Charismatic Renewal*, 109.
51. Bridge and Phypers, *More Than Tongues*, 128–31. See also Quebedeaux, *New Charismatics II*, 4–5; Coleman, *Globalization of Charismatic Christianity*, 68.
52. Green, *I Believe*, 305.

in more liberal Protestant denominations as well as in Catholicism and has transdenominational acceptance and achievements.[53] Accordingly, it is regarded as sound evangelistic, functional charismatic, reformist and restorationist in character which has had a speedy acceptance in all the historic denominations.[54] The movement is also regarded as the largest influential religious movement in the history of Christianity that has had a profound effect on Christianity around the world, and is still the fastest growing, expanding, and influential movement of the time.[55] With this commitment and approach, the Charismatic movement became a renewal movement of the whole of Christendom and has challenged all of Christendom's traditional thinking in relation to the presence, gifts, power, and works of the Holy Spirit in the church's life, worship, ministry, and mission.[56]

11.3. SUMMARY

Given these accounts and discussion, four factors seem worth noting in concluding the chapter.

First, why did the *Pentecostal-charismatic* experience break out and revive in the small Bethel Bible School in Topeka rather than in the large theological institutions of the established churches of the time? Was it because it was seriously and earnestly sought after and prayed for by those in the Bethel Bible School but ignored and avoided by those in the major established theological institutions of the time? Or was it God's response to Parham's longing and prayer for the renewed Pentecostal coming of the Holy Spirit and as a means to put to shame all those who ignored this aspect of Christianity? Berkhof would answer these two questions by saying, "Yes, this was the case!" as he affirms that "the Pentecostal movement is God's judgment upon a church which lost its inner growth and its outward extension, its character as a vertical as well as a horizontal movement."[57] Indeed, from an evangelical Christian perspective, especially tracing Jesus' rhetorical question recorded in Luke 11:13, it could be said, in agreement with Berkhof, "Yes, so it is!" However, the

---

53. Hyatt, *2000 Years*, 179–80.
54. Quebedeaux, *New Charismatics II*, 4–5.
55. Williams, *Renewal Theology*, 2:194; cf. Welker, *God the Spirit*, 8.
56. Badcock, *Light of Truth*, 136–37.
57. Berkhof, *Doctrine of the Holy Spirit*, 93.

challenge we may face is that, as discussed in chapter 3, none of the early church's *Pentecostal-charismatic* phenomena happened in response to believers' longing, prayer, and enthusiastic expectation. Why, then, did the phenomenon occur in the Bethel Bible School in response to people's longing, prayer, and enthusiastic expectation? Could this be one of the dilemmas for some, if not for all of us, in relation to claims and experiences of the ongoing manifestations and workings of the Holy Spirit in the present time? Such questions seem to require scholarly attention but do not appear to have been addressed by scholars. Despite the existence of a wide range of scholarly discussions and related in-depth examinations of the nature and effects of the PCMs, these questions seem to have not been given attention.

Second, as discussed in chapter 3, the coming of the Holy Spirit in biblical times sometimes entailed both objective gifts of divine reality for salvation and subjective experience resulting from the gifts and power imparted along with the Holy Spirit. There was objective imparting of the Holy Spirit and subjective experience resulting from the gifts and power of the Holy Spirit. Having given individuals either audible utterances or visible performances of charismatic gifts and empowered them, the Holy Spirit then inspired and moved those individuals towards practical implementation through subjective experience as an expression of his presence, gifting, and empowering of believers. In biblical times it was God who made his own arrangements, gave gifts, and moved his people by his initiative toward subjective experiences, but never, in any circumstance, in response to human enthusiastic expectation and nagging prayers. Subjective experiences of biblical times, therefore, had authentic theological and pneumatological roots and genuine practical affirmation. Nevertheless, such divinely delivered and divinely initiated genuine subjective experience of the Holy Spirit did not continue in the church of successive generations due to many different challenges confronting the church, as well as the church's adaptation of different kinds of non-biblical traditions. Since 1901, however, subjective experience of the Holy Spirit seems to have reemerged through the Pentecostal movement. The Charismatic movement of the mid-twentieth century has also been significant in promoting the subjective experience of the Holy Spirit as it joined alongside the Pentecostal movement and has continued to promulgate this experience to the present day.

Third, as discussed in chapter 2, the concept and practice of baptism in the Holy Spirit are spoken of in the New Testament only three times.

Thereafter, claims of such concept and practice seem to have remained outside the church's thought and practice. Even in the Montanist movement of the second century, baptism in the Holy Spirit does not seem to have been part of the movement's core emphases. When closely examined through the historical accounts consulted in the preceding chapters, the only person who emphasized, longed for and prayed for the experience of baptism in the Holy Spirit, in the entire postapostolic history of the church, seems to be the evangelist Charles F. Parham in the early twentieth century. Interestingly, then, when considering the inception events of the Pentecostal movement, it seems that God willed to positively respond to the human's longing, nagging prayers, and enthusiastic expectation of baptism in the Holy Spirit, which was not the case during biblical times. Furthermore, when viewed in the light of the reappearance of the experience of baptism in the Holy Spirit in the early twentieth century, it seems that the church's long-lasting lack of interest in it does not necessarily mean that its theological content and practical significance were absent. Despite the authenticity of its claim and experience remaining a questionable issue, the theological content and spiritual significance of the Spirit baptism appear to be convincingly evident.

Fourth, although the Pentecostal movement is half a century older than the Charismatic movement, evaluations of its nature suggest that the Pentecostal movement did not spread quickly and widely before the rise of the Charismatic movement. Momentum to increase and extend its aspired influence to bring about tangible changes took place only after the rise of the Charismatic movement. As the accounts consulted above indicate, the two movements joined hands and continued to spread joint aims and objectives beginning in the 1960s. From then on both movements had a common emphasis on worship and spiritual experiences and have an "underlying unity."[58] Their commonly held renewalist views are such that it becomes impossible to distinguish between the two movements. When the emphases and practices of both movements are closely considered, there seems to be no Pentecostal or charismatic Christian who does not emphasize fresh reception of the gifts, empowerment, and workings of the Holy Spirit. The theological and practical departure point of the two movements seems to be only the emphasis on speaking in different tongues. While Pentecostals emphasize speaking in different tongues as evidence of Spirit baptism, charismatics do not. Otherwise,

---

58. Hyatt, *2000 Years*, 3.

the two movements' overall aims and objectives overlap and it often becomes difficult to distinguish between their particular identities. As both movements hold a "renewalist" view as the "umbrella" of their practices, the "criteria for distinguishing between them is becoming confusing"[59] and may even be said that it is "impossible to distinguish between Pentecostals and Charismatics."[60] Both movements have much in common, they offer or contribute much to each other, and are soundly symbiotic. Therefore, the very terms "Pentecostal" and "charismatic," as cited above, are sometimes "applied in a rather bewildering range of senses." They travel together and have challenged the whole of Christendom's traditional thinking about the fresh reception of and experience of the gifts, power, and workings of the Holy Spirit through the *Pentecostal-charismatic* form of worship and spiritual experiences. Thus, these inexpressibly symbiotic and "widely variegated" spiritual movements have been viewed as the "greatest revival movements in the history of the church" and have brought the practice of "Holy Spirit empowerment to the front burner and challenged Christians from all traditions."[61]

Thus, it is evident that the PCMs of the twentieth century most often heed converging, yet on occasions diverging, paths and have become the common renewal movements of an entire Christendom with their symbiotic power and energy. Despite this, scholarly observations from different theological traditions and geographical territories attribute more weight to the influential role and power of the Charismatic movement. Such observations attest, as presented above, that the Charismatic movement is viewed as transdenominational, transconfessional, and as a new form of ecumenical movement that has been touching the whole of Christendom with charismatic effects and a new interest in the theology of the Holy Spirit. With this quality of spirituality and inclusivity, the Charismatic movement has continued to influence all the established Christian denominations and peoples across the world since the 1960s. To this, we now turn our examination.

---

59. Adogame, "Reconfiguring the Global Religious Economy," 185–86.
60. Anderson, *Introduction to Pentecostalism*, 157.
61. Hurt, "Spirit Baptism," 261–62.

CHAPTER 12

Expansion and Influence of the Charismatic Movement on the Established Churches' Traditional Teaching and Practice of the Person, Gifts, and Workings of the Holy Spirit

THE RISE, EMPHASIS, DESIGNATION, and expansion of the Charismatic movement are briefly examined in chapter 11. This chapter examines the nature of the expansion, influence, and effects of the Charismatic movement on the traditional doctrine of the Holy Spirit. The examination of the chapter focuses on four features: (1) how the Charismatic movement expanded and reached different Christian denominations in different continents; (2) how it impacted the established churches' traditional teaching and practice of the presence, gifts, and works of the Holy Spirit; (3) how changes have come about in the established churches' traditional doctrine of the Holy Spirit; and (4) how academic and scholarly interests and conversions emerged and heated up concerning contemporary Christendom's teaching and practice of the presence, gifts, and works of the Holy Spirit.

12.1. EXPANSION OF THE CHARISMATIC MOVEMENT

Indeed, many scholarly evaluations and observations are offered on how the Charismatic movement expanded different continents and reached different Christian denominations in the second half of the twentieth century. One detailed account of the expansion of the movement can be found in Kilian McDonnell's three edited volumes entitled *Presence, Power, Praise: Documents on the Charismatic Renewal*. In this work, McDonnell recorded how the Charismatic movement expanded and reached the American, Latin American, European, African, Asian, and Australian established churches in the years between 1960 and 1980. He provided us with evidence from regional, national, continental, and international documents which were produced by the established churches in response to the influence of the Charismatic movement. His work provides us with insights into how the Charismatic movement reached different parts of the world in the years between 1960 and 1980 and how it influenced the established churches' traditional understanding and practice of the presence, gifts, and workings of the Holy Spirit.[1] McDonnell reports a detailed account of the emergence and expansion of the Charismatic movement in American churches in *Charismatic Renewal and the Churches*. In the third chapter, entitled "Enthusiasm and Institution: The Responses of the Churches," McDonnell reports that the period between 1960 and 1975 was a time of heated challenges by the Charismatic movement to the established Protestant and Catholic churches of America. He reports that Protestant churches such as the Episcopalians, the American Lutheran Church, the United Presbyterian Church, the Presbyterian Church in the United States, the Lutheran Church in America, and the Catholic Church have all been influenced by the Charismatic movement in that period. All of these churches, says McDonnell, were forced to appoint special committees or commissions to examine the nature and effects of the impact of the movement on their congregations. The common features on which the committees or commissions focused were the person, gifts, baptism, and works of the Holy Spirit, speaking in tongues, and enthusiastic and spontaneous experiences. Based on the findings and reports of the commissions, says McDonnell, some churches decided to resist the movement, some decided to remain cautiously open to it, and some decided to remain neutral—neither to condemn nor to commend. He asserts that the movement took the upper hand in many of those churches to the extent that it attracted ordained ministers, including some who left their positions of ministry and joined the movement.[2] Balmer concurs that the Charismatic movement "took root" in those churches identified by McDonnell and others such as the American Baptist Church, the

---

1. McDonnell, *Presence, Power, Praise*.
2. McDonnell, *Charismatic Renewal*, 41–70.

United Methodists, the Mennonites, the Church of Christ, and the United Church of Christ. Apart from the Lutheran Church Missouri Synod and the Southern Baptist Convention, says Balmer, all Protestant churches in America have been influenced by the movement from 1960 onwards.[3]

There is nevertheless a documented story, which Balmer might have not had an access, that informs us that the Charismatic movement spread to the Lutheran Church—Missouri Synod congregations in the early 1960s. In certain congregations of the Synod, the influence of the movement caused tensions and division over such charismatic experiences as "speaking in tongues, miraculous healings, prophecy," and claims of the "possession of special baptism in the Holy Spirit." The report states that at the request of the president of Missouri Synod, the "Commission on Theology and Church Relations" began to study the nature of the charismatic movement in 1968 with a focus on the baptism in the Holy Spirit. It states that the first "gathering of Missouri Synod charismatic pastors" was held at Crystal City, Missouri, in April 1968. The meeting was attended by "44 pastors across the Synod," who claimed to have been baptized in the Holy Spirit. The synodical convention held in 1969, says the document, further directed the commission to undertake a "comprehensive study of the charismatic movement" by involving some of the pastors who claimed to have "received the baptism of the Holy Spirit" and some charismatic gifts. Hence, beginning in 1969 the commission sought possible, practical means to "acquaint itself with the theology of the charismatic movement." It endeavored to learn the views of "representative Lutheran charismatics" and to address the features of the movement that are a "matter of interest or concern" within the Synod. Accordingly, it had consulted privately with Lutheran pastors who were involved in the movement on different occasions at different places. The commission also intensively examined such documents as "position papers . . . official reports . . . booklets . . . study documents" produced both by Lutheran charismatics and non-Lutheran church bodies on the Charismatic movement. The commission also held a conference of Lutheran charismatic pastors at Concordia Seminary, St. Louis, in May 1971. By that time the commission learnt that the number of pastors claiming to have received baptism in the Holy Spirit amounted to over two hundred. In its final report to the Missouri Synod, in January 1972, the commission stated "baptism in the Holy Spirit, speaking in tongues, and . . . miraculous

---

3. Balmer, *Encyclopedia of Evangelicalism*, 150.

healing" as the most frequent and experienced phenomena within the Synod.[4]

Concerning the American Roman Catholic Church, Leonard and Crainshaw report that the Charismatic movement took root in 1967 when "students and faculty at Duquesne University in Pittsburgh, Pennsylvania, experienced the baptism in the Holy Spirit with speaking in tongues." They state that the movement spread rapidly and "received uninterrupted papal support and operates today as a conglomeration of local, regional, and national gatherings."[5] Thiselton affirms these observations and describes another similar event that took place at the University of Notre Dame in 1967. He states that the Catholic believers involved in the movement "saw the outpouring of the Holy Spirit as God's answer to Pope John's prayer for a new Pentecost."[6] Synan affirms these two cases and confirms the event with a precise date of Saturday, February 18, 1967. Synan considers that day as a day "chosen by God to become another day of Pentecost for the Roman Catholic Church." He notes that it was on this particular date that the Holy Spirit fell upon a group of believers in Pennsylvania and the charismatic experiences took root in the Catholic Church. Synan affirms that the movement was successful in influencing and raising the Catholic Church's awareness of the functions and operations of the Holy Spirit through charismatic experience.[7] Consequently, reports McDonnell, the Catholic bishops of the United States held two successive national conferences in 1969 and 1975 to discuss the impact of the Charismatic movement. Comparing the proceedings of the two conferences, McDonnell writes that the first conference was restrictive, with a "wait and see" statement, but the latter was more positive about the charismatic renewal in the church and resolved to go beyond such limitations. He cites these statements from the 1975 conference resolution: "The bishops strongly encourage priests to take an interest in the movement" and "we encourage those who already belong and we support the positive and desirable directions of the charismatic renewal."[8] Kärkkäinen further clarifies it by stating that Vatican II of the Catholic Church

---

4. *Charismatic Movement and Lutheran Theology*, 3–7.

5. Leonard and Crainshaw, *Encyclopedia of Religious Controversies*, 1:163.

6. Thiselton, *Holy Spirit*, 368.

7. Synan, *Century of the Holy Spirit*, 209; cf. pp. 222, 230.

8. McDonnell, *Charismatic Renewal and the Churches*, 49; cf. p 70. See also O'Connor, "Literature of Catholic Charismatic Renewal," 145–47; Gelpi, "Pentecostal Theology," 87–89.

"sanctioned the Catholic Charismatic renewal that was so quickly incorporated into the main church life."[9]

Scholarly evaluations also indicate that beginning in 1960 the Charismatic movement spread out from the shores of America and reached churches on other continents. Thiselton, for instance, reports that from 1960 onwards the Charismatic movement spread through Europe to countries such as England, Germany, France, Holland, Belgium, and the Scandinavian nations. He adds that in the same period, the movement spread to South American countries such as Brazil, Argentina, and Chile, and churches such as "Methodists, Presbyterians, and Congregationalists" began to lose their members to the Charismatic movement.[10] McDonnell adds that the movement reached to countries such as Puerto Rico, Panama, Scotland, and Canada in the same period.[11] From the years 1962 to 1982, Sullivan notes, the Protestant Churches in many parts of the world saw a remarkable outbreak of the Charismatic movement. Sullivan describes how many Protestant pastors were involved in introducing charismatic renewal to their churches and lists the names of some prominent pastors, including ministers of the Presbyterian, Reformed, Lutheran, Anglican, and Episcopalian churches.[12] In the same period, says Synan, the Charismatic movement reached countries with Hispanic, Haitian, Korean, and Filipino ethnic groups. He states that before 1960 many of the Protestant churches' ministers suffered bitter reactions from their churches when they became involved in Pentecostal experiences but this has not been the case since the 1960s. Since most of those churches became involved in charismatic experiences in the 1960s, the ministers of these churches seized the opportunity to become formally involved in the charismatic experiences.[13]

A detailed account of the emergence of the Charismatic movement in African churches is offered by Kalu in his book *African Pentecostalism*. In part 2 of his book, Kalu reports how charismatic experiences took root in African churches from the 1970s onwards.[14] Anderson reports that

9. Kärkkäinen, *Holy Spirit and Salvation*, 300, in particular, and pp. 294–301, in general.

10. Thiselton, *Holy Spirit*, 366–68.

11. McDonnell, *Charismatic Renewal and the Churches*, 59–72.

12. Sullivan, *Charisms and Charismatic Renewal*, 55.

13. Synan, *Century of the Holy Spirit*, 151; cf. pp. 222–23. For further detailed information of how the Charismatic movement "massively penetrated and permeated" the entire Churches by its "distinctive features" in "worship and in forms of ministry," see Hocken, "Charismatic Movement," esp. p. 501; and *Challenges of the Pentecostal*, 53–89.

14. Kalu, *African Pentecostalism*, 42–100.

African Pentecostal Christianity primarily draws its roots not only from the Charismatic movement of the 1960s but also from the Azusa Street Pentecostal movement beginning in 1907 through Pentecostal missionaries. Anderson affirms that Pentecostalism has celebrated a "century" in Africa and that Pentecostal and Charismatic Christianity are still "fast-growing and dominant forms of Christianity on the continent."[15] Thus, scholarly evaluations show that the 1960s were a significant time during which Charismatic movement reached all parts of the world. In light of these accounts, it seems that no established denomination of Christianity has remained untouched by the Charismatic movement since the 1960s. In the light of this evidence, it can be noted that it is inevitable that considerable changes have occurred in every established denomination's traditional belief, teaching, and practice of the Holy Spirit as a result of the influence of both the PCMs since the 1960s.

12.2. THE IMPACT OF THE CHARISMATIC MOVEMENT ON THE ESTABLISHED CHURCHES

Different evaluations indicate that the influence of the Charismatic movement has brought about a remarkable change in all of Christendom's traditional belief, teaching and practice of the Holy Spirit. William R. Barr and Rena M. Yocom, for instance, suggest that the established churches used to profess that the Holy Spirit worked through their structured practices, and yet their structures often resisted or even denied believers' involvement in the movement and workings of the Holy Spirit. However, say Barr and Yocom, this traditional resistance of the established churches has been broken through by the current charismatic renewal movement. As a result of the influence of the Charismatic movement, remarkable prophetic-charismatic voices have arisen, and have challenged and changed such traditional structural resistances. This prophetic-charismatic challenge, as the writers note, has observably convinced the established churches to reconsider, review, and redefine their traditional structures in light of the effects of the current charismatic experiences.[16] Christenson suggests that wherever the Charismatic movement was introduced, it focused on engaging believers in a

---

15. Anderson, *Introduction to Pentecostalism*, 103–4.
16. Barr and Yocom, *Church in the Movement*, 2–8.

renewed and fresh experience of the gifts and power of the Holy Spirit.[17] In another volume of his work, Christenson affirms that wherever the Charismatic movement is introduced, it has tangibly offered "one of the basic raw materials for spiritual power and renewal."[18] In support of this view, Heron states that wherever the Charismatic movement was introduced, charismatic groups emerged with the accompanying experiences of "tongues, healings, prophecies, visions, and revelations." He considers these experiences as the most "striking features of Neo-Pentecostalism."[19] Similarly, Kärkkäinen notes that although the established churches strongly opposed the PCMs in the beginning, they eventually adopted the charismatic emphases in their churches. He asserts that the movement convincingly delivered to the established churches the "restoration of apostolic signs: healing, miracles, prophecy, speaking in tongues and so on."[20] Concurring in this, Bradford suggests that traditionally denominational churches had "deprived" their members from "faith-building" charismatic experiences. Currently, however, these churches have been "grateful for the charismatic renewal, for through it they have been able to experience what they believe makes the reality of God come alive."[21]

Hence, instead of resisting, says Thiselton, the established denominations began to promote agreement and mutual acceptance of charismatics. He writes, "Rather than nurturing a mutually critical and suspicious relationship with the traditional denominations, both sides have recognized an urgent need for mutual respect and mutual listening." Accordingly, Thiselton concludes, the established churches began to consider "how the riches of the movement may be conserved for the good of the church."[22] Discussing on the twentieth- and early twenty-first-century Christian understanding and interpretation of the place and role of the Holy Spirit, Kärkkäinen notes that pneumatological traditions of many Christian churches and believers are being "revisited, reinterpreted, and reconfigured as an essential part of the continuing constructive work" and accordingly a "new breed of pneumatological interpretation is . . . emerging."[23] Horgan further elaborates on some of the questions raised

17. Christenson, *Charismatic Renewal Among Lutherans*, 33–34.
18. Christenson, *Message to the Charismatic Movement*, 23.
19. Heron, *Holy Spirit*, 132.
20. Kärkkäinen, *Toward a Pneumatological Theology*, 109–10.
21. Bradford, *Releasing the Power*, 17–18.
22. Thiselton, *Holy Spirit*, 368–70.
23. Kärkkäinen, *Pneumatology*, 97–98.

by the established churches regarding how charismatic experiences could be integrated into their structured worship practices and how authentic experiences might be discerned from imitations. He states that many established churches have come to agree upon a renewed understanding and experience of the gifts and workings of the Holy Spirit. However, they have struggled with discernment questions such as: How precisely does Scripture provide basic guidelines for discerning the true work of the Holy Spirit? How much are the current charismatic manifestations and their experiences in agreement with Scripture? How can one distinguish authentic manifestations of the gifts of the Holy Spirit from imitations by mere sentimentality or other evil spiritual realities? Since there are often phenomenological similarities between both realities, how can one discern which is of the divine and which is not? By what rules or format can the form, content, words, and actions of such movements be discerned? How can believers genuinely share in God's liberating and transforming movement through the Holy Spirit with all humility, patience, and gentleness while preserving the unity of the Spirit in the church?[24]

These scholarly evaluations and suggestions remind us of two main considerations. *Firstly*, they remind us that in contemporary Christendom, the thought and practice of the gifts and workings of the Holy Spirit through *Pentecostal-charismatic* experiences have been given proper attention by established churches. The established churches have conceded to the necessity of coping with and balancing two different theological perspectives of the Holy Spirit: doctrinal belief, which is their traditionalist position, and subjective experience, which has been imposed on them by the PCMs and has led them to reconsider their traditional thought and practice of the subjective experiential content of the manifestation of the Holy Spirit. *Secondly*, they remind us that established churches have been asking important theological and practical questions in order to realize genuine charismatic experiences. Scripture indeed teaches that at times those who promote the *Pentecostal-charismatic* form of spiritual experiences may take the appearance of sheep while in reality being wolves in their actions intent upon leading even the elect astray (Matt 7:15–23). It is also evident that evil spiritual realities always strive to take advantage of opportunities created by enthusiastic experiences to mar genuine spiritual experiences. It is, therefore, relevant to ask: what enables the church to discern whether everything held in contemporary

---

24. Horgan, *Biblical Basis*, 27–28.

charismatic experience is of the Holy Spirit or is of other pretending spiritual realities? Since there is no clearly set guidance about the nature of authentic charismatic experiences either in Scripture or in tradition, except through their fruits, it is indeed the case that churches can face real challenges when making decisions or judgments either to commend or to condemn the experiences at hand.

12.3. CHANGES IN THE TRADITIONAL TEACHING AND PRACTICE OF THE HOLY SPIRIT

Evaluations of the effects of the impact of the Charismatic movement on the established churches suggest that the movement has convinced those churches to reconsider their traditional views on the doctrine of the Holy Spirit. Dunn, for example, observes that the Charismatic movement has challenged mainstream churches to "recognize the importance of the emotional and non-rational in a fully integrated faith life, to give place to these less structured and less predictable elements in our worship, and to take seriously the third article of the Creed 'I believe in the Holy Spirit, the Lord, the Life-giver.'"[25] Williams supports this view and suggests that despite the church's formulation of the "ontological equality" of the Son and the Holy Spirit, there has been an obvious "functional subordination" of the Holy Spirit to the Son such that the entire role and function of the Holy Spirit was viewed only as an "applicative instrumentality" to Christ's works and that the fundamental purposes of the Pentecostal coming of the Holy Spirit, his gifts, and works were seriously neglected. He then affirms that as a result of the influence of the Charismatic movement, this situation has been changed and that the Holy Spirit is now being understood both objectively and subjectively by his own unique and distinctive gifts and works.[26] Indeed, the Charismatic movement, says Clement, has clearly pointed out the age-long neglect of the third person of the Trinity. Since the influence of the movement the Holy Spirit, "who . . . seemed little more than a token figure before" has now become "vividly real and personal" and an "imminent pervasive presence" for established churches.[27] Strengthening these observations, Samuel C. Storms suggests that since the influence of the Charismatic movement, there has been a painful

---

25. Dunn, *Ministry and The Ministry*, 81.
26. Williams, *Renewal Theology*, 2:137; cf. p 207.
27. Clement, *Pentecost or Pretense?*, 121.

and prayerful cry throughout Christendom saying, "Come Holy Spirit!" and a longing for his coming with power to work, to bestow gifts and to empower the church with the full range of charismata listed in Scripture.[28]

Accounts also indicate that longing for the coming and working of the Holy Spirit extended beyond denominational boundaries and became a recognized ecumenical issue. Evidence for this emerges from two different meetings of the World Council of Churches (WCC). The first was the WCC Consultation on the Significance of the Charismatic Renewal for the Churches held in Bossey, Geneva, in March 1980 with the theme "Towards a Church Renewed and United in the Holy Spirit." One of the five papers presented at the Consultation was put forward by Philip Potter, General Secretary of the WCC at the time, on the topic of "Charismatic Renewal and the World Council of Churches."[29] Potter begins his presentation by expressing his surprise at "how vast the phenomenon of the Charismatic Renewal" was, "how vast the literature" produced on the subject was, and how he "did not realize" the phenomenon until then. He explained how he visited the library in Geneva, perhaps during the composition of that presentation, and found out that there were "four shelves of books" written on the Charismatic movement during the preceding ten to fifteen years, which he considered to be "quite a discovery" for him.[30] Potter argued that the WCC was represented by churches that were "unreformed, unrenewed, official, and ununited" and that the Charismatic movement was reacting against these and was "uniting people"[31] beyond denominational boundaries. He asks, "Now, why is the World Council of Churches interested in the Charismatic Renewal?" The following extracts are taken from many of the reasons he enumerated why the WCC was interested in the Charismatic Renewal. He states that the Charismatic Renewal

> certainly confirms the goal of the ecumenical movement. It is a means of drawing people of different communions together. It has done that very clearly. All the reports of people who, in local situations caught in their confessional boxes and patterns, suddenly are exploded out and meet each other, pray, are able to express their doubts together, even to break through the rules

---

28. Storms, "Third Wave View," 175.
29. Potter, "Charismatic Renewal," 75.
30. Potter, "Charismatic Renewal," 75.
31. Potter, "Charismatic Renewal," 75.

of worshiping together ... so that is one of the reasons we are interested in Charismatic Renewal.[32]

[The Charismatic renewal] provides a link between the churches of the Reformation ... the Roman Catholic, the conservative Evangelicals, and with the Orthodox being true to their historic faith.... Now, we have learned ... the Charismatic Renewal has involved a great many Protestants and Roman Catholics.... Therefore it has enabled us to have a new kind of dialogue both with Roman Catholics at the base level and conservative Evangelicals. And that is important for the ecumenical movement.[33]

Potter claimed that the Charismatic movement was enabling believers to express the way of life in the Spirit against "hard and fast-whether traditional cultures and forms of church life,"[34] that it had tangibly broken through the traditional "denominational views" and "approaches" to the "unity of the churches" and had "thrown the people of all traditions in unity." He acknowledged that the movement was important for helping the WCC to work towards achieving the aim of the unity of God's people and the unity of all the people of the world, which is the work of the Holy Spirit through the church. He asserted that the Charismatic Renewal of the time was not only a renewal of the unity of peoples but was also the "renewal of the whole of Creation." He concluded by asking this question: "How far is the Charismatic Renewal opening us to the work of renewal of the whole of God's creation?"[35] Consideration seems to have been given to this question continuously which was reflected during the next assembly of the WCC.

The second meeting was the Seventh Assembly of the WCC, held in Canberra, Australia, in February 1989, with its theme "Come Holy Spirit—Renew the Whole Creation." The report adopted by the Council contains this statement:

The renewal of all life through God's pouring out of the Spirit is one of the powerful images in the Old Testament. In the New Testament, the outpouring of the Holy Spirit on the day of Pentecost is seen as the event that gathered the believers as a community of faith—the church. The first disciples experienced the

32. Potter, "Charismatic Renewal," 79.
33. Potter, "Charismatic Renewal," 79–80.
34. Potter, "Charismatic Renewal," 80.
35. Potter, "Charismatic Renewal," 84–86.

> Holy Spirit as the source of their faith, hope, and joy and as the power at work among them.... We are built up through the gifts of the Spirit into a people empowered to do God's will, to share the good news, and to become a community of sharing.... Indeed the Spirit lifts up our vision and points us to the renewal of the whole created order.... As we pray for this renewal, we seek to discern and participate in the activity of the Holy Spirit.[36]

Although this statement does not identify and address any specific results of the workings of the Holy Spirit through the Charismatic movement, it appears to stem from a renewed understanding and longing for the coming, gifting, empowering, renewing, and transforming works of the Holy Spirit. This renewed ecumenical interest seems to have raised an ecumenical awareness of the presence, gifts, power, and workings of the Holy Spirit in the church and in the whole creation.

These WCC statements are indicative of a turning point in Christendom's doctrine of the Holy Spirit. They are clear indicators that the impact of the Charismatic movement has contributed to an ecumenical reconsideration and rethinking of the traditionalist stance towards the place and role of the Holy Spirit both in the church and the wider world. The 1980 WCC Consultation, in particular, seems to be the most important and played a significant role in initiating a new pneumatological dimension and interest. Subsequent conferences, such as the one in 1989, seem to be referential to and reflective of the consultation of 1980 and influenced a deeper and broader discussion of the need for seeking the coming and working of the Holy Spirit. It appears that a remarkable conviction and consensus about a renewed understanding and experience of the Holy Spirit have emerged from the 1990s meetings of the WCC and spread throughout the whole of Christendom. This in itself is sufficient evidence of the renewal and transformation of Christendom's perspective regarding the place and role of the Holy Spirit in the church and the whole creation. This also ensures that as this pneumatological renewal formally took place, a renewal that had been ignored since the early post-apostolic period, a precise ecclesiastical theological breakthrough also took place. Thus, it seems, at least from my point of view, that it was these ecumenical pneumatological discussions that resulted in renewed pneumatological conversations between scholars of different theological traditions as can be seen from the examples presented below.

36. World Council of Churches, *Come Holy Spirit*, 7–8.

12.4. ACADEMIC AND SCHOLARLY INTEREST IN THE CONVERSATIONS OF THE PRESENCE AND ROLE OF THE HOLY SPIRIT IN THE CHURCH

As discussed in chapter 10, the Holy Spirit was an ignored member of the Trinity from the church's teaching and worship practices, and the subject of his gifts, empowerment, and working remained almost a moot point for centuries. The scholarly evaluations and observations of the place and role of the Holy Spirit presented in chapter 10, indicate that the Holy Spirit was made a "shy," "silent," "eclipsed," "dark-sided," and "Cinderella" member of the Trinity in the church's theological teaching, academic writings, and worship practice. In line with Christianity's neglect of the Holy Spirit for centuries, academic theological studies also isolated the Holy Spirit's place and role from theological and biblical studies.[37] Elaborating on this view, Yong writes that the Holy Spirit was traditionally made out to be the "shy or silent member of the trinity" and his role was marginalized in the history of Christian thought, practice, and academic theological works.[38] In contrast to this, however, the Holy Spirit has now become a matter of academic concern and scholarly attention with frequent flows of scholarly evaluations in line with the effects of the influence of the Charismatic movement and resulting contributions to theological studies and worship practices. For example, McGrath, who previously argued that the Holy Spirit had long been made the "Cinderella of the Trinity," affirms that this is not now the case in contemporary theological studies. He points out how the change has come about within established churches and how it has "ensured that the Holy Spirit figures prominently on the theological agenda."[39] Supporting this argument, Cartledge suggests that the Holy Spirit, who was viewed as the "Cinderella of theology," is now allowed to "attend the ball," which means, instead of being ignored, the Holy Spirit is being appreciated for his independent presence, manifestation, gifts, and independent workings.[40]

Kärkkäinen suggests that in traditional theology the Holy Spirit was "quite reserved and limited." Accordingly, traditional theology was "often perceived as dry and abstract." This traditional position has been "challenged in many ways by contemporary Pneumatologies." In contrast to the

37. Anderson, *Shape of Practical Theology*, 322–25.
38. Yong, "Ruach," 183.
39. McGrath, *Christian Theology*, 240.
40. Cartledge, *Encountering the Spirit*, 134.

traditional perception, there is a "new appreciation of the experience and spirituality" of the Holy Spirit and that there is an observable "attempt to give the [Holy] Spirit a more integral and central role." In the "beginning of the third millennium," says Kärkkäinen, many "public issues" which include "political, social, environmental" and worship are being invoked by theologians to give a more integral and central role to the Holy Spirit.[41] Yong suggests that in contemporary theology, pneumatology has been given a renewed emphasis in the church's doctrine of the Trinity. The current scholarship seems to be interested in, attracted to, and willing to read pneumatological passages of the Scriptures and biblical teaching in relation to Christian understanding, interpretation, and practice of them mostly regarding presence, gifts, and works of the Holy Spirit. Yong asserts that Christianity has been experiencing a "kind of renaissance in Christian theological reflections on the Holy Spirit that has invigorated the study of pneumatology proper and provided pneumatological perspectives on other themes of the traditional theological loci."[42] Discussing further on the idea of the "Pneumatological Renaissance," Kärkkäinen suggests that "in recent years, one of the most exciting developments in the theology has been an unprecedented interest in the Holy Spirit." He adds, "A renaissance concerning the doctrine and spirituality of the Holy Spirit has stirred much interest and even enthusiasm from all theological corners."[43]

Thiselton suggests that since around 1990 in particular, a "wealth of more scholarly literature has sprung up" on the issue of the doctrine of the Holy Spirit.[44] Barr and Yocom strengthen these suggestions by saying that the ecumenical study of the doctrine of the Holy Spirit is leading scholars to deeper insights into the movements and activities of the Holy Spirit in the church, in individual believers, and the world. They note that such insightful scholarly explorations, as they note, have come to commend that "essential to apostolic faith and believers' common confession of and witness to it is a fuller and deeper life in the Spirit." Barr and Yocom state that this recognition has deepened insightful scholarly explorations of the mysterious *Pentecostal-charismatic* role of the Holy Spirit and its significance to the faith community. Accordingly, they conclude, scholars have come to suggest that the source and power of the church's life are the gifts and works of the Holy Spirit; that the church's

---

41. Kärkkäinen, *Guide to Christian Theology*, 104.
42. Yong, "Ruach," 183; cf. pp. 190–91.
43. Kärkkäinen, *Pneumatology*, 1.
44. Thiselton, *Holy Spirit*, 366. See also Kärkkäinen, *Pneumatology*, 97–98.

life and ministry are to be shaped in and by the Holy Spirit; and that the church has to live in expectation and experiencing of the gifts, power, and works of the Holy Spirit.[45] Similarly, Leron F. Shults and Andrea Hollingsworth have observed that "most treatments of the doctrine of the Holy Spirit in the middle of the twentieth century began with a complaint about the inadequacy of the Christian tradition's treatment of the 'third person' of the Trinity." Currently, however, "Christian theology is in the midst of an academic revival of interest in pneumatology." They assert that over the last few decades "reflection on the Spirit has come to the forefront of discussions within and across theological disciplines" and that "pneumatology has increasingly become a generative theme around which creative dialogue across religious traditions has flourished."[46]

These scholarly observations of an increasingly growing pneumatological dialogue across denominations seem to be based on the existing reality. Conversations held between theologians of different theological traditions and published in books constitute examples of this. For example, *The Work of the Holy Spirit: Pneumatology and Pentecostalism*, published in 2006 and edited by Michael Welker, contains conversations of many prominent scholars. An acknowledgement page of the book explains:

> This book is the result of a consultation entitled "Pneumatology: Exploring the Work of the Spirit from Contemporary Perspectives," held in New York City in November 2004. . . . The interdisciplinary discourse on the topic had a specific profile as scholars with Pentecostal and Charismatic religious backgrounds and scholars with Anglican, Reformed, Lutheran, Methodist, and Roman Catholic heritage entered into a dialogue with each other.[47]

A similar conversation appears in the book *The Church in the Movement of the Spirit*, published in 1994 and edited by William R. Barr and Rena M. Yocom. People from a wide variety of theological and ecclesiastical traditions gathered together to discuss how the Holy Spirit is present and experienced in their worship and spiritual experiences. The book contains a heartfelt appreciation of the participants regarding their experience in the conversation: "In this discussion, we ourselves experienced the leading of the Spirit as we struggled to grasp the meaning of ways of perceiving and speaking of the Spirit in

---

45. Barr and Yocom, *Church in the Movement of the Spirit*, 5.
46. Shults and Hollingsworth, *Holy Spirit*, 1.
47. Welker, *Work of the Holy Spirit*, vii.

other traditions, in theological perspectives different from our own, and in others' personal experiences of the Spirit."[48] The contributors to these books shared important insights and made incisive suggestions for further scholarly conversations on the subject matter. These exemplary contributions are important gate openers to the increasingly growing scholarly conversation about contemporary Christendom's understanding and experience of the role of the Holy Spirit in the life, worship, spirituality, and mission of the church. They indicate the global engagement of scholars in renewed understanding, interpretation, and application of the subjective experiential content of the manifestation of the Holy Spirit. When records of those conversations are closely observed, the proposals of the participants demonstrate that scholars from different theological traditions have put forward a common view that their own churches' ages-long traditionalist pneumatic perceptions and practices have been impacted by the Charismatic movement and observable changes have come about. It appears that through the scholarly dialogues, a degree of consensus has been reached in that both objective doctrinal belief and subjective experience of the Holy Spirit must be uplifted. Indeed, these scholars seem to concur with Bradford who says, "We have to strike the balance."[49]

Further affirming these conclusions, Horgan suggests that many scholars have focused on the experiential aspect of the Holy Spirit in various branches of the church and from the perspectives of various theological traditions and they have come to recognize and appreciate more fully the work of the Holy Spirit across different theological traditions and in different ways. He states that as scholars have attempted to investigate the nature of contemporary claims of the gifts and works of the Holy Spirit, they have found that varying theological traditions have provided them with important insights into establishing a background for their evaluations, findings, and proposals. Such insights, as Horgan notes, have helped scholars of varying theological traditions discern more carefully the witnesses of Scripture regarding the gifts and workings of the Holy Spirit. Horgan asserts that most of those scholarly findings concur that the Holy Spirit plays a key role in the inspiration, empowerment, equipping, guidance, and communication of the church's gospel proclamation. Through such scholarly

48. Barr and Yocom, *Church in the Movement*, xi.
49. Bradford, *Releasing the Power*, 17–18.

findings and proposals, concludes Horgan, various traditionalist denominations have come to agree on a renewed understanding and experience of the workings of the Holy Spirit in the life and function of the church.[50] Insightfully comparing and contrasting the traditionalist and contemporary understandings and practices of the Holy Spirit, Horton further asserts that "all talk of the Spirit as the vulnerable person of the Trinity, the shy one, the 'still-small voice' which often becomes the Archimedean point for finding a weak spot in the Godhead, must be put to flight."[51]

In light of these scholarly observations and affirmations, it might be noted that over the last five decades, scholarship has produced a steady stream of books addressing and witnessing the established churches' recognition of and openness to the subjective experience of the Holy Spirit from a variety of theological and traditional perspectives. Horton's comment, in particular, seems to provide assurance that the churches of established denominations no longer downplay the importance of subjective experiential content of the Holy Spirit. There would, therefore, appear no future for traditionalist churches that remain intent on being held captive to their long-standing institutionalist, conservative pneumatological attitudes. Horton's reminder cited here indeed appears indicative that a broad agreement is being reached regarding the theological reality, practical importance, and inevitability of the subjective experience of the Holy Spirit. Thus, generally speaking, it would seem that the influence of the Charismatic movement has sparked a new interest in the doctrine of the Holy Spirit, both in terms of believers' subjective experience and scholarly study. This seems to remind us that the doctrine of the Holy Spirit has become a new and quite interesting ecumenical field of teaching, research, debate, and spiritual practice in contemporary Christian theology.

12.5. SUMMARY

In light of the above accounts and discussion, three points seem to be worthy of attention in concluding the chapter.

Firstly, the scholarly accounts consulted in this chapter attest that the rise and expansion of the Charismatic movement have been

---

50. Horgan, *Biblical Basis*, 27–28.
51. Horton, *Rediscovering the Holy Spirit*, 177.

swift. The movement has reached every corner of the world and has profoundly challenged all of Christendom with pneumatic power and charismatic effects. The movement's infusion of its objectives and convincing power is strong, and effective, and has reawakened a new interest in the theology and doctrine of the Holy Spirit throughout contemporary Christendom. Accordingly, all of Christendom has been touched by and recognized the gifting and workings of the Holy Spirit through Pentecostal-charismatic forms of worship and spiritual experiences. The fast and far-reaching achievement of the Charismatic movement may lead us to raise further questions such as: Why has the Charismatic movement gained such swift acceptance in churches throughout the world? Is it because established churches have conceded their past mistakes of allowing Christianity to enter a "long dryness" as discussed in chapter 8? Is it just a random religious and ecclesiastical phenomenon? Has the movement been genuinely meeting a spiritual hunger of believers in every church in contrast to the so-called "institutional cerebral rationalism, nominal formal religiosity, and anaemic conservative spirituality"? We have seen in this chapter how unprejudiced scholarly evaluations attest that the movement has been offering "the basic raw materials for spiritual power and renewal" for both individual believers and for the church as a whole. If this has truly been the nature of the movement, then it may be assumed that it is the Holy Spirit who has been working in churches tangibly and visibly through the charismatic experiences since the 1960s rather than a result of the established churches' conceding and confessing to past mistakes.

Viewed through the scholarly evaluations, observations, and suggestions presented in this chapter, the impact of the Charismatic movement appears to have resulted in the integration of the *institutional-organizational* and *Pentecostal-charismatic* nature of the church's life and ministry. These accounts inform us that contemporary Christianity has gone far beyond a traditional reluctance to combine doctrinal belief and subjective experience of the Holy Spirit. The perennial nervous tension that existed between the *institutional-organizational* and *Pentecostal-charismatic* forms of religious practice, which has endured since the repudiation of the Montanist movement, in particular, seems to have been remarkably broken and the wall of hostility erected between the two views has been shaken. Leaving behind the old hostile view, there is a renewed interest, longing, and prayer for the reception and experience of the gifts, power, and works of the Holy Spirit. This renewed interest has impacted the traditional worship and liturgical patterns of the established churches both conceptually and experientially. Accordingly, the liturgies of established churches have been undergoing revision and reformation in response to the question of integrated, inclusive, and participatory forms of worship. These changes may remind us about the fruitful contribution of charismatic experiences to the church's life and ministry.

Despite all these remarkable changes, however, it cannot be concluded that recognition of and adoption of the subjective experience of the Holy Spirit in established denominations means that the divisions of "for" and "against" views of these experiences are completely absent from those churches. Nor does it mean that all Christians are comfortable with a renewed emphasis on charismatic experiences and new measures being taken in churches to integrate both the institutional structures and the charismatic emphases of the Holy Spirit. Rather, there may still remain an unidentified and unaddressed tension, resistance, and rejection of charismatic experiences that run between the views of those groups either "for" or "against." Unlike the Spirit-initiated genuine subjective experience of biblical times, in contemporary charismatic experiences practitioners may at times mix up and confuse empirical experience with experimental experience and cause the charismatic experience to take an entirely experimental image, about which Paul alerted Corinthian believers (1 Cor 12). In particular, given a mixture of confused and scandalized enthusiastic charismatic experiences, such as those being observed in contemporary Ethiopian Para churches, established denominations' reverting to their traditionalist position and systematic suppression of charismatic experience may not be a matter of doubt. However, this study suggests that what ought to be sincerely considered by the church is *not the behavior of practitioners but the subjective experiential content of the manifestation and function of the Holy Spirit and divine purpose through Spirit-initiated subjective experience.*

Secondly, it would seem that the impact of the Charismatic movement has contributed to renewed interest in academic study regarding the reality of the workings of the Holy Spirit in and through subjective experience. As already stated in the preceding discussions, the subject of the Holy Spirit's presence in and working through subjective experience was almost a moot point for centuries. Currently, however, it has become a matter of worship practice, academic attention, and scholarly conversation. Indeed, scholarly critiques of traditional forms of pneumatological doctrine are increasingly emerging and calling the established churches to reconsider and redefine their traditional pneumatic position. Influenced both by on-the-ground experiences and scholarly proposals, theological institutions of established churches have established new units in pneumatology in their study programs and courses. Indeed, many scholars have suggested that objective theological and biblical studies are embracing the doctrine of the Holy Spirit. Most importantly, the phrases "baptism in the Holy Spirit" and "the gifts of the Holy Spirit" have taken on a renewed emphasis and meaning in contemporary theological and biblical studies. The current case of the Mekane Yesus Seminary constitutes an example of this. Since 1991—the time when the EECMY began to be greatly influenced by the Charismatic movement—the subject of the Charismatic movement, charismatic gifts, and baptism in the Holy Spirit have become issues for seminar presentations, discussions of consultations and assemblies, essay writing, term papers, theses, dissertations, etc. within the EECMY. Finally, the subject became one of the major courses with greater credit hours at Mekane Yesus Seminary with the title "Issues in Pneumatology." Although Mekane Yesus Seminary was established in 1960, it was only in 2011 that a course entitled "Issues in Pneumatology" appeared in the curriculum as a result of and in response to the influence of the Charismatic movement. The stated aim and objective of the course, in the course description, is to maintain and promote interaction between doctrinal belief and subjective experience of the Holy Spirit, thereby developing the knowledge and skills to ensure a balance between academic education and spiritual formation. This has also been the case in most of the evangelical churches across Ethiopia since 1991. Herein lies one of the major impulses prompting this study and leading to the writing of this book. As indicated in the introduction, however, the case of EECMY and the evangelical churches across Ethiopia will be pursued at great length in the subsequent volume of this work.

Thirdly, in light of the accounts and discussions held in this chapter, the subject seems worthy of consideration of further questions. For example:

(1) To whom should all these pneumatological changes be credited? Could it be to Charles F. Parham, founder of Bethel Bible School in Topeka, Kansas, in 1900? Can he be counted as the twentieth-century reformer regarding the Pentecostal-charismatic nature and function of Christianity, while the sixteenth-century reformers were reformers regarding the evangelical nature of Christianity? Or can it be said that it was God who restored the doctrine of justification by faith through the sixteenth-century

reformers and the doctrine of the subjective experience of the Holy Spirit through Parham in the twentieth century? While Pentecostal denominations may credit it to Parham, what do others think or say?

(2) Would there be a lesson to be learned by churches of every denomination from accounts of Parham's perseverance and the event of Bethel Bible School? The answer to this question seems to be "yes" since this event reminds us that the periphery has most often been the place where renewal, transformation, empowerment, and inspiration have taken place in the history of Christianity. The New Testament, for instance, clearly indicates that Jesus' ministry and redemptive work began on the periphery of the powerful Jewish religious institution of the time. However, his work became convincingly powerful and continuously victorious. Later, after Jesus' ascension and the coming of the Holy Spirit at Pentecost, Christianity as a movement began on the periphery of that same religious institution but continued to flourish, blossom, and win millions across the globe as predicted in Matt 13:31–32. The same principle seems to be the case concerning the twentieth-century PCMs. Parham focused on the *Pentecostal-charismatic* life and function of the church, which had been ignored or even avoided by the powerful institutional churches of the preceding eighteen centuries. His vision, longing, and prayer for the coming, baptizing, gifting, empowering, and working of the Holy Spirit in believers' lives and ministry brought an astonishing pneumatological fact to light, which the established and prestigious churches not only failed to do but also opposed most vehemently for centuries. Through Parham's perseverance in longing and praying for this particular Christian experience, the whole of Christendom has now embraced the values of the *Pentecostal-charismatic* nature and functions of the church.

In whichever way we may perceive and interpret his longing and constant prayer for this experience, and by whatever name we call it, Parham seems to have insightfully used his gifts of vision, teaching, and leadership, which prevailed over and penetrated the opposing established churches to their surprise and consequent silencing of their traditional resistance. Parham thus appears to have a special place within the contemporary *Pentecostal-charismatic* stream and there is a lesson to be learned from his perseverance. Furthermore, although historical accounts examined in this study indicate that experience of a *Pentecostal-charismatic* form of worship and spirituality was not upheld by the church between the post-apostolic time and the early twentieth century, this does not necessarily mean that its content and substance have been absent from Christian belief, teaching, and practice. Since such an experience is a divinely destined and divinely delivered gift and a divinely initiated practice of the church, it continues in its function and shall last until the end of this age. Therefore, while Parham's perseverance may remain both valid and appreciated, his Pentecostal experience cannot be regarded as an innovation but as a revival of the long-neglected gift and practice of the Church of Christ.

CHAPTER 13

Summary, Personal Reflections, and Conclusions

As stated in the introduction, the purpose of this study has been to examine the person, gifts, and works of the Holy Spirit in biblical teaching and historical Christian belief, teaching, and practice through the centuries and then to provide theologically, biblically, and historically reasonable answers to the questions which prompted this study and finally led to the writing of this book. To this effect, the exploration of the study has focused on three major parts. The first part examined the biblical teaching about the theology, manifestation, gifts, and works of the Holy Spirit. The second part explored historical Christian belief, teaching, and practice of the person, gifts, and works of the Holy Spirit beginning in the apostolic time down to the end of the nineteenth century. The third part explored contemporary Christendom's thought, teaching, and practice of the person, gifts, and works of the Holy Spirit. Stories and features analyzed in each chapter of each part have been selected as carefully as possible from among many others as accurate and the most significant for this study. In general, the study has attempted to make two important issues very clear and to bring them to light, that is, *two distinct Christian views* on the doctrine of the Holy Spirit: (1) the *institutional-organizational* view, which emphasizes objective reception and doctrinal belief of the Holy Spirit; and (2) the *Pentecostal-charismatic* view, which strives to add the subjective experience of the Holy Spirit to the doctrinal belief. The theological, theoretical, and practical developments of both views have been examined and analyzed.

This chapter will conclude that examination and its findings with a summary of the issues raised and features covered in the study. Indeed, major points of the findings of the study have already been summarized at the end of each chapter. Chapter 10, in particular, has summarized the overall situation of the place and role of the Holy Spirit in Christian belief, teaching, and practice in the centuries between AD 100 and 1900. Nevertheless, it is appropriate at the conclusion of the study to draw together the main threads of the examinations and to conclude with personal reflection. To do this, there are relevant questions to be addressed and answered. For example, what are the findings of this study concerning (1) what the Bible teaches about the Holy Spirit; (2) how and why the nature, gifts, and works of the Holy Spirit appear to cause doubts, questions, confusions, and controversies; and (3) how and why the subjective experience of the Holy Spirit, in particular, appears to cause confusion, tension, and division in the church. Finally, it concludes by underscoring how the mysteries of the objective gift and subjective experiential contents of the manifestation of the Holy Spirit should be understood and practiced in the church in an equal measure.

13.1. WHAT DOES THE BIBLE TEACH ABOUT THE PERSON, GIFTS, AND WORKS OF THE HOLY SPIRIT?

As examined and analyzed in chapters 1 to 4, the Bible teaches four major features about the person, gifts, and works of the Holy Spirit:

First, the Bible teaches about the essence, transcendence, manifestation, gifts, and activities of the Holy Spirit beginning in the inception of creation. The Old Testament teaches that the *Spirit of God* implemented divine purpose for creation from day one and exercised a continuous function in giving and sustaining life. All the divinely destined and divinely initiated actions and events in the Old Testament were illumined, gifted, empowered, and guided by the *Spirit of God* as a way of displaying that God himself was present and acting out his purpose through the invisible personality of his Spirit. Accordingly, the being, manifestation, gifts, and works of the *Spirit of God* were identified with the transcendent divine—God. We have seen that what is referred to as the "Spirit of God" or the "Spirit of the LORD" in the Old Testament is what is believed and described as the "Holy Spirit" in the New Testament. This marks clearly who the Holy Spirit is and what he does and thus, clearly implies that there is no difference between the being of God the Creator and the Spirit of God—the Holy Spirit.

Second, the Bible teaches about the independent personality and independent operations of the Holy Spirit within the Godhead. The New Testament presents that the Holy Spirit is an independent divine person within the Godhead with consciousness, will, knowledge, intelligence, and all personal senses. As discussed in chapters 1 and 4, the Holy Spirit's role as an independent personal being can be seen in a wide range of situations within the post-Pentecostal life and functions of the early church. For example, he played the divine role as a guide in leadership appointment by permitting and forbidding believers to do certain things, by providing intelligence for missionary movement, by commanding the church to set aside individuals for the ministry in which he wanted them to serve, etc. This biblical evidence presents a picture of the Holy Spirit as a full personal being who does things only a real personal being can do. In view of this biblical evidence, the issue of the Holy Spirit's deity, independent personality, authority, and independent operation within the Godhead appears to be *incontestable*. This biblical teaching provided the church of the patristic period with the theological and biblical grounds on which it formulated the doctrine of the Holy Spirit's deity, authority, and independent personality in the second ecumenical council in 381.

Third, the Bible teaches about the objective gift and subjective experiential contents of manifestations of the Holy Spirit. As discussed in chapters 2 and 3, in biblical times there was objective salvific imparting of the Holy Spirit from the divine side, and subjective experiential movement from the human side, which resulted from the gift and power imparted by the Holy Spirit. When God imparts the Holy Spirit to his people, his audibly uttered or visibly performed charismatic gifts are also imparted. According to accounts of the experience of the early church, it was the divine objective impartation of the Holy Spirit that resulted in initiating subjective charismatic forms of worship and spiritual experiences in the lives of believers. In such Spirit-provided and Spirit-initiated incidents the subjective experience of believers was accompanied by genuine exuberant worship, praise, and audibly uttered or visibly performed charismatic experiences. Manifestation and reception of the Holy Spirit in biblical times, therefore, seems to mean an experience of evident presence, gifts, power, and acts of the Holy Spirit in equal measure. This seems to be clear biblical ground for why the Holy Spirit has historically been associated with, and represented by, audible and visible charismatic experiences, as well as practices of enthusiastic praise, spontaneity, exuberance, inspiration, and awakening.

Fourth, the Bible contains accounts regarding the manifest connection of the Holy Spirit with charismatic gifts. As discussed in chapters 1 to 3, the Bible is clear enough in attesting that the Holy Spirit dispensed different kinds of charismatic gifts and empowered individuals for divinely related actions. All the divinely destined and divinely initiated messages, utterances, and actions of the biblical times followed the coming of the Holy Spirit, resulted from the possessing, gifting, empowering, inspiration, and guidance of the Holy Spirit, and were experienced as the gifts of the Holy Spirit. This biblical evidence assures us that it was God himself who purposely connected the manifestation of the Holy Spirit with the manifestation of charismatic gifts, empowerment, and inspired utterances of audible charismata or performances of visible charismata. This again appears to be clear biblical ground for why the Holy Spirit has traditionally been associated with audibly uttered and visibly performed charismatic gifts, as well as spiritual practices of enthusiastic praise, spontaneity, exuberance, inspiration, and awakening.

These four biblical accounts indicate who the Holy Spirit is, what he does, how his manifestation, presence, gifts, and activities are related to the life, ministry, and mission of the church, and how the church's life and functions are dependent on the presence, gifts, and works of the Holy Spirit. Nevertheless, despite this biblical evidence, two factors have caused doubts, questions, confusions, controversies, and divisions within the church concerning the doctrine of the Holy Spirit: *firstly*, the nature of the Holy Spirit; and, *secondly*, subjective experience of the Holy Spirit. Each of these factors will be analyzed briefly as follows.

13.2. HOW DOES THE NATURE OF THE HOLY SPIRIT CAUSE QUESTIONS AND CONTROVERSIES?

As examined and analyzed in chapter 6, there were different perceptions of the Holy Spirit in the early church which eventually led some people to disputes with the church over the nature of the Holy Spirit. The finding of the examination shows that some people of the time felt that Scripture was silent about the nature, authority, independent personality, and independent operations of the Holy Spirit. Others felt that Scripture subordinated the Holy Spirit to the other two persons of the Trinity. Still, others felt that Scripture never calls or mentions the Holy Spirit as God but only a minister of God. Such different views of the Holy Spirit, therefore, contributed to questions, confusion, controversies, and divisions over the nature of the Holy Spirit. However, the findings of this study have attempted to provide evidence that Scripture is not silent about the deity, independent personality in the Godhead, manifestation, independent authoritative operations, gifts, and workings of the Holy Spirit. Neither does Scripture explicitly subordinate the Holy Spirit to the Father and the Son. Nevertheless, certain texts in Scripture seem to have the potential to lead to arguments and disputes over the subordinate state of the Holy Spirit. This can be seen in the following three examples:

First, when taken at face value, biblical passages like John 16:13–15 appear to contain the idea of the Holy Spirit's subordination to the Father and the Son. When taken at face value such words that the Holy Spirit "will not speak on his own; he will speak only what he hears. . . . He will bring glory to me by taking from what is mine" appear to present a degree of the inferiority of the Holy Spirit to both the Father and the Son. Indeed when considering Gregory of Nyssa's citations of the questions and arguments of the Macedonians, analyzed in chapter 6, it appears that most of the questions, confusions, and controversies of the period over the nature of the Holy Spirit drawn from and revolved around this Scriptural reference. This text appears to continue to raise questions and confusion to this day for those who engage in academic Pneumatology. For example, there were many questions raised by my students at MYS when I taught the "Issues in Pneumatology" course. Different classes of students raised the same questions year after year over John 16:13–15. One of the common questions raised by different classes of students is: "How can we answer theological and doctrinal questions on the nature of the Holy Spirit that arise from John 16:13–15?" Particularly, the students who have been teaching in the regional seminaries always express how they have been challenged by their students on the nature of the Holy Spirit in reference to this text. This may indicate that those who engage in academic pneumatology may encounter continuing grappling with the ambiguities and questions arising from the words of John 16:13–15. Viewed in light of this text, the disputers' perception of subordination of the Holy Spirit may not be criticized as mere groundless fantasy. However, such perception cannot be favored when viewed over other wider perspectives of the biblical teaching about the Holy Spirit as well as the relationship between Jesus and the Holy Spirit. Further light will be shed on this below.

Second, there are similar other questions about the nature of the Holy Spirit in reference to certain biblical accounts. For example, different classes of my students at MYS raised the same questions year after year over texts that speak about the nature of the Holy Spirit. The students consider that in all his works in creation, incarnation, redemption, salvation, and the founding and organizing of the church, the Holy Spirit manifests and acts as one of the persons in the Godhead. However, the students express their ambiguity with the features the Holy Spirit is symbolized in the Bible. They wonder why God the Father, who himself is the Spirit, is symbolized by a human personality while God the Holy Spirit is symbolized by fire (Matt 3:11–12), water (John 4:10–14; 7:37–39), wind (John 3:8), oil/ointment (1 John 2:20, 27), a dove (John 1:32), a seal (Eph 1:13–14), or even by rays of light which strike from the transcendent down to earth (Acts 9:3–5). The students expressed how this induces them to question how the living, speaking, and acting God the Holy Spirit can be symbolized by these non-living things. Even when the Holy Spirit is symbolized by a living being, the students argue, it is in the form of a bird, the dove. They ask: how can these living and non-living entities give Christians an accurate glimpse of the truly personal nature of the Holy Spirit? These biblical texts, the students assert, continue to raise difficulties in providing a convincing or satisfying answer to the question: in what sense can the Holy Spirit be perceived and spoken of as a personal being? My meek suggestion to them is simply to say, "Yes, of course, it seems difficult to make an academic analysis and give a satisfying answer to these and similar questions drawing from Scripture. . . . However, the features by which the Holy Spirit is symbolized do not seem to represent the precise nature or identity of the Holy Spirit. Rather, they would seem to symbolize or represent the Holy Spirit's presence and action in historical affairs through human-involving subjective experiences. . . . Each of these features appears to have a mysterious connection to the presence and action of the Holy Spirit in historical ecclesiastical life and function in the world." For some students, my suggestion appears likely but for others it is unlikely. Hence, we often conclude our discussions without reaching any satisfying answer or consensus. This again indicates that those who engage in academic pneumatology may keep encountering the continuing questions and ambiguities arising from these biblical references.

Third, added to all these contestable features are the various ways of reception of the Holy Spirit. As discussed in chapter 2, there are different accounts, images, and indications of how the Holy Spirit was received in early New Testament times. Scripture clearly presents that in the early New Testament times the Holy Spirit was sometimes received in and through water baptism; sometimes after a certain length of time after the reception of water baptism; sometimes by the laying on of hands; sometimes those who had already received him received him over and over again; and sometimes nonbelievers received him even before they had come to faith and water baptism. In light of this biblical evidence, particularly from an academic point of view, it seems that there is no clearly defined answer regarding how to perceive, interpret, and act with the mystery of the ways of reception of the Holy Spirit. As mentioned earlier, one of the impetuses of this study was the search for answers to these ambiguities, questions, and confusion. After a thorough examination of the Scriptures the deity, manifestation, independent personality in the Godhead and independent authoritative activities of the Holy Spirit, this study has established that doubts, questions, confusions, and ambiguities arising over the nature of the Holy Spirit are rooted in both the divine side and human side. From the divine side, it appears evident that God did not reveal to humankind what is in his mind about the status of each person of the Trinity. From the human side, it is clear that academics struggle with how to understand, interpret, and clarify certain unclear biblical passages such as are at issue here. Accordingly, a huge gap seems to be evident between both sides. The question that might be asked in this respect is: can this gap be bridged in any way? The answer to this question seems to be both "no" this gap cannot be bridged, and "yes," it may be bridged. Why the answers are both "no" and "yes" requires a brief explanation of each.

First, the answer "no," this gap cannot be bridged in any way, may be considered in the light of the following four theological and biblical features:

1. According to the Scriptures, God's concern about humankind is saving and reconciling it with himself (John 3:16–17) but not for its academic knowledge. Concerning salvation, God has revealed the three persons of the Godhead in the way he thinks would suffice for salvation. He may not consider the need for providing further definition regarding the status of each person of the Godhead in such a way that answers the questions or solves the problems of academic knowledge beyond what he has already revealed in the redemptive

activities and which is preserved in the Scriptures. If this is so, then the gap at issue here may never be bridged until cows come home.

2. According to the Scriptures, it is God who sends the Holy Spirit sometimes as an invisible personality and other times as a visible personality such as in the form of a dove. Since God is sovereign and free to act in the way he wills and wants to act for his purposes, can futile human academic excellence ask him why this is so? Can human academic elitism ask God why he allows his Holy Spirit to be symbolized by non-living features such as fire, water, wind, oil/ointment, etc. while he, who is the Spirit himself (John 4:24), is symbolized by human personality? Would he be willing to answer such academic questions and satisfy the academics? Thus, if God does not reveal what is in his mind and answer such academic questions, then academically motivated efforts to know about this particular aspect of the Holy Spirit would remain futile.

3. According to John 16, it was Jesus who declared that the Holy Spirit would say or do nothing from himself but receive from Jesus and deliver to Jesus' followers, thus bringing glory to Jesus. Can it be possible for academics to examine whether this speech of Jesus might have minimized the credibility of the Holy Spirit in any way? Can Jesus be questioned as to why he seems to have subordinated the Holy Spirit under himself in this speech, while giving him equal status on another occasion with the Father and himself by saying, "Go . . . baptize . . . teach in the name of the Father and of the Son and of the Holy Spirit"? If Jesus does not give the kind of definition or explanation academics would like to have for this speech, then academically motivated efforts to know about this particular point would remain futile.

4. Christian belief and teaching asserts that Scripture is the God-breathed word of God and that the Holy Spirit inspired and guided the writings of the Scriptures (2 Tim 3:16–17; 1 Pet 1:20–21). If this is an ascertained fact, then the biblical passages presented above, which seem to cause questions, confusions, and controversies regarding the nature of the Holy Spirit, are also God-breathed words of God and were written under the inspiration and guidance of the same Holy Spirit. If these passages, John 16:13–15 in particular, minimize his credibility in any way, then why did the Holy Spirit not guide the writers to write them differently? Why did he not illumine

the writers regarding the status of his position in the Godhead and the nature of his relationship with the other two persons in the Godhead? If the Holy Spirit does not answer these questions with what is in his mind, then the academically motivated efforts to know about this particular case would again remain futile.

In the light of these unanswerable questions and insoluble ensuing problems, the gap at issue here may not be bridged. Unless God answers every question and provides a solution for every doubt, confusion, and controversy arising in reference to the nature, ways of reception, and workings of the Holy Spirit through a new revelation or in any other means, the gaps at issue here may never be bridged. Indeed it is difficult to predict whether God may bring a new revelation or any other means to answer questions or to solve confusion regarding the relationship and hierarchy between the three persons of Godhead. Therefore, since humankind's academic elite cannot examine God's deepest secrets, which he has reserved for himself, finding the most probable answers or solutions to bridge the gap at issue here seems to be a matter of impossible possibility. Given this, what the second ecumenical council of the church attributed to the Holy Spirit and formulated as his doctrine in 381 ever remains fundamentally right. It answers all questions and solves all confusion regarding the nature of the Holy Spirit in a very simple, clear, and general way. Standing firm and remaining bound in it is a valuable conclusion.

Second, the answer "yes" to the "gap at issue here may be bridged" may be considered in the light of the following two important factors:

1. The gap at issue here may be bridged simply by interpreting and applying texts such as John 16:13–15 in the light of other discourses of Jesus. Two factors can be presented as examples. *First*, according to the testimonies of the gospels, Jesus asserted how he and the Father are one, are working together in his earthly ministry, and that whatever belongs to the Father also belongs to him (John 5:19–24, 30; 7:16–18; 8:16, 27–30; 12:49–50; and 14:8–11). He asserted that the words he spoke and actions he did during his earthly ministry are the words and actions of the Father and they fulfil the will and purpose of the Father. He assured his audiences that the words and actions of the Son mean at the same time the words and actions of the Father and vice-versa. Believing in one of them, therefore, means at the same time believing in the other of them. Thus, Jesus' discourses in John 16:13–15 can also be perceived to mean that the words and

actions of any one of the three persons within the Godhead mean at the same time the words and actions of the other two. *Second,* accounts of the Gospels present Jesus' ministry as conducted in the power of the Holy Spirit. Jesus was anointed with and by the Holy Spirit (Luke 4:18-20; Acts 10:38) and was led into the wilderness to be tempted by Satan (Luke 4:1-13). After temptation he was led back to Galilee in the power of the Holy Spirit (Luke 4:14). He cast out demonic spirits in the power of the Holy Spirit (Matt 12:28; Acts 10:38). If Jesus' anointment, empowerment, and serving by the power of the Holy Spirit minimize his credibility in any way, then couldn't he express the event in different way? Jesus is aware that his discourses are intended not to declare the subordination or hierarchical status of the three persons in the Godhead. Rather, his discourses clearly teach his audiences about the mystery of how the three persons of the Godhead relate to one another and how they work together towards bringing salvation for humankind. His discourse in John 16:13-15, therefore, is the same and asserts that the cycle of the involvement and activity of the one person within the Trinity in redemptive activity means the involvement and activity of all three persons of Godhead. The lesson the reader may grasp from Jesus' discourse in John 16:13-15 is that there is "no mission of the Son in which the Spirit of God does not participate and there is no mission of the Spirit in which the Son of God does not participate."[1] This strictly reminds the reader about the mystery of how the three persons of the Godhead relate to one another and how they work together towards bringing salvation for humankind. In light of this, an intended message of John 16:13-15, does not appear to subordinate the Holy Spirit to the Father and the Son.

2. The gap at issue here can be best bridged through engaging in a personal experience of the Holy Spirit rather than striving to know him through frail and finite human academic elitism. Any doubt, question, or confusion arising from longing for proper knowledge of the nature, gifts, power, and workings of the Holy Spirit can be radically answered or solved only when one engages in the knowledge of him through simple personal experience. Those who have personal experience of the Holy Spirit have been possessed (controlled), gifted, empowered, illumined, inspired, and guided by the Holy Spirit.

---

1. Nafzger et al., *Confessing the Gospel,* 555.

They engaged in Spirit-endowed and Spirit-initiated audibly uttered and visible performed extraordinary experiences. As an expression of this, they have advanced their knowledge of the nature, presence, gifts, power, and workings of the Holy Spirit, as well as the depths of their spirituality. Returning to and engaging in the personal experience of the Holy Spirit is an earnest suggestion of this study.

13.3. HOW AND WHY THE SUBJECTIVE EXPERIENCE OF THE HOLY SPIRIT CAUSES QUESTIONS, CONFUSION, TENSION, AND DIVISION IN THE CHURCH

As considered in the earlier discussions, the second main reason why the nature of the Holy Spirit has been viewed as controversial arises from the Holy Spirit's manifest connection with charismatic gifts and resultant subjective experience. The study has attempted to identify some of the biblical and historical reasons regarding why and how the concept and practice of subjective experience of the Holy Spirit became features of question, confusion, tension, and division within the doctrine of the Holy Spirit. We have seen in chapters 2 and 3, how the Scriptures assert that in biblical times there was objective imparting of the Holy Spirit, from the divine side, and subjective experiential movement, from the human side, resulting from the gift endowed and the power imparted along with the Holy Spirit. The Scriptures inform us that the coming of the Holy Spirit entailed two phenomena: the objective manifestation of divine reality and the subjective experience of the presence, gifts, power, and workings of the Holy Spirit. These twofold manifestations of the Holy Spirit were fundamental means and instruments of life in and experience of the Holy Spirit in biblical times. Scripture accounts ascertain that subjective experience of the Holy Spirit, in biblical times, was not constituted by human enthusiastic and emotional experiences. Rather, it was divinely destined, divinely delivered, and divinely initiated for the fulfillment of the divine purpose in the world. Therefore, it was a genuine expression of the reception of the Holy Spirit, his gifts, and moving power, which took place only through the expression of the Spirit-initiated, audibly uttered or visibly performed charismatic gifts. The manifestation of audibly uttered and visibly performed charismata acted as the means of the Holy Spirit's

SUMMARY, PERSONAL REFLECTIONS, AND CONCLUSIONS

objective gift and people's expression of it through the Spirit-initiated experiences.

Biblical accounts examined in chapters 1 to 3 attest that it was not human enthusiastic, emotional, ecstatic, and spontaneous experiences that constitute the subjective experience of the Holy Spirit. Rather, it is God who constitutes both objective impartation and subjective experiential dimensions of the Holy Spirit's manifestation. In biblical times it was God who took the initiative for subjective experience by giving either audible utterances or visible performance of charismatic gifts through his Spirit and thereby working towards his purpose through human subjective experience. All the origin, manifestation, and function of the Holy Spirit and related manifestations of the audibly uttered or visibly performed charismata, in biblical times, were God's intervention in the concerns of salvation, renewal, transformation, and empowerment of his people. For this purpose it was God himself who constituted both objective impartation and subjective experiential dimensions of the Holy Spirit's manifestation and introduced it to the world as the fulfillment of his promise (Joel 2:28). This reminds the church that both the objective impartation and subjective experiential content of the Holy Spirit's manifestation have sound theological and biblical objectivity and an indispensable authoritative functional role in the life, worship, ministry, and mission of the church. Despite this biblical fact, the church historically paid greater attention to conceptual doctrinal belief and ignored the subjective experience of the Holy Spirit. Consequently, subjective experience of the Holy Spirit remained for centuries a matter of question, confusion, tension, and division in the church. As discussed in chapters 5 to 9 and briefly summarized in chapter 10, this study has attempted to identify and highlight some of the reasons for the church's ignoring of subjective experience and how such a position continued until the 1960s when the Charismatic movement emerged, expanded, and impacted the whole of Christendom and revived the concept and practice of subjective experience of the Holy Spirit.

Thus, in light of the findings of this study, two points, from many others, appear to require particular attention regarding the subjective experience of the Holy Spirit.

Firstly, it is evident that the Bible clearly teaches that the Holy Spirit is an objectively given gift of salvation and yet gives gifts of salvation ministry that are realized and demonstrated through subjective experience. In the objective nature of his manifestation, the Holy Spirit is the objective gift of God to his people to indwell and endow them with supernatural gifts of God's grace. Through the subjective nature of his manifestation, the Holy Spirit often provides God's people with audibly uttered or visibly performed charismatic gifts and with empowered, awakened, inspired, and devotional worship, spiritual experience, and ministry. The subjective experience of the Holy Spirit, therefore, is an *original theological input* from the divine *just like the objective impartation* of the Holy Spirit. Thus, viewed through biblical teachings of the subjective experiential nature of the Holy Spirit's manifestation, subjective experience is not something alien and shameful for the church to claim and experience. Rather, it is divinely destined, divinely delivered, and divinely initiated theological, functional, and spiritual reality for the church. While maintaining the objective reception of the Holy Spirit through baptismal sacrament and formulating doctrinal belief of the Holy Spirit is valid, valuable, and of lasting importance, this should not obscure the subjective experience of the Holy Spirit. Rather, doctrinal belief should shape and guide the practical appropriation of the subjective experience.

Scholars who have critically examined the theological reality and practical significance of subjective experience of the Holy Spirit suggest that the subjective experiential dimension of the Holy Spirit's manifestation should not be underplayed. Horgan, for example, suggests that the experience of the Holy Spirit makes the church the sacramental presence of Christ; the sacrament of humanity's union with God in his grace which enlivens, empowers, transforms, enhances, and uses the gifts of the church to share in God's world-redeeming mission. The church, therefore, asserts Horgan, cannot live and serve by its human resources because its true resource comes from God's grace through the experience of the Holy Spirit.[2] The experience of the Holy Spirit, concurs Dunn, is the "power of inner life which lives far behind all the merely ritual and outward and makes a faith in God and worship of God existentially real," the "power which transforms a man from the inside out, so that metaphors of cleansing and consecration become matters of actual experience in daily life" and is the "source of the wave of love and joy which overwhelms the forces that oppose from without."[3] Neglecting the experience of the presence, gifts, movements, and workings of the Holy Spirit in the church only "distorts the whole content of faith" and is an "accomplice to

---

2. Horgan, *Biblical Basis*, 13.
3. Dunn, *Jesus and the Spirit*, 201–2.

the individualistic and institutionalistic introversion" as well as "egotism," which still is the case in many of the established churches.⁴ In order to maintain the theological and spiritual health of the church, it is a must that the church's "*theology* of the Spirit" and "its *experience* of the Spirit" must "correspond more closely."⁵ Moule asserts that "to experience the power of the Spirit" is "obviously far more important than to talk about it" and that it is a "gross mistake to try to squeeze New Testament language into the mould of later doctrinal formulations."⁶ A similar opinion is offered by Clark H. Pinnock who asserts that the effectiveness of the church's worship, ministry, and mission are always dependent on the gifts, power, and activities of the Holy Spirit. For this reason, the Holy Spirit indwells the church as a perpetual Pentecost, communicates the gifts of grace, and manifests the transforming power of the day of Pentecost in all ages. Pinnock adds, "Any church that denies the Spirit freedom stands in danger of becoming a lifeless and self-glorifying church"⁷ and thus having an insipid ministry. These scholarly suggestions are in accord with, and a reflection of, biblical teachings examined in this study. In light of these scholarly suggestions two points appear to require particular attention:

(1) The doctrinal belief of objective reception must be strongly maintained and preserved as the ruling norm of the Christian doctrine of the Holy Spirit but not to the exclusion of subjective experience. It must be noted that there is no theological or scriptural ground for justification of doctrinal belief that does not comprise the subjective experiential nature of the Holy Spirit's manifestation. The divine nature of the Holy Spirit must indeed be doctrinally believed and worshiped, in which the church abides by the objective reality of the Holy Spirit. At the same time, however, the presence, gifts, and workings of the Holy Spirit must also be realized and preserved through Spirit-initiated and Spirit-guided subjective experience. As the formulation of objective doctrine attempts to constitute knowledge of and belief in the Holy Spirit, subjective experience of him, too, attempts to constitute absolute realization of his presence, gifts, power, and activities in the collective life of the church, as well as in the life of individual believers. Conceptual doctrinal belief formulated by humankind can only describe the doctrine of the Holy Spirit, whereas Spirit-endowed, Spirit-initiated, and Spirit-guided subjective experience

---

4. Berkhof, *Doctrine of the Holy Spirit*, 34.
5. Fee, *God's Empowering Presence*, 2.
6. Moule, *Holy Spirit*, 4; cf. p. 24.
7. Pinnock, *Flame of Love*, 114-15, 131.

can put this doctrinal belief into the tangible practice of the Holy Spirit in the life and function of the church. The Holy Spirit must, therefore, be objectively received as God's gift of salvation, doctrinally believed and worshiped as the divine, and subjectively experienced as the means of experiencing the charismatic gifts of God. Christianity should, therefore, not insist only on the formulation of doctrinal belief and act against the possibility of subjective experience of the Holy Spirit. It is an earnest suggestion of this study that the church's belief, teaching, and practice have to create a hunger for this gift of God and exhort believers toward its genuine realization and experience.

(2) The church must be reminded that any doctrine formulated by humans towards the divine can neither be an absolute criterion for the divine truth nor does it determine further revelation and action of the divine. Doctrinal formulas set by humans with a human concept of divine truth and action cannot limit divine intervention and action through the subjectively experienced gifts of the divine. Thus, it is important to consider the theological reality and practical significance of the subjective experiential nature of the Holy Spirit's manifestation instead of insisting on a set doctrinal formula. Integrated realization of both the objective gift and subjective experience of the Holy Spirit may even lead Christians to the far-reaching authentic Scriptural doctrine of the saving, renewing, transforming, gifting, empowering, sanctifying, and edifying role of the Holy Spirit. This is because Spirit-provided and Spirit-initiated subjective experience can lead the practitioners to the most reliable form of understanding and binding to the objective doctrine, which cannot be achieved through only a set formula of doctrinal belief. The church, therefore, ought to attain and benefit from the indwelling and endowment of the Holy Spirit through these twofold manifestations: *objective reception* and *subjective experience*. As already discussed, these twofold manifestations of the Holy Spirit have been fundamental means and instruments of the church's foundation and organization from its very inception. Thus, the church must be reminded that what ought to be sincerely and seriously considered is not the behavior of practitioners of the subjective, but the theological reality and practical significance of subjective experiential content of the Holy Spirit's manifestation, which is experienced through audibly uttered or visibly performed charismatic gifts.

Second, as discussed in chapters 1 to 4, charismatic gifts of the Holy Spirit in their origin are not based on mere human aspiration or driven merely by human subjectivity. They are rather divinely destined, divinely delivered, divinely arranged, and divinely initiated gifts for the church. The Scriptures clearly inform us that the divine-human communication tradition has always been based upon and dependent on divine intervention through audibly uttered or visibly performed charismata. God's message to, and purpose for, the world has often been communicated, accompanied, and evidenced by divine actions manifest through signs, miracles, healing, raising of the dead, casting out of evil spirits, as well as prophetic and revelational utterances. These gifts, therefore, are the divine side of reality and are quite different from the human side in their origin and dispensation. They are divinely originated, divinely set, divinely distributed, and divinely initiated means of the realization of divinely supplied gifts and power of Christian life, worship, ministry, and mission. As the Holy Spirit proceeds from God (John 15:26) the gifts and power of the Holy Spirit, too, spring from God. All manifestations of the charismatic gifts and their experience are God's manifestation, intervention, communication, and touch to save, renew, transform, gift, empower, and guide his church. It is only God who possesses and dispenses charismatic gifts and accomplishes his purpose through them. Yet he works through individuals whom he counts deserving to be given these gifts and to be used. Charismatic gifts, therefore, are sound objective theological ways for God's people to experience and demonstrate the presence, gifts, and power of the Holy Spirit working in, with, through, and among them. There is nothing shameful for the church to long and pray for, to receive and experience these gifts, to integrate the use of them in its worship, to create a hunger for reception and experience of them, and to encourage believers to realize and genuinely practice them.

As considered in chapter 4, the ecclesiastical functional significance of the charismatic gifts for enhancing gospel proclamation through accompanying and validating supernatural power is indeed far-reaching. When viewed through the gospel proclamation of Jesus and the apostles, charismatic gifts contain an unparalleled theological, missiological, and spiritual significance for faith life, ministry, and mission. Bearing this in mind, Jesus pledged to endow his disciples with his prophetic gospel proclamation, which was often accompanied by supernatural signs, wonders, miracles, healings, discerning spirits, casting out of demonic spirits, and raising the dead (Matt 10:1–15; Mark 3:14–15; 16:17–18; Luke 9:1–10; 24:49; John 14:12–14). These references point out that Jesus pledged to provide his disciples with all the possible supernatural resources with which he served. This demonstrates the dynamic continuity between the gospel proclamation of Jesus, of his disciples, and of the church. This dynamic continuity emerged when the apostles received the gift of the Holy Spirit and were endowed with the promised gifts and clothed with the power from on high on the day of Pentecost. From the day of Pentecost, the gospel proclamation of the apostles was accompanied by signs, wonders, miracles, healings, prophecies, raising the dead, exorcising demonic spirits, and with the confidence of power and authority (Acts 2:43; 3:1–10; 8:5–11; 9:39–41; 14:3–11). Not only the apostles, but the Holy Spirit also continued in anointing, gifting, empowering, equipping, and guiding many other believers with the same gifts and power. As analyzed in chapter 3, the book of Acts refers to many of the early Christians who were experiencing the prophetic gospel proclamation content of Jesus' ministry through a variety of charismatic gifts. This reminds the church of every generation that the Holy Spirit, who anointed, gifted, empowered, and guided Jesus, continued to anoint, gift, empower, equip, and guide the apostles, prophets, teachers, leaders, and miracle workers in the church. This demonstrates that the church continued living, practicing, and serving the Spirit-anointed, Spirit-gifted, Spirit-empowered, and Spirit-guided life and ministry of Jesus. Hence, there are obvious theological and biblical grounds for the church to realize, experience, and preserve charismatic gifts as important theological, spiritual, and sociological parts of its life and function.

When and where the charismatic gifts are objectively manifested and genuinely realized and practiced, they manifest a tangible divine power and the resulting impact bends the knees of the dark powers of the world. When the gospel proclamation is accompanied by these gifts, it cuts through the power and resistance of evil realities, disease, deformity, etc. Through the divine power manifesting and acting through charismata, the oppressed are freed, the sick are healed, the hungry are fed, the dying are given new life, the dead are raised, lives are inspired, and the new covenant's life and ministry are leavened (Luke 4). This makes charismatic spirituality liberating from the kinds of oppressions from which Jesus himself had liberated during his earthly ministry. This affirms that charismatic gifts have been effective in validating the message of the gospel to the world through audibly uttered and visibly performed supernatural manifestations resulting in the conviction, confession, and conversion of nonbelieving people both in the past and still now. They always contain and manifest dynamic, transdenominational, transconfessional, universal, global, local, and crosscultural significance and impacts. Wherever they are genuinely realized and practiced, they invaluably contribute to the spiritual, moral, ethical, missiological, and social life of the church as well as individual believers. Therefore, the life, worship, ministry, and mission of the church, which does not integrate practices of charismatic gifts, may indeed lack the dynamic that makes the church effective and influential in its life and worldwide mission.

Scholars who have closely observed the reality of the inextricable connection between charismatic gifts of the Holy Spirit and the church's life, ministry, and mission, have offered some insightful suggestions. For instance, Barr and Yocom suggest that the church was born in the creating, life-giving, gift-giving, empowering, and transforming movement of the Holy Spirit. The church, therefore, "bears witness to and serves as a means of the [Holy] Spirit's ongoing activity." The presence, gift, and activity of the Holy Spirit in the church, note Barr and Yocom, means God's continuous gifts of grace to his church.[8] Macchia concurs with this view and suggests that the church is a grace-gifted, grace-empowered, and grace-guided fellowship of the followers of Jesus. In this fellowship, charismatic gifts are specific divine means and instruments that make the church a fellowship of "engraced" community. Charismatic gifts, asserts Macchia, can be considered to facilitate the "engraced" capacity, fellowship, and mission of the church and make the church open to God's ongoing gracious activities for a graceless world.[9] Charismatic gifts, as Dunn observes, are particular manifestations of, and actual revelation of, God's grace and are the expressions of divine movement within, among, and upon humankind that establish renewing, transforming, and edifying relation and interaction between God and humans.[10] The source of transforming power of the church's mission, notes Berkhof, is always dependent on the demonstration of the gifts of the Holy Spirit. Therefore, the church that does not appropriate the gifts of the Holy Spirit may not achieve much in its mission.[11]

In a further assertion of these scholarly suggestions, Lindberg states that charismatic gifts are not meant to be merely options that the church includes in its religious practice only if it desires them. Rather, they are the divinely appointed, essential, and mandatory instruments of the church's life and mission. Active openness to and experiences of charismatic gifts,

8. Barr and Yocom, *Church in the Movement*, 1.
9. Macchia, "Signs of Grace," 148–49.
10. Dunn, *Jesus and the Spirit*, 202; cf. p. 254.
11. Berkhof, *Doctrine of the Holy Spirit*, 39.

in Lindberg's view, is the church's proper response to divine manifestation and presence. In the church where these divinely appointed gifts are ignored, concludes Lindberg, the charismatic power and ministry of the church become weakened or even crippled.[12] A church that recognizes and realizes the charismatic gifts can experience divine intimacy and involvement in its life and an ongoing divine revelation over fixed canons, traditions, and church disciplines.[13] George Vandervelde and William R. Barr also affirm that the church's existence is "ultimately a work of the Spirit" and the church lives and proclaims by the power of the Holy Spirit. Through the presence, gifts, and work of the Holy Spirit "human lives are changed" because the Holy Spirit "works a radical transformation of human life." Therefore, the Holy Spirit for the church, conclude Vandervelde and Barr, is always "God's *gift* filling in the church, transforming, reforming, and renewing it, and sending it in power."[14] Dunn concurs with these convictions when he states that the Holy Spirit is truly a "power that shakes the foundations, and shatters old moulds, a perennial challenge rebuke to all narrow factionalism and mere traditionalism." He alerts the church by stating that a church's failure to realize the presence, gifts, power, and working of the Holy Spirit inevitably causes impotence in spirituality, ministry, and mission.[15]

These insightful scholarly observations and suggestions, again, are in accord with and a reflection of biblical accounts regarding the significance of the presence, gifts, and activities of the Holy Spirit in the life and function of the church. They remind the church that charismatic gifts of the Holy Spirit are the most treasured theological resources and divinely supplemented power instruments for the life, function, and mission of the church. From a theological and biblical point of view, there is nothing shameful for the church, for any denominational theological tradition, or individual believers, to long and pray for the charismatic gifts, to receive and experience them. From a historical point of view, as carefully examined and analyzed in this study, there is no accounted detrimental effect where charismatic gifts have been incorporated into Christian worship and spiritual practice. Even the accounts of trusted church fathers such as Eusebius, Cyril of Jerusalem, Basil, and Hippolytus, which contain some defective

---

12. Lindberg, *Third Reformation?*, 232–33.
13. Crumbley, "Sanctified Saints," 93.
14. Vandervelde and Barr, "Spirit in the Proclamation," 77–81.
15 Dunn, "Towards the Spirit of Christ," 21–26.

practices and ethical issues in the Montanist charismatic experience, did not identify detrimental effects of the charismatic gifts. The same is true regarding churches' responses to charismatic experiences during the medieval, Reformation, and post-Reformation periods. Therefore, there is no historical, practical reason for withholding the church from praying for, receiving, and experiencing the charismatic gifts today and beyond. If any church body or any given denominational theological tradition bluntly ignores or systematically avoids the practice of charismatic gifts from its life without clearly identifying potential detrimental effects, then this can be considered heretical from both a theological and canonical point of view. Established churches of conservative theological traditions must, therefore, carefully consider that striving to maintain and preserve a historically conservative tradition is one thing, but identifying and applying what is most important to empower and transform the lives of their congregations is another matter. They must insightfully consider the theological reality, spiritual significance, and positive contributions of the workings of God through charismatic gifts and positively respond to them for the sake of the effectiveness and edification of their congregations. They must also consider that if any denominational theological tradition chooses to remain only institutional, organizational, and structural, and systematically works to remain closed to the practice of charismatic gifts, it is evident that it loses its gifting, empowering, and transforming function only enabled within the practice of the gifts, power, and works of the Holy Spirit. Therefore, to conclude in Kärkkäinen's words, it is "vital for the church of the third millennium to rediscover the charismatic structure of the church and its integral link with the diaconic structure of ministry" and that "taking the charismatic structure of the church as the starting point means that the [Holy] Spirit . . . is the leader of the church."[16]

CONCLUSION

In earnestly suggesting all these points, however, I am not ignorant of possible obstacles that may afflict the church and prevent the realization and experience of the charismatic gifts. To mention two simple examples of these:

---

16. Kärkkäinen, *Hope and Community*, 408.

Firstly, Scripture warns that those who are presumed to attain charismatic gifts may take, at times, the appearance of sheep while in reality being wolves in their actions, intent upon leading even the elect astray (Matt 7:15–23). This passage stands as a reminder to the church that charismatic experiences are subject to pretensions and abuses. Evil spiritual realities strive to take advantage of opportunities created by enthusiastic experiences to mar genuine charismatic experiences. Not only evil spiritual realities but practitioners of charismata may also confuse empirical experience with experimental experience and cause it to take on an experimental image, the kind to which Matt 7:15–23 alerts the church. This is an existing reality in the contemporary church. The ministry of TB Joshua of Nigeria can constitute an example of this. TB Joshua was one of the famous charismatic evangelists of the first two decades of the twenty-first century. Due to certain charismatic phenomena that occurred in his ministry, he was viewed as a prophet of God. Sadly, however, evidence continued to emerge revealing how his ministry was a mixture of the divine and the evil spiritual realities. Some evidence is offered by BBC News Africa. This media outlet has carefully examined the nature of Joshua's ministry and released some of its findings in a three-part documentary which was posted online. The first episode, described as "a ground-breaking investigation into the world famous televangelical preacher, TB Joshua" began by asking a question: "Man of God or predatory cult leader?" It then goes on to enumerate many heartbreaking, devilish, inhuman, and scandalous experiences of TB Joshua.[17] Such self-appointing prophets, with their abusive, scandalous, and business-making use of charismatic gifts, can in a very real way be said to undermine the church's confidence in those presumed to be endowed with charismatic gifts. Given such abusive—even what could be termed scandalous false—experimental experiences, the systematic suppression of charismatic experiences by established churches may not be a matter of doubt. Yet there is no set formula or guidance in Scripture about the nature of genuine charismatic experiences, except to recognize them by their fruits, sooner or later. Thus, the church faces real challenges when making decisions or judgments on pretension and abusive and genuine charismatic experiences. It is evident that on such confusing grounds, the established churches would push towards further systematic suppression of charismatic experience, along with their reverting to a traditionalist conservative position.

---

17. BBC Africa, *Disciples*.

Secondly, as repeatedly highlighted in this study, it is understandable that there has been intentional suppression of a charismatic experience by the dictatorial church hierarchies throughout church history. Such dictatorial hierarchies have always been reluctant to accept the gifts and workings of the Holy Spirit through charismatic experiences and have been resistant to these. As a result of this human-set dominant tradition, Christianity has for centuries struggled to evangelize the world with a mission movement devoid of the gifts and workings of the Holy Spirit. Consequently, the nature of apostolic Christianity and the nature of historical Christianity followed parallel but separate spiritual traditions up until the 1960s when the Charismatic movement emerged and impacted this long-standing parallelism. Nevertheless, despite the significant impact of the Charismatic movement, it is evident that such dictatorial and bureaucratic hierarchies, ordained hierarchies in particular, have continued to experience unreserved power and authority in the contemporary church, albeit under a different name and a different guise. It cannot, therefore, be a matter of doubt that such dictatorial hierarchies would still give priority to their own choices, interests, and privileges, and continue to imperil the claim and experience of the charismatic gifts.

Despite these and similar challenging factors, there are obvious theological and biblical grounds for the church to realize, experience, and preserve charismatic gifts as standing, important parts of its life and function. Therefore, what ought to be sincerely, carefully, and responsibly considered by any church body or an individual believer is that:

1. Initiating the objective gift of the Holy Spirit and endowing believers with charismatic gifts was, is, and will forever remain the possession and prerogative of God. These, as repeatedly mentioned in this study, are the divine side of reality and are quite different from the human side in their origin, dispensation, function, and effects. They are divinely originated, divinely set, divinely distributed, and divinely initiated means of the realization of divinely supplied gifts and power of Christian life, worship, ministry, and mission. Therefore, on the one hand, the church's belief, teaching, and spiritual practice must create a hunger for charismatic gifts and exhort believers toward genuine realization and experience. On the other hand, it is up to each believer to long for, seek, pray for, receive, and realize or ignore these gifts.

2. What ought to be carefully considered is not the behavior of practitioners of the charismatic gifts, but the theological reality and practical significance of the subjective experiential content of the Holy Spirit's manifestation, which is experienced through audibly uttered or visibly performed charismatic gifts. It must be noted that believers are not meant to experience the choices, interests, or feelings of the practitioners, but the divine reality of the charismatic content of the manifestation of the Holy Spirit: the pneumatic-charismatic nature of the church and the divine purpose for the world delivered through charismatic gifts. It must be noted that God's gracious gifts should not be weighed and judged by frail, wicked, finite, and futile human enthusiastic practices.

3. It must be noted that Scripture teaches that Christians have a Christly heart and mind (1 Cor 2:16), which is a perfect charismatic heart that receives the content of God's heart, knows the will and the path of God, and lives and acts accordingly. If the church of Christ as a whole or individual believers insightfully and prayerfully realize a Christly heart and mind, then they can insightfully distinguish between the results that can be gained from the views, choices, and interests of human hierarchies or pretending practitioners and genuine realization and experiences of the charismatic gifts. The church as whole and individual believers, in particular, must carefully and responsibly consider whether they are realizing Christly heart and mind in their entire being and dong.

Hence, this book comes with my earnest and heartfelt prayer that the Triune God, who has designed and founded the church on the *prophetic-charismatic gospel proclamation* and *humble servant leadership-administration* methods of Jesus' ministry, who gives his Spirit to indwell his people and endow them with charismatic gifts to be experienced through Spirit-initiated subjective experience, may enlighten the hearts and minds of the church as whole and individual hierarchies and help them to insightfully realize a Christly heart—a sound, charismatic-prophetic heart—that receives the content of God's heart, knows the will and the path of God, and lives and acts accordingly.

SUMMARY, PERSONAL REFLECTIONS, AND CONCLUSIONS

Bibliography

Acts of the Holy Apostles Peter and Paul. Ante-Nicene Fathers. Vol. 8. Edited by Alexander Roberts and James Donaldson. Grand Rapids: Eerdmans, 1951.
Adogame, Afe. "Reconfiguring the Global Religious Economy: The Role of African Pentecostalism." In S*pirit and Power: The Growth and Global Impact of Pentecostalism*, edited by Donald E. Miller et al., 185–203. New York: Oxford University Press, 2013.
Alexander, Estrelda Y. *Black Fire: One Hundred Years of African-American Pentecostalism.* Downers Grove, IL: IVP Academic, 2011.
Allen, David. *The Unfailing Stream: A Charismatic Church History in Outline.* Tonbridge, UK: Sovereign World, 1994.
Althaus, Paul. *The Theology of Martin Luther.* Philadelphia: Fortress, 1966.
Anderson, Ray S. *The Shape of Practical Theology: Empowering Ministry with Theological Praxis.* Downers Grove, IL: InterVarsity, 2001.
Anderson, Allan H. *An Introduction to Pentecostalism.* Cambridge: Cambridge University Press, 2004.
———. *An Introduction to Pentecostalism.* 2nd ed. Cambridge: Cambridge University Press, 2014.
Aquinas, Thomas. *On Nature and Grace: Selections from the Summa Theologica.* Translated and edited by A. M. Fairweather. Philadelphia: Westminster, 1954.
Arndt, William F., and F. Wilbur Gingrich. *A Greek-English Lexicon of the New Testament and Other Early Christian Literature.* Chicago: University of Chicago Press, 1957.
Athanasius. *Letters to Serapion on the Holy Spirit.* Translated by Mark DelCogliano et al. New York: St. Vladimir's Seminary Press, 2011.
Augustine. *The City of God; Christian Doctrine.* Nicene and Post Nicene Fathers. Series 1, vol. 2. Edited by Philip Schaff. Grand Rapids: Eerdmans, 1979.
Badcock, Gary D. *Light of Truth and Fire of Love: A Theology of the Holy Spirit.* Grand Rapids: Eerdmans, 1997.
Balmer, Randall. *Encyclopaedia of Evangelicalism.* Rev. ed. Waco, TX: Baylor University Press, 2004.
Balz, Horst, and Gerhard Schneider, eds. *Exegetical Dictionary of the New Testament.* Vol. 3. Grand Rapids: Eerdmans, 1993.
Barr, William R., and Rena M. Yocom. *The Church in the Movement of the Spirit.* Grand Rapids: Eerdmans, 1994.
Barth, Karl. *Church Dogmatics.* 1/1: *The Doctrine of the Word of God.* Translated by G. W. Bromiley. Edited by G. W. Bromiley and T. F. Torrance. Edinburgh: T&T Clark, 1975.

———. *Church Dogmatics*. 4/1: *The Doctrine of Reconciliation*. Translated by G. W. Bromiley. Edited by G. W. Bromiley and T. F. Torrance. New York: Charles Scribner's Sons, 1956.

———. *Church Dogmatics*. 4/2: *The Doctrine of Reconciliation*. Translated by G. W. Bromiley. Edited by G. W. Bromiley and T. F. Torrance. Edinburgh: T&T Clark, 1958.

———. *Church Dogmatics*. 4/4: *The Doctrine of Reconciliation*. Translated by G. W. Bromiley. Edited by G. W. Bromiley and T. F. Torrance. Edinburgh: T&T Clark, 1969.

Basil of Caesarea. *Letter 188*. Nicene and Post-Nicene Fathers. Series 2, vol. 8. Edited by Philip Schaff and Henry Wace. Edinburgh: T&T Clark, 1986.

———. *Oration on The Spirit*. Nicene and Post-Nicene Fathers. Series 2, vol. 8. Edited by Philip Schaff and Henry Wace. Edinburgh: T&T Clark, 1986.

BBC News Africa. *Disciples: The Cult of TB Joshua*. Ep. 1: "Miracle Makers," Jan. 7, 2024. https://www.youtube.com/watch?v=UZZVQxjXWCg.

Beasley-Murray, George R. *John*. Word Biblical Commentary 36. Waco, TX: Word, 1987.

Beckwith, Carl L. *The Holy Trinity: Confessional Lutheran Dogmatics*. Vol. 3. Fort Wayne, IN: Luther Academy, 2016.

Beckwith, R. T. "Purgatory." In *New Dictionary of Theology*, edited by Sinclair B. Ferguson and David F. Wright, 549. Leicester: InterVarsity, 1988.

Bergmann, Sigurd. "Revisioning Pneumatology in Transcultural Spaces." In *Spirits of Globalization: The Growth of Pentecostalism and Experiential Spiritualities in a Global Age*, edited by Sturla J. Stålsett, 183–87. London: SCM Press, 2006.

Berkhof, Hendrikus. *The Doctrine of the Holy Spirit*. Atlanta: John Knox, 1976.

Berkhof, Louis. *The History of Christian Doctrines*. Edinburgh: Banner of Truth Trust, 1937.

Bittlinger, Arnold. *The Church Is Charismatic*. Geneva: WCC, 1981.

Bloesch, Donald G. *A Theology of Word and Spirit: Authority and Method in Theology*. Downers Grove, IL: InterVarsity, 1992.

Bouyer, Louis. "Some Charismatic Movements in the History of the Church." In *Perspectives on Charismatic Renewal*, edited by Edward D. O'Connor, 113–20. Notre Dame: University of Notre Dame, 1975.

Bradford, Brick. *Releasing the Power of the Holy Spirit*. Oklahoma City: Presbyterian Charismatic Communion, 1983.

Brecht, Martin. *Martin Luther: His Road to Reformation, 1483-1521*. Minneapolis: Fortress, 1993.

———. *Martin Luther: Shaping and Defining the Reformation, 1521-1532*. Minneapolis: Fortress, 1994.

Bridge, Donald, and David Phypers. *More Than Tongues Can Tell: Reflection on Charismatic Renewal*. London: Hodder and Stoughton, 1982.

———. *Spiritual Gifts and the Church*. Rev. ed. Fearn, UK: Christian Focus, 1995.

Brown, Colin. *The New International Dictionary of New Testament Theology*. Exetere, UK: Paternoster, 1986.

Bruce, F. F. *The Book of Acts*. New International Commentary on the New Testament. Rev. ed. Grand Rapids: Eerdmans, 1988.

Bruner, Dale F. "Of Water and the Spirit: Christian Baptism is the Baptism in the Holy Spirit." In *The Holy Spirit: Shy Member of the Trinity*, Dale F. Bruner and William Hordern, 35–64. Eugene, OR: Wipf & Stock Publishers, 2001.

———. "The Shy Member of the Trinity: Expository Preaching Gives the Filling of the Holy Spirit." In *The Holy Spirit: Shy Member of the Trinity*, Dale F. Bruner and William Hordern, 11–33. Eugene, OR: Wipf & Stock, 2001.

———. *A Theology of the Holy Spirit: The Pentecostal Experience and the New Testament Witness*. Eugene, OR: Wipf & Stock, 1997.

Bruner, Dale F., and William Hordern. *The Holy Spirit: Shy Member of the Trinity*. Eugene, OR: Wipf & Stock, 2001.

Brunner, Emil. *The Christian Doctrine of the Church, Faith, and the Consummation*. In *Dogmatics*, vol. 3. Translated by David Cairns. Philadelphia: Westminster, 1962.

———. *The Christian Doctrine of Creation and Redemption*. In *Dogmatics*, vol. 2. Translated by Olive Wyon. Philadelphia: Westminster, 1952.

Bultmann, Rudolf. *Theology of the New Testament*. 2 vols. Translated by Kendrick Grobel. New York: Charles Scribner's Sons, 1951–55.

Bundy, David D. "European Pietist Roots of Pentecostalism." In *The New International Dictionary of Pentecostal and Charismatic Movements*, edited by Stanley M. Burgess and Eduard M. Van Der Maas, 610–13. Rev. ed. Grand Rapids: Zondervan, 2003.

Bundy, D. D. *European Pietist Roots of Pentecostalism*, in Dictionary of Pentecostal and Charismatic Movements, edited by Stanley M. Burgess and Gary B. McGee. Grand Rapids, Michigan: Regency-Zondervan Publishing House, 1988.

Burgess, Stanley M. "Change and Continuity Among Twentieth-Century Peoples of the Spirit." In *Spirit-Empowered Christianity in the 21st Century*, edited by Vinson Synan, 47–54. Lake Mary, FL: Charisma, 2011.

———. "Holy Spirit" in *Encyclopaedia of Pentecostal and Charismatic Christianity*, edited by Stanley M. Burgess. New York: Routledge, 2006.

———. *Encyclopaedia of Pentecostal and Charismatic Christianity Movements*. New York: Routledge, 2006.

———. *The Holy Spirit, Doctrine of: The Medieval Churches*, in Dictionary of Pentecostal and Charismatic Movements, edited by Stanley M. Burgess and Gary B. McGee. Grand Rapids, Michigan: Regency-Zondervan Publishing House, 1988.

———. *The Holy Spirit: Ancient Christian Traditions*. Peabody, MA: Hendrickson, 1984.

———. *The Holy Spirit: Medieval Roman Catholic and Reformation Traditions*. Peabody, MA: Hendrickson, 1997.

———. "Quakers (Society of Friends)." *The New International Dictionary of Pentecostal and Charismatic Movements*, edited by Stanley M. Burgess and Eduard M. Van Der Maas, 1014. Rev. ed. Grand Rapids: Zondervan, 2003.

———. *The Holy Spirit, Doctrine of: The Ancient Fathers*, in Dictionary of Pentecostal and Charismatic Movements, edited by Stanley M. Burgess and Gary B. McGee. Grand Rapids, Michigan: Regency-Zondervan Publishing House, 1988.

Burgess, Stanley M., and Eduard M. Van Der Maas. *The New International Dictionary of Pentecostal and Charismatic Movements*. Rev. ed. Grand Rapids: Zondervan, 2003.

Burgess, Stanley M., and Gary B. McGee. *Dictionary of Pentecostal and Charismatic Movements*. Grand Rapids: Regency-Zondervan, 1988.

Buschart, David W. *Exploring Protestant Traditions: An Invitation to Theological Hospitality*. Downers Grove, IL: InterVarsity, 2006.

Cairns, Earle E. *Christianity Through the Centuries*. 3rd ed. Grand Rapids: Zondervan, 1996.

Calvin, John. *Institute of Christian Religion*. 2 vols. Translated by Ford Lewis Battles. Edited by John T. McNeill. London: Westminster John Knox, 2006.

Cartledge, Mark J. *Encountering the Spirit: The Charismatic Tradition*. New York: Orbis, 2006.

Chadwick, Henry. *The Early Church*. London: Penguin, 1967.

The Charismatic Movement and Lutheran Theology: A Report of the Commission on Theology and Church Relations of the Lutheran Church—Missouri Synod. January 1972. https://files.lcms.org/file/preview/98E8ACF8-F3DE-45D6-8081-BE1ED38C065F.

Christenson, Larry. *The Charismatic Renewal Among Lutherans*. Minneapolis: International Lutheran Renewal Centre, 1985.

———. *A Message to the Charismatic Movement*. Minneapolis: Dimension, 1972.

———. *Welcome Holy Spirit: A Study of Charismatic Renewal in the Church*. Minneapolis: Augsburg, 1987.

Clement, Arthur J. *Pentecost or Pretense? An Examination of the Pentecostal and Charismatic Movements*. Milwaukee: Northwestern, 1981.

Clement of Rome. *First Epistle to the Corinthians*. Ante-Nicene Fathers. Vol. 1. Edited by Alexander Robert and James Donaldson. Grand Rapids: Eerdmans, 1956.

Coleman, Simon. *The Globalization of Charismatic Christianity*. Cambridge: Cambridge University Press, 2000.

Congar, Yves. *I Believe in the Holy Spirit*. 3 vols. New York: Herder and Herder, 1997.

Constitutions of the Holy Apostles. Ante-Nicene Fathers. Vol. 7. Edited by Alexander Roberts and James Donaldson. Grand Rapids: Eerdmans, 1975.

Cook, Chris. *The Routledge Companion to Christian History*. London: Routledge, 2008.

Cox, Harvey. *Fire from Heaven: The Rise of Pentecostal Spirituality and Reshaping of Religion in the Twenty-First Century*. Cambridge: Da Capo, 2001.

———. "Spirits of Globalization: Pentecostalism and Experiential Spirituality in a Global Era." In *Spirits of Globalization: The Growth of Pentecostalism and Experiential Spiritualities in a Global Age*, edited by Sturla J. Stålsett, 11–22. London: SCM, 2006.

Crumbley, Deidre H. "Sanctified Saints—Impure Prophetesses." In *Philip's Daughters; Women in Pentecostal-Charismatic Leadership*, edited by Estrelda Alexander and Amos Yong, 74–94. Eugene, OR: Pickwick, 2009.

Culpepper, Robert H. *Evaluating the Charismatic Movement: A Theological and Biblical Appraisal*. Valley Forge, PA: Judson Press, 1977.

Cyril of Jerusalem. *Catechetical Lectures*. Nicene and Post-Nicene Fathers. Series 2, vol. 7. Edited by Philip Schaff and Henry Wace. Edinburgh: T&T Clark, 1986.

Davids, Peter H. *The First Epistle of Peter*. New International Commentary on the New Testament. Grand Rapids: Eerdmans, 1990.

Davis, Leo Donald. *The First Seven Ecumenical Councils: Their History and Theology*. Collegeville, MN: Liturgical, 1999.

Dayton, Donald W. *Theological Roots of Pentecostalism*. Peabody, MA: Hendrickson, 1987.

Decker, Rodney J. *Reading Koine Greek: An Introduction and Integrated Workbook*. Grand Rapids: Baker Academic, 2014.

Deer, Jack. *Surprised By the Power of the Holy Spirit*. Eastbourne, UK: Kingsway, 2006.

Doles, Jeff. *Miracles and the Manifestations of the Holy Spirit in the History of the Church*. Milton Keynes, UK: Lightning Source, 2008.

Dreyer, Elizabeth A. *Holy Power, Holy Presence: Rediscovering Medieval Metaphors for the Holy Spirit*. New York: Paulist, 2007.

Dunn, James D. G. *Baptism in the Holy Spirit.* Philadelphia: Westminster, 1970.

———. *Jesus and the Spirit: A Study of the Religious and Charismatic Experience of Jesus and the First Christians as Reflected in the New Testament.* London: SCM, 1975.

———. "Ministry and the Ministry: The Charismatic Renewal's Challenge to Traditional Ecclesiology." In *Charismatic Experiences in History,* edited by Cecil M. Robeck Jr., 81–101. Peabody, MA: Hendrickson, 1985.

———. "Towards the Spirit of Christ: The Emergence of the Distinctive Features of Christian Pneumatology." In *The Work of the Spirit: Pneumatology and Pentecostalism,* edited by Michael Welker, 3–26. Grand Rapids: Eerdmans, 2006.

Duquoc, Christian, and Casiano Floristan. *Charisms in the Church.* New York: Seabury, 1978.

Elowsky, Joel C. *We Believe in the Holy Spirit.* Ancient Christian Doctrine 4. Downers Grove, IL: IVP Academic, 2009.

Esser, H. H. *Grace, Spiritual Gifts,* in The New International Dictionary of New Testament Theology Vol. 2, edited by Colin Brown. UK: Paternoster Press, 1986.

Eusebius. *Church History.* Nicene and Post-Nicene Fathers. Series 2, vol. 1. Edited by Philip Schaff and Henry Wace. Grand Rapids: Eerdmans, 1979.

Fee, Gordon D. *God's Empowering Presence: The Holy Spirit in the Letters of Paul.* Peabody, MA: Hendrickson, 1994.

Ferm, Robert L. *Readings in the History of Christian Thought.* New York: Rinehart & Winston, 1964.

Freedman, David Noel. *The Anchor Bible Dictionary.* 6 vols. New York: Doubleday, 1992.

Gaffin, Richard B. *Perspectives on Pentecost: New Testament Teaching on the Gifts of the Holy Spirit.* Phillipsburg, NJ: Presbyterian and Reformed, 1979.

Gassmann, Gunther, and Scott Hendrix. *Fortress Introduction to the Lutheran Confessions.* Minneapolis: Fortress, 1999.

Gause, Hollis R. "Issues in Pentecostalism." In *Perspectives on the New Pentecostalism,* edited by Russell P. Spittler, 106–16. Grand Rapids: Baker, 1976.

Gelpi, Donald L., SJ. "Pentecostal Theology: A Roman Catholic Viewpoint." In *Perspectives on the New Pentecostalism,* edited by Russell P. Spittler, 86–103. Grand Rapids: Baker, 1976.

Gerberding, George Henry. *The Way of Salvation in the Lutheran Church.* 1887. N.p.: Dodo, n.d.

Green, Michael. *I Believe in the Holy Spirit.* Rev. ed. Grand Rapids: Eerdmans, 2004.

Gregory of Nazianzus. *Against Arians.* Nicene and Post-Nicene Fathers. Series 2, vol. 7. Edited by Philip Schaff and Henry Wace. Edinburgh: T&T Clark, 1986.

———. *The Fifth Theological Oration: On The Holy Spirit.* Nicene and Post-Nicene Fathers. Series 2, vol. 7. Edited by Philip Schaff and Henry Wace. Edinburgh: T&T Clark, 1986.

Gregory of Nyssa. *On the Holy Spirit.* Nicene and Post-Nicene Fathers. Series 2, vol. 5. Edited by Philip Schaff and Henry Wace. New York: Charles Scribner's Sons, 1986.

Gregory the Great. *Dialogues.* Fathers of the Church 39. Translated by Odo John Zimmerman. Washington, DC: Catholic University of America Press, 1959.

Gulley, Norman R. *Systematic Theology.* Vol. 1: *Prolegomena.* Berrien Springs, MI: Andrews University Press, 2003.

Hagglund, Bengt. *History of Theology.* Translated by Gene J. Lund. Saint Louis: Concordia, 1968.

Hamilton, Michael P. *The Charismatic Movement*. Grand Rapids: Eerdmans, 1975.
Hartely, John E. *The Book of Job*. New International Commentary on the Old Testament. Grand Rapids: Eerdmans, 1988.
Hayford, Jack W., and S. David Moore. *The Charismatic Century: The Enduring Impact of the Azusa Street Revival*. New York: Warner Faith, 2006.
Heron, Alasdair I. C. *The Holy Spirit*. Philadelphia: Westminster, 1983.
Hilary of Poitiers. *On the Trinity*. Nicene and Post-Nicene Fathers. Series 2, vol. 9. Edited by Philip Schaff and Henry Wace. Grand Rapids: Eerdmans, 1979.
Hippolytus. *The Refutation of All Heresies*. Ante-Nicene Fathers. Vol. 6. Edited by Alexander Roberts and James Donalson. Edinburgh: T&T Clark, 1868.
Hocken. P. D. *European Pentecostalism*, in Dictionary of Pentecostal and Charismatic Movements, edited by Stanley M. Burgess and Gary B. McGee. Grand Rapids, Michigan: Regency-Zondervan Publishing House, 1988.
Hocken, Peter. *The Challenges of the Pentecostal, Charismatic and Messianic Jewish Movements: The Tensions of the Spirit*. Farnham, UK: Ashgate, 2009.
Hocken, P. D. *Charismatic Movement*, in Dictionary of Pentecostal and Charismatic Movements, edited by Stanley M. Burgess and Gary B. McGee. Grand Rapids, Michigan:Regency-Zondervan Publishing House, 1988.
———. "Charismatic Movement." In *The New International Dictionary of Pentecostal and Charismatic Movements*, edited by Stanley M. Burgess and Eduard M. Van Der Maas, 477–519. Grand Rapids: Zondervan, 2003.
Horgan, Taddeus D., SA. "Biblical Basis and Guidelines." In *The Church in the Movement of the Spirit*, edited by William R. Barr and Rena M. Yocom, 11–28. Grand Rapids: Eerdmans, 1994.
Horn, F. W. "Holy Spirit" in The Anchor Bible Dictionary Vol. 3, H-J, edited by David Noel Freedman. New York: Doubleday, 1992.
Horton, Michael. *Rediscovering the Holy Spirit: God's Perfecting Presence in Creation, Redemption, and Everyday Life*. Grand Rapids: Zondervan, 2017.
Horton, S. M. *The Holy Spirit, Doctrine of The*: in Dictionary of Pentecostal and Charismatic Movements, edited by Stanley M. Burgess and Gary B. McGee. Grand Rapids, Michigan: Regency-Zondervan Publishing House, 1988.
Hummel, Charles E. *Fire in the Fireplace: Charismatic Renewal in the Nineties*. Downers Grove, IL: InterVarsity, 1993.
Hurt, Larry. "Spirit Baptism." In *Spirit-Empowered Christianity in the 21st Century*, edited by Vinson Synan, 261–86. Lake Mary, FL: Charisma, 2011.
Hyatt, Eddie L. *2000 Years of Charismatic Christianity*. Lake Mary, FL: Charisma, 2002.
Ignatius. *Epistles to the Ephesians, Magnesians, Trallians, Philadelphians, and Smyrnaeans*. Ante-Nicene Fathers. Vol. 1. Edited by Alexander Roberts and James Donaldson. Grand Rapids: Eerdmans, 1956.
Irenaeus. *Against Heresies*. Ante-Nicene Fathers. Vol. 1. Edited by Alexander Roberts and James Donaldson. Grand Rapids: Eerdmans, 1981.
Jefford, Clayton N. *Apostolic Constitutions and Canons*, in The Anchor Bible Dictionary Vol. I, A–C, edited by David Noel Freedman. New York: Doubleday, 1992.
John of Damascus. *Exposition of the Orthodox Faith*. Nicene and Post-Nicene Fathers. Series 2, vol. 9. Translated by Philip Schaff and Henry Wace. Grand Rapids: Eerdmans, 1979.
Judisch, Douglas. *An Evaluation of Claims to the Charismatic Gifts*. Grand Rapids,: Baker, 1978.

Justin, Martyr. *Dialogue with Trypho.* Ante-Nicene Fathers. Vol. 1. Edited by Alexander Roberts and James Donaldson. Grand Rapids: Eerdmans, 1981.

———. *The Second Apology.* Ante-Nicene Fathers. Vol. 1. Edited by Alexander Roberts and James Donaldson. Grand Rapids: Eerdmans, 1981.

Kalu, Ogbu. *African Pentecostalism: An Introduction.* New York: Oxford University Press, 2008.

Kamlah, E., Dunn, J. D. G., and Brown, C. *Spirit, Holy Spirit,* in New International Dictionary of New Testament Theology, Vol. 3, edited by Colin Brown. UK: The Paternoster Press, 1992.

Kärkäinnen, Veli-Matti. *Christian Understandings of the Trinity: The Historical Trajectory.* Minneapolis: Fortress, 2017.

———. *A Constructive Christian Theology for the Pluralistic World.* Vol. 1: *Christ and Reconciliation.* Grand Rapids: Eerdmans, 2013.

———. *A Constructive Christian Theology for the Pluralistic World.* Vol. 2: *Trinity and Revelation.* Grand Rapids: Eerdmans, 2014.

———. *A Constructive Christian Theology for the Pluralistic World.* Vol. 4: *Spirit and Salvation.* Grand Rapids: Eerdmans, 2016.

———. *A Constructive Christian Theology for the Pluralistic World.* Vol. 5: *Hope and Community.* Grand Rapids: Eerdmans, 2017.

———. *A Guide to Christian Theology: The Holy Spirit.* Louisville: Westminster John Knox, 2012.

———. *Holy Spirit and Salvation: The Sources of Christian Theology.* Louisville: Westminster John Knox, 2010.

———. *Pneumatology: The Holy Spirit in Ecumenical, International, and Contextual Perspective.* 2nd ed. Grand Rapids: Baker Academic, 2018.

———. *Toward a Pneumatological Theology: Pentecostal and Ecumenical Perspectives on Ecclesiology, Soteriology, and Theology of Mission.* Lanham, MD: University Press of America, 2002.

Keener, Craig S. *A Commentary on the Gospel of Matthew.* Grand Rapids: Eerdmans, 1999.

Kistemaker, Simon J. *Exposition of the Acts of the Apostles.* New Testament Commentary. Grand Rapids: Baker, 1990.

———. *Exposition of the Epistle of James and the Epistles of John.* New Testament Commentary. Grand Rapids: Baker, 1986.

Koenig, John. *Charismata: God's Gifts for God's People.* Philadelphia: Westminster, 1978.

Kremer, J. *Pnuema* in Exegetical Dictionary of the New Testament, Vol. 3, edited by Horst Balz and Gerhard Schneider. Grand Rapids, Michigan: Eerdmans Publishing Company, 1993.

Kydd, Ronald A. N. *Charismatic Gifts in the Early Church: An Exploration into the Gifts of the Spirit During the First Three Centuries of the Christian Church.* Peabody, MA: Hendrickson, 1984.

Land, Steven Jacker. *Pentecostal Spirituality: A Passion for the Kingdom.* Cleveland: CPT, 2010.

Lederle, Henry I. *Theology with Spirit: The Future of the Pentecostal and Charismatic Movements in the 21st Century.* Oklahoma: Word & Spirit, 2010.

———. *Treasures Old and New: Interpretation of Spirit-Baptism in the Charismatic Renewal Movement.* Peabody, MA: Hendrickson, 1988.

Leonard, Bill J., and Jill Y. Crainshaw. *Encyclopedia of Religious Controversies in the United States*. 2 vols. 2nd ed. California: ABC-CLIO, 2013.

Letham, Robert. *The Holy Trinity in Scripture, History, Theology and Worship*. New Jersey: P & R, 2004.

Lindberg, Carter. *The Pietist Theologians*. Oxford: Blackwell, 2005.

———. *The Third Reformation? Charismatic Movement and the Lutheran Tradition*. Macon: Mercer University Press, 1983.

Littell, Franklin H. *The Origins of Sectarian Protestantism*. New York: Beacon, 1964.

Lohse, Bernhard. *Martin Luther's Theology: Its Historical and Systematic Development*. Translated and edited by Roy A. Harrisville. Edinburgh: T&T Clark, 1999.

Lovelace, Richard F. *Dynamics of Spiritual Life: An Evangelical Theology of Renewal*. Downers Grove, IL: InterVarsity, 1978.

Lull, Timothy E. *Martin Luther's Basic Theological Teaching*. Minneapolis: Fortress, 1989.

Luther, Martin. *Letters of Spiritual Counsel*. Translated and edited by Theodore G. Tappert. Louisville: Westminster John Knox, 1955.

———. *Luther's Table Talk*. Translated by William Hazlitt. Updated and revised. Orlando: Bridge-Logos, 2004.

———. *Luther's Works*. Vol. 14: *Selected Psalms III*. Edited by Jaroslav Pelikan. Saint Louis: Concordia, 1958.

———. *Luther's Works*. Vol. 16: *Lectures on Isaiah 1–39*. Edited by Jaroslav Pelikan. Saint Louis: Concordia, 1969.

———. *Luther's Works*. Vol. 21: *The Sermon on The Mount*. Edited by Jaroslav Pelikan. Saint Louis: Concordia, 1956.

———. *Luther's Works*. Vol. 24: *Sermons on the Gospel of John 14–16*. Edited by Jaroslav Pelikan. Saint Louis: Concordia, 1961.

———. *Luther's Works*. Vol. 31: *Treatise on Christian Liberty (The Freedom of a Christian)*. In *Career of the Reformer: I*. Edited by Harold J. Grimm. Philadelphia: Muhlenberg, 1957.

———. *Luther's Works*. Vol. 36: *Word and Sacrament II: The Babylonian Captivity of the Church, 1520*. Translated By A. T. W. Steinhauser. Edited by Abdel Ross Wentz. Philadelphia: Muhlenberg, 1959.

———. *Luther's Works*. Vol. 40: *Lectures on Church and Ministry*. Edited by Conrad Bergendoff. Philadelphia: Muhlenberg, 1958.

———. *Luther's Works*. Vol. 53: *Lectures on Liturgy and Hymns*. Edited by Helmut T. Lehmann. Philadelphia: Fortress, 1965.

———. *Ninety-Five Theses*. Edited by Kurt Aland. St. Louis: Concordia, 2004.

MacArthur, John Jr. *Charismatic Chaos*. Grand Rapids: Zondervan, 1992.

Macchia, Frank D. "The Kingdom and the Power: Spirit Baptism in Pentecostal and Ecumenical Perspective." In *The Work of The Holy Spirit: Pneumatology and Pentecostalism*, edited by Michael Welker, 109–25. Grand Rapids: Eerdmans, 2006.

———. *Baptism in the Holy Spirit*, in Encyclopaedia of Pentecostal and Charismatic Christianity, edited by Stanley M. Burgess. New York: Routledge, 2006.

———. "Signs of Grace in a Graceless World: The Pentecostal Challenge to the Church." In *Spirit-Empowered Christianity in the 21st Century*, edited by Vinson Synan, 141–58. Lake Mary, FL: Charisma, 2011.

MacCulloch, Diarmaid. *A History of Christianity: The First Three Thousand Years*. London: Penguin, 2010.

———. *Reformation: Europe's House Divided, 1490–1700*. London: Penguin, 2004.

McDonnell, Kilian. *The Baptism in the Holy Spirit*. Notre Dame: Charismatic Renewal Service, 1972.

———. *Charismatic Renewal and the Churches*. New York: Seabury, 1976.

———. *The Holy Spirit and Power: The Catholic Charismatic Renewal*. New York: Doubleday, 1975.

———. *Presence, Power, Praise: Documents on the Charismatic Renewal*. 3 vols. Minnesota: Liturgical, 1980.

McDonnell, Kilian, and George T Montague. *Christian Initiation and Baptism in the Holy Spirit: Evidence from the First Eight Centuries*. 2nd ed. Minneapolis: Liturgical, 1990.

McGee, Gary B. *Miracles, Missions, and American Pentecostalism*. American Society of Missiology Series 45. New York: Orbis, 2010.

McGrath, Alister E. *Christian Theology: An Introduction*. Oxford: Blackwell, 1994.

———. *Historical Theology: An Introduction to the History of Christian Thought*. Oxford: Blackwell, 1998.

———. *Reformation Thought: An Introduction*. 3rd ed. Oxford: Blackwell Publishing, 1999.

Menzies, Robert P. *Empowered for Witness: The Spirit in Luke-Acts*. Sheffield: Sheffield Academic Press, 1994.

Metcalfe, John. *The Gifts and Baptism of the Spirit*. Buckingham: John Metcalfe Publishing Trust, 2001.

Michaels, Ramsey J. *1 Peter*. Word Biblical Commentary 49. Waco, TX: Word, 1988.

Middlemiss, David. *Interpreting Charismatic Experience*. London: SCM, 1996.

Milne, Bruce. *Know the Truth: A Handbook of Christian Belief*. 2nd ed. Leicester: InterVarsity, 1998.

Moltmann, Jürgen. *The Church in the Power of the Spirit*. Translated by Margaret Kohl. London: SCM, 1977.

———. *The Church in the Power of the Spirit*. New York: HarperCollins, 1991.

———. *The Spirit of Life: A Universal Affirmation*. Translated by Margaret Kohl. Minneapolis: Fortress, 1992.

Moule, C. F. D. *The Holy Spirit: Contemporary Christian Insights*. London: Continuum, 2000.

Nafzger, Samuel H., et al., eds. *Confessing the Gospel: A Lutheran Approach to Systematic Theology*. Vol. 1. Saint Louis: Concordia, 2017.

O'Brein, T. C. *Corpus Dictionary of Western Churches*. Washington: Corpus Publications, 1970.

O'Connor, Edward D., CSC. "The Literature of Catholic Charismatic Renewal, 1967–1974." In *Perspectives on Charismatic Renewal*, edited by Edward D. O'Connor, CSC, 145–52. Notre Dame: University of Notre Dame Press, 1975.

Opsahl, Paul D. *The Holy Spirit in the Life of the Church*. Minneapolis: Augsburg, 1978.

Origen. *Against Celsus*. Ante-Nicene Fathers. Vol. 4. Edited by Alexander Robertson and James Donaldson. Grand Rapids: Eerdmans, 1963.

Oyer, John S. *Lutheran Reformers Against Anabaptists*. Paris: Baptist Standard Bearer, 1964.

Packer, J. I. "Holy Spirit." In *New Dictionary of Theology*, edited by Sinclair B. Ferguson and David F. Wright, 316–19. Leicester: InterVarsity, 1992.

Pannenberg, Wofart. *Systematic Theology*. Vol. 2. Translated by Geoffrey W. Bromiley. Grand Rapids: Eerdmans, 1994.

Pierson, Paul E. *The Dynamics of Christian Mission: History Through a Missiological Perspective*. Pasadena: William Carey International University Press, 2009.

Pinnock, Clark H. *Flame of Love: A Theology of the Holy Spirit*. Downers Grove, IL: InterVarsity, 1996.

Poewe, Karla. *Charismatic Christianity as a Global Culture*. Columbia: University of South Carolina Press, 1994.

Pomerville, Paul A. *The Third Force in Mission: A Pentecostal Contribution to Contemporary Mission Theology*. Peabody, MA: Hendrickson, 1985.

Potter, Philip. "Charismatic Renewal and the World Council of Churches." In *The Church Is Charismatic: The World Council of Churches and the Charismatic Movement*, edited by Arnold Bittlinger, 73–87. Geneva: WCC, 1981.

Quebedeaux, Richard. *The New Charismatics II*. San Francisco: Harper and Row, 1982.

Rahner, Karl. *The Spirit in the Church*. New York: Seabury, 1979.

Rahner, Karl, and Herbert Vorgrimler. *Theological Dictionary*. 2nd ed. London: Burns & Oates, 1965.

Robinson, Maurice A., and Mark A. House, eds. *Analytical Lexicon of New Testament Greek*. Rev. ed. Peabody, MA: Hendrickson, 2012.

Sasse, Hermann. *Letters to Lutheran Pastors*. Vol. 1: *Remarks on the Dogma of the Assumption of Mary*. Translated by Matthew C. Harrison. Saint Louis: Concordia, 2013.

———. *Letters to Lutheran Pastors*. Vol. 3: *On the Doctrine of the Holy Spirit*. Translated by Norman Nagel. Saint Louis: Concordia, 2015.

Schatzmann, Siegfried. *A Pauline Theology of Charismata*. Peabody, MA: Hendrickson, 1987.

Schuchard, Bruce G. *1–3 John*. Concordia Commentary. Saint Louis: Concordia, 2012.

Seven Ecumenical Councils of the Undivided Church. Nicene and Post-Nicene Fathers. Series 2, vol. 14. Edited by Philip Schaff and Henry Wace. Grand Rapids: Eerdmans, 1979.

Shults, Leron F., and Andrea Hollingsworth. *The Holy Spirit*. Grand Rapids: Eerdmans, 2008.

Smail, Tom, et al. *Charismatic Renewal*. London: SPCK, 1995.

Smalley, Stephen S. *1, 2, 3 John*. Word Biblical Commentary 51. Waco, TX: Word, 1984.

Sproul, R. C. *Faith Alone: The Evangelical Doctrine of Justification*. Grand Rapids: Baker, 1995.

Steinmann, Andrew E. *1 Samuel*. Concordia Commentary. Saint Louis: Concordia, 2016.

Storms, Samuel C. "A Third Wave View." In *Are Miraculous Gifts for Today? Four Views*, edited by Wayne A. Grudem, 173–223. Grand Rapids: Zondervan, 1996.

Sullivan, Francis A. *Charisms and Charismatic Renewal: A Biblical and Theological Study*. Grand Rapids: Servant, 1982.

Synan, Vinson. *Aspects of Pentecostal-Charismatic Origins*. Plainfield, NJ: Logos International, 1975.

———. *The Century of the Holy Spirit: 100 Years of Pentecostal and Charismatic Renewal 1991–2001*. Nashville: Thomas Nelson, 2001.

———. *Spirit-Empowered Christianity in the 21st Century*. Lake Mary, FL: Charisma, 2011.

Tappert, Theodore G. *The Book of Concord: The Confessions of the Evangelical Lutheran Churches*. Philadelphia: Fortress, 1959.

The Teaching of the Twelve Apostles (Didache). Ante-Nicene Fathers. Vol. 7. Edited by Alexander Roberts and James Donaldson. Grand Rapids: Eerdmans, 1975.

Tertullian. *Treatise on the Soul.* Ante-Nicene Fathers. Vol. 3. Edited by Alexander Roberts and James Donaldson. Grand Rapids: Eerdmans, 1963.

Thiselton, Anthony C. *The First Epistle to the Corinthians: A Commentary on the Greek Text.* Grand Rapids: Eerdmans, 2000.

———. *The Holy Spirit: In Biblical Teaching, Through the Centuries, and Today.* Grand Rapids: Eerdmans, 2013.

———. *A Short Guide to the Holy Spirit: Bible, Doctrine, Experience.* Grand Rapids: Eerdmans, 2016.

Thomas, W. H. Griffith. *The Holy Spirit.* Grand Rapids: Kregel, 1986.

Tillich, Paul. *A History of Christian Thought.* Edited by Carl E. Braaten. New York: Harper & Row, 1968.

———. *Systematic Theology.* Vol. 3: *Life and the Spirit History, and the Kingdom of God.* Chicago: University of Chicago Press, 1963.

Tixeront, J. *History of Dogmas.* Vol. 1: *The Ante-Nicene Theology.* Westminster, MD: Christian Classics, 1984.

———. *History of Dogmas.* Vol. 2: *From St. Athanasius to St. Augustine.* Westminster, MD: Christian Classics, 1984.

———. *History of Dogmas.* Vol. 3: *The End of the Patristic Age.* Westminster, MD: Christian Classics, 1984.

Turner, Max. *The Holy Spirit and Spiritual Gifts Then and Now.* Carlisle, UK: Paternoster Press, 1996.

———. *Power from on High: The Spirit in Israel's Restoration, and Witness in Luke-Acts.* Sheffield: Sheffield Academic Press, 1996.

Vandervelde George, and William R. Barr. "The Spirit in the Proclamation of the Church." In *The Church in the Movement of the Spirit,* edited by William R. Barr and Rena M. Yocom, 75–90. Grand Rapids: Eerdmans, 1994.

Verburgge, V. D. *The NIV Theological Dictionary of New Testament Words.* Grand Rapids: Zondervan, 2000.

Waldron, Samuel E. *To Be Continued? Are the Miraculous Gifts for Today?* Merrick, NY: Calvary, 2005.

Walls, Andrew F. "Eusebius Tries Again: Reconceiving the Study of Christian History." *International Bulletin of Missionary Research* 24:3 (2000) 105–11.

Warfield, Benjamin B. *Counterfeit Miracles.* Edinburgh: Banner of Truth, 1972.

Weinrich, William C. *John 1:1—7:1.* Concordia Commentary. Saint Louis: Concordia, 2015.

Welker, Michael. *God the Spirit.* Translated by John F. Hoffmeyer. Minneapolis: Fortress, 1994.

———. *The Work of the Holy Spirit: Pneumatology and Pentecostalism.* Grand Rapids: Eerdmans, 2006.

Wesselschmidt, Quentin F. *Ancient Christian Commentary on Scripture: Old Testament VIII; Psalms 51–150.* Downers Grove, IL: InterVarsity, 2007.

Williams, C. P. "Protestantism." In *New Dictionary of Theology,* edited by Sinclair B. Ferguson and David F. Wright, 540. Leicester: InterVarsity, 1988.

Williams, Rodman J. *Renewal Theology: Systematic Theology from a Charismatic Perspective; Three Volumes in One.* Grand Rapids: Zondervan, 1996.

World Council of Churches. *Come Holy Spirit: Renew the Whole Creation; Six Bible Studies.* Geneva: WCC, 1989.

Yong, Amos. "Pentecostalism and Ecumenism: Past, Present, and Future." In *Pentecostals in the 21st Century: Identity, Beliefs, Praxis*, edited by Corneliu Constantineanu and Christopher J. Scobie, 202–36. Eugene, OR: Cascade, 2018.

———. "Ruach, the Primordial Chaos and the Breath of Life: Emergence Theory and the Creation Narratives in Pneumatological Perspective." In *The Work of the Spirit: Pneumatology and Pentecostalism*, edited by Michael Welker, 183–204. Grand Rapids: Eerdmans, 2006.

Zahl, Simeon. *Pneumatology and Theology of the Cross in the Preaching of Christopher Friedrich Blumhardt: The Holy Spirit Between Wittenberg and Azusa Street*. London: T&T Clark, 2010.

———. "Reformation Pessimism or Pietist Personalism? The Problem of The Holy Spirit in Evangelical Theology." In *New Perspective for Evangelical Theology: Engaging with God, Scripture and the World*, edited by Tom Greggs, 78–92. London: Routledge, 2010.

General Index

African Pentecostalism (Kalu), 258–59
Against Arians (Gregory of Nazianzus), 149
Against Celsus (Origen of Alexandria), 153–54
Against Heresies (Irenaeus), 102, 113–14, 141–42
Against Marcion (Tertullian), 142
Alexander, Estrelda Y., 243–44
Allen, David, 103, 118, 146, 151, 164, 190, 238–39
Anderson, Allan H., 237–38, 246–47, 258–59
Anderson, Ray S., 117
apostolic succession, 102–3, 164–65
apostolic transmission, 81–111
    authority to the bishops, 100–103
    leadership-administration functions of the church, 96–100
    prophetic-charismatic gospel proclamation method, 88–96
    ways of reception, gifts, and workings of the Holy Spirit, 84–88
Arianism, 126–27
Athanasius, 127–29
Augustine of Hippo, 154–56
Azusa Street revival movement, 239–40, 259

The Babylonian Captivity of the Christian Church (Luther), 179
Badcock, Gary D., 176, 198
Balmer, Randall, 255–56

baptism in the Holy Spirit, 26–30, 239–40, 241–43, 244–45, 247–48, 256–57
Barr, William R., 259, 267–69, 293, 294
Barth, Karl, 29, 39, 206–7
Basil of Caesarea, 132–33, 148–49, 157
Beckwith, Carl L., 20
Bennet, Dennis, 245
Berkhof, Hendrikus, 51, 115, 116–17, 167–68, 206, 293
Berkhof, Louis, 126, 175–76
Bethel Bible School, 238–40
Bible, 277–79
Birgitta of Sweden, 182
bishop of Rome, 122–24, 146, 164–65
Bradford, Brick, 219, 260, 269
Brecht, Martin, 177–78, 189–90, 191, 197, 207
Bridge, Donald, 29, 34
Bruner, Dale F., 34–35, 220
Brunner, Emil, 39, 207, 219
Bultmann, Rudolf, 38–39, 103, 114
Burgess, Stanley M., 116, 123, 125, 169, 176, 220, 238, 244
Buschart, David W., 200

Caesarea, 35–36, 85
Cairns, Earle E., 115, 122, 164–65, 169
Calvin, John, 194–98
canon of Scripture, 224–25
Cartledge, Mark J., 219–20, 239–40, 245–46, 248, 266
Catechetical Lectures (Cyril of Jerusalem), 148–49
Catherine of Siena, 182

Catholic Church, 88, 185–89, 190, 197–98, 255, 257–58
charismata
  biblical teaching about, 52–55
  linguistic origin and development, 43–44
  theological origin and meaning, 45–49
  visibly performed, 49–52, 286–87, 291
Charismatic Chaos (MacArthur), 223–25
charismatic experiences, 25, 50, 52–54, 71, 89–91, 94, 100, 103, 145, 151–53, 153–56, 168–69, 180–82, 215, 222, 248, 256–59, 260–62, 278, 295
charismatic gifts
  in the Bible, 278–79
  cessationist view, 221–25
  Charismatic movement, 247–49
  manifest connection with the Holy Spirit, 49–52
  and the papacy, 166
  in the patristic church, 141–43
  Pentecostal movement, 241–43
  and subjective experience, 286–95
  visibly performed, 49, 53, 278–79, 286, 290
Charismatic movement, 209
  established churches, impact on, 259–62
  expansion of the, 254–59
  Pentecostal movement, 243–44, 247–48
  rise and growth of the, 244–50
  scholarly evaluations, 266–70
  subjective experience of the Holy Spirit, 218, 287
  traditional views on the Holy Spirit, 262–65
charismatic renewal, 245, 257–58, 260, 263–64
Charismatic Renewal and the Churches (McDonnell), 255–58
Christenson, Larry, 28, 34, 45, 113, 152, 165–66, 259–60
Christology, 116–18

Church History (Eusebius), 147–48
The Church in the Movement of the Spirit (Barr and Yocom), 268–69
City of God (Augustine of Hippo), 154–56
Clement, Arthur, 207–8, 248, 262
"Commission on Theology and Church Relations," 256–57
Congar, Yves, 145–46, 166–67, 170–71, 176, 210
Constantine (Emperor), 118–25, 164, 223
Constitutions of the Holy Apostles, 24, 32–33, 87–88, 91–96, 96–100, 100–101, 102–3
Counterfeit Miracles (Warfield), 222–25
Crainshaw, Jill Y., 239, 257
Culpepper, Robert H., 149
Cyril of Jerusalem, 148–49

Davis, Leo Donald, 135, 173–74
Dempster, Murray W., 238
Dialogues (Gregory the Great), 180–81
Dialogue with Trypho (Justin Martyr), 141
Didache, 91–92
doctrine of subsequence, 241–42
Doles, Jeff, 182
double procession, 175–77
Dreyer, Elizabeth A., 219
Dunn, James D. G., 25–26, 34–35, 36, 39, 45–46, 51, 143–44, 189, 240–42, 262, 288, 293–94
Duquoc, Christian, 45, 168

early church, 19, 24, 31–37, 38–39, 50–51, 64, 86, 115, 123–24, 125–26, 175, 186–87, 192, 195–96, 278–79
Ephesus, 36–37, 85–86
Ephesus Council, 169–70
Esser, H. H., 45
established churches, 244–46, 247–49, 254–55, 259–65, 266, 289, 295
Eucharist, 166–67
Eusebius, 118–24, 147–48

GENERAL INDEX

faith as means of salvation, 59–60
Fee, Gordon D., 44, 48
Fifth Theological Oration (Gregory of Nazianzu), 129–31
filioque doctrine, 175–77
Firrer, Vincent, 182
Floristan, Casiano, 45, 168
Fountain Trust, 245–46
Francis of Assisi, 181–82

Gaffin, Richard B., Jr., 223–25
Gassmann, Gunther, 165
Gelasius I, 165
generalized prophetic ministries, 9
Gertrude of Helfta, 182
gift of the Holy Spirit as means of salvation, 63–64
gifts in the Old Testament, 7–12
The Globalization of Pentecostalism (Dempster, Klaus, and Petersen), 238
Gnosticism, 113–15, 150
Great Commission, 132–33
Green, Michael, 22
Gregory of Nazianzus, 129–31, 135, 149
Gregory of Nyssa, 131–32, 135, 280
Gregory of Palamas, 182
Gregory the Great, 174, 180–81

Harper, Michael, 245
Hendrix, Scott, 165
Heron, Alasdair I. C., 260
Hilary, 154
Hildegard of Bingen, 181
Hippolytus, 149–50
Hocken, Peter D., 244, 247–48
Hollingsworth, Andrea, 268
holy baptism as means of salvation, 60–61
Holy Communion/Lord's Supper as means of salvation, 61
Holy Power, Holy Presence (Dreyer), 219
Holy Spirit
    apostolic transmission, 84–88
    authority to the bishops, 100–103

    baptism in the, 26–30, 239–40, 241–43, 244–45, 247–48, 256–57
    in the Bible, 277–79
    cessationist view of charismatic gifts of the, 221–25
    changes in traditional views on, 262–65
    charismatic gifts, manifest connection with, 49–55
    charismatic gifts and subjective experience, 286–95
    Christology, emphasis on, 116–18
    Constantine's favor towards Christianity, 118–25
    disputes over nature of, 279–86
    disputes over the nature of, 125–34
    future coming of, 7, 13–15, 16, 21–22
    gifts of in the medieval church, waning existence, 180–83
    Jesus' ministry, methods of, 65–73
    linguistic and theological meaning, 5–6
    magisterial reformers response to radical reformers, 193–99
    Mary substituted the gifts and works of the, 169–71
    Montanist movement, 143–53
    neglected member of the Trinity, 219–21
    New Testament teaching, 16–22
    nonbiblical traditions, 177–80
    Old Testament teaching, 6–15
    papacy substituted the gifts and works of the, 164–69
    patristic church, 141–43
    Pentecost, day of, 23–26
    place and role from A. D. 100 TO 1900, 215–19
    post-Pentecostal early church, 31–37
    presence and role in creation, 7
    prophetic gifts and ministries, 8–12
    reception of, 31–37, 51–52, 52–55, 63–64, 71, 84–88, 215–16, 221, 241, 278–79, 281–82, 288

Holy Spirit (continued)
  religious movements, 113–16
  in renewal and transformation activities, 12–13
  repeated reception experiences in the early church, 38–39
  sacred images/icons substituted the gifts and works of the, 171–75
  and salvation, 59–64
  scholarly evaluations, 266–70
  subjective experience of the, 215–18
  supernatural gifts for divine-related activities, 7–8
  water baptism and laying on of hands, 37
  wider church's response to disputes, 134–36
  See also Charismatic movement
Horgan, Taddeus D., 208, 260–61, 269–70, 288
Horton, Michael, 17, 34, 270
Horton, S. M., 114–15
house church movement, 245
Hummel, Charles E., 122–23
Hyatt, Eddie L., 102–3, 118, 144–46, 149–50, 151, 153

I Believe in the Holy Spirit (Congar), 166
Ignatius, 100–102
image of the cross, 119–21, 171–73
indulgences, 177–78, 187
Institute of Christian Religion (Calvin), 195–96
An Introduction to Pentecostalism (Anderson), 237–38
Irenaeus, 101–2, 113–14, 141–42

Jesus, 59–73
  anointment and ministry, 17–18
  baptism in the Holy Spirit, 27–29
  charismatic gifts, 291–93
  future coming of the Holy Spirit, 21–22
  Holy Spirit and charismatic gifts, 50
  Holy Spirit in the life and ministry of, 16–18

leadership/administration method of ministry, 72–73
Methodist movement, 206–7
ministry methods, 65–73
nature of the Holy Spirit, 283–85
office functions of ministry, 65–69
post-Pentecostal early church, 32–37
sacred images/icons, 171–73
salvation, five features as means of, 59–64
teachings of the theology and doctrine of the Holy Spirit, 19–20
John of Damascus, 172–73
Judisch, Douglas, 224
Julian of Norwich, 182
justification by faith, 187–88, 189
Justin Martyr, 125, 141

Kalu, 258–59
Kärkkäinen, Veli-Matti, 47–48, 125–26, 257–58, 260, 266–67, 295
Klaus, Byron D., 238
Koenig, John, 247

Land, Steven J., 240
laying on of hands, 34, 37, 66, 88, 103, 282
leadership-administration, 69, 72–73, 96–100, 102
Leo I, 165
Leonard, Bill J., 239, 257
Letham, Robert, 17–18
Life of Constantine (Eusebius), 119–23
Lindberg, Carter, 192, 293–94
Logos-Christology, 116–17
Lovelace, Richard F., 178–79
Luther, Martin, 178–79, 186–88, 189–90, 191–92, 194–95, 197–98
Lutheran churches, 200–201, 206, 256–57
Lutheran Church—Missouri Synod congregations, 256–57

MacArthur, John F., Jr., 223–25
Macchia, Frank D., 29, 242, 293

MacCulloch, Diarmaid, 174, 177–78, 200–201
Macedonians, 126–28, 131, 135
magisterial reformers, 218
    continued influence on successors, 199–209
    Radical Reformation, rise of the, 191–92
    radical reformers, response to, 193–99
Margery of Kempe, 182
Mary, 164–74
McDonnell, Kilian, 25–26, 146, 255–58
McGee, Gary B., 220, 240, 244
McGrath, Alister E., 126, 179, 189, 199–200, 220, 266
Menzies, Robert P., 242
Metcalfe, John, 224
Methodist movement, 200–209
Middlemiss, David, 45
Moltmann, Jurgen, 45, 117, 209
Montague, George T., 146
Montanist movement, 143–53, 216–17
Moravians, 203–4
Moule, C. F. D., 117, 289

Neo-Pentecostalism, 247, 260
The New International Dictionary of Pentecostal and Charismatic Movements (Burgess and Van Der Maas), 238
New Testament
    apostolic transmission, 84–85, 90–91
    cessationist view of charismatic gifts of the Holy Spirit, 221–25
    charismata, 47–48
    post-Pentecostal early church, 34–35
    reception of the Holy Spirit, 282
    sacred images/icons, 175
    subjective experiences of the Holy Spirit, 215–16
    teaching of, 16–22, 277–78
Nicene-Constantinopolitan Creed of 381, 136
Nicene Creed, 126, 135, 176
Ninety-Five Theses (Luther), 178

nonbiblical traditions, 177–80, 185–87, 217

objective reception, 288–90
Old Testament
    baptism in the Holy Spirit, 30
    charismata, 44, 46–47
    Holy Spirit and charismatic gifts, 49
    Jesus' anointment and ministry, 17–18
    office functions of ministry, 65–69
    Pentecost, day of, 23–26
    sacred images/icons, 175
    Spirit, linguistic and theological meaning, 3–6
    teaching of, 6–15, 277–78
On the Holy Spirit (Athanasius), 127–29
On the Holy Spirit (Gregory of Nyssa), 131–32
On the Spirit (Basil of Caesarea), 132–33
On the Trinity (Hilary), 154
Origen of Alexandria, 125–26, 153–54
Ozman, Agnes, 239

Pannenberg, Wolfart, 68
papacy, 118, 164–69, 191
Parham, Charles F., 238–40, 243
patristic church, 116, 117–18, 141–43, 153–56, 216, 217
Pentecost, day of, 23–26, 50–51, 240–43
Pentecostal-charismatic, 71–72, 95, 102, 115–16, 117, 123, 152–53, 216–19, 244, 261–62, 267
Pentecostal movement, 210, 237–44, 247–48
people-targeted and response-required prophetic ministries, 9–10
Petersen, Douglas, 238
Peter's key, 122–24, 164
Phypers, David, 29, 34
Pierson, Paul E., 118, 178–79
Pietist movement, 200–203
Pinnock, Clark H., 289

pneumatology, 116–18, 198, 266–70, 280–81
Potter, Philip, 263–64
Presence, Power, Praise (McDonnell), 255
prophetic utterances, 10–12, 147–48, 181
Protestant churches, 198–99, 199–201, 205–6, 209, 218, 244, 246, 255–56, 258
purgatory, 177–78

Quakers, 210

Radical Reformation, 190–91, 191–92, 193–99, 205, 209–10, 218
Rahner, Karl, 29
Reformation movement, 178–79, 184–91
Reformation theology, 188, 191, 206
Reformation tradition churches, 199–209
Refutation of All Heresies (Hippolytus), 149
regional councils, 146–47
religious movements, 113–16, 216, 250

sacred images/icons, 171–75
salvation, 59–64, 170–71
salvation theology, 45, 117–18
Samaria, 31–35, 85
Samaritans, 241–42
Schatzmann, Siegfried, 45, 48
Second Apology (Justin Martyr), 141
second council, 125, 136, 149, 164, 175–76, 217
Seymour, William, 239–40
Shults, Leron F., 268
speaking in tongues, 11, 24, 35, 36, 47, 144–45, 171, 181–82, 238–39, 241, 245, 248, 255–57
Spirit, linguistic and theological meaning, 3–6
Spirit baptism. *See* baptism in the Holy Spirit
Spirit-charismata, 94–96, 219, 221–22

spiritual renewal, 146, 178, 185, 190–91, 201, 208
Spreading Fires (Anderson), 237–38
Storms, Samuel C., 262–63
subjective experience of the Holy Spirit, 215–18, 286–95
Sullivan, Francis A., 258
Symeon the New Theologian, 181
Synan, Vinson, 257–58

Teaching of the Twelve Apostles, 91–92
Tertullian, 142–43, 145–46
Theodosius I, 134–35
third council, 175–76
Thiselton, Anthony C., 29–30, 44, 145, 149, 238, 257–58, 260, 267
Thomas, W. H. Griffith, 143
Thomas Aquinas, 182
Tillich, Paul, 102–3, 143, 151–52, 166
Tixeront, 127, 169–70, 171–72
traditional views on the Holy Spirit, 262–65
Treatise on the Soul (Tertullian), 142
Turner, Max, 16–17, 22, 29, 48

Van Der Maas, Eduard M., 238
Vandervelde, George, 294
Venerable Bede, 181
Verbrugge, V. D., 43–44

Waldron, Samuel E., 224
Warfield, Benjamin B., 222–25
water baptism, 27, 37, 282
Welker, Michael, 29–30, 268
Wesley, John, 203–4
Western churches, 175–77, 179–80, 202–3, 217, 219–21
Williams, C. P., 200–201
Williams, Rodman J., 51, 262
word of God as means of salvation, 62
The Work of the Holy Spirit (Welker), 268
World Council of Churches (WCC), 263–65

Yocom, Rena M., 259, 267–69, 293
Yong, Amos, 220, 245, 266–67

Scripture Index

OLD TESTAMENT

Genesis
1:2	3-4, 6, 7, 19
1:26	174
1:30	4
2:7	4
20:7	9
41:38	12

Exodus
7-12	46
14	46
15:25	46
16	46
17	46
20:7	20
23:16	24
25:9	175
25:18	175
25:40	175
26:30-31	175
28-29	66
28:41	17, 68-69
30:10	66
31:1-4	8
31:3	6
35:30-35	8

Leviticus
4:3	68-69
4:5	68-69
4:16	68-69
16:20-22	66
23:9-14	24

Numbers
11:16-17	9
11:25	10, 15
11:26	10
12:6-8	9
16:31-5	46
24:1-2	10
27:18	12
27:18-21	15

Deuteronomy
16:9-12	24
18:15-19	9
18:15-22	65
29:5	46
34:9	6, 11, 15

Joshua
3:16	46
10:12-14	46

Judges
3:10	6, 8
4:4-20	9
6:34	8, 11
11:29	6, 8
13:25	6, 8
14:6	6, 8
14:19	6, 8

Judges (continued)

15:4–5	8
15:14	8
15:14–16	6
15:15	8
15:9	46
16:28–30	8

1 Samuel

9:16	69
10:1	17, 69
10:6	6
10:6–11	10
11:6	11
16:13	8
16:23	11
19:20	10
19:23–24	10
20:14	6
24:6	69
24:20	6

2 Samuel

7:16	67

1 Kings

3:10–13	72
14:1–16	31
14:21–24	31
16:21–34	31
17	9, 46
18:38	46
19:15–16	17
19:16	69

2 Kings

1:10–12	46
2:15	15
2:19–22	46
4:32–35	46
5:12–14	46
6:6–7	46
6:18–19	46
9:1–16	69
13:20–21	46
17:7–22	31
17:24–41	31
18:9–16	31
20:8–11	46

2 Chronicles

15:1	6

Ezra

9	31

Nehemiah

9:30	9

Job

33:4	6
34:14–15	7

Psalms

51:11	6
89:3	67
89:19–24	11
89:20–36	67
104: 29–30	7
105:14–15	9

Isaiah

6:8	9
9:1–7	67
9:6–7	67
11:1–2	12, 17
11:1–3	67
11:1–4	14
11:1–5	13
11:2	6
32:15–20	12
35:5–6	194
41:1–2	17
42:1–4	11, 14
42:1–5	13
44:3	13
48:16	9
53	66
59:21	13

61:1	6, 9, 11
61:1–4	13, 17
63:10	6, 15
63:10–11	6

Jeremiah

29:10–11	31
31:31–34	12

Ezekiel

11:18–20	13
36:25–32	13
36:27	12
36:37	12
37:1–14	5, 13
39:29	13

Daniel

3:16–17	46
4:8	12
6:16–24	46

Hosea

9:7	9
12:13	9

Joel

2:28	6, 12, 24, 30, 40, 94, 287
2:28–29	14, 28

Micah

3:8	9

Haggai

2:5	13

Zechariah

4:6	13
7:12	9–10
9:9–10	67

Malachi

4:5	9

NEW TESTAMENT

Matthew

3:11	27, 39
3:11–12	281
3:16	17
4:23–25	66
5–7	106
7:15–23	261, 296
7:20–23	143
8:14–17	66
8:27	17
9:6	17, 72
10:1	72
10:1–4	21
10:1–8	69
10:1–15	70, 291
10:5	32
10:5–9	69
10:7–8	47, 50
10:15	72, 108
10:23	104, 107
10:32–33	93
10:40	72
11:2–6	65, 66
11:4–6	50
11:9	17
12:8	17
12:28	285
12:28–29	72
12:32	20
12:42	67
13:31–32	274
13:53–58	68
13:57	65
16:18–19	72
16:28	104, 107
18:11	18
20:24–28	68
20:28	66
21:46	65
23	169
24:29–31	67

Matthew (continued)

24:34	104
25:31–34	68
26:26–28	61, 66
27:12–14	66
28:18–20	21, 67, 68, 69, 133
28:19	5, 20
28:19–20	128

Mark

3:7–11	66
3:13–15	72
3:13–19	21
3:14–15	70, 291
6:1–3	65
6:53–56	66
10:45	66
13:20	104, 107
13:30	104, 107
16:17–18	70, 93, 94, 291

Luke

1:32–33	67
1:35	16
4:1–13	285
4:14	285
4:18–19	17
4:18–20	17, 18, 50, 65, 69, 75, 285
4:31–37	68
4:31–41	50
4:31–43	66
7:11–23	65
7:16	65
9:1–6	21, 47, 50, 69
9:1–10	70, 291
9:10	21
9:52	32
10:16	72
10:19	72
10:20	241
11:13	250
11:37–52	169
17:15–19	32
22:20	66
22:24–27	68
24:49	21, 25, 63, 70, 107, 291

John

1:12	18
1:16–17	18
1:29	67
1:32	281
1:33	14, 17, 27, 39
3:1–8	60
3:1–11	27, 55
3:8	106, 281
3:14–18	60
3:16	18
3:16–17	282
3:16–18	94
3:18	60
3:19	60
3:34–35	62
3:36	60
3:44	65
4:4–9	32
4:10–14	281
4:24	283
4:44	65
5:19–22	18
5:19–24	18, 62, 284
5:30	284
5:36–38	65
6:35	61
6:37–40	94
6:40	60
6:47	60, 94
6:47–58	61
6:63	19, 62, 170
7:16–18	284
7:37–39	281
8:12	18
8:16	284
8:25–29	65
8:27–30	284
8:31	62
8:42–45	65
8:48	32
8:51	62
9:17	65
10:9	18

10:11	66	2:38	28, 33		
10:15	66	2:43	50, 70, 89, 292		
12:44–45	60	2:47	54		
12:47–48	62	3:1–10	50, 70, 89, 292		
12:49–50	284	3:1–11	50		
13:2–17	68	3:22–24	66		
13:4–17	68	4:8	38		
13:10	241	4:28–30	50		
13:20	69	4:31	38, 56		
14:6	18	5:1–11	72		
14:8–11	284	5:1–12	54		
14:12	194	5:12	50, 89		
14:12–14	70, 291	5:12–14	54		
14:15–17	38, 63	5:12–16	50, 89		
14:16	6, 21	6:1–6	19		
14:25–26	19	6:5	32		
14:26	21, 63	6:8	70, 89		
14:30–31	194	8:4–6	70		
15:3	241	8:4–7	50, 89		
15:12–13	66	8:4–17	31–35		
15:16	241	8:5–11	70, 291		
15:26	21, 22, 291	8:5–13	50		
16:7	21	8:15	28		
16:13	63	8:17	28		
16:13–15	21, 138, 280, 283, 284–85	8:26–29	19		
		8:29	19		
16:14	21, 22	9:3–5	281		
17:3	92	9:17	28		
17:20–23	69	9:32	50		
17:20–26	61, 67	9:32–43	89		
20:22	38, 241	9:39–41	50, 70, 292		
20:23	72	10:19	19		
21:15–17	72, 96	10:19–20	19		
		10:38	285		

Acts

		10:44–46	35
1:4	21	10:44–48	35–36
1:4–8	21	10:45	28
1:5	28	10:47	28
1:5–8	29, 39, 107	11:12	19
1:8	28, 32, 69, 70	11:13–18	36
2	38	11:15	28
2:1–4	6	11:15–17	35–36
2:4	11, 24, 28	11:16	28, 29, 40
2:14–18	24	11:27–28	50
2:29–36	68	11:27–30	70
2:33	14, 28	13:1–3	70
2:37–41	25	13:1–4	19
		13:8–12	72

Acts (continued)

13:9	38
13:52	38, 56
14:1–3	50, 89
14:3–11	50, 70, 292
14:8–12	89
14:16	19
14:17	22
14:23	73
14:26	22
15:4	73
15:12	50
15:23	73
15:28–29	19
16:6–7	19
16:7	21
16:7–11	22
16:13	22
18:9–10	19
19:1–6	36–37, 86
19:2	28
19:6	28
19:11–12	89
20:7–12	89
20:22–24	19
20:28	19, 73
21:9	70
21:10–11	70
23:11	19
26:17–18	60
28:3–6	89
28:8–12	50

Romans

6:5–11	106
6:6–13	105
8:5–11	105
8:11	63, 105
8:12–14	105
8:27	19
11:16	106
12:1–4	106
12:6–8	47, 89, 90, 92
13:11–12	105
15:19	50
16:1	73

1 Corinthians

2:11–12	19
2:13	19
2:16	19, 298
3:16–17	105
6:9–11	105
6:12–20	106
6:15–20	105
7:29	86
7:29–31	105
10:21	105
12:4–11	19, 47, 74, 89, 90, 92
12:8–11	47, 51
12:18	11
12:28	47, 73, 74, 91

2 Corinthians

5:17	63, 105
6:16	105
15:1–2	11
20:14–17	11
24:20	11

Galatians

3:1–5	105
3:5	51
5:22	63, 105
5:24	105

Ephesians

1:13–14	281
2:12–16	66
2:20	91
4:4–6	224
4:10–11	47
4:11	73, 91
4:17–24	63, 105
4:30	19
5:18	63, 86, 105

1 Thessalonians

1:5–6	51
3:11–13	106
5:12–13	96, 231
5:19	90

5:23	106

Philippians

1:1	73
2:9–10	68
2:9–11	16

1 Timothy

3:1–7	73, 96
3:1–13	73
3:8–12	73
5:17	96, 231

2 Timothy

3:16–17	283

Titus

1:5–9	73, 96
2:1–6	73

Hebrews

2:4	51
2:8	16
7:23–27	67
9	67
9:23–28	67
10:10–18	67
12:1–9	106
13:17	96, 231

1 John

2:18	105
2:20	105, 281
2:27	105, 281

1 Peter

1:20–21	283
4:7	105
4:17	105
5:1–5	96

2 Peter

3:8–15	105

James

5:7–9	105

Revelation

5:9–13	67, 69
19:11–21	68
21:22–27	68

www.ingramcontent.com/pod-product-compliance
Lightning Source LLC
Chambersburg PA
CBHW052144300426
44115CB00011B/1509